The Dialectic of Ch

FROM THE LIBRARY OF

V

The Dialectic of Change

BORIS KAGARLITSKY

Translated by Rick Simon

VERSO

London · New York

First published by Verso 1990
© Boris Kagarlitsky 1990
Translation © Rick Simon 1990

Verso
UK: 6 Meard Street, London W1V 3HR
USA: 29 West 35th Street, New York, NY 10001-2291

Verso is the imprint of New Left Books

British Library Cataloguing in Publication Data

Kagarlitsky, Boris, *1958-*
    The dialectic of change.
    1. Eastern Europe. Political developments History
    I. Title
    320.947

    ISBN 0-86091-258-2
    ISBN 0-86091-973-0 (pbk)

US Library of Congress Cataloging-in-Publication Data

Kagarlitsky, Boris, 1958-
    The dialectic of change/Boris Kagarlitsky; translated by Rick Simon.
        p.   cm.
    Translated from the Russian.
    ISBN 0-86091-258-2 (hard) — ISBN 0-86091-973-0 (pbk.)
        1. Soviet Union—Politics and government—1985- 2. Europe, Eastern—Politics
and government—1945- 3. Socialism—Europe, Eastern—History—20th
century.   I. Title.
    DK288.K34   1989
    947.084—dc20

Typeset by Leaper & Gard Ltd, Bristol
Printed in Finland by Werner Söderström Oy

Contents

Preface: A Letter to the Reader

The main part of the this book was written in 1983–85. This was far from the best time for Soviet society. The economic situation was slowly and steadily worsening, a silent but bitter struggle was going on in the ruling group, but in the country it was if everything had been frozen. The stability of the 1970s had already receded into the past but changes had not yet arrived. Nevertheless, the inevitability of change was obvious enough — only Sovietologists and emigrés, commentating on the progress of events in the USSR in the pages of popular Western publications, could have any doubts about it.

For me, working on this book was first of all a means of preparing myself for future political conflicts and of elaborating a definite approach to the analysis of the crisis situations which we would patently have to experience in the near future. It is hoped that this book will also be of assistance to other people, in other parts of the world, who are seriously involved in the struggle for the transformation of society.

A great deal has altered in the time that has elapsed between writing the first draft of the book and its publication. In an effort not to be behind the times I have inserted various additions and amendments into the text as events occurred. Frequently, conclusions which five or six years ago one had to try and argue today seem almost banal. The second half of the 1980s has proved rich in all kinds of political crisis, revolution and attempts at reform. The crisis of technocratic dictatorships in the Third World has led to the re-establishment of democratic norms of rule in many countries, but the new democratic governments have been unable to propose a socio-economic strategy which guarantees the strengthening and development of political freedoms. The East European regimes are experiencing the most severe crisis and, for the first time since 1956, this crisis is affecting not simply one country or another but, to a greater or lesser extent, the entire region. In Hungary, the carefully erected edifice of historic compromise between the statocracy and society is falling to pieces. The Party leadership is taking one decision after another, in many respects going far beyond anything done in Czechoslovakia at the time of the 'Prague Spring' in its radicalism, while still being unable to regain either its authority or society's confidence. In Poland, the military government has completely lost control of the situation and has been forced to sit at the negotiating table with Solidarity, the total collapse of which the authorities had repeatedly and triumphantly declared. Meanwhile, neither in Poland nor in Hungary has the opposition been able to advance a conception of socio-economic reform which differs radically from that being carried out or proposed by the government. The opposition itself is in the thrall of traditional technocratic schemas, hoping that the market will miraculously solve all problems at a stroke. The authorities and the opposition have been equally hypnotized by the successes of Western capitalism without giving a thought to the price of these successes. They strive in equal measure to utilize as much as possible from the experience of capitalist management and are equally surprised when these borrowings merely intensify the problems. The opposition has, for the time being, an 'alibi' since all the government's failures can be put down to bad management, bureaucratism, inconsistency and so on; but the authorities, sensing the real significance of the ideological unity which has been achieved in society for the first time in many years, are striving to draw the opposition into the administration and thereby shift a portion of the responsibility onto it for the actions which it has itself prepared through its theoretical utterances. The Third World and Eastern Europe are playing out an amazingly similar drama and in both cases the profoundly conscious desire for democracy is not being reinforced by a programme of socio-economic transformations which could guarantee the viability of that democracy. As a result the crisis of dictatorship is giving way to (or being united with) a crisis of democracy. Political reforms by themselves do not allow society the opportunity to overcome its social death-agony.

A radical democratic strategy can only be found if the question of political institutions is tightly linked with the question of the fundamental needs and interests of working people. It is essential not simply to change laws but to transform the class nature of the state, and reorient it from defending the interests of privileged elites to working in the interests of the majority. This means reviewing the most important priorities of development, rejecting many dogmas and creating a mechanism of democratic decision-making which operates at the most diverse levels. It is no longer a question of the 'optimal' correlation between plan and market (in various specific situations, very different correlations can be 'optimal') but, first and foremost, of society gaining the possibility of working out this correlation on the basis of a democratic process.

The key moment in Marx's notion of socialism was the ability of society to determine consciously the perspectives of its own development. In this sense democratic politics and socialist politics are indivisible. A consistently implemented democratization is already in itself a movement towards socialism. But consistent democratization demands a decisive repudiation of any form of market or plan fetishism, of the defence of the privilege of an elite, or of any attempt to overcome the crisis at the expense of the workers. It requires a decisive defence of social ownership and, at the same time, a no less decisive struggle against any concentration of economic power. It requires replacing the principle 'the bigger, the better' with the principle 'small is beautiful', recognizing the necessity of workers' self-management as the basis of development, and reorientating to new priorities, ecologically clean and 'alternative' technologies. Both plan and market should serve the aims given them by society in accordance with the place allotted to them in a democratically formulated strategy. The problem is that a new mass movement, free from the dogmas of the past, is needed for these transformations to be realized, a movement capable of carrying out the reforms in a revolutionary manner and of preserving reformist moderation in the course of the revolution.

The numerous practical suggestions as to how to improve the situation, ensure greater efficiency and take care of social justice are, in themselves, of no help to anyone if the forces capable of realizing them do not exist. Reforms from above, even of the most radical variety, are today demonstrating their historical limitedness. The Chinese miracle is turning into a nightmare before our eyes: inflation, poverty and food shortages are making China one of the poorest countries in the Third World. The Gorbachev reforms, which have enraptured the Western press, are more and more evidently reaching an impasse. The crowds of many thousands, demonstrating in Moscow in March 1989 in support of the disgraced Party figure Boris Yeltsin, demanded not only that the elections be conducted honestly but also respect for workers' social rights, equality and real participation in decision-making. At the same time as the Gorbachev leadership is staking more and more on technocratic solutions, on the maximum utilization of capitalist methods in order to shift the burden of the crisis onto the shoulders of the workers, the masses are striving ever harder to take their destiny into their own hands.

Questions which five years ago I endeavoured to resolve theoretically while sitting in my study are now becoming practical everyday questions for all of us. For the first time the opportunity has arisen for the Left in the Soviet Union to found its own mass organization, the Popular Front, and try not only to play the role of critics and commentators but also the role of active participants in the reforms. But this means that we are living through a complex and risky transition from reform from above to reformist revolution from below.

Nowadays the attention of the world is riveted on Russia. Our country has merited this through its tragic history. But it is to be very much desired that the world has not simply followed the 'Russian drama' through curiosity, but has drawn from it some lessons. In this sense our crisis and our struggle do not only affect ourselves, just as the sufferings of the Third World and the conflict of political forces in Western countries are not only of national but global significance. We live in one world and changing it requires common efforts.

That, in essence, is what this book is about.

In the West it is often assumed that Russians love to lecture foreigners. The utterances of many of our emigrés who left the Soviet Union in the 1970s would appear to confirm this. I must make it clear from the outset that I, at least, have no intention of lecturing anybody. We can like or dislike this or that event but we must never force our opinions and evaluations onto others. In this book some Western politics and groupings come in for quite sharp criticism. The reader can either agree or disagree with my appraisals: I only wish to show things as they appear from Moscow, through the prism of our historical and political experience.

Unfortunately, I cannot name those people who have assisted me in collecting material and preparing the manuscript. I have been helped a great deal by colleagues from several British universities and also by Roy A. Medvedev, the only name which can be mentioned here. The idea of writing this book first came to me during our discussions at his cosy flat on Dybenko Street, and his help has played an enormous role in various stages of the work. As regards my other colleagues and friends, they can be certain that I constantly think of them and thank them.

Moscow, 29 March 1989

PART ONE

Introduction

If, back in 1968, revolution was the major theme of theoretical discussion on the Left, by the mid 1980s the question of reformism had moved to the forefront. The Italian Communists call themselves a reformist party; Hungarian dissidents speak of the politics of radical reform; the triumphal success of social democrat Alan Garcia in the 1985 Presidential Elections in Peru indicates that, even in the Third World, reformism is gaining more established positions.

In such circumstances it is especially important to study the general strategic principles of reformism. While there exist many works on individual questions, this is patently inadequate. A generalizing theoretical analysis is required, free from ideological preconceptions. In most theoretical discussions among the Western Left, the problem of reformism is examined without utilizing the vast historical experience accumulated by the world's socialist and workers' movement over the past fifty years. Theoreticians indulge themselves in abstractions; practical people, pre-occupied with their own affairs, become immersed in individual questions. Because of this, revolutionary mythology is gradually being replaced by a reformist mythology which is adopting all of its shortcomings. This was shown in 1985 by the discussion 'What Sort of Reformism?' in *MondOperaio*, the journal of the Italian Socialist Party.

In exactly the same way as the revolutionary myth repudiated reform from the beginning, the current reformist myth is forcing the question of revolution out of ideological circulation. The latter would appear to be beyond the field of vision of those theoreticians for whom reformism is the sole possible form of progressive politics. In such a view, Marxist theory, with its revolutionary problematic, seems of purely historical interest. But behind the slogan of a break with utopia, nothing but a restructuring of utopian consciousness is taking place.

Marxism is not an ideology of revolution but a theory of social development. Many revolutionaries have failed to grasp this and their error has been replicated by the reformists. As a result of this one-sided view, neither the former nor the latter have been able to use Marxism effectively in their struggle.

This work is an attempt at a Marxist analysis of the problems of reformism in material from the West, Eastern Europe and the Soviet Union. Of course, it is not able to 'provide answers to all questions'; rather it endeavours to pose theoretical questions, the definitive answers to which can only be given by practice.

Reformism is not a homogeneous concept. History knows of the conservative reformism of the ruling classes, the essence of which was splendidly expressed by a young French aristocrat on the eve of the 1830 Revolution: 'For everything to remain the same, everything must change.' Social democratic reforms within the framework of the capitalist system and Janos Kadar's reforms in Hungary are efforts at a more profound transformation – but one which remains within definite, previously drawn boundaries. Nevertheless, there are examples of more radical reformist politics consciously breaking through or pushing aside such limitations. In the end such reformism merges into revolution.

Conservatives have traditionally been considered the major enemies, and revolutionaries the rivals, of reformism. But in the twentieth century, the technocratic project of rationalizing and regulating the system has also been opposed to that of reformism. Technocratic ideology outwardly appears to be a variety of reformism, but the ideas of the democratization of life, the transformation (albeit partial) of the social mechanisms of society and the expansion within it of the role of the working masses are alien to it. It is precisely technocracy which proves reformism's chief historical adversary and although moderate reformist groups have, at times, united with technocrats to isolate revolutionaries, effective struggle for the transformation of society requires a directly opposite course.

In preparing this book I have been assisted by people with a wide range of views (from liberals and social democrats to Eurocommunists and Trotskyists) from a wide range of countries. While discussing my own ideas with them I not only tested the applicability of these and other general positions to specific situations, but I also satisfied myself once more that the unity of all on the Left, irrespective of ideological and geographical differences, is not only possible but essential. I remain an advocate of such unity and should therefore warn the reader in good time against attempts to reduce the author's position to support for one or another of the ideological-political currents in the contemporary West. The true dividing line passes not between parties but between classes. In the end, the real historical choice must be made not between ideological doctrines but between that politics which strives to perpetuate exploitation and inequality and that which derives from the workers' interests.

On the Left today the Trotskyists are evidently the most ideologically oriented group. Of all radical currents they most consistently reject reformism, considering themselves the mouthpiece of the working class's revolutionary will and uncompromising proponents of pure socialist politics. This self-evaluation is, in my view, not so very mistaken but, insofar as the working class in the industrial democracies displays no real revolutionary will, the Trotskyists remain a small group with limited influence on the masses. When real conditions arise for arousing its revolutionary will, the working class expresses it through its own traditional mass organizations, which in such circumstances inevitably 'move to the left'.

The Trotskyists' misfortune lies not in being 'too' revolutionary but, it seems to me, in their insufficiently dialectical appreciation of revolution. Each move to the right and defeat of radical initiatives is explained by the machinations of opportunists in the labour movement while the masses are seen as invariably revolutionary. In the meantime, the proletariat, on which such hopes have been pinned, continues to support social democratic reformist politics while failing to heed the revolutionaries' inflammatory calls.

To orthodox Trotskyists all reformism is class collaboration and all class collaboration the result of opportunist activity. Indeed, without class collaboration the process of capitalist production would be totally unviable. This means that class collaboration is as much an objective law of any exploitative society as class struggle. A reformist politics derives from this reality: the real task of radical socialist forces is not to condemn this state of affairs but to seek the means of overcoming it, but it is impossible to achieve this aim through revolutionary slogans alone. Furthermore, there must inevitably be a reformist element in any authentically revolutionary programme.

The specificity of the 1980s lay in the fact that the crisis of reformism was coupled with the glaring absence of a revolutionary alternative in the West. The Left's task is to provide a fresh impulse to reformist activity through a revival of the revolutionary ideal. The whole Left must accomplish this task together. Every current, from Trotskyists to social democrats, can make its contribution to the common cause, co-operate with others and change without losing the originality of its own best traditions. One aim of this study is to formulate some general strategic principles which can unite the contemporary Left in the East, West and Third World. On the basis of such principles an international dialogue might then become possible in which all radical forces could participate irrespective of their ideological conceptions and geographical separation.

1

Marxism and Reformism

'Marxism is the science of social revolution.' This definition has become so commonplace that it is difficult to find a book where it is not repeated in one form or another. As that science becomes widely disseminated and turned into an ideology, 'revolution' appears as absolute good and everything opposed to it absolute evil. But what about reforms? What about partial changes? This problem has traditionally troubled Marxists. Lenin declared that

> a reform is a concession made by the ruling classes *in order* to stem, weaken or conceal the revolutionary struggle, in order to split the forces and energy of the revolutionary classes, to befog their consciousness, etc.[1]

True, he did later concede that the contrast between reform and revolution 'is not something absolute, this line is not something dead, but alive and changing, and one must be able to define it in each particular case.'[2] The trouble is that in twentieth-century Europe not a single successful social revolution has so far occurred — at least in Western Europe. Having set their sights on revolution, the theoreticians of the Left studied what in reality was not there and ignored what was happening in front of their eyes. At the turn of the century, a French socialist wrote that 'reformism was the product of a short phase of universal history' and that, in particular, 'reformist illusions' had been assigned a life of all of four years 'between 1898 and 1902 when all states to a greater or lesser degree experienced a revival of exchange.' As soon as this period of revival was over, reformism was finished and 'the triumph of the revolutionary spirit' had begun.[3] Consoled by such reasoning,

7

Marxists entered the new epoch while striving with all their might to convince themselves and others that we were still in the old.

This may seem an exaggeration, but it is an indisputable fact that the question of reform has been less discussed in socialist, and particularly Marxist, literature than that of revolution. But without the one it is impossible to understand the other. From the very beginning, the dialectic of large and small social conflicts, reform and revolution, consent and coercion attracted Marx's attention. If, in devoting our attention to one side of his theory, we forget the other, the blame is not with the author of *Capital*, but only with ourselves.

Repeating the words of the Master as an answer to all questions is naive, but the theoretical analysis made by Marx in the nineteenth century still retains its validity as a methodological paradigm to which it is continually necessary to return. Thus, 'what Marx really said' is of interest not only to historians but also to people concerned with contemporary problems.

The idea of a revolutionary transition to socialism undoubtedly occupies a central place in Marx's political works, but only those incapable of grasping what they have read can ignore the patently reformist themes of *Capital*.

First of all, Marx devotes special attention to English factory legisl-ation not only because this had been achieved through prolonged struggle but also because it is 'that first conscious and methodical reaction of society against the spontaneously developed form of its production process'.[4] It is strikingly apparent that when he characterized the British reforms in these terms, Marx was emphasizing their socialist tendency. 'Conscious and methodical' social regulation is counterposed to the spontaneous development of market capitalism. This counterposi-tion is especially important when we recall that Marx avoided using the term 'socialism' in *Capital*, confining himself merely to an indication of the possibility of restructuring social production on a new basis.

Anybody now characterizing, in a similar fashion, measures taken by Western governments to protect labour would immediately be accused of opportunism. If, all in all, it was a question of an insignificant reduction in the working day, and this reform in no way undermined the power of capital, why did Marx value it so highly?

Marx was no opportunist, but a scholar whose starting point was reality, not slogans. A close examination of the analysis of British factory legislation in *Capital* enables a whole series of elements to be defined more precisely, and not only clarifies Marx's thought but is of major interest to the contemporary socialist movement.

Initial demands for reform are frequently advanced in an elemental fashion by the workers themselves, but they are formulated by the intelligentsia, who turn a class slogan into a demand of public opinion by obtaining support from all strata of society among those who are 'competent' and 'free from partisanship and respect of persons'.[5] These demands can gain the sympathy of the mass of people remote from socialism and the working class precisely because they do not threaten the basis of the social system. But, even in a democratic country, public opinion cannot carry the day without a struggle. Reform encounters fierce opposition from the manufacturers who favour the old arrangements. The first legislative attempts to introduce public regulation of labour relations provoke a veritable 'revolt of capital' — a particularly senseless revolt as, in the end, reform increases industrial efficiency even in a capitalist sense. After restrictions were placed on exploitation, manufacturers were obliged to modernize production by introducing more productive machinery and labour-saving technology. In this way social progress furthers technical progress. The higher cost of labour power is accompanied by an increase in the quality of labour and the introduction of improved equipment. Society is raised to a new level of development.[6]

Shlomo Avineri writes, with reference to Marx, that factory legislation brings 'aspects of community-oriented considerations' into the economy and 'contributes further to social change'.[7] And yet there has been no revolution! The contradiction between labour and capital has been preserved. Without a doubt. So does it not follow from this that reform strengthens the old regime by alleviating its contradictions and averting revolution? Lenin and many other of Marx's followers considered this to be the case. Marx himself thought otherwise.

Firstly, capitalist society 'is no solid crystal, but an organism capable of change, and constantly engaged in a process of change'.[8] In the course of this development 'a radical change in the existing relations between capital and labour' must inevitably begin long before the revolution.[9] Reforms not only represent a victory for socialist principles, and not only introduce elements of socialism into the existing structure, but also demonstrate the viability of these very principles and the progressiveness of these elements. They become a school of socialism for the labouring classes and a practical preparation for revolution. They cannot substitute for it because they do not resolve the system's basic contradiction, but neither can they stave off more profound changes. According to Marx,

the transformation of some elements of the social structure is essential to
create the conditions for the peaceful development of the revolution and
for a painless transition to the new system.

Marx, we would add, knew that a painless transition to the new
system would by no means be equivalent to universal compromise.
Revolution without struggle is inconceivable, but the class struggle
assumes forms 'more brutal or more humane according to the degree of
development of the working class itself'.[10] The point of partial changes is
to raise this level. And here Marx was addressing himself not just to the
proletariat but also to its class antagonists — who, in the struggle for
reform, can prove its greatest allies:

> Apart from any higher motives, then, the most basic interests of the present
> ruling classes dictate to them that they clear out of the way all the legally
> removable obstacles to the development of the working class. For this
> reason, among others, I have devoted a great deal of space in this volume to
> the history, the details, and the results of the English factory legislation. One
> nation can and should learn from others. Even when a society has begun to
> track down the natural laws of its movement — and it is the ultimate aim of
> this work to reveal the economic law of motion of modern society — it can
> neither leap over the natural phases of its development nor remove them by
> decree. But it can shorten and lessen the birth-pangs.[11]

The preparation for socialism consequently begins within the old
system and on the success of this preparation depend, to a significant
degree, the conditions, forms and methods of the subsequent struggle.
The Soviet researcher, G.G. Vodolazov, has written that, in Marx, there is
an inherent striving 'to place reformist activity in a revolutionary
context'. Furthermore, 'within the single act of political action, within
the single act of socialist struggle, reform and revolution are combined in
a close, organic unity.'[12] Jean Jaurès defined this position most precisely
in his speech to the French Socialist Congress in Bordeaux in 1903:

> It is not a question of counterposing reform and revolution as if they are
> mutually exclusive, as those who have an interest in confusing the issue
> attempt to demonstrate. Reform and revolution, far from being mutually
> exclusive, augment and are conditioned by each other.

Marx's primary idea had however been much more profound. Jaurès
emphasized that successful reforms become 'an unrivalled stimulus for
the working class, aroused to hasten the achievement of its own liber-

ation with a powerful hand.'[13] Thus, the whole value of reforms is in being a preparation for revolution. Marx was convinced that they prepare not only the revolution, but also socialism. In other words, for Marx, the value of reforms was not in that they undermined the old system — sometimes they even strengthen it — but in their creation of elements of the new system within the framework of the old society.

This theme in Marx's theory has been completely ignored by revolutionaries and reformist social democracy alike. It is also absent from Marx's and Engels's later works. It is indeed possible that, after the first volume of *Capital* was published, Marx himself to some degree changed his point of view. The Paris Commune and the revolutionary struggle on the Continent compelled him to take a more decisive stance: the seemingly imminent revolution rendered reform a less immediate problem.

We do not have the right, however, to pass over Marx's reformist ideas, if only for one reason: the original conception of *Capital*'s author was that it is precisely reformative activity within the old system which provides an answer to the question 'What is socialism?' This formulation may seem somewhat paradoxical — did Marx not know what socialism is? An explanation is required.

In *The German Ideology*, Marx and Engels wrote that socialism (or 'communism' as they then termed it) 'is for us not a *state of affairs* which is to be established, an *ideal* to which reality [will] have to adjust itself. We call communism the *real* movement which abolishes the present state of things.'[14] And intended reforms formed part of this movement. But this is not the whole picture. Marx, unlike the utopians, refused to describe future society in advance, as he did not wish to construct 'models' artificially. His unwillingness to discuss some sort of social 'ideal' to be striven for was demonstratively emphasized in his works, particularly in the period before 1871. The scientific character of Marx's socialism does not consist in its being free from error. Mistakes can be made in science, and sometimes utopians brilliantly guess truths unknown to science. The difference between science and utopia consists in the fact that the former derives from reality, the latter from an ideal. While socialism remained only an ideal, a hypothesis, a thought, Marx did not consider it possible to provide a description of the future system. He could only catalogue capitalism's flaws and thereby establish the tasks which had to be accomplished. Nevertheless, Marx did not decline to examine the question of socialism. There is only an apparent contradiction here. The author of *Capital* sought elements of the future in the present and through his analysis of capitalism he originated socialist theory. Reforms which are achieved, or can be achieved, in bourgeois society do not, in and of themselves, create socialism but they can serve as material for theory, thereby rendering Marx's notions of socialism more specific.

For Marxists, the goal of change has always been freedom — that state in which 'the free development of each is the condition for the free development of all.'[15] Consequently, reforms which extend democracy and social control over the economy are simultaneously experiments in socialism. Eduard Bernstein related this chiefly to the expansion of the role of trades unions under capitalism: 'Their tendency is to undermine the absolutism of capital and give the worker an opportunity to influence the management of industry.'[16] But while Bernstein was concerned primarily with what sort of benefits the proletariat derived from one reform or another, Marx was much more interested in the theoretical lessons which could be drawn from them.

In the nineteenth century, however, the harvest from reform was not a bountiful one. Under pressure from activists in the labour movement who demanded definite programmatic slogans, Marx and Engels were forced more and more into concessions to the old utopian socialism with which they had fought at the commencement of their activity. These compromises later attracted the attention of all of Marx's critics, from Bernstein to Professor Alec Nove of Glasgow, who have counterposed their own scientific theses to Marx's 'utopian' socialism.

Let us take the most straightforward example. Everyone writes that Marx underestimated the significance of the market for a socialist society. This is already so well known that one feels somehow ashamed to repeat it. One can, of course, like Nove, dig up forgotten quotations from Marx's later works just to repudiate once again all of the principles enunciated in them: but this game is not worth the candle. The Scottish Professor is seemingly tilting at windmills. Fortunately or unfortunately, even in Marx's later works there is no comprehensive characterization of socialism: he was interested in capitalism. He studied the system's contradictions, which would have to be resolved. The socialist system arises naturally from measures directed at eliminating these contradictions.

Nove might have produced a more useful work if, instead of returning again and again to Marx's errors (detected long since by his followers), he had added to his cited quotations an even greater number of others which say the *direct opposite*.

The young Marx and Engels had much to say on the eradication of private property but nothing on the elimination of the market. Not a single word can be found about this in either *The Communist Manifesto* or *The Principles of Communism*! There is no mention of any anti-market slogans nor any discussion of the abolition of commodity production and so forth. This is completely natural, for both authors started out from the idea, perfectly correct for their time, that the prolonged existence of a mixed economy was essential. Engels wrote that the immediate elimination of private property 'would be just as impossible as at *one* stroke to increase the existing productive forces to the degree necessary for instituting community of property.' Proletarian power 'will transform existing society only gradually, and be able to abolish private property only when the necessary quantity of the means of production has been created.'[17]

True, Engels was referring here to the fact that, in the end, this will all lead at some time to the disappearance of money, exchange and commodity-production, but it was perfectly clear to him that such a utopia is something for the very distant future and not a practical programme. Something completely different is brought to the fore, for here the politics of reform is proposed not only as a preparation for revolution but also as its continuation. Revolution is conceived as a definite and necessary stage, a qualitative leap, in the process of reform. The existence of non-commodity production in the conditions of a mixed economy is inconceivable. The market and commodity–money relations are essential for its development. In this sense, advocates of 'market socialism' could base themselves entirely on the ideas of the young Marx and Engels. Towards the end of his life, however, the views of the author of *Capital* changed. Anti-market sentiments are much more in evidence in works written after the first volume of his magnum opus. After Marx's death, Engels quite bluntly characterized socialism as a system of non-commodity production. The scholars had succumbed to the influence of the ideology which had traditionally possessed the workers' minds. Thus one comes across utterances, written in the last years of Marx's life, strikingly reminiscent of Proudhon's ideas — which Marx had slated in *The Poverty of Philosophy*. Marx had patently fallen under the influence of Proudhonism when, in the *Critique of the Gotha Programme*, he discussed the future organization of production and distribution.

One could say that, as a scholar, the 'young' Marx was more consistent and sober-minded than the 'old'. But this is of purely historical significance. Essentially there is no longer any argument with anybody, apart from a few romantics and dogmatists among orthodox Trotskyists and Maoists in the West. As is well known, the Chinese Maoists have turned out to be the more realistic, but leading theoreticians of neo-Trotskyism, such as Ernest Mandel, have shifted away from the old dogmas. All socialists understand the need for a market; on the agenda are other questions — questions of strategy.

For Marxists, the word 'reformism' is no longer the term of abuse it was at the turn of the century. History has all too sternly demonstrated that one should be much more wary of the empty chatter of revolution-ary phrases and demagogic promises. In the last analysis, 'opportunists' have caused less damage than extremists. Lenin himself wrote in 1921 that

> the greatest, perhaps the only danger to the genuine revolutionary is that of exaggerated revolutionism, ignoring the limits and conditions in which revolutionary methods are appropriate and can be successfully employed. True revolutionaries have mostly come a cropper when they began to write 'revolution' with a capital R, to elevate 'revolution' to something almost divine, to lose their heads, to lose the ability to reflect, weigh and ascertain in the coolest and most dispassionate manner....

Untimely revolutionism, to use Lenin's term, is capable of inflicting (and has inflicted) major harm on the Left, particularly in periods of society's calm and 'peaceful' development. Lenin continues:

> True revolutionaries will perish only if they abandon their sober outlook and take it into their heads that the 'great, victorious, world' revolution can and must solve all problems in a revolutionary manner under all circum-stances and in all spheres of action.[18]

The thorniest problem still concerns that of the paths of transition to socialism in the specific conditions of each country. In the nineteenth century, revolutionaries' notions of future society remained at quite an abstract and, at times, naive level, but twentieth-century experience has permitted Marxists to elaborate a more substantial programme of social reorganization. Numerous socialist experiments in a variety of countries have, despite their many failures, enriched the Left theoretically. For the Left today it is clear that socialism cannot exist without political democ-racy, workers' self-management of production, market relations in the economy, or without nationalization and planning. The transition from the old to the new society still remains, however, an acute and frequently unresolved problem.

Nicos Poulantzas has written that Marx did not touch upon this question but 'left only a few general observations on the close relationship between socialism and democracy'.[19] But here the Eurocommunist theoretician is certainly not thinking about either the internal dynamic or historical meaning of Marx's thought.

Marx always evaluated the prospects for progress towards socialism, and revolutionary or reformist transformations, within the context of the democratic state. The young Marx began with a defence of press freedom under the conditions of the repressive, Prussian police system. 'Freedom of the press,' he exclaimed, 'too, has its beauty — if not exactly a feminine one — which one must have loved to be able to defend it.'[20] Every curtailment of freedom of expression is a denial of reason, an attempt on the very essence of man as a thinking being. The anti-democratic actions of the state are, therefore, not only inhuman but unnatural.[21] But the suppression of the opposition press, the twisting of dissidents' arms, the government's mendacity and the people's lack of will, are only differing manifestations of an unfree society. Democracy is needed to eradicate this unnatural state of affairs.

> One form of freedom governs another just as one limb of the body does another. Whenever a particular freedom is put in question, freedom in general is put in question. Whenever one form of freedom is rejected, freedom in general is rejected and henceforth can have only a semblance of existence, since the sphere in which absence of freedom is dominant becomes a matter of pure chance. Absence of freedom is the rule and freedom an exception, a fortuitous and arbitrary occurrence.[22]

Evidently, Marx understood the problem much more profoundly than many Western 'defenders of democracy' who suppose that a partial restriction of civil liberties is permissible in the name of the higher goals of strengthening the foundations of the 'free world'. Marx, by contrast, was convinced that, in order to defend democracy and save freedom, they must be extended. This was the starting point of Marx's socialist programme. He subjected bureaucratic ideology and 'barrack communism' to a withering critique, contrasting them with his ideas of social transformation. A British author writes that Marx's socialism 'as a political programme may be most quickly defined as *the complete democratization of society*, not merely of political forms.'[23]

Capitalist society and parliamentary democracy must be transformed because they are insufficiently democratic. If, in extending our freedom, we do not go beyond the limits of traditional bourgeois institutions, we risk losing it. Marx was indignant that democracy and civil liberty adapt themselves 'to the narrow limits of private property'.[24] Engels declared, in 1845, that 'democracy nowadays is communism'. Being a consistent democrat meant being an advocate of socialism.

> Democracy has become the proletarian principle, the principle of the masses. The masses may be more or less clear about this, the only correct meaning of democracy, but all have at least an obscure feeling that social equality of rights is implicit in democracy.[25]

The interests of the ruling class have always been the source not only of economic oppression but also of political restrictions, repressions and prohibitions. Antagonisms between classes must be eliminated: consequently, a revolution is necessary. It is stated directly in *The Communist Manifesto* that the task of revolution is to turn the proletariat into the ruling class, 'to win the battle of democracy'.[26] The West German political scientist, K. Lenk, notes in this regard that

> Marx calls 'democracy' the situation where society is dominant over its own productive development. The establishment of such an order is only possible by overcoming economic obstacles: the contradictions between labour and capital. Having changed their relations in the course of a social revolution, society will rid itself of state violence and the corresponding apparatus of coercion by replacing it with a union of free and equal people'.[27]

Existing democratic institutions, however, already constitute an element of the future. Marx's words to the effect that in England and other free countries the transition to socialism can be achieved by peaceful means, but that, on the Continent, it would most probably become necessary to resort to force, have become well known. Everything depends on the political system existing in a particular country: 'heed must be paid to the institutions, customs and traditions of the various countries.'[28] Unfortunately, this statement has often been interpreted in a narrowly tactical sense. Marx saw that democratic institutions in Britain had already attained such maturity and stability that, in and of themselves, they opened up the possibility of society's transition to socialism. This transition was, of course, inconceivable without a struggle, without the bourgeoisie's opposition; but this struggle could be conducted roughly along the lines of the campaign for factory legislation and universal suffrage. At a definite stage of development, democratic institutions *per se* assume a socialist character. They should not be eliminated during the transition to socialism, but strengthened. Towards the end of his life, Engels wrote:

> One can conceive that the old society may develop peacefully into the new one in countries where the representatives of the people concentrate all power in their hands, where, if one has the support of the majority of the people, one can do as one sees fit in a constitutional way: in democratic republics such as France and the USA, in monarchies such as Britain, where the imminent abdication of the dynasty in return for financial compensation is discussed in the press daily and where this dynasty is powerless against the people.[29]

At the beginning of the twentieth century all Marxists agreed, in principle, with this assessment of the parliamentary system. In any case the discussion was, for the time being, about England (although Engels had mentioned other countries ...). Lenin, however, concluded only that one must combine 'the struggle for democracy and the struggle for the socialist revolution, *subordinating* the first to the second.'[30] In this formulation, democracy and socialism are divorced and turned into quite separate goals (political freedom being valued primarily as a means of struggling for socialism). Bernstein was much closer to Marx when he said that 'democracy is at one and the same time both a means and an end',[31] for it is in democratic institutions that the prototype of socialist institutions is to be found.

Democracy enables reform and revolution to be united in a single strategy of class struggle. It is only if one acknowledges this that one can understand Marx's reasoning on the 'dictatorship of the proletariat', which generates so much disquiet among present-day Western communists.

The French Communist Party (PCF) officially abolished the slogan of the 'dictatorship of the proletariat' at its 22nd Congress. It was declared outmoded and incompatible with the new conditions:

> Democracy not only creates the spirit of the regime when power resides in the workers' hands, it is not only the outcome of such power, it is one of its foundations. Without it workers' power can neither triumph nor be built.[32]

Pious words! But the French communists have simultaneously maintained that, although power in the Soviet Union resides in the workers' hands, genuine democracy does not, in their opinion, exist. How this contradiction is resolved remains quite incomprehensible. It is even less understandable why such wonderful words about democracy only became a reality in the 1970s. Was not the idea of socialism's democratic foundations as justified fifty years ago as it is today? Concealed behind the debate on the dictatorship of the proletariat — and this is no secret to anybody — is the desire of Western communists to cleanse themselves of their past, of Stalinism, and to contrast their programmatic positions with the political practice of the Soviet state. All this is clear. But it is no less clear that from moral or propagandistic considerations (both, in fact), they have remained silent about the very essence of the problem.

The term 'dictatorship of the proletariat' does not appear immediately in Marx's work and is encountered quite infrequently. Nevertheless, it is not employed in a chance fashion, nor is it a 'slip of the pen' or a 'slip of the tongue'. Robert Tucker writes that

> Admittedly the teaching on proletarian dictatorship had a significant place in classical Marxism, and one which later social-democratic Marxists, including even Engels in his old age, were inclined to downgrade. But it had not the central place accorded to it in Lenin's Marxism, nor was the proletarian dictatorship conceived by Marx and Engels as a dictatorship of a revolutionary party on behalf of the proletariat. They did not imagine that the working people, once in power, would have need of a party as their 'teacher, guide and leader' in building a new life on socialist lines.[33]

Lenin reinterpreted Marxism in the spirit of the Russian Populist tradition and the realities of Russian conditions by utilizing Marx's teaching on the dictatorship of the proletariat as the theoretical foundation of the Bolsheviks' political line from 1917 to 1922.[34] Stalin, in his turn, reinterpreted Lenin by converting the slogan of proletarian dictatorship into the ideological foundation of terror.

Since Marx demanded unlimited social democracy, and Stalin unlimited personal power, some theoretical contradictions were, at first sight, unavoidable. How could the total negation of Marxism by Stalin and his disciples (from Mao to Pol Pot) be presented as genuine loyalty to the old revolutionary banner? Trotsky attempted to establish the deviants' guilt by accusing Stalin of revisionism:

> With the utmost stretch of fancy it would be difficult to imagine a contrast more striking than that which exists between the schema of the workers' state according to Marx, Engels and Lenin, and the actual state now headed by Stalin.[35]

In reality, however, it was very easy to counter Trotsky's allegation.

Stalin's point of view was brilliantly defended during one discussion by a certain E. Habibi from Israel, who asked: 'Is not *any* restriction of rights and freedoms an infringement of democracy?'[36] I do not know which is the greater here — naive stupidity or blatant cynicism — but it is a standpoint with its own kind of logic: the real triumph of democracy consists in its self-liquidation. Yes, in precisely this. Democracy is unstable; democratic rights can be used to undermine the existing system, in 'groundless criticism', and so on. Consequently, freedoms must be curbed in the name of stabilizing democracy. The more we restrict them the more stable democracy becomes. A 'democratic' regime attains the highest degree of stability when freedoms and civil rights have been abolished altogether. Absurd? No, it is irreproachable sophistry. And if you think that only a Stalinist would reason in this manner you would be mistaken. Other pro-Western liberals argue in exactly the same fashion.

However, we are not, at this moment, interested in how Lenin, Stalin or Trotsky interpreted Marx, but what Marx himself had in mind. The question is essentially quite straightforward. By analysing the social structure of society, Marx came to the conclusion that, in conditions of class struggle, the state cannot be an organ which takes care of the 'common good'. It implements the ruling class's will and ensures the implementation of adopted decisions by force. In other words, every power has a class character and every power contains an element of coercion. This fact was recognized, incidentally, a long time before Marx. Take the *Reminiscences of Socrates* by Xenophon of Athens. From this book we know of a debate of some interest to us that took place at least two thousand years before *Capital* was written. Alcibiades demanded from Pericles, the leader of Athenian democracy, an answer to the question: what is the difference between democracy and tyranny? Pericles replied that tyranny rests on force, but democracy on law; tyranny on coercion, but democracy on persuasion. Alcibiades retorted that the defence of laws also requires force and that the democratic majority compels the minority to recognize its will 'without having persuaded' it. As a result, Pericles had to acknowledge that everything 'the dominant class in the state writes down, after consideration of what must be done, is called law.'[37] Evidently, a connection between the law and class interests, and between the state and coercion already existed. In the new European philosophy we find a developed exposition of this latter idea in Hobbes's *Leviathan*. Marx was the first in history to give a theoretical and, as distinct from Hobbes, socio-economic foundation to the theory of state and law. It was clear to him that even the most democratic power remains a power all the same.

Eurocommunist ideologues, especially in Spain, insist that democracy 'permits an advance towards socialist transformation based on consensus and hegemony and not on coercion'.[38] Marx would never have agreed with these words even though he was a democrat to his very core. Unlike contemporary Western communists, he was not inclined to take his desires for reality and mix emotions with theory. Marx understood that *every* state utilizes coercion but that, in a democracy, it is not only applied in a different way from an authoritarian regime, but is a totally different kind of coercion. Lenk writes, with reference to Marx, that although democracy does not eliminate coercion in a democratic country, 'state force assumes a legal form and is recognized as lawful by the governed masses themselves who constitute the majority of citizens.'[39] In other words, democracy does not do away with class struggle but confines it within a definite legal framework acceptable to all classes.

It is, of course, impossible to speak of the state's 'neutrality'. The regime of the Fifth Republic was defined in a thoroughly Marxist fashion by François Mitterrand as a state where 'behind a mask of benign institutions a class dictatorship is exercised' for which democracy serves merely as a 'cover'.[40] He arrived at such a conclusion, not through reading Marx, but through his own experience. A liberal democrat, he was later drawn into the socialist movement by following the same logic of the struggle for freedom as Marx and Jaurès. There is nowhere in Mitterrand's reasoning a denial or underestimation of the civil rights of the French people, for a class state of the democratic type is qualitatively different from an authoritarian or totalitarian system where force is directed against the majority.

Marx's viewpoint might be considered one-sided but its correctness has, in general, been confirmed by history. Roy Medvedev accuses Lenin of being prepared to say that 'power, any kind of power, amounts to dictatorship.' Lenin's teaching on the state was, consequently, 'imprecise and false'.[41] But, in saying that a state sysem always means 'the organized, systematic use of force against persons', Lenin was only repeating Marx and Engels's words.[42] Medvedev starts out from moral and political considerations: 'If we describe all power and systems of government as dictatorial, we are guilty not only of a logical error but a political one too.'[43] This is indisputable. But what is under discussion here is not theory but tactics and party phraseology. As for theoretical analysis, that is a different matter.

Police and bureaucracy are organs of coercion in even the freest country. If anybody believes that the activities of the tax inspectorate are unnecessary because of people's general desire to share their money voluntarily with their state, then we can only envy their faith in humanity.... The modern state is not reducible to coercion, but a state without coercion would be a state without power.

Karl Kautsky correctly emphasized that when Marx spoke of proletarian 'dictatorship', he was not speaking about the elimination of liberties but 'about the sole political power of the proletariat'.[44] Lenin understood Marx perfectly correctly, but what conclusions he drew is another question. First, by constantly accusing his opponents — Kautsky, Plekhanov, Martov and other social democrats — of confusing the question of the class essence of power with the question of the form of power, he was making exactly the same mistake himself at every step. If, in one instance, he is in agreement with Engels by stressing that the dictatorship of the proletariat does not mean 'the abolition of democracy' for the workers,[45] elsewhere he writes that:

> Dictatorship is rule based directly upon force and unrestricted by any laws. The revolutionary dictatorship of the proletariat is rule won and maintained by the use of violence by the proletariat against the bourgeoisie, rule that is unrestricted by any laws.[46]

What sort of democracy is this! Even an official Soviet political commentator, in an oblique polemic with Lenin, has remarked that the elimination of all legality would reduce society 'to a state of total anarchy'.[47] This, incidentally, is incorrect, for a despotic, authoritarian state is quite capable of maintaining order on a foundation of lawlessness, but we can congratulate the author for making a legitimate point.

It is clear that Marx would not have agreed with interpretations of proletarian dictatorship in which no place remained for democracy. Lenin attempts to resolve the contradiction by saying that the dictatorship of the proletariat 'does not mean the abolition (or very material restriction, which is also a form of abolition) of democracy for the class over which, or against which, the dictatorship is exercised.'[48] So are legality, civil rights and liberties consequently preserved for the workers? Even if we adopt a 'purely theoretical' stance, forgetting about the practice of Lenin's, and even more so Stalin's time, it becomes immediately obvious that we are falling into a new contradiction. Bourgeois parliamentary democracy guarantees, albeit formally, the equality of rights of all citizens irrespective of class, nationality and political views. Rosa Luxemburg, whom nobody could accuse of having a bourgeois attitude, saw that the great merit of Western democracy is in that it leads to 'the participation of all popular strata in political life.'[49] How can the proletarian state be a higher form if it cannot guarantee this? But Lenin continually insists that the new power is 'a *million times* more democratic than any bourgeois democracy.'[50] The question is not whether such a state is a step forward as Lenin supposed, or a step back as other Marxists thought. It is simply that such a solution is, in practice, completely unrealizable. There can be no democracy without universal formal equality, for this is its starting principle which links it with socialism. Wherever complete equality of civil rights is absent there can be no democracy in general let alone socialist democracy. However, we must here return to the author of *Capital.*

Since Marx saw the state's principal function precisely in organized coercion, it was clear to him that the greater the democracy, the less the state apparatus. In his opinion the role of coercion will be reduced to a minimum in a socialist society and this provided him with the grounds for speaking of the withering away of the state (evidently, it would be more correct to speak of the withering away, or at least weakening, of one of the state's functions inasmuch as the modern state system is not, in practice, reducible to organized coercion). There is, therefore, no inconsistency whatsoever in Marx's thought between the idea of the proletarian dictatorship and the striving for freedom: indeed, one presupposes the other. In *The Critique of the Gotha Programme*, which is devoted precisely to the dictatorship of the proletariat, Marx emphasizes that 'freedom consists in converting the state from an organ superimposed on society into one thoroughly subordinate to it.'[51] Rosa Luxemburg had truly grasped this idea when she wrote that the proletarian dictatorship must display in practice 'the distinct extension of democracy and not its abolition.'[52] Lenin could raise no objection to this in theory but made the reservation that the extension of democracy could 'in essence' be accompanied by the restriction of 'formal' rights and liberties – a notion profoundly alien to Marx.

Marx understood the dictatorship of the proletariat as the state of the transition period when power has already been wrested from the hands of the bourgeoisie but the new system has not yet been definitively established and there is ongoing class struggle. Marx related the dictatorship of the proletariat directly to '*the permanence of the revolution*' which would lead to 'the *abolition of class differences in general*'.[53] The seizure of power by a socialist working class must be the beginning of a whole period of socio-economic transformations which Marx envisaged as either an uninterrupted chain of radical reforms (when discussing England) or a series of revolutionary acts (in France). The character of the revolutionary power clearly depends on the character of the struggle, but Marx and Engels emphasized that the model form of proletarian dictatorship must be the democratic republic: 'our Party and the working class can only come to power under [this] form.'[54] It follows from this that all state institutions necessary for the realization of the dictatorship of the proletariat can be created under the old system and within the framework of bourgeois society. In the end Eurocommunism's strategy in the 1970s was reduced to this, although the term 'dictatorship of the proletariat' was not mentioned for perfectly understandable reasons. The slogan of 'the establishment of a new, advanced democracy' was announced which included 'active workers' participation and control.' The idea of smashing the bourgeois state, undemocratically interpreted by communists in Stalin's time, was given a new meaning. According to the theoretical journal of the French communists, 'smashing the state means developing a democratic state system capable of realizing its social tasks in their entirety.'[55] Their Spanish comrades went even further:

> We are for establishing a political democracy capable not only of intervening into economic life in order to ensure justice but of contributing to the progress of the relations of production and the replacement of the ruling classes.[56]

The expansion of democracy consequently becomes the starting point and key means of profound social transformation.

There is nothing novel about these thoughts. The forces of the Left have not arrived at the last quarter of the twentieth century with outstanding results. During the youth rebellion of the 1960s, Jean-Paul Sartre wrote that 'the classical left-wing parties have remained in the nineteenth century.'[57] He suggested that their outmoded concepts made them incapable of comprehending new problems. However, the 'historical delay' was, in reality, related as much to the fact that, even at the turn of the century, the Left could not answer a whole series of questions satisfactorily. New problems seemed difficult because the old ones had not been resolved. It was therefore quite natural that Western Marxists, awoken from the ideological nightmare of Stalinism, once again encountered those problems which had occupied a central place in the theoretical discussions of the pre-Stalin period. The polemic of the late 1970s is vividly reminiscent of the battles of ideas among the ranks of Western social democracy at the beginning of the century. In the main the terminology has changed but the themes of the arguments remain as before. Today, however, we possess the advantage of historical experience which enables us to appraise old conceptions in a new light.

At the turn of the century the question of reform and revolution was debated with incredible passion in all socialist parties. Eastern European socialists were drawn indirectly into the dispute, but in Russia, there was no choice. In an unfree land no other path remained to the opposition but revolution, as all possibility of reformist activity was closed to it. This does not mean that reforms were inconceivable but that, in any case, democratic Left forces could only promote reform through revolutionary means by exerting pressure on the authorities 'from below'. Matters were somewhat different in the democratic states of the West.

Official Soviet historians put the growth of reformist moods down to the fact that 'the influx of non-proletarian elements into the social democratic party had intensified.' But this is just a generality which explains precisely nothing: Marx and Engels were 'non-proletarian elements'. Among the Russian Bolsheviks, especially before 1906, the proportion of intellectuals was far greater than in any of the Western social democratic parties which, according to an official Soviet historian, proved to be 'in the hands of inveterate reformists.'[59] The fact is that the growth and strengthening of the Left in the West had already, by the turn of the century, created new opportunities and a new political situation which demanded a review of tactics and, in part, of strategy.

The discussion was concentrated around two 'individual cases'. In France, where a high degree of freedom had already been achieved, the practical activity of Millerand, a socialist who had entered the bourgeois parliament, became the subject of stormy debates. The Germans, with their traditional penchant for abstract philosophizing, and in conditions where the largest mass social democratic party was bound hand and foot by anti-democratic legislation and had no real access to power, engaged in a quite vacuous polemic around the theoretical pronouncements of Bernstein and von Vollmar. Both discussions, despite all their differences, were united by a common problem: what does a socialist party do in bourgeois society? A revolutionary party must seize power and, having gained the support of the majority of the population, transform society. But what is to be done until then?

Scheidemann expressed the viewpoint of the official social democratic centre quite precisely:

> It is possible to calculate with certainty that in 10 to 15 years — and what is
> 15 years in the life of a people! — the revolutionary party will almost auto-
> matically attract to its side the majority of the people and, at the same time,
> win the indisputable right to exercise political power.[60]

All that was necessary, meanwhile, was agitation and cultural work. There was no need for the party even to make special efforts to democratize the state — crucial, at first glance, in the struggle for power. Marx and Engels, in their critique of the programme of German social democracy, always stressed that the workers' party could come to power 'only ... under the form of the democratic republic.'[61] Their followers among the 'orthodox Marxists' thought otherwise. They acknowledged the superiority of English and French democracy but made the proviso that 'however much we desire this for ourselves, we are not in favour of racking our brains over it.'[62] Power itself will fall into the hands of the proletariat, and one need only await the longed-for day. And although this wretched theory was a product of the bureaucratization of German social democracy, similar ideas can also be encountered among left-wing socialists. On the eve of the 1910 Elections, Jules Guesde declared: 'If eight million French workers vote for their class on 24th April ... then by that same evening a revolution will have been achieved.'[63] A great and victorious revolution solves all problems at a stroke, and the damnable old society can only be destroyed at once and as a whole. There were people, however, who realized that such a tactic was suicidal, that it would lead to the demoralization of the masses and to the self-imposed isolation of the party which assumed the role of eternal opposition. The workers would inevitably give their preference to those prepared to carry on the difficult, day-to-day struggle for their interests even though from a 'revolutionary social democratic' standpoint, such a struggle, by improving the lot of the masses under capitalism, postponed the social revolution.

The ineffectiveness of such a line was apparent to many representa-
tives of both left and right wings of the workers' movement. Even Lenin wrote that there were questions which could not be put to one side 'until socialism has been achieved' but had to be resolved quickly, utilizing 'the democratic state system'.[64] It should be noted that, at that time, there was a general recognition of the value of democracy among all currents of international socialism. But 'what to do with democracy',

how to make use of free institutions in the struggle for socialism, remained an open question.

When Bernstein emphasized the link between democracy and socialism, nobody argued with him. When he said that *Capital* was already inadequate for explaining the new economic processes of the twentieth century, such representatives of the Left as Luxemburg and Lenin indirectly agreed with him, the only difference being that, instead of advancing the usual arguments about the book being 'outdated', they attempted to formulate new theories which generalized the new facts.[65] But when Bernstein and his French friends called for a re-examination of social democracy's tactics, a very fierce polemic flared up.

Attacking Bernstein, who had preached rejection of consistent revolutionism in favour of an orientation to gradual reforms in collaboration with the liberal bourgeoisie, Auguste Bebel declared that 'the tried and victorious tactic of class struggle' could not be repudiated.[66] Kautsky insisted on the exacerbation of social contradictions and accused Bernstein of incorrectly grasping the spirit of the times: 'We are heading towards a revolutionary epoch', he reiterated.[67] This meant there was no sense in discussing reforms. They would not be necessary. The facts to which Bernstein referred to justify himself were of no value: 'the fact that political revolution has not yet arrived does not give the slightest grounds for concluding that revolution has receded into the past and there will be no more of them.'[68] Plekhanov wrote that reformists were going over 'to the point of view of bourgeois democracy';[69] Luxemburg spoke of 'a rejection of independent proletarian politics',[70] and Lenin simply called for opportunists of Bernstein's type to be hounded 'with all our might'.[71]

What, however, did the other side say? Although international social democracy attached considerable significance to the Bernstein affair, it was only part, and not the most important part at that, of a general polemic. The discussions among the French Socialists are deserving of much greater attention. The Germans discussed theoretical ideas, the French discussed actual, practical policy. German socialists talked, the French acted.

Millerand declared:

If we consider violence so worthy of condemnation, as well as useless, if legal reforms seem to be our immediate task and the sole practical means capable of bringing us closer to our distant goal, then we should boldly call ourselves by our proper name — 'reformists'. For we really are reformists.[72]

In his capacity as a Minister in the French Government, Millerand managed to introduce legislation on the length of the working day and on new regulations for capitalist contractors undertaking public works. These regulations gave workers additional opportunities for defending their rights. The social insurance system was also improved. In other words, Millerand utilized his parliamentary powers to ameliorate the proletariat's material position. But, clearly, not one of these measures was a threat to the system. Not one of them directly affected the bourgeoisie's position or eliminated exploitation. Furthermore, not one of them, *in and of itself*, was even transitional to socialism.

In this regard the German reformist, von Vollmar, who publicized and supported Millerand's actions in every way possible among his Party comrades, was forced to declare:

> No, insurance in the event of sickness, old age or misfortune is important in itself — so little can be called the main and most important goal of our efforts — for example, the concern, recently expressed with more and more urgency, about the provision of workers' housing.[73]

There can be no objections to this. Millerand's preparedness to enter a bourgeois government to promote social reform, which aroused the ire of left-wing social democrats, is not at all sinful. Engels wrote, in his time, that socialists must conclude agreements with other democratic parties if they are 'progressive as regards economic development or political freedom.' He added that he was 'enough of a revolutionary not to renounce even this means'.[74] True revolutionism presupposes tactical flexibility and readiness to compromise. The question is, under what conditions to compromise?

Here we encounter a very important problem which evidently became the stumbling block for both reformists and revolutionaries in the Second International: how to make the transition from individual reforms to global demands, from improving the system to its replacement. French right-wing socialists, dealing with a constitutional republic, attempted to dispose of the Left's criticism with generalities to the effect that democracy itself would resolve all problems: 'Democracy is clearly the negation of a class state.' Political freedom was here turned into the same sort of ideological fetish as revolution was for the traditional leaders of the Second International. If one side declared that reforms are unnecessary because revolution will solve all problems without them, then the other pinned the same sort of absolute hopes on the automatic operation of the parliamentary mechanism. At the French Socialist Congress in Bordeaux, Sarreau said that

> once the state has been democratised and equal rights granted to all, both capitalists and proletarians; once the regime of the majority has superseded the class oligarchy and regime of property qualification it is already contradictory and senseless to speak of a class state. Political and social institutions cease to be tools of the possessing classes; they become the work and fruit of the hands of the majority; they can be directed and operated in the general interest.[75]

Formal equality does not, however, signify real equality; equal rights are not the same as equal opportunities. If Sarreau's viewpoint is accepted then socialism becomes completely unnecessary for democracy 'replaces' it; and although, as a Party member, Sarreau could not himself draw such a conclusion, it follows precisely from what he had said.

Rosa Luxeumburg noticed the Right's weak position on this score. In her opinion, 'democracy is indispenable not because it renders superfluous the conquest of political power by the proletariat, but because it renders this conquest of power both *necessary* and *possible*.' Class struggle does not exclude the democratic road; indeed, in the end it must exclude any other road, for 'the fate of democracy is bound with the socialist movement.'[76] Wherever democratic freedoms call into question the existence of the whole socio-economic system, the old ruling class prefers to get rid of them by resorting to naked force or a coup d'état. As Engels wrote at the end of his life: 'They will shoot first.'[77] All subsequent experience has confirmed this — it is sufficient to recall General Pinochet's coup in Chile in 1973 or General Jaruzelski's in Poland in 1981. Rosa Luxemburg justifiably concluded from Engels's words that the struggle for democracy is an essential part of the struggle for socialism but that this does not exclude acute class conflicts.

German reformists, in conditions of Empire, pinned rather less hope on the parliamentary machine. But it was a belief no less characteristic of them than of the French that it was only necessary to win essential freedoms and everything would improve by itself. Bernstein quite justifiably insisted that, in the end, the alternative to parliamentary democracy was either despotism or 'the power of an oligarchy'.[78] However, he was inclined, precisely because of this, to idealize the Western political system, excuse its many shortcomings and underestimate the possibilities for further democratization. All the same, this was not Right social democracy's main problem at the turn of the century.

Millerand, von Vollmar and Bernstein all failed to advance their own strategy of reform, a strategy of reformist struggle for socialism in conditions of freedom. They proposed numerous, unconnected alterations, possible and essential in a given specific situation, instead of concerning themselves with a desirable change in the situation itself. This was reformist ideology without a reformist programme.

Jean Jaurès was apparently one of the first to become aware of, and address, this contradiction. To go down this road, he declared, 'would mean confining socialism forever within the framework of a programme of business which, of necessity, is not unfavourable to the bourgeois spirit.'[79] Taking Millerand's activities apart, he stressed that

> a great danger is concealed in this policy: it breaks the socialist programme into two parts. It is as if we see before us a tree of a certain height — this is the programme — and only its lower part is connected to reality: all the rest — the top — has been cut off from the roots; and the part of the programme which we have thus ceased to promote, which we have not introduced at the very least into the everyday life of our party, this part ceases to receive the life-giving juices of activity and vitality and soon turns into something like a mere barren flower, a useless survival.[80]

We may well say that these words proved prophetic.

In his criticism of the 'revisionists', Antonio Gramsci recalled Bernstein's famous phrase 'the goal is nothing, the movement everything.' In the opinion of this remarkable Italian Marxist, Bernstein's formula reveals the methodological weakness of the whole 'revisionist' approach. 'Without a perspective of specific goals, the movement in general cannot exist', remarked Gramsci, predicting the future degeneration of 'revisionist' reformism:

> Can such a movement retain its vitality and effectiveness when it is devoid of the prospect of achieving any of its nearest or more distant goals? Bernstein's conviction, according to which the movement is everything, the final goal nothing ... conceals a mechanistic conception of life and the historical process: human forces are considered to be passive and without consciousness, an element indistinguishable from material phenomena, and the notion of vulgar evolution in the naturalistic sense is substituted for the concept of coming into being and development.[81]

Gramsci exaggerates somewhat (and corrects himself later — 'the role of people is not altogether excluded' by Bernstein[82]), but he is right to point out that, since they elevated the movement to a goal in itself, the Right social democrats proved incapable of elaborating a conscious strategy of struggle and their 'movement' began to fade away.

If Millerand encountered this problem at the level of everyday politics, Bernstein did so at the level of theory. Here is evidently the key to understanding Bernstein's proposed 'revision' of Marxism. The critique he undertook of Marx is not systematic (as opposed to the critiques of Hegel, Proudhon or Dühring in the works of Marx and Engels themselves). In his defence against the attacks of the dogmatists, Bernstein made reference to Marx and his heritage of ideas:

> Thus errors in doctrine can be overcome when they are realized by followers of the doctrine themselves. One can say with confidence that, in freeing oneself from what is recognised to be mistaken — allow me to use Lassalle's expression — it is precisely Marx who disproves Marx.[83]

In principle this is true, but in itself the method of Bernstein's critique manifests a 'decline of doctrine'. His 'revisionism' is the sum of various observations, sometimes true, sometimes erroneous, sometimes debatable, sometimes based on misunderstandings. Rejecting the dialectic means simultaneously rejecting the whole system of thinking. As a result, Bernstein has no unified theoretical conception, scientific generalization or strategic plan. It should be noted that subsequent critics of Marx, from Tugan-Baranovsky and Bernstein to Galbraith and Popper, have started 'from the facts' — that is, by counterposing separate, individual events to separate, individual points of theory. But theory is generalization and is aware that it cannot reflect the complete diversity of living facts. Theory is grey, my friend, but the tree of life is evergreen!

Theory can only make known general tendencies and laws. When such a critique reveals a discrepancy between an isolated fact and an isolated specific position of Marx's, his critics see a 'fundamental error'. Typically, they all have their own 'fundamental error' and so they can never agree among themselves. What is required is a new general explanation of facts and theoretical ideas, ideological errors and their causes. Marx's critical method consists in precisely this, whereas his detractors confine themselves to a few odd remarks. Unlike Marxist critical philosophy, such a critique does not, as a rule, produce new ideas. In creating his own system, Ralph Dahrendorf borrowed a bit from Marx and rejected a bit, added a bit from the new sociology and ended up with a collection of applied explanations for a mass of individual facts instead of a generalizing theory.

The upshot of this would be that we would have to concur with Karl Popper's idea that it is impossible to create any serious philosophy of history and, consequently, any general theory of social development. At the level of political practice such thinking gives rise to inconsistent, timorous reformism implemented through a series of fortuitous, disconnected measures, the final outcome of which is unpredictable and incomprehensible even to the 'reformists' themselves. Popper called this a movement 'into the unknown, the indeterminate and the insecure.'[85] Every attempt at social progress bears a significant risk, but here we have an unjustified historical risk, not even a movement without a goal but merely a marking of time.

Early-twentieth-century 'revisionists' were much more careful in their handling of theory but they had already come up against this problem. 'New' facts cannot be analysed in isolation from 'old' ones — just as the simple comparison of theory with facts which, at first glance, do not fit into it explains nothing in itself. And in the meantime a sizeable volume of such facts had accumulated.

Bernstein's utterances were extremely useful and opportune as they inflicted a blow against the dogmatism which prevailed among the theoreticians of the Second International.[86] Roy Medvedev has remarked that 'moderate dogmatism' is sometimes 'necessary and useful both in science and in politics.'[87] Of course the dogmatism of the Second International was moderate when compared to the communist dogmatism of the 1930s, but it was hardly useful. Moreover, the aggressive dogmatism of the Stalinized communist parties was historically prepared by the 'moderate dogmatism' of old social democracy.

Bernstein, however, provided only a negative and not a positive answer to the question. More precisely, he simply pointed to some questions which the dogmatists had tried hard not to notice. Vodolazov justifiably remarks that the 'really new social problems' which lay behind Bernstein's statements had to be revealed 'and a positive Marxist response given to these new problems and questions.'[88]

The attack on Bernstein within German social democracy was led at once by two factions. Both the Party leadership, defending the old dogmas, and the Party's left wing spoke out against 'revisionism' and 'reformist illusions'. In theory this opposition was headed by Kautsky and Luxemburg respectively.

Both Kautsky's and Plekhanov's works directed against Bernstein contain many true observations, and are quite logical — if excessively tedious. With the obstinacy of a German schoolmaster Kautsky explained banal general points of theory as if to a disobedient pupil, while keeping clear of sharp corners and diligently avoiding any original thought. Kautsky, in common with all Marxists, defended the democratic road to socialism which, compared to the violent struggle of nineteenth-century bourgeois revolutionaries, is 'less dramatic and striking, but demands fewer sacrifices.' Socialism is possible only in a democratic state and in conditions where the proletariat 'has grown into a considerable mass' and constitutes a majority of voters.[89] Plekhanov expressed a somewhat different point of view, which anticipated Lenin's future position. In 1903 he declared that it was not especially necessary to respect formal, democratic legality, which would have no relevance during a revolution. To ensure the success of the revolution it might be necessary to 'limit temporarily the operation of one democratic principle or another', and he advised Russian revolutionaries, 'if elections turn out unsuccessfully' after the seizure of power, to abolish parliament 'not in two years but, if possible, in two weeks.'[90] It must be said that in 1918 Lenin followed this advice and dispersed the Constituent Assembly. By that time, Plekhanov could only make indignant protests. He was never an opponent of democracy and his position during the 1917 Revolution confirms this. Nevertheless, unlike Kautsky, he had posed a difficult question and not been afraid to answer it. What should be done if the logic of revolution requires going beyond the bounds of existing democratic legality?

Here another very important question arises: if the revolution has already superseded the bounds of constitutional politics, how can the restoration of democracy be guaranteed at the post-revolutionary stage? This problem later confronted the forces of the Left in the Third World in a sharp and, at times, tragic fashion. We have referred already to the Russian experience: even if one disagrees with Plekhanov, he should be accorded his due for his decisiveness in dealing with unpleasant matters. Kautsky was afraid even to consider such terrible questions. He wrote that

> we have now entered the period of struggle for state institutions and state power, a period of battles which might extend over decades with the most varied changes in fortune — battles, the forms and duration of which it is still difficult to ascertain, but which will, in all probability, lead in the very near future to a significant shift in the balance of forces in favour of the proletariat, if not to its absolute rule in Western Europe.[91]

How this new alignment of forces could be utilized or how it would be expressed was, for Kautsky, pure speculation. In any event, he totally rejected the idea of a compromise with the bourgeoisie and the formation of a reformist coalition with the socialists' participation. Any such government 'must collapse'.[92] This conclusion was based on nothing other than general references to the class struggle. The reality of the class struggle, its dialectic, is more complex, however, than any schema. Each side in a compromise pursues its own goals. In any compromise between opposing forces there is a winner and a loser. For socialists, an agreement with the ruling class is not for that reason always impossible or inconceivable (even in defence of democracy?), but such an agreement must be to the proletariat's advantage and part of an overall strategy.

A Soviet specialist writes with regard to this problem that 'of major significance is the fact that reformist activity has its own logic.... Any serious complex of reforms, in the process of its realization, creates a new situation with a new inertia of development.' Attempts to restrain or turn back such a development might have an unfavourable impact on the 'equilibrium of the system as a whole.'[93] This very important idea will prove useful to us later. At present we need mention only one aspect. Reformist and liberal groupings in the ruling class sometimes enter into agreement with the Left in the pursuit of quite limited goals, but the logic of the struggle for reform takes them at times beyond their own initial intentions and forces them to act more decisively. In such a situation either the workers' movement secures a shift of the whole reformist coalition to the left (as happened in Spain in 1936–37, in Hungary, and partially in Poland in 1956 and Czechoslovakia in 1968) or, on the other hand, the Left finds itself in crisis and loses its support (as in France in the 1930s and Italy at the end of the 1960s).

It would, of course, be impossible to establish that, at the turn of the century, Kautsky and 'orthodox' social democracy rejected reforms completely; but the problem was resolved at a very superficial level. For Kautsky everything was reduced to the political aspects of the struggle and, even more narrowly, to the question of power. The difference between reform and revolution lay in 'the gaining of power by a new class' and in that alone. Kautsky recognized neither 'revolution from above' nor crisis situations where the young class temporarily seizes power not for purposes of revolution but in order to implement a reformist programme or to defend civil liberties.

Legal and state measures are *reforms* if they have their origin in the ruling classes. They are reforms even when they are not granted voluntarily but extorted by pressure on the part of the oppressed classes or by force of circumstance. On the other hand, such measures are acts of *revolution* if they have their origin in the class which up to that time had been oppressed but has now gained political power for itself.[94]

Everything is reduced in this fashion to politics. Hypertrophy of the political aspects of the class struggle in western conditions led to 'parliamentary cretinism'. In Russian conditions, the same mode of thought resulted in the Bolshevism of Lenin and Trotsky. Plekhanov's position in 1903 bridged the divide between 'orthodox' social democratic thinking and the Bolsheviks' anti-parliamentarism; there exists a direct link between them.[95] Rosa Luxemburg had a rather more profound understanding of the problem. Reformists, she wrote, assume that

> 'one's appetite grows with eating', and the working class will not supposedly content itself with reforms till the final socialist transformation is realised. Now the last-mentioned condition is quite real. Its effectiveness is guaranteed by the very insufficiency of capitalist reforms. But the conclusion drawn from it could only be true if it were possible to construct an unbroken chain of augmented reforms leading from the capitalism of today to socialism. This is, of course, sheer fantasy. In accordance with the nature of things as they are, the chain breaks quickly and the paths that the supposed movement can take from that point on are many and varied.[96]

The fusion of illogical and strange reasoning with splendid and original ideas was always a hallmark of this remarkable woman. Here, however, she was doubly mistaken — but mistaken, it could be said, in a very gifted way. First, the proletariat can, for a certain period, be totally satisfied with reforms, as Western experience since the Second World War has demonstrated. Second, reform within the framework of the system does not in principle alter the proletariat's position in society. Consequently, revolution can be postponed because of a reform's success but it cannot be put off indefinitely. The possibility of the working class breaking with the system always remains, but it can only be realized under certain conditions.

But we are anticipating. Another point is of more interest. In speaking of an unbroken chain of social transformations, Luxemburg has given us a brilliantly conceived schema of revolutionary, anti-capitalist reforms. And yet she declares her own brilliant idea 'a fantasy'. Why? Because, in the last analysis, the 'natural limits of social reform' are determined by the interests of capital. The problem is to overcome these limitations and cross over to the revolutionary stage of the struggle. But, instead of resolving this question, Luxemburg simply condemns reformism by saying that 'in the capitalist world, social reform has always been and still is a dead end.'[97]

Alone among activists in the Second International, Jaurès and his supporters genuinely understood the depth and complexity of this problem. Alone among revolutionaries, Jaurès grasped the value of reformist work, proclaiming it necessary 'to take up the business of reform from the beginning and, through reform, to begin the business of revolution.'[98] Alone among reformists in the International, Jaurès attempted to elaborate an entire offensive, socialist strategy of struggle for state power in the conditions of democracy. As the supporters of Jaurès put it: 'our weapon has two edges, one is the spirit of gradual reform, the other is revolution.'[99]

The starting point of Jaurès's strategic concept, termed the 'new method', was Engels's idea that, in conditions of freedom, the proletariat can struggle initially for a share of power, 'and then the whole of that power, in order to become enabled to change existing laws in conformity with their own interests and requirements.'[100] The democratic state, unlike other forms of power, does not permit the bourgeoisie's complete and undivided rule. This rule is limited by certain conditions, and the class essence of democracy therefore consists in a compromise between the contending forces. In a polemic with Right social democracy, Jaurès said that, in French conditions, class antagonism

> exists and develops within democracy and is subordinate to the conditions of the democratic regime. The struggle between the two opposing classes, between the two groups of interests resisting each other, cannot assume an identical form, character and means in both a democratic republic and a despotic state. This is true and indisputable.[101]

History also disproves the notion of the bourgeoisie's absolute rule in conditions of democracy. Against those extremists who demanded a rejection of the Chilean Constitution, Allende insisted that this was impossible because political freedoms are 'the achievements of the people.'[102] Vodolazov in turn reminds us that there is 'nothing specifically bourgeois about freedom of expression, conscience and assembly.'[103] These rights have not been 'granted', but won, at times against the wishes of the bourgeoisie. Lenin said that in 1905 the proletariat was the hegemon of the democratic revolution, and this did not apply only in the

Russian case. In the struggle for democracy the decisive force has almost always been precisely the proletariat and not the bourgeoisie. The history of the three revolutions in France in the nineteenth century is testimony to this. The bourgeoisie were completely satisfied with a liberal monarchy and even an Empire, while the proletariat favoured a republic. Universal suffrage was introduced by the West's ruling circles, as a British historian acknowledges, 'slowly and reluctantly', under pressure from the workers. In Belgium, a general strike was needed. 'The acceptance of the new system presented the capitalist class in all countries with exceptionally difficult problems.'[104]

Jaurès was quite correct to see the achievement of democracy as a vital step on the road to socialism and the starting-point of the struggle for it. The Spanish Marxist, L. Gomez Laurente, has rightly insisted that only democracy creates 'the political space for actions which transform society.'[105] Of course we are not here referring to parliamentary actions but to the political activity of the masses. This is only possible in a free country, and without it the socialist reconstruction of life is inconceivable. To recognize this fact is not to idealize existing forms of parliamentarism and Western society.[106]

This was perfectly clear to Jaurès. It should not be thought, he said, that 'political democracy has assumed its final form, as if it could attain this by itself while remaining in contradiction with economic forms not yet imbued with democracy.'[107] The socialist movement, he continued, must inevitably pass through 'a transitional stage in which governmental power is simultaneously in the hands of both bourgeoisie and proletariat.'[108] The task of this transitional stage is to refine democracy, to weaken and paralyse the possibility of class coercion, and to ensure the peaceful character of the revolution at the next stage of the struggle. 'For the proletariat in a democracy, in a republic with universal suffrage, the state does not represent some sort of solid, completely impregnable stronghold.' Despite ruling class resistance, 'the influence of socialism and the proletariat partially penetrates the state' long before the revolution.[109] Both compromise and participation in a ruling majority are useful in the course of the struggle, which allows 'one of our own to be left behind in the fortress of bourgeois government.'[110] However, one should have no illusions: 'we can and must hope, with total justification, for the complete assimilation and metamorphosis of the democratic state into the socialist', but we should remember at the same time that at present

it is only ours in part and continues to be a force hostile to us. Against this hostile force in the state we must bring forth another force from our side which can neutralise it — the force of the full socialist ideal which groups and unites the proletarians around it.[111]

In the end, this viewpoint has triumphed among contemporary Left socialists. A.B. Reznikov, expounding their conception of political struggle, writes that 'democracy is of great value in itself. Its individual institutions — parliament, universal suffrage, freedom of speech, the press, etc. — are of considerable significance.'[112] Democracy is not, however, something once and for all:

> On the one hand, genuine democracy which ensures real freedoms, justice, equality and fraternity has yet to be created and there is still a long way to go. On the other hand, on the road to genuine democracy, one cannot violate its existing principles.

If we lose even what little we have, this would hardly constitute a step forward. A democratic state system must 'be seized, but under no circumstances must it be smashed, destabilized or endangered';[113] it must be refashioned from within. This is precisely what Jaurès stood for.

Thus, *the goal of reformism is not in petty and partial improvements but in the transformation of the state.* But here a new problem of a tactical character arises: why must the basis of reformism necessarily be compromise? P. Lui wrote in a critique of Bernstein and right-wing socialists that 'daily deals have not given us a single wide-ranging reform.' But events of a revolutionary character have often resulted in reform from above. One need only recall the winning of universal suffrage in Belgium.

> When you run through the complex series of texts which everywhere regulate the length of the working day, hygiene, insurance and the elementary rights of the proletariat, then you become convinced that they were wrested by persistent pressure from without.[114]

Neither compromise nor negotiation, but *direct action* played the major role.

Right social democrats have often been accused of 'parliamentary cretinism'. They did undervalue extra-parliamentary actions, or reduce them to purely agitational tasks. In their opinion, political questions were to be resolved through the system of state institutions. True, Bernstein saw the limitations of such a point of view. He devoted a book to the strike as a weapon of proletarian struggle, and acknowledged in particular first, that the aims of a strike may be not only economic but may include 'socio-legal improvements and even a combination of both one and the other'; and second, that any strike, even if no political demands are advanced, is of 'political as well as merely economic significance.'[115] It was Bernstein's view, however, that the development of democratic forms of power, in and of itself, renders strike action unnecessary. The resort to extra-parliamentary means results from the imperfection of the parliamentary system or shortcomings in the country's democracy.

Extra-parliamentary action seemed to Bernstein intrinsically undesirable and undemocratic. This is a very vulnerable position. As a rule in a democracy it is, of course, the minority, defending its rights against a government elected by the majority of the population, that resorts to political strikes, demonstrations, boycotts and hunger strikes. But there is nothing anti-democratic in acts of protest. The majority is not always right. Direct action and political protests by the opposition should draw society's attention to the cause in the name of which the struggle is taking place. Extra-parliamentary politics is, therefore, as essential in a free country as parliamentary politics. On numerous occasions extra-parliamentary opposition has achieved its aims while not taking part in elections. One has only to recall the lessons of the 1960s and the struggle against the war in Vietnam.

Orthodox social democrats treated the idea of political strikes with suspicion for quite different reasons than did Bernstein. In the idea of the political strike, and above all of the general strike, they heard an echo of anarcho-syndicalist theories, which rejected parliamentary struggle on principle and placed all hopes on 'the revolutionary might of the strike in the process conceived of as disorganizing capital.'[116] According to Georges Sorel, Antonio Labriola and other theoreticians of this current, the general strike, 'with arms folded', will be sufficient to destroy the old society and the capitalist mode of production. Political demands and party leadership become superfluous, for the entire work of destruction is performed by the strike, and the positive element by workers' self-organization in the course of the struggle.

> This revolution, happening 'everywhere and nowhere', will be accompanied by the seizure of the instruments of production. As opposed to the plans of such revolutionaries as Blanqui, no sort of 'insurgent government' will be formed nor any kind of dictatorship established. The bakers of each bakery, the miners of each mine, etc., will be united on the basis of free production

into a free association. Syndicates and labour exchanges will be superior instruments of revolution. Beginning one day, the strike is generalized, i.e., draws under its influence all workers and all branches of production, becomes total and then no forces can stop it.[117]

In the course of the struggle, the armed workers will successfully unite and become completely conscious of their class interests; the 'myth' of the great strike mobilizes the masses and will awaken their hidden strengths and aspirations. According to Sorel, this is the only way the proletariat will succeed 'in driving the capitalists out of the sphere of production and taking their place in the workshops created by capitalism.'[118]

For Sorel, only the social aspect of the revolution, driving out the bourgeoisie, is achieved by this. Its political and economic sides are simply ignored. Sorel's position rather resembles Kautsky's — only inside out. For the one, only the state-political aspect of the class struggle is important; for the other, only the social aspect. The bankruptcy of the 'orthodox' strategy inevitably gave rise to such a 'counterweight'. For all its naivety, this theory contains an element of truth: the 1905 Russian Revolution, like the Polish events of 1970 and 1980, demonstrated the massive organizing power of a strike and its role in revolutionizing the consciousness of the masses. But the same experience also showed that *direct action does not have unlimited potential.* We will return to this question.

At first, social democrats disclaimed direct action just as decisively as anarcho-syndicalists disclaimed political struggle. One 'orthodox' social democratic author even wrote that 'all strikes that are *not opportunistic* are doomed to impotence' — that is, a strike cannot be a principled instrument of political and revolutionary struggle (!).[119] However, as socialists grasped the experience of the real workers' movement they were compelled to change their views.

Luxemburg was one of the first Marxists to detect the rational kernel in the doctrine of direct action, by demonstrating that a strike, irrespective of its specific objectives, is the means by which the proletariat organizes and educates itself. She emphasized that in Russia in 1905, strikes helped the workers become conscious of their *class* position:

And this increasing class feeling was expressed in the fact that millions of proletarians unexpectedly clearly and sharply sensed the intolerability of their social and economic existence whereas, before, they had patiently borne the chains of capitalism for decades.[120]

Thus, in any strike, 'the economic and political aspects are indivisible', and, consequently, the strike movement can become a means of political action. Luxemburg vigorously assailed right-wing reformists who 'reduce the political struggle of the working class to parliamentary struggle.'[121] We have already seen that this accusation is exaggerated, but it should be remembered that her position within German social democracy was considered heretical and that she had to present her arguments in their sharpest form. To the horror of the 'orthodox', there was almost no place for the party in Luxemburg's notion of the strike. The *masses' spontaneous self-education* in the process of revolution completely removes from the agenda the question of the organizing and directing role of the Marxist party, the conscious vanguard of the class, and so forth. To the centralized and bureaucratic organization that German social democracy had become, such a theory was self-evidently unacceptable. Moreover, Luxemburg's ideas had something in common with those of the 'revisionists', for the party was reduced to playing the role of the class's parliamentary representative, which would reinforce through legislative acts the gains of the revolution as it spontaneously developed 'from below'. This amounts to something like 'parliamentary cretinism' inside out, although Luxemburg herself — and this was her strength — refused to draw the necessary conclusions from her own ideas.

Official social democracy was forced to elaborate a counterweight to Luxemburgism, in the shape of its own centralist–bureaucratic conception of the strike carried out under the party's control and at its behest at the appointed hour and on the appointed day. Jaurès remarked ironically in this regard that

> there was a widespread notion that the general strike is like a mechanism sitting in one pocket with the key to it in the other so that the police cannot seize both mechanism and key at the same time. But, at a given moment, the machine appears, the hour of revolution has sounded and the revolution is ready.[122]

Jaurès understood, unlike Luxemburg, that workers' self-organization and self-education during the course of a strike 'cannot substitute for consistent, systematic efforts nor relieve the working class of the need for organization.' The task of the political vanguard is to unite disparate actions into a single whole subordinate to an overall strategy of struggle. A strike in itself does not represent some sort of 'miraculous means' or 'marvellous treasure'.[123]

It would be wrong to suspect Jaurès's supporters of underestimating the general strike. They probably stood alone in evaluating correctly the role of direct action in the struggle for socialism, without going to one extreme or the other; to them, both worship of blind spontaneity and the social democrats' ultra-centralist tendencies were equally alien. The difference between Luxemburg and Jaurès is that between a revolutionary romantic and a realist. The crude pragmatism of Right social democracy was absolutely foreign to Jaurès; he was a man of principle and even, if you like, an idealist. But his idealism was combined with a sober practical streak and a French rationality, both of which Luxemburg altogether lacked.

Such national–cultural specificities should not be dismissed. They may play different roles at different times and in different countries, but the more we try to eliminate cultural problems, the more they resurface. At all events, the French socialists stood alone in the Second International, if the Belgian Party, which was close to them, is not taken into account. The latter also seemed unique in its time. Commentators acknowledged that 'it was only there that "reformists" and "revolutionaries" complemented rather than restricting and hindering one another.'[124] Jaurès's realism was manifested in his reformism. As distinct from Luxemburg, who had created an abstract theory of a spontaneous revolutionary movement, Jaurès's starting point was the *dialectic of reform and revolution.* This dialectic was quite beyond the conception of most of his contemporaries. At the Amsterdam Congress of the International, both Right and Left came down on the French. Hardly anybody accepted Jaurès's assessment of the strike as a revolutionary means for achieving reformist aims. Jaurèsism was repudiated by the International and it exerted no material influence upon even minority groups in other socialist parties. Nowhere else did the working class have such rich political experience and traditions as in France, but it was precisely because of this that the French Left shot too far ahead, leaving behind their colleagues in other countries. Trotsky declared that Jaurèsism was 'organized opportunism',[125] and at the Amsterdam Congress the French remained completely isolated (the more so as Jules Guesde exacerbated the situation by his factional speeches).

The practice of the Second International envisaged a unity of strategic line, and overall leadership of the movement from a single centre. In fact this meant the domination of the German party-bureaucratic machine over the world socialist movement. The German social democrats monopolized power over other parties to such an extent that their role can be compared with that of the Soviet Communists in the first period of the Third International. The supremacy of the German social bureaucrats within the workers' movement at the turn of the century helped ensure that the Jaurèsists' practical and theoretical experiences remained substantially inaccessible to other parties. An ideological prohibition, a taboo, was placed upon it and it was *collectively condemned.* Naturally enough, the very people who had argued so furiously against Jaurès and his 'new method' found it extraordinarily easy to enter into agreement with the bourgeoisie during the World War. Guesde joined the government — not, like Millerand, to promote social reform, but to help the ruling class mobilize workers for the War: disgracefully, he did not elicit even minimal concessions in exchange for his treachery. Jaurès, by contrast, called for peace until the last day of his life and was killed, in Antonov-Ovseenko's phrase, 'at a timely moment by a crazed fanatic of patriotism' on 1 August 1914.[126]

After Jaurès's death and the split in the Socialist Party, the ideas of the 'new method' were widely aired within the French workers' movement itself. Both Socialist and Communist parties declared themselves Jaurès's lineal successors, but this was little more than rhetoric. The formation of communist parties, which drew in most of the Left, pushed social democracy even further to the right, changing the balance of forces inside the Second International. In France, it was particularly noticeable that social democratic opportunism was increasing in direct proportion to communist dogmatism. The Socialist Party (SFIO) became more and more a part of the capitalist system. The Communists (PCF), who remained under Moscow's control until the mid 1950s, turned their backs on democracy (apart from the brief periods of the Popular Front and Resistance), and conducted a dogmatic campaign against all dissidents in the Left camp. It was notable that many of the victims of this persecution were quite ready to forgive their tormentors, so strong was the general hostility to the social democrats' opportunism. In her reminiscences, Simone de Beauvoir expresses her preference for the Communists over the 'bourgeoisified SFIO': one had to support the PCF for 'socialism can only be victorious with its help.' The Communists successfully attracted a significant section of workers but the SFIO 'recruited the majority of its adherents among the petty bourgeoisie.'[127] But the PCF for its part was in no sense a party capable of guaranteeing the victory for socialism. As one French commentator accurately expressed it, the PCF stood not to the socialists' left but to their East.

The Communist International took Bolshevik practice in 1917 as a universally applicable method. Irrespective of whether their methods were good or bad in themselves, they were obviously engendered by a specific situation, and were simply unsuited to Western conditions. By mechanically imitating the tactics of the Russian Bolsheviks, the communists closed themselves off from the democratic road to power. The idea was promoted that the direct democracy of workers' councils (on the 1917 model) was incompatible with a representative parliamentary system. It was necessary to eliminate the latter in the name of the former: 'There is no choice: either the proletarian Soviets disorganise the bourgeois state apparatus, or the latter succeeds in corrupting the Soviets into a pseudo-existence and in thus destroying them.'[128] In Western conditions such arguments sounded simply absurd.

Lenin himself recognized this problem by writing the pamphlet *Left-wing Communism: An Infantile Disorder*, in which he argued against transposing Bolshevik methods to the West. He called on Western marxists to elaborate their own line of struggle, recalling that:

> Tactics must be based on a sober and strictly objective appraisal of *all* the class forces in a particular state (and of the states that surround it, and of all the states the world over) as well as of the experience of the revolutionary movements.[129]

He spoke of 'communist parliamentarism' and of the need to collaborate with reformist trade unions. M. Kheveshi has quite correctly remarked that Lenin recommended his Western friends 'to resort to manoeuvre and compromise.'[130] In the last analysis, however, there is no clear-cut strategic line in Lenin's pamphlet, only the general notion that communists should participate (in the West) in the democratic life of the state.

This was a first step in the right direction. Paradoxical as it may seem, it was precisely in Moscow that the idea of the possibility of different roads to socialism, which had been repudiated both by old social democracy and by Stalinist communists, was expressed for the first time since Marx. Lenin, however, vehemently advocated the idea of a democratic road to socialism to his supporters in the West, who had drawn only one 'lesson' from the Russian experience — that of the 'superiority' (that is, the 'simplicity', 'purity') of violent methods. The socio-political changes which had occurred in Russia — the reinforcement of the Party-bureaucratic apparatus under Zinoviev, and then Stalin's victory over the Opposition and the establishment of a new order as a result of collectivization — could not but have an influence on the

Comintern. Even official Soviet historians concede that the organization became even more centralized and less democratic and effective. Not everything, though, should be blamed on Stalin and events in the USSR. Corresponding tendencies could already be observed in the 1920s among Western communists. Lukàcs wrote that, for communists, legality 'has become a purely tactical question' and appealed for all 'illusions in democracy and the peaceful transition to socialism' to be cast aside.[131] As early as 1924 he had written that social democrats were indistinguishable from the Right: 'opportunism is the class enemy of the proletariat in its own camp.' The refusal to collaborate with other Left forces, the rejection of 'bourgeois' freedoms and the aggressive dogmatism of Western communists at that time led to defeat after defeat. The social democrats fared no better. Their political programmes became ever feebler and their actions ever more indecisive and inconsistent. Piece-meal reformism 'from the right' perfectly complemented the narrow-minded dogmatism then triumphant among the communists. The culmination of this process was the inability of the Left in Germany to stop Hitler.

The victory of fascism in Germany, followed by the complete rout of the Communist Party, forced the Comintern, in the interests of self-preservation, to make peace with the socialists. The hero of the day was Georgi Dimitrov, who succeeded in putting forward the idea of an anti-fascist front of all Left forces in Europe without exposing to direct criticism Stalin's dogma of the communists' exclusive role. The new course, propounded in 1935, contained a whole series of constructive elements. Communists in the West not only gained the right to enter into alliance with social democrats but were obliged, 'in the capitalist countries, to defend every inch of bourgeois–democratic freedom on which fascism and bourgeois reaction are encroaching.'[133] For the first time, the slogan of critical support for social-democratic reforms was advanced. True, anti-fascist unity was often understood in a quite specific manner. In the 1940s, Spanish socialists remarked ironically that communist proposals for a joint struggle against Franco's dictatorship seemed like threats: 'The relationship with the communists can be summarized as follows: one is a traitor, the next is fit for nothing, the third is a criminal. We are securing unity with them.'[134] Clearly, where a united front policy was conducted in a serious fashion, such an approach had to be rejected. It was evidently at the Seventh Comintern Congress that the preconditions were created for the later conversion of several Western communist parties to the principles of democratic socialism. A considerable role was also played by the Resistance and the experience of communist participation in Left-reformist coalitions in France and Italy after the crushing of fascism.

A genuine reappraisal of values only took place in the 1970s, but we should not forget that it was the communist movement itself which nurtured the thinker who endeavoured to create a general theory of the reformist struggle of the proletariat in conditions of democracy. We are referring to Antonio Gramsci. Gramsci formulated his ideas while in a fascist jail, and for a long period they were unknown to a wide public. It might be said that Gramsci was fortunate: in the 1930s, when he was working on his *Prison Notebooks*, neither social democrats nor communists were ready to grasp his theories. If the *Prison Notebooks* had become known during their author's lifetime he would certainly have been accused of revisionism and, most likely, expelled from the Party.

The French Eurocommunist (or Eurostalinist), F. Inker, later wrote, with reference to the specific conditions of the struggle for socialism in the free countries of the West, that 'Gramsci was the first who resolved to formulate these questions and provide something like an answer to them.'[135] The correct answer, of course, was given by the French Communist Party, headed by comrades Georges Marchais and F. Inker. As we have already seen, Gramsci was not the first, and Inker displays a startling ignorance when he overlooks the contributions of Marx, Engels and Jaurès. This is forgiveable, however, for no mention of these contributions is found in the textbooks of the PCF. What is more serious is that Eurocommunist party theoreticians in France and Spain not only went no further than Gramsci in solving the problems of the democratic road to socialism, they were not even capable of fully understanding his ideas.

Gramsci, as distinct from Marx, concentrated his attention on consent rather than coercion. He showed that no state system could be sustained for long through coercion alone. The ruling class not only relies on organs of repression but also on an *'apparatus of hegemony'*. Marx had made some reference to this when he said that the ideas of the ruling class are the ruling ideas in society, but Gramsci explored the problem in much more detail.

The ruling class is capable of carrying the majority of society along with it and of securing mass support. The state with its coercive apparatus is only part of the system of class rule. Alongside it exists *civil society*. Mass political parties, cultural institutions and the press are elements of civil society through which the hegemony of the ruling group is realized. A characteristic of civil society is its pluralism: of necessity, it is like a mosaic, contradictory and the arena for a perpetual struggle. This distinguishes it from the unified state apparatus. Here the will of the ruling class is realized, in the last analysis, through the resolution of conflicting wills. The ruling ideology is developed through interaction with opposing ideologies. The actual fact of their coexistence within a unified system is of benefit to the ruling class, which controls the key positions in this system. In a democracy, institutions arise which simultaneously belong to both civil society and the state:

> Parliament [is] more closely linked to civil society; the judiciary power, between government and Parliament, represents the continuity of the written law (even against the government). Naturally all three powers are also organs of political hegemony, but in different degrees: 1. Legislature; 2. Judiciary; 3. Executive.[136]

In a democracy, the Left parties — socialists, communists, social democrats — conduct an ideological struggle with the ruling class at the level of civil society. The winning of key positions in civil society by the proletariat can signal a crisis for the entire system of domination, when the exploiters must either resort to *anti-democratic force* (as has happened repeatedly in Latin America where, through the weakness of bourgeois traditions, left-wing culture has easily achieved predominance in civil society) or retreat. The seizure of power by the Left does not itself create the conditions for socialist revolution without the capture of key positions in civil society. Gramsci thus repudiates two preconceptions that have taken root in both social democratic and Leninist–communist versions of Marxism: first, that economic shocks inevitably lead to crisis and the collapse of power and, second, that the resolution of the question of power resolves all other questions.[137] Gramsci writes that in the most developed states of the West, civil society

> has become a very complex structure and one which is resistant to the catastrophic 'incursions' of the immediate economic element (crises, depressions, etc.). The superstructures of modern society are like the trench-systems of modern warfare.[138]

Here the difference between a democratic and an undemocratic society is very important. In the conditions of an undemocratic regime, where the institutions of civil society are poorly developed or absent, Lenin's tactics work: in a crisis, the conservative–repressive system disintegrates or, in any case, fissures and then the whole political structure collapses. In a certain sense, achieving radical change in an unfree country is easier than in a democratic one for which 'a relatively rudimentary State apparatus, and greater autonomy of civil society from State activity' is characteristic. Russia is an example of the first case and the West of the second:

> In Russia the State was everything, civil society was primordial and gelatinous; in the West there was a proper relation between State and civil society, and when the State trembled a sturdy structure of civil society was at once revealed. The State was only an outer ditch, behind which there stood a powerful system of fortresses and earthworks: more or less numerous from one State to the next, it goes without saying — but this precisely necessitated an accurate reconnaissance of each individual country.[139]

It should be noted that even before Gramsci, Trotsky had spoken in almost identical terms when he was discussing England; but they came to quite different conclusions.[140] To be more precise, Trotsky did not come to any serious conclusions. Gramsci counterposed a 'war of manoeuvre' in the East — especially in Russia, where a frontal attack on the state power was conceivable — to a 'war of position' in the West, where the Left systematically lays siege to civil society, occupying one 'trench' after another. The Italian communist, M. Spinella, emphasizes in this regard the need to found a revolutionary party of a new type. The goal of the struggle becomes, to a significant extent, 'a radical change in reality not only in a socio-economic, but also in an intellectual and a moral sense.'[141]

Referring to *Left-wing Communism: An Infantile Disorder*, Gramsci wrote that Lenin already 'understood that a change was necessary from the war of manoeuvre applied victoriously in the East in 1917, to a war of position which was the only form possible in the West', but 'did not have time to expand his formula.'[142] Here again there is some exaggeration. Lenin, like Trotsky, sensed a difference between Russia and the West but did not think his ideas through to the end. Gramsci, unlike Lenin, was himself a Westerner brought up in a relatively free country. Type of culture is of more significance here than level of knowledge. In this case the difference between the Bolsheviks and Gramsci is one of principle: we are witnessing a different mode of thinking.

The European cultural tradition and the dialectical approach to history enabled Gramsci to draw a remarkably important conclusion as to the relationship between reformism and revolutionary struggle. In his analysis of the process of Italian unification in the nineteenth century (the Risorgimento), he compared the reformist Cavour to the revolutionary Mazzini, writing that 'whereas Cavour was aware of his role (at least up to a certain point) in as much as he understood the role of Mazzini, the latter does not seem to have been aware of his own or Cavour's.' It follows from this that reformists and revolutionaries must not only mutually reinforce each other in the common struggle, but must understand each other's position. They must interact not blindly, but consciously. There is no 'golden mean' between reformism and revolutionism: each must 'seek to be itself totally.'[143] This contradiction can be resolved, however, by the general revolutionary–reformist practice of the Left.[144] 'Moderates' and 'radicals' can establish a new kind of mutual relationship.[145]

The Italian communists have assimilated Gramsci's ideas comparatively easily. By the 1940s, they already saw Stalinism as foreign ideological ballast, and they ditched it at the first opportunity. Things have been different with the French and Spanish Communist Parties, where the Eurocommunists theoreticians, while referring to Gramsci, have tried to combine the ideas of liberalism and the old dogmatism in an eclectic manner. They inform us that democracy and hegemony exclude any coercion. But this is patently absurd in a society divided into contending classes, and merely provides the foundation for new illusions and liberal placidity. While sheltering behind Gramsci's name, they are clearly trying to achieve a theoretical transition from Marxism to nineteenth-century Liberalism. Because of this, their practical politics sometimes remains totally Stalinist.

It goes without saying that, compared to 'classical' Stalinism, liberal ideology is a massive step forward, but a more serious and sober-minded analysis is required. A complete renunciation of coercion is only possible in a classless society. It was precisely because of this that Gramsci did not counterpose the theory of hegemony to Marx's 'dictatorship of the proletariat' but, on the contrary, demonstrated the direct link between these ideas.

There is, however, an opposite interpretation. The entire system of the institutions of civil society can be depicted as simply the continuation of the repressive apparatus of power, as the 'ideological apparatus of the state'. The autonomous role of civil society is ignored or reduced to a technical function — for example, the reproduction of labour power. Althusser wrote:

Scientifically speaking, the reproduction of labour power requires not only the reproduction of its level of skill, but also the reproduction of obedience to the existing system, the reproduction of the workers' subordination to the dominant ideology

— and so forth, so as to ensure 'the ruling class's rule'.[146] These arguments, expressed moreover in monstrously pseudo-philosophical language, were essential for Althusser to reduce Marx and Gramsci's dialectical ideas to the primitive schema of a Comintern textbook. Long before Althusser, Lukács wrote that ideology is not only a product of society's economic conditions, 'but simultaneously a condition of its peaceful functioning.'[147] This was quite a step forward for its time. But to recapitulate the ideas of the 1920s *after* Gramsci is a step backwards.[148] Civil society and the apparatus of hegemony cannot be considered simply as part of the state apparatus or as 'the ideological apparatus of the state.' They are autonomous and lead their own lives. Wherever the apparatus of hegemony is indeed turned into 'the ideological apparatus of the state' (and the history of the twentieth century can provide several examples) civil society withers away and a totalitarian dictatorship of a fascist or of another kind is established. In such cases, the consent of the masses proves to be coerced and hegemony forced — in other words, ideological and spiritual influences are turned into their opposites. Ideas can be foisted on both society and the individual through terror and threats, but this does not signify the triumph of these ideas. As Miguel de Unamuno said to Francoists celebrating the crushing of the Spanish Republic — you can be victorious but not have the power to convince.

The development of Marxism in the West did not cease with Gramsci's works. Nevertheless, it has taken around forty years for communists in Spain and France to become familiar with even some of his ideas. Such a lag is cause for concern. That renewal has sometimes proved very superficial is demonstrated by the example of the Spanish Communist Party's former leader, Santiago Carrillo, author of the scandalous book *Eurocommunism and the State*. When this book was published Carrillo was an extreme liberal but when he lost his position as leader, he underwent an unexpected transformation and became an extreme dogmatist. The superficial liberalism turned out to be merely a cover for the old dogmatism. Most communist parties have had to undergo profound internal changes in order to cleanse themselves of Stalin's heritage, but this process is only now beginning.

It does not follow, however, that the socialists, who by and large escaped the influence of Stalinism, have been able to resolve their own theoretical and organizational problems. The right wing of the workers' movement has been under the sway of other ideas, but this does not prove that it has always trodden the correct path. The politics of inconsistent and indecisive reforms has led many parties to lose their socialist perspective. Attempts to generalize such a practice in a scientific and theoretical manner have pushed social democrats towards techno-cratic ideology, which has nothing in common with socialism.

Social democracy's errors have also been far from inoffensive, although compared to that of other contemporary parties its activity seems more or less attractive. The road to the future is, in the last analysis, the road of self-criticism. For the Left throughout the whole world, hopes for the future now rest on internal renewal. Renewal is not only essential for the communist parties if they are to try and play some sort of active role in democratic development; it is also essential for social democracy. Earlier we spoke of 'reformist' and 'revolutionary' politics. What is needed now is socialist and realistic politics.

Notes

1. V.I. Lenin, *Collected Works*, 4th edn, English version (hereafter CW), vol. 12, p. 237.
2. Ibid., vol. 17, p. 116.
3. P. Lui, *Budushchee Sotsializma*, Moscow 1906, pp. 192, 193–4.
4. Karl Marx, *Capital*, vol. 1, London 1976, p. 610.
5. See ibid., p. 91.
6. Today's events have turned out somewhat differently. In the nineteenth century, England was the sole completely developed capitalist country. Capital had nowhere to run. In the twentieth century, reforms might initially provoke an outflow of capital into other countries capable of taking up the same production. But democratic labour reforms will have to follow there too, and capital will be forced to speed up its technical re-equipping. In other words, Marx's logic holds true in a long-term perspective even today, helping us to comprehend the significance of the technological revolution of the 1980s.
7. Shlomo Avineri, *The Social and Political Thought of Karl Marx*, Cambridge 1968, pp. 159–60.
8. Marx, *Capital*, p. 93.
9. Ibid., pp. 92–3.
10. Ibid., p. 92.
11. Ibid.
12. G.G. Vodolazov, *Dialektika i Revoliutsiya*, Moscow 1975, pp. 197–8.
13. *Sovremenniy Sotsializm*, R. Enzor, ed., Moscow 1906, p. 243. (Original translation edited by B.K.)
14. Marx and Engels, *The German Ideology*, London 1970, pp. 56–7.

15. Marx and Engels, *The Manifesto of the Communist Party*, in *The Revolutions of 1848*, David Fernbach, ed., London 1973, p. 87.

16. E. Bernstein, *Die Voraussetzungen des Sozialismus und die Aufgaben der Sozialdemokratie*, Berlin 1923, p. 174.

17. Marx and Engels, *Socnineniya*, vol. 4, p. 332.

18. Lenin, CW. vol. 33, p. 111. Such utterances are evidence of the fact that Lenin's views had gradually changed.

19. N. Poulantzas, 'Towards a Democratic Socialism', *New Left Review*, 109, 1978, p. 76.

20. Marx and Engels, *Collected Works*, vol. 1, p. 137.

21. 'The censored press remains bad even when it turns out good products, for these products are good only insofar as they represent the free press within the censored press, and insofar as it is not in their character to be products of the censored press. The free press remains good even when it produces bad products, for the latter are deviations from the essential nature of the free press. A eunuch remains a bad human being even when he has a good voice. Nature remains good even when she produces monstrosities.

    'The essence of the free press is the characterful, rational, moral essence of freedom. The character of the censored press is the characterless monster of unfreedom; it is a civilised monster, a perfumed abortion' (Marx and Engels, *Collected Works*, vol. 1, p. 158).

    'It is the *censored press* that has a *demoralising* effect. Inseparable from it is the most powerful vice, hypocrisy, and from this, its basic vice, come all its other defects, which lack even the rudiments of virtue, and its vice of passivity, loathsome even from the aesthetic point of view. The government hears only its *own voice*, it knows that it hears only its own voice, yet it harbours the illusion that it hears the voice of the people, and it demands that the people, too, should itself harbour this illusion. For its part, therefore, the people sinks partly into political superstition, partly into political disbelief, or, completely turning away from political life, becomes a *rabble of private individuals* ... in the way that God spoke of His Creation only on the Sixth day: "And, behold, it was *very* good", and since, however, one day necessarily contradicts the other, the press lies continually and has to deny even any consciousness of lying, and must cast off all shame' (Marx and Engels, *Collected Works*, vol. 1, pp. 167–8).

22. Marx and Engels, *Collected Works*, vol. 1, p. 181.

23. Hal Draper, *Karl Marx's Theory of Revolution, Volume 1: State and Bureaucracy*, New York 1977, p. 282 (emphasis in original).

24. Marx and Engels, *Collected Works*, vol. 1, p. 241.

25. Marx and Engels, *Collected Works*, vol. 6, p. 5.

26. Marx and Engels, *Manifesto of the Communist Party*, p. 86.

27. K. Lenk, *Politische Wissenschaft*, Stuttgart u.a., 1975, p. 123.

28. K. Marx, 'Speech on the Hague Congress', in *The First International and After*, ed. and introduced by David Fernbach, London 1974, p. 324.

29. Marx and Engels, *Selected Works*, vol. 3, Moscow, p. 434.

30. Lenin, CW, vol. 35, p. 267.

31. Bernstein, *Voraussetzung des Sozialismus*, p. 178.

32. S. Goffard, 'La question du pouvoir est à l'ordre du jour', *Nouvelle Critique*, no. 93, April 1976, p. 19.
33. R.C. Tucker, *Stalin as Revolutionary*, New York 1974, pp. 16–17.
34. This is graphically illustrated by the Soviet anthology of Marx, Engels and Lenin, *On the Dictatorship of the Proletariat*, Moscow 1978. Even the number of items is curious. Included in the volume are twenty-five excerpts from Marx and Engels and forty from Lenin. The number of excerpts from Lenin could have been doubled.
35. L. Trotsky, *The Revolution Betrayed*, New York pp. 51–2.
36. *Revoliutsiya i Demokratiya*, Prague 1980, p. 51.
37. Ksenofont Afinskii, *Socraticheskie Sochineniya, Academia*, Moscow–Leningrad 1935, p. 34. Xenophon Athenensis, *Memorabilia*, I, 2, 43.
38. *Revoliutsiya i Demokratiya*, p. 68.
39. Lenk, *Politike Wissenschaft*, p. 124.
40. *Mitterrand, l'homme, les idées*, Paris 1974, p. 70.
41. Roy Medvedev, *Leninism and Western Socialism*, London 1980, p. 44.
42. Lenin, CW, vol. 25, p. 360.
43. Medvedev, *Leninism*, p. 42.
44. K. Kautsky, *Put'k Vlasti*, Moscow–Petrograd 1923, p. 18.
45. See Lenin, CW, vol. 28, p. 235.
46. Ibid., p. 236.
47. Yu. Krasin, *Revoliutsiei Ustrashennye*, Moscow 1975, p. 285. Quoted in Medvedev, *Leninism*, p. 48.
48. Lenin, CW, vol. 28, p. 235.
49. Rosa Luxemburg, 'Social Reform or Revolution', in *Rosa Luxemburg Speaks*, M.A. Waters, ed., New York 1970, p. 80.
50. Lenin, CW, vol. 28, p. 248.
51. Marx, *Critique of the Gotha Programme*, in *The First International and After*, London 1974, p. 354.
52. R. Luxemburg, *Gesammelte Werke*, Band 4, Berlin 1974, p. 363.
53. Marx, 'The Class Struggles in France, 1848–1850', in *Surveys from Exile*, ed. and introduced by David Fernbach, London 1973, p. 123. The Soviet publishers shamefully replaced the word 'permanent' with the word 'uninterrupted' so that nobody would surmise that Trotsky had borrowed his idea from Marx.
54. Marx and Engels, *Selected Works*, vol. 3, p. 435.
55. *Nouvelle Critique*, no. 93, 1976, pp. 19, 9.
56. *Revoliutsiya i Demokratiya*, p. 68.
57. J.-P. Sartre, *Situations X*, Paris 1976, p. 47.
58. The question has not lost its relevance over the last 50 years, even if it has not been resolved ...
59. *Istoriya II Internatsionala*, Moscow 1966, vol. 2, p. 42 and elsewhere.
60. F. Scheidemann, *Krushenie Germanskoi Imperii*, Moscow–Petrograd 1923, p. 22. Written in 1922. '10–15 years later' in Germany, not 'revolutionary social democracy' but fascism was in power.
61. Marx and Engels, *Selected Works*, vol. 3, p. 435.
62. Quoted in *Istoriya II Internatsionala*, vol. 2, p. 110.
63. *Le Socialisme*, 28 May 1910.

64. Lenin, CW, vol. 22, pp. 146–7.
65. See Rosa Luxemburg, *The Accumulation of Capital* and Lenin, *Imperialism, The Highest Stage of Capitalism.* The latter work, despite its oversimplified approach to the problem, played an important role in showing the shifts in the structure of capitalist society and production.
66. Quoted in *Istoriya II Internatsionala*, p. 43.
67. K. Kautsky, *Sotsial'naya Revoliutsiya*, Moscow 1918, p. 60.
68. K. Kautsky, *Put'k Vlasti*, p. 18.
69. G.V. Plekhanov, *V Amsterdame*, Moscow 1923, p. 9.
70. R. Luxemburg, *Izbrannye Sochineniya*, vol. 1, ch. 2, Moscow 1930, p. 89.
71. Lenin, CW, vol. 43, p. 397.
72. *Sovremennyi Sotsializm*, p. 106.
73. Ibid., p. 193.
74. Marx and Engels, *Sochineniya*, 2nd edn., vol. 37, p. 275.
75. *Sovremennyi Sotsializm*, p. 221.
76. Rosa Luxemburg, *Social Reform or Revolution*, pp. 81, 76.
77. *Neue Zeit*, vol. X, I, p. 583.
78. E. Bernstein, *Parlamentarismus und Sozialdemokratie*, Berlin 1906, p. 59.
79. *Sovremennyi Sotsializm*, p. 232.
80. Ibid., pp. 233–4.
81. A. Gramsci, *Izbrannye Proizvedeniya*, Moscow 1980, pp. 329, 328.
82. Ibid., p. 329.
83. E. Bernstein, *Voraussetzungen des Sozialismus*, p. 51.
84. R. Dahrendorf, *Soziale Klassen und Klassenkonflikt*, Stuttgart 1957.
85. K.R. Popper, *The Open Society and Its Enemies*, London 1966, p. 201.
86. L. Kolakowski in his three-volume *Main Currents in Marxism* (Oxford 1978) assesses this period as the 'Golden Age' of theory, completely ignoring the real state of affairs. It was an age precisely of scholastic dogmatism and philosophical decline.
87. Medvedev, *Leninism*, p. 8.
88. Vodolazov, *Dialektika u Revoliutsiya*, p. 160.
89. K. Kautsky, *Put'k Vlasti*, pp. 46, 14.
90. *II S'ezd RSDRP, Protokoly*, Moscow 1959, p. 182.
91. K. Kautsky, *Put'k Vlasti*, p. 52.
92. Ibid., p. 17.
93. *Sotsial-demokraticheskii i Burzhuaznyi Reformizm v Sisteme Gosudarstvenno-Monopoliticheskogo Kapitalizma*, Moscow 1980, p. 13. This collective monograph is one of the best examples of Soviet political science. It is also interesting for the authors' objective and almost sympathetic attitude to the Western Left.
94. K. Kautsky, *Sotsial'naya Revoliutsiya*, p. 3.
95. The Bolsheviks participated in the State Duma but saw it purely as a platform for exposing the system (in Tsarist conditions this was most probably correct). The same approach led, however. to the dispersal of the Constituent Assembly.
96. Rosa Luxemburg, *Social Reform or Revolution*, p. 59.
97. Ibid.
98. *Les deux méthodes, Conference par J. Jaurès et J. Guesde*, Paris 1925, p. 24.
99. *Sovremennyi Sotsializm*, p. 218.

100. F. Engels, *Selected Writings*, W.O. Henderson, ed., London 1967, p. 152.
101. *Sovremennyi Sotsializm*, p. 222.
102. S. Allende, *Istoriya prinadlezhit nam*, Moscow 1974, p. 188.
103. Vodolazov, *Dialektika i Revoliutsiya*, p. 197.
104. *Obshchestvennye Deyateli Anglii v Bor'be za Peredovuyu Ideologiyu*, Moscow 1954, p. 69.
105. *Teoria socialista del Estado*, Madrid 1978, p. 6.
106. One has to agree with the Spanish Socialist leader, Felipe Gonzalez, who has repeated time and again that, limited as freedoms are under capitalism, 'without respect for what is termed formal or bourgeois democracy, there can be no socialism' (*Der Spiegel*, 7 May 1976, p. 137).
107. *Sovremennyi Sotsializm*, p. 222.
108. *Istoriya II Internatsionala*, vol. 2, p. 103.
109. *Sovremennyi Sotsializm*, p. 225. One inevitably comes to the conclusion that in such circumstances the fortress of state power must repeatedly change hands until socialism is finally triumphant. This is confirmed by events in Western Europe in the 1980s.
110. *Les deux méthodes*, p. 20.
111. *Sovremennyi Sotsializm*, pp. 226–7.
112. *Sotsial-demokraticheskii i Burzhuaznyi Reformizm*, pp. 19–20.
113. Ibid., pp. 20–21.
114. P. Lui, *Budushchee Sotsializma*, pp. 90–91.
115. E. Bernstein, *Der Streik, Sein Wesen und Sein Wirken*, Frankfurt-am-Main 1906, p. 210.
116. P. Strel'skii, *Novaya Sekta v Ryadakh Sotsialistov*, Moscow 1908, p. 151.
117. *Stachki: Istoriya i Sovremennost'*, Moscow, 1978, p. 211.
118. *Le Mouvement Socialiste*, 15 March 1906, p. 297.
119. Strel'skii, *Novaya Sekta*, p. 151.
120. R. Luxemburg, *Politische Schriften*, Leipzig 1969, p. 152.
121. Ibid., pp. 171, 209.
122. *Sovremennyi Sotsializm*, pp. 249–50.
123. Ibid., pp. 251, 250.
124. Ibid., p. 7.
125. *II S'ezd RSDRP*, p. 274.
126. Quoted in I. Feinberg, *1914-i*, Moscow 1934, p. 84.
127. S. de Beauvoir, *La Force des Choses*, Paris 1963, vol. 1, pp. 18, 152.
128. G. Lukács, *Lenin*, London 1970, p. 63.
129. Lenin, CW, vol. 31, p. 63.
130. *Voprosy Filosofii*, no. 12, 1980, p. 116.
131. G. Lukács, *Geschichte und Klassenbewusstsein*, Berlin 1924, pp. 269–70.
132. Lukács, *Lenin*, p. 58.
133. G. Dimitrov, *Nastuplenie Fashizma i Zadachi Kommunisticheskogo Internatsionala v Bor'be za Edinstvo Rabochego Klassa protiv Fashizma*, Moscow 1935, p. 33.
134. J. Barras, *Politica de los Exilados Espanoles, 1944–50*, Paris 1976, p. 103.
135. *Nouvelle Critique*, no. 93, 1976, p. 7.
136. A. Gramsci, *Selections from the Prison Notebooks*, trans. and ed. Quintin Hoare and Geoffrey Nowell Smith, London 1971, p. 246.

137. We shall return to these problems, so we will not linger on specific examples.
138. Gramsci, *Prison Notebooks*, p. 235.
139. Ibid., pp. 243, 238.
140. See L. Trotsky, *Kommunizm i Masonstvo*. Trotsky's theory of 'permanent revolution' does not answer the question of socialist tactics in the conditions of Western democracy, but avoids it.
141. M. Spinella, 'Preface', in A. Gramsci, *Elementi di Politica*, Rome 1978, p. 16.
142. Gramsci, *Prison Notebooks*, pp. 237–8.
143. Ibid., pp. 108–9.
144. If I were a radical philosopher I would in this instance write unhesitatingly about the 'totalizing' or 'generalizing' practice of the class struggle. But I am not a philosopher. Fortunately.
145. This 'love-hate' relationship began to form between Communists and Socialists in Italy after Stalinism had been overcome. (It should be remembered that the Italian Socialist Party (PSI) was even more Stalinist than the Communist Party (PCI) and the 20th Congress was as much a shock for it as for the Communists. Even after the 20th Congress, PSI figures wrote that the Soviet people should be grateful to Comrade Stalin for he had 'made the Soviet Union what it is today.') The new relations with the PCI in the 1960s did not, however, progress.
146. *La Pensée*, no. 151, June 1970, pp. 6–7.
147. G. Lukács, *Geschichte und Klassenbewusstsein*, p. 266.
148. These days it is rather embarrassing to attack Althusser who has suffered a profound personal tragedy. But, first, I had begun to write this chapter before I discovered what had happened to him and, second, it is not a matter of Althusser himself but of the neo-dogmatic (in Garaudy's expression) tendencies he has displayed.

Technocracy

The conflicting classes continue the traditions of the nineteenth century. This statement is just as true at the end of our century as it was at its beginning. The basic goals and slogans of the contending parties were advanced in the middle of the last century, for it was at that time that both proletariat and bourgeoisie definitively came into being in Western Europe. The comparative stability of ideological principles in the conditions of a modern, dynamic, developing society may appear paradoxical or even 'unnatural', but in reality it is easily explained: while the major problems remain unresolved, the ideological objectives which such problems engender retain their relevance for all social forces. It is another matter that the problems themselves are becoming more complex, are being exacerbated or eased — in short, are changing their historical form. This naturally encourages many to elaborate completely new principles. Such a desire is not in general 'illegitimate', though practical experience reminds the innovators at every turn that the ideas of the nineteenth century have not yet lost their relevance and it would be premature to jettison them.

The firmness of the Left's ideological principles seems, on the surface, to be inertia and conservatism. This impression is reinforced when the Left at times really is inclined to both one and the other, at least in the field of theory. For example, left Labourites doggedly adhered to one and the same strategic doctrine (rejection of European integration, statization of the economy, and so on) through almost two decades. They showed no desire to modify it in the light of new conditions, and realized how backward their programme was only after their catastrophic defeat in the 1983 elections.[1] This reluctance suggests a poverty of ideas.

By comparison with the Left, technocrats at first seem very free-thinking and modern people. They have no 'preconceived' ideas and — so they believe — no ideology. They are certain they live in a world of real problems, not philosophical theories. They consider themselves above such matters. They generally examine the problems of socialism, capitalism, bureaucracy and dictatorship only from the point of view of efficiency. Efficiency is their one and only God, their sole criterion, their sole aim. But here arises the first perplexity: what precisely is it? Typically, 'efficiency', like a biblical deity, does not lend itself to definition. It is ineffable and inexplicable. Nowhere have I been able to discover a developed definition of efficiency. Evidently we can each understand this deity in our own way. However, the generally accepted opinion is as follows: to be efficient means to achieve one's stated goals with the least waste, quickly and completely. Economic efficiency assumes that goods are produced with minimal costs and reach the market in the shortest possible time. Political efficiency presupposes that the tasks set by a government or political party are completely fulfilled through the projected means — and so forth. The trouble is that these goals can be varied and, at times, mutually exclusive. Even economic efficiency is not something continual and steady. The same production may prove, in different social conditions, to be either efficient or inefficient. It depends on the cost of labour power, on social needs, norms and conditions, and in the end on social culture and psychology. The state sector in developing countries often lowers the prices of its goods and thereby maintains its competitiveness by sacrificing a portion of its profits. But, in similar conditions, a private firm prefers to cut wages or even go into liquidation. It is obvious that capitalists and socialists, bureaucrats and workers, democracy and dictatorship, will set themselves different goals. Thus, in the end, every major political movement begets its 'own' variety of technocrat. In the same way, technocrats will behave differently in differing socio-political systems. They can be left-wing, right-wing, centrist or 'neutral' depending on external circumstances. Thus technocracy, which began by rejecting ideology and attempting to stand above parties, usually ends up by placing itself at the service of all conceivable parties and ideologies.

There have however been attempts to elaborate a system of 'pure' technocratic ideas. Efficiency for efficiency's sake sounds rather awful but it is, nevertheless, the only approach by which technocracy can preserve its virginal purity. Here difficulties of quite another order arise.

It is quite easy to define what constitutes 'maximum economic efficiency'. All work, all effort, must be subordinated to it. But how is this to be achieved? The technocrat's answer is simple: the economy must be freed from ideology and politics. Concrete problems as such must be solved, but all others are unnecessary complications. Philosophers and ideologists, making calls to 'liberate the individual' or 'rescue mankind', are idiots (if not worse). From the viewpoint of such a 'practical worker' there is little to distinguish priests from left-wing activists. The rule of technocracy appears to its supporters as the power of specialists and experts — if you like, the power of scientists — and, consequently, as the triumph of science. But there are things beyond the bounds of economic or social science in the narrow sense of the word. It was the twentieth century's greatest scholar, Albert Einstein, who wrote that 'we must be careful and not exaggerate the possibilities of science or scientific methods when we speak of the problems of mankind, and we must not think that only experts have the right to express themselves on questions relating to the organisation of society.'[2] Professional narrowness is as essential to scientists and economists as it is to everyone else, but knowing one's specialism does not mean knowing the truth.

'Economists by profession' fail to notice that by refusing to consider or simply overlooking various 'secondary' factors — political, social, cultural, historical, ideological, religious, moral, and so on — they do not take into account life itself. And outside of life, economics ceases to exist. The people who constitute the object of economic planning possess consciousness and free will. In the end this will have its effects on economics, and a high price will have to be paid for attempting to ignore the extra-economic aspects of economic problems. The sorry fate of the last Shah of Iran, that crowned technocrat, may serve as a lesson.

Of course, not all technocrats come to such a bad end. In essence the force of technocratic ideology lies in its perfectly real and comparatively broad social base — managers, administrative apparatus and the most dynamic and educated elements of the bureaucracy. These social groups have grown appreciably in recent times in both numbers and significance. The ideologist of technocracy, J.K. Galbraith, wrote in the 1960s that 'the men who now run the large corporations own no appreciable share of the enterprise.'[3] Still earlier James Burnham had gone so far as to conclude that a 'managerial revolution' had taken place in contemporary society.[4] In the West, managers had successfully become a new ruling class (and, in the opinion of supporters of this theory, the same thing would happen sooner or later in the East). The individual capitalist had been replaced by a group of technocrats directing the company in his name.

Often, the 'depersonalization of capitalism' had gone even further: it was impossible to determine who really owned a firm. (If, for example, you try to find out who Marks and Spencers belongs to, you will hardly receive an intelligible answer.) Joint-stock companies have replaced the individual owner by a faceless collective of people who may, perhaps, never see each other in their lives.

Marx had noted this tendency back in the nineteenth century, emphasizing that in a joint-stock company 'function is separated from capital ownership.'[5] Later Engels observed 'the transfer of major productive enterprises and means of communication into the hands of joint-stock companies and state ownership', forcing the bourgeoisie away from the levers of day-to-day management: 'All of the capitalist's social functions are now fulfilled by salaried employees.'[6] Thus the managerial revolution was described in Engels's *Anti-Dühring* and Marx's *Capital* long before Burnham introduced the term into circulation.

Of course, this does not signify the 'end of capitalism'. On the contrary: Marx's *Paris Manuscripts*, and his theory of alienation, irresistibly come to mind. The depersonalization of capital — the universal rule of a new form of social alienation — only aggravates many psychological problems. It is one thing when a worker is opposed by a flesh–and–blood human being, and quite another when it is an anonymous and faceless organization. The problem of responsibility, and above all irresponsibility, arises because in a large organization (even if within it there is comparative openness) it is extremely difficult to determine who indeed took this or that decision.

Galbraith writes of 'a shift of power from owners to managers',[7] but this changes little in essence for, to the technocrats' horror, both owners and managers are subject to one and the same objective general laws of capitalist production. In the last analysis, it is not the capitalist who engenders capitalism but the other way round. The redistribution of power within the framework of the ruling group or organization does not radically change the nature of the organization or its relations with society. Only the redistribution of power on a societal scale can have decisive significance and, in this regard, something has really changed in the West compared to Marx's time. Something, but not everything: one cannot speak of a qualitative, revolutionary shift changing the essence of society. Even more dubious is Galbraith's thesis that this 'shift of power', accomplished within the framework of Western capitalism, is 'enduring'.[8] Of course, the shift in power towards the managers or, as Galbraith puts it, the technostructure, is very important as it has already placed in doubt the whole ideological foundation of private property: the capitalist has turned into a parasitical figure, superfluous even under capitalism! But practical experience shows that the technostructure's real opportunities are limited by existing social and economic relations. The techno-structure depends on the ruling 'parasitical' groups, even if it is reluctant to recognize this. Furthermore, it cannot be completely counterposed to them. In Galbraith's opinion, the technostructure does not in general exist in Soviet conditions as an independent entity; it has not even been able to differentiate itself definitively from the traditional bureaucratic apparatus, remaining a fraction of it. The creation of specialized production associations might lead to the birth of a technostructure but it is evidently too soon to say.

Of equal importance is the fact that owners of capital, in the opinion of both Soviet and American sociologists, 'while transferring the function of management to managers, can retain control for themselves over the choice of company policy and strategy.'[9] Thus the 'old' bourgeoisie, while being removed from routine management, is not being removed from power. In addition, power is now being exercised as *control over management.* Max Weber wrote that 'a wide degree of control over the policies of management may rest in hands outside the organiz-ation.'[10] But even this is not the most important thing. The system possesses a general logic that appears as a kind of mechanism of objective control. Whoever goes against the system is, so to speak, 'punished by life'. Technocrats therefore act within the framework of each system according to its laws and not their own. A Soviet researcher asserts that 'it can be established that the interests of the proprietors are defended even in those companies which are controlled by managers.'[11] The final means of control can be 'cadre policy' — the dismissal of those who are obstinate and the appointment of obedient figures in their posts. It is, moreover, a well-known fact that it is enough to punish one person to make others stop and think (and change their minds).

The social effectiveness of the technostructure's activity would, however, be considerable if it could present itself as the homogenous body Galbraith tries to depict. But the reality is different. Research shows that intense social stratification and blatant inequality exist within the technostructure. The topmost groups converge with the 'old' ruling class and those at the bottom with the proletariat. Research has indicated that 'managers, prominent in their economic position and social standing, approximate to proprietors. Their remuneration ... reaches astronomical heights.'[12] As a result, the technostructure proves incapable of acting as a united whole, some of its groups oppressing and exploiting others: it is as riven with internal contradictions as society itself. In time of profound socio-political crisis it can not only lose all effectiveness but simply fall apart. Even in conditions of comparatively 'stable' development, there are instances were one section of the technostructure has sabotaged the efforts of other sections to carry through reforms within the organiz-ation. The classic example of this is the 1965–68 economic reforms in the Soviet Union and Poland which, despite the full support of the government, encountered desperate opposition from various groups within the economic apparatus (the opposition in Poland was so serious that not even the first steps could be taken!). Group interests fracture the technostructure not only 'horizontally' but also 'vertically'. Everyone knows that the struggle between departments and sections is found not only among bureaucrats but even at the highest levels in the managerial apparatus of production. It clearly follows from all this that Galbraith's notion of unity is an illusion and self-deception. More precisely, a *techno-illusion.*

We will now examine technocrats 'in action'. In his celebrated book *The New Industrial State*, Galbraith delights in detailing the principles by which an organization operates. True, this techno-delight is not shared by everybody. Technocrats maintain that there is a massive difference between the work-methods of bureaucracy and their own. But at bottom there lies one general principle: 'the superiority of the organization over the individual.'[13] Protest in such a case can only pose the question, not solve it. In reality it is not a question of who takes decisions, an individual or an organization, but under what conditions, in whose interests and towards what goal they are acting: what sort of decision-making mechanism exists — in other words, what are the general rules of the game. The behaviour of an organization is subordinate to these general rules to an even greater extent than the behaviour of an individual. An individual's advantage over an organization, incidentally, lies in the fact that a person can take a subjective decision, in other words in the fact that the range of possibilities is somewhat broader than for an imper-sonal organization reacting automatically to external stimuli. Subjective decisions are not always mistaken but they always carry a heightened degree of risk. They are either a direct breach of the 'rules of the game' or a deviation from those rules. In both cases the issue is the same: glory or dishonour. In principle the 'transgressors' must be punished ... apart from those instances when a breach of the rules, through its sheer effrontery and ill intent, goes beyond conceivable bounds. A footballer, accidentally touching the ball with his hand, is penalized, but a chap from Rugby, picking up the ball and carrying it towards his opponents' goal, created the basis for a completely new set of rules. And it is the same in politics. It is no accident that from the late 1970s strong-willed individuals, capable of taking the risk of an independent decision, have been so highly valued in all parties, of both Left and Right. In this sense Margaret Thatcher and François Mitterrand embody one and the same principle.

Galbraith's book is a veritable hymn to the limitless possibilities of mediocrity. In his opinion the systematic organization of scientific research renders genius superfluous, but it has 'greatly increased the need of the industrial enterprise for specialized talent.'[14] In actual fact, these new conditions generate a special need for people capable of breaking free from standard modes of thought and opening up new directions in scientific research. Mediocrity can elaborate ready-made ideas but it cannot create new ones. The strength of an organization lies in its tendency towards the average — an organization cannot be too stupid but neither, as a rule, can it be brilliant (unless it is an association of geniuses like the Frankfurt School of Social Research in the 1930s). Moreover, the cultural level of managers in most countries can hardly be said to be too high. Sociologists recognize that 'if representatives of the intellectual elite find themselves in the technostructure they do not determine its cast of mind.' Here one encounters people whose spiritual world is staggering in its poverty. Professionalism takes the place of genuine education. E. Ambartsumov writes:

These people are devotees of semi-knowledge, specialists without culture and intellectuals without horizons. They have replaced nobility with cunning, independence of mind with conformism. The author of this article has, at times, utilized the expression "quasi-intelligentsia". It is precisely almost an intelligentsia which mimics its external appearance but, in no sense, its function as a creator of spiritual values.[15]

Technocratic organization is dominated by the Principle of the Gory-nych Serpent: one head is good, but two are better. But this ancient principle is far from justified everywhere and at all times: it should not be forgotten what filled those two heads. If conditions are favourable, one idiot can paralyse the work of an entire committee of wise men, but the opposite is, alas, improbable....

The technostructure strives to escape petty surveillance from above,

Administrative interference from without, in Galbraith's words, reduces its 'reliability and efficiency' (and, in Soviet conditions, even prevents the formation of the technostructure as an independent organization). It is thoroughly bad when external interference becomes systematic. Galbraith emphasizes that 'it will develop the same tendencies to irresponsibility as an individual similarly treated.'[16] Incidentally, despite everything said above, Galbraith recognizes that, in the end, what matters is not who takes the decisions, a group or an 'individual', but the circumstances in which such actions are taken. But an individual enjoys certain advantages. It is a well-known fact that individuals can be found even in unfavourable conditions who are not subject to external pressure and continue to work well despite everything (through love of the job, integrity or simply stupidity). In such cases bureaucratic interference from above is powerless. Such instances are well known to anyone who has had dealings with the economic practice of Eastern Europe (for some reason, such individuals are found most of all in Germany). On the other hand, if the anonymous, averaging group does not directly set itself the goal of resisting bureaucratic interference, it is totally subordinate to it. Collective irresponsibility is thus more dangerous than individual irresponsibility. Any cohesive group at any level produces its own kind of collective security: no-one knows who is to blame, no-one knows what to look for.

In the end Galbraith's starting-point is the idea that the techno-structure always makes an optimal decision on the basis of collective analysis. However, this is no more than a hypothesis and, in my view, a debatable one. In the first place, the probability of error, although lowered, is not removed and, second, it should not be forgotten that the group taking the decisions depends on the quality of information transmitted 'from below' and on the general directions received 'from above'. Thus the situation can arise where even the finest experts, having received incorrect information or not having carried out instructions, take not simply unsuccessful but blatantly idiotic decisions. And the principle of collective security forces these decisions to be consistently implemented in real life....

Of course any group consists of individuals, and this should not be forgotten. But people are different. Galbraith indicates that the individual stimulus in both technostructure and bureaucracy is that of a career. But advancement up the ladder of service for both technocrats and bureaucrats is inevitably related to the fulfilment of definite tasks, and they do not set these tasks for themselves: they are set for them. A manager's career in the West entails furthering the aims of the capitalist, and in Eastern Europe those of the Party or state. Managers can be indifferent to these aims, a career being more important in itself, but it is precisely this indifference which makes them ideal executors.

The technostructure does not especially strive for profit and enrichment. If it has its own social goal then it is steady, stable self-reproduction and, if possible, expanded self-reproduction. But, alas, such a goal is also typical of a bureaucratic apparatus. In order to achieve its objective the technostructure is governed by the principle of the *minimalization of risk*. Galbraith writes that 'if, as will often happen, the maximization of revenues invites increased risk of loss, then the technostructure, as a matter of elementary interest, should forgo it.'[17] This feature is very important. The experience of the 1970s shows that in many cases small and medium firms outstripped major corporations in the introduction of new technology. It is not just that small firms are more dynamic but that they are readier to run risks. In fact the risk related to technological revolutions is far smaller for a corporation but, because of the 'minimalization principle', major corporations are more conservative and let themselves be overtaken by those that are bolder. In the case of bureaucratic organization, the principle of minimalization of risk degenerates into the principle of *avoidance of responsibility* where decisions entailing even minimal risk are simply not implemented at all.... Thus for all their differences, technocracy and bureaucracy have quite a lot in common. Ideally, any bureaucratic structure can be reorganized and turned into a more or less (preferably less) effective technostructure, but in practice, for some reason, it always happens the other way round: the technostructure degenerates into some variety of traditional bureaucratic apparatus. Technocracy constitutes the ideal of a 'model' bureaucracy; bureaucracy is a caricature of real technocracy.

The reasons for this are legion but, in my view, the major cause of the technocracy's principled ineffectiveness is the fact that this model does not take into account the existence of the human individual. For the technocrat a human is an automaton, some sort of two-legged computer. There are several objective reasons for this. The development of cybernetics created the possibility of building machines possessing certain 'human' features but this, in turn, revived old scientific prejudices. In the eighteenth century Lamaître wrote a book entitled *Man the Machine*. The modern-day technocrat could write a book called *Man the Computer*. If for a representative of the eighteenth-century Enlightenment human beings were thought of as mechanical machines, then the twentieth-century technocrat sees them as cybernetic machines.[18] In turn, if man is like a computer, then computer technology is like a god: it is capable of anything. But this is a double illusion. There exist, says E.F. Schumacher, 'serious and difficult questions. It is not possible to programme a computer and get an answer. The really serious matters of life cannot be calculated.'[19] Nevertheless, this goal is what technocrats are doggedly pursuing.

The American philosopher, Hwa Yol Jung, has written that, despite all its alluring consistency, this theory is 'unable to understand the intentional structure of human consciousness.' In any case, 'the machine may be either superhuman or subhuman but never be human.'[20] Humans remain simultaneously natural and social beings, which, fortunately, cannot be said of a machine. On the other hand, the technocratic concept of the individual totally ignores both the unconscious in human thinking and behaviour as well as ideological, moral, cultural, religious, and other factors. We are returning to our starting point. Human beings possess free will and consciousness, but they also possess unconscious complexes, unrecognized desires, impulsive needs. In the end humans have characteristic beliefs, convictions, illusions and prejudices. This is all *absolutely real.*

M. Weiss wrote in 1977 that 'the decline of ideology is irreversible.'[21] This was a most typical ideological illusion. Such a declaration could only have been made by someone with a mistaken image of both the structure of modern society and the psychology of the individual personality. The technocrats have often thought that the development of science renders ideology superfluous. But the functions of the former and the latter are different. 'Science', wrote Schumacher, 'cannot produce ideas by which we could live.'[22] An oversimplified picture of the world gives rise to the technocrat's one-sided and primitive conclusions. Toffler observes that technocrats 'start from the premise that even non-economic problems can be solved with economic remedies.'[23] They encounter a reality in which even purely economic questions are closely bound up with political, social and, last but not least, moral contradictions. Information fetishism and computer cretinism create for the 'practical man' a totally distorted image of the world. Enlightened Europeans, blindly believing in the omnipotence of technology, are in the end indistinguishable from primitive peoples convinced of the omnipotence of their idol. Pragmatists think they are above ideology, whereas in fact their 'anti-ideologism' is simply the worst variety of ideology. They live in a world of illusion, for they endeavour to ignore perfectly real cultural and ideological facts. They are, moreover, also human beings, although you would not guess it, and they have the same inherent weaknesses as other people. Technocratic pragmatism is precisely the worst kind of ideology in so far as the pragmatists do not realize their ideological limitedness and revere their illusions above reality itself. They are uncritical. W. Akin, in a sympathetic analysis of early technocratic utopias in America at the time of the great depression, recognizes the patent impracticality of many of the projects. But the technocrats themselves did not suspect or even think about this. They were incapable of sober self-evaluation: 'Their self-image was one of engineer-scientist guided to their conclusions by rational and empirical methodology.'[24] They recognized neither the subjectivity of their conclusions nor the problems of the human personality. The celebrated French philosopher, E. Mounier, wrote that:

> Psychological and spiritual trouble is related to economic trouble and can, in the long term, undermine decisions of a purely economic order. The most rational economic structure, if it ignores the individual's basic requirements, is doomed to destruction.[25]

J.M. Keynes once accurately remarked that 'professional economists', as a rule, 'were apparently unmoved by the lack of correspondence between the results of their theory and the facts of observation.'[26] But the position of those declaring 'so much the worse for the facts' is not as invulnerable as it would seem at first glance.

A pragmatist is indeed an impractical being to the highest degree. 'Technocrat' and 'failure' are, in the final analysis, one and the same. However, after the collapse of each technocratic experiment (the most recent and most shattering being in Iran), their advocates convince themselves and their associates that it is not a matter of the method itself being defective but of the insufficient purity and consistency of the experiment. They prepare a new, still 'purer' experiment which collapses in even more catastrophic fashion, and so on *ad infinitum*. They do not understand that, despite their own calls to free economic policy from 'ideological ballast', they themselves totally subordinate their strategy to ideological illusions. 'Pure' economics is an illusion, for economics cannot be divorced from social structures and human psychology, and a policy constructed on illusions sooner or later suffers defeat. One should not be surprised by the failures of 'sober-minded people', by their striking naivety and the truly heroic stubbornness with which they continue to defend their positions while refusing to make even the slightest concession to reality....

As we mentioned above, there are both right-wing and left-wing technocrats. Right-wing technocrats are conservatives in politics and monetarists in theory. We shall return to them later. Left-wing techno-crats are liberals or social democrats in policy and Keynesians in theory. They have no love for each other. There are extremes on both sides. From time to time one encounters extreme right-wing and even extreme left-wing technocrats but these are exceptions. Here we are interested in social–liberal technocracy, which has exerted enormous influence on the development of the West in the post-war period. And Galbraith is closest of all to this.

John Maynard Keynes, who created the foundations of a new economic theory in the West, was undoubtedly an outstanding thinker. However, this idol of technocratic ideologues in the 1960s could scarcely be called a technocrat. The schematism and primitivism of thought of modern pragmatists were foreign to him, and his books today seem somewhat sentimental (especially when one recalls that he was a professional economist). In his political views he was above all a liberal, and he never adhered to social democracy. True, Keynes sometimes displayed sympathy towards the Left, corresponding with George Bernard Shaw and speaking out against the economic blockade of Russia in 1918; and he was even one of the few British intellectuals who tried to obtain an entry visa into Britain for Trotsky. But on the whole, he was a long way from socialism. He was an enlightened, humane, liberal English bourgeois in the very best sense of the word, but a bourgeois nonetheless.

While aware of capitalism's defects, he never wished to liquidate the capitalist system as a whole. His pupil, Joan Robinson, wrote that he criticized capitalism 'for moral and aesthetic reasons, but he was by no means a socialist.'[27] In 1925 he said: 'I can be influenced by what seems to me to be Justice and good sense; but the class war will find me on the side of the educated bourgeoisie.'[28] When he spoke in favour of the re-establishment of economic links with Russia, he was in no way guided by love of the Bolsheviks (who by and large bewildered him), but by considerations of common sense: in this he had much in common with Shaw. The blockade of Russia, he wrote, is 'a foolish and shortsighted proceeding; we are blockading not so much Russia as ourselves.'[29] Trade with the Russians was necessary precisely so as to temper the existing revolutionary regime, for whether or not the form of communism represented by Soviet government proves permanently suited to the Russian temperament, the revival of trade, of the comforts of life and of ordinary economic motive are not likely to promote the extreme forms of those doctrines of violence and tyranny which are the children of war and of despair.[30]

The lessons of the First World War were indeed particularly important to Keynes himself. Global conflict did not only mean the destruction of productive forces and economic crisis. In a series of countries, significant experience of state regulation of economic life had been accumulated. Lenin even wrote, perhaps a little prematurely, of the beginnings of 'state-controlled capitalist production, combining the colossal power of capitalism with the colossal power of the state into a single mechanism.'[31] Keynes, in his turn, called for this experience to be utilized in peacetime and for crises to be eliminated by resorting 'to such all-embracing measures as were previously allowed only for war and destruction.'[32] Western society, emerging from the World War, had clearly outgrown the old forms of economic organization. Marx had predicted in *Capital* that the development of powerful joint-stock companies 'gives rise to monopoly in certain spheres and hence provokes state intervention.'[33] Keynes, however, posed the question in practical terms. He focused his attention on an analysis of variable economic factors which 'can be deliberately controlled or managed by central authority in the kind of system in which we actually live'[34] — that is, within the capitalist system.

It seems somewhat paradoxical that in Western Europe it was actually workers' parties which adopted Keynes's ideas. This is, however, very easily explained. The working class in the West in the 1930s and post-war period desired not the eradiction of capitalism, but reforms. Lenin once said that two political courses are open to the working class. The first of these is for a break with capitalism, for socialist revolution; the second is for the amelioration of its position and a broadening of its rights within the capitalist system. This Lenin called 'the bourgeois politics of the working class.' The proletariat makes a choice in favour of one of these two strategic lines or vacillates between the two. Both policies accord with the class's interests, but they do so, so to speak, at different levels. In choosing reformism, workers give capitalism a respite. The reformist choice is, of course, conditioned by circumstances: but at all events, it was this choice which determined the fate of Western society in the post-war period. Capitalism, wrote N.I. Bukharin, exists only while the working class 'silently "consents"' to it.[36] The conclusion is simple enough and, as far as we know, no one disagrees ('this is true', noted Lenin in the margin of Bukharin's book[37]). But two points should be mentioned: first, the consent of the proletariat entails some 'corresponding' concessions — which may sometimes be substantial — on the part of the ruling class; and second, the rejection by Western workers of the revolutionary road was predetermined by the historical events of the 1930s and 1940s. It is explained not by a love of capitalism, but by a mistrust of the Marxist programme. In conditions where Stalinism was advancing from the East under the banner of 'socialism', where millions of people in the West (this unpleasant fact should be recognized) came to associate Marxist slogans voluntarily or involuntarily with the 'Gulag' and socialism was compromised in the eyes of the European public, the revolutionary mood of the proletariat in capitalist countries clearly declined. It was this and not some mythical 'betrayal' by its leaders that caused the transition of Western social democracy to more moderate positions. The rejection of the revolutionary course occurred under pressure from below. Ideologues attempted to counterpose new slogans to this pressure but they could do nothing. Research provides evidence of the fact that those who vote for the British Labour Party (in their majority skilled workers) 'are only slightly more "left-wing" than Conservative electors.'[38] The French sociologist Maurice Duverger remarks that, in a series of cases, 'voters transferred to the left parties but the latter themselves moved towards the centre.'[39] On the other hand, organizations adopting strongly revolutionary positions were unable to improve their position in the 1950s or 1960s. Even the crises of the 1970s did not provoke a mass movement for a radical restructuring of the system, although they did alter the relationship of forces.

This could be called 'postponed revolution'.[40] But the sharp decline in the western proletariat's revolutionism did not signify a rejection of opposition to capitalism. This opposition was expressed through the demand for reforms. Before 1945 the social democratic parties, expressing such a mood in the working class, remained formally Marxist although in practice they inclined towards liberal reformism. In the postwar period an explicit re-examination of ideological principles became unavoidable. The German social democrats held their Congress in Bad-Godesberg, and 'Bad-Godesberg' became symbolic. For some it was associated with betrayal, for others with wise realism. In any event, it was Keynes who came to social democracy's rescue. He criticized existing capitalism in the name of social justice and equality, but did not call for the system's overthrow and confined himself to reforms within it. This was the very thing needed by workers' parties in the post-war West.

Keynes died in 1946, having written his major works in the mid-1930s. 'Left Keynesianism', paradoxically, had originated even earlier. The Polish economist, M. Kalecki, developed analogous ideas several years before his British colleague. This is not surprising: Keynes, while he had a brilliant knowledge of nineteenth-century 'classical' political economy, had never even tried to read *Capital* and had only an incidental notion of Marxism. Kalecki, for his part, had never been interested in 'classical' theory: 'The only economics he had studied', remarks Joan Robinson, 'was in Marx.'[41] Keynes spent much time rediscovering Marx's theory of reproduction, while Kalecki found it ready-made in *Capital*. Robinson writes: 'The interesting thing is that two thinkers, from completely different political and intellectual starting points, should come to the same conclusion.'[42] This is a very important observation. Kalecki was a convinced opponent of capitalism and Keynes its defender, trying to cure the system's defects with the help of the latest methods. The simplest explanation may be that scientific truth proves to be higher than party loyalty. In this case, though, it is irrelevant. A certain duality exists in Keynes's theory itself. It can be used by both right- and left-wing. This duality is generally inherent in reformist ideas. Some turn to them in order to strengthen the system by means of partial improvements; others so as to change the system itself and transform its basis. 'Left Keynesianism' has given rise to a whole school of contemporary economists: Joan Robinson, Pierro Sraffa, J. von Neumann and others. Typically, however, actual social democratic practice tended to be much more moderate than that proposed by theoreticians of this tendency. If 'Left Keynesians' moved from Keynes to Marx, then the 'practical people' of social-technocracy travelled in the opposite direction.

Thus Right social democrats did not go beyond the boundaries of the existing system. On the other hand, as Soviet experts have correctly observed, modernizing this system in European conditions 'proved practically impossible without the more or less active participation of social democratic parties in the process of government.'[43] The traditional political groupings of the ruling class, when in office, hold fast to the old order even when changes are necessary in their own interests. Such is conservatism's ideological and psychological logic, and such a situation can be observed not only in the example of twentieth-century European capitalism but in other historical instances. As one of our political commentators has written, conservatives 'are oriented not so much to altering as to preserving this order. Such parties, therefore, approach imminent changes with procrastination, indecision and inconsistency etc.'[44] As a result it frequently happens that reform of the system is carried out by forces which, in a class sense, are opposed to it.

Reforms have been comparatively successful. The strategy of Right social democracy in Europe has been to increase state involvement in the economy, redistribute national income through the state budget, and utilize some socialist methods of economic management and elements of democratic planning. In the United States the same measures have been advanced, albeit less consistently, by liberal Democratic Party administrations. The outcome of this 'Keynesian revolution', as Galbraith puts it, was that from 1947 to 1966 'there was no serious depression.' The triumph of the new principles was universal. Capitalism had been altered. In the 1960s, Keynes's views were shared by virtually all economists, 'a nostalgic and romantic minority apart.'[45]

Western society seemed totally stable. Keynesian methods of state regulation had enabled more or less steady economic growth and lowered social tension. True, a side effect of such a policy was a comparatively high rate of inflation but this had been foreseen earlier. The expansion of state expenditures, even the most absurd and senseless, by increasing the purchasing power of the population, revives economic life. As demand grows, prices rise but production also expands. Additional demand is created artificially and is short-lived, but it does its job. The state 'deceives' the market. Thus even the arms race proves to be a positive factor for Western economies. Keynes's renowned reasoning should be recalled: 'If the Treasury were to fill old bottles with banknotes, bury them at suitable depths in disused coal-mines' and so on, and then private entrepreneurs be permitted, in accordance with existing laws on leasing the land, to dig them up,

> there need be no more unemployment and, with the help of the repercussions, the real income of the community, and its capital wealth also, would probably become a good deal greater than it actually is. It would indeed be more sensible to build houses and the like; but if there are political and practical difficulties in the way of this, the above would be better than nothing.[46]

Keynes understood perfectly that house building would encounter more opposition than the patently idiotic project of burying money in the ground. But this was not the point. His point was that, under certain conditions, even perfectly nonsensical behaviour by the state has a positive economic effect, for it can promote the growth of employment:

> When employment increases, aggregate real income is increased. The psychology of the community is such that when aggregate real income is increased aggregate consumption is increased.[47]

And consumption stimulates production. Nineteenth-century 'classical' theory saw the chief means of combating unemployment in the lowering of wages so that it became profitable to hire additional workers. But this, objects Keynes, reduces aggregate demand and thereby production, provoking further redundancies, another decrease in wages and so on. Consequently, such methods are not appropriate for fighting unemployment in crisis conditions. The state must give people work at any price even if this work is of no use to anybody:

> But the incomes from this fruitless labour will be expended on food, clothing, shelter, medical care and recreation. The incomes of the producers of these commodities and services will grow and so will their own spending. Thus, even totally wasteful employment has the result of increasing useful output and useful labour.[48]

The successes of social democratic governments in this field in the 1960s have been recognized even by pro-Soviet communists. 'The anti-cyclical conjunctural policy of the Austrian state has proved completely effective,' wrote E. Fial and F. Mura, 'although it has major inadequacies'. Austrian socialists were able to prevent and attenuate crises through changes in the state budget: 'During the boom small increases in expenditure were made but when the economic situation deteriorated, social expenditure was sharply increased by means of "deficit spending".' The government consequently acted precisely in line with Keynesian methods. The result was the almost complete elimination of unemployment in the 1960s and a rise in living standards. The communist authors recognized that 'in reality, the high level of employment achieved in the preceding years strengthens the position of workers and employees in negotiations over the redistribution of wages both at a trade-union and an individual level.'[49]

In this system inflation appears as an inevitable evil but it performs a definite positive 'role'. It forces the bourgeoisie to invest money in production, and workers in consumption: money, lying as a 'dead weight', and unrealized accumulations depreciate. Thus

> most Keynesian–type economists, basing their prognoses on the experience
> of the 'Great Depression' of the 1930s, have considered the growth of
> inflation into a serious and destructive process to be improbable. A little
> 'controlled' inflation is, they suggest, useful for injecting dynamism into
> economic development.[50]

It is crucially important to Keynesians that the rise of classical crises of
overproduction is averted at any price. If financial crises of a new type
appear in their place they are considered in any case to be a lesser evil.
And not without justification. A contemporary American follower of
Keynes has indicated that 'the decline in inflation rates in the USA has
only at one point ended badly and that was in the $200 billion underpro-
duction as a result of contracting employment and a drop in active
capacity.'[51] The growth of production and 'full employment', being a
strategic goal, must be achieved at any price.

Here, it is true, one more general question arises. The strategy of
growth allows the material position of exploited social layers to be
improved without altering their subordinate role in society and without
liberating them. But this very goal is rendered unattainable in conditions
of recession. Here any improvement in the lives of those at the bottom
must be gained at the expense of those at the top and at the expense of a
reorganization of social structures. Thus continual economic growth
appears a necessary condition, not for the survival of civilization, as some
assume, but for the maintenance of social equilibrium in a system based
on exploitation. But, in the end, the illusion appears that growth of gross
national product is necessary in itself, is an objective in itself. An orientation to growth for the sake of growth originates which is characteristic
not only of capitalist regimes but also of bureaucratic and statocratic
ruling groups in other countries.[52] New problems and contradictions
arise. As E.F. Schumacher has said, under such conditions, which have
been prevalent throughout the whole of the twentieth century, 'the
dangers have grown even faster than the opportunities.'[53] Pollution of the
natural environment, alienation of the individual, disproportions and
disequilibria in the economy, the accumulation of unresolved social
problems — these are the direct consequences of such 'progress'.
Moreover, the means which could be spent on improving the quality of
life are devoted to accumulation and, even worse, accumulation for the
sake of accumulation. If at first growth was necessary to ensure a higher

standard of living, then at a certain stage the inertia of the very same policy leads to ruling groups striving to lower the masses' standard of living in the name of accelerating growth. The means replaces the end. D. Goulet writes of how 'development's blind forces will make men into their own image: process without goals, power and abundance without freedom.'[54] Our criticism of the technocratic 'growth strategy' should not, however, make us lose sight of its real successes in the 1960s.

So state regulation created a serious problem in inflation, but it also ensured a prolonged period of uninterrupted growth. This greatly increased the social stability of the system. As Galbraith wrote: 'Instead of revolution, there would be a budget deficit.'[55] Steady economic growth made for a real improvement in the lives of many categories of workers. Official ideologists in the United States announced with pride that 'almost 84 per cent of American workers travel to work in their own automobiles.'[56] In western European countries, where social democrats have been in power for long periods since the War, standards of living have approached those of the Americans and social inequality is perceptibly much less than in the USA. A British Labour Party commentator writes:

> The walls that had, for so long, segregated class from class were, by dint of war, at last starting to crack and crumble. They did not collapse completely then, and they are still largely standing today. But the cruelly stratified society of pre-1939 Britain could never, after 1945, be wholly revived.[57]

In the 1970s, however, the situation changed dramatically. 'We had lived through a blossoming punctuated by small and brief crises,' wrote Olaf Palme, leader of Sweden's social democrats. 'And suddenly we were faced with a situation with which we could not so easily cope.'[58] Crises followed one another with incredible rapidity, each one more acute than its precursor. Experts remarked that 'the present exacerbation of cyclical crises gives no ground for any doubt that, in the 1970s and early 1980s, the economy of the USA had experienced three "full-blooded" crises of overproduction – in 1970, in 1973–75 and in 1980–82.'[59] Furthermore, there existed, in addition to cyclical crises of overproduction, a lingering structural crisis which had led to the collapse of whole branches of the economy in such countries as Britain and France, and a crisis of the world economic order which had caused the indisputable exacerbation of the contradictions both between the leading centres of industrial capitalism and between countries of the 'wealthy North' (including

Eastern Europe) and the 'poor South' (including China). Unfortunately, Soviet experts are perfectly correct when they say that the crisis took liberals and social democrats 'unawares' and that 'they were unprepared for it either at a theoretical or a practical level.'[60] Neo-conservatives threw down a challenge to Keynesian theory and the monetarists, headed by Milton Friedman, called for a return to the good old days of 'classical' capitalism. Despite the absurdity and naivety of such ideologies, their wide success has been revealing: their strength is in the impotence of Keynesianism. It is a reaction to the defeat of reformism. And as we shall see later on, even if conservative critics of Keynes propose nothing new (compared to the nineteenth century) they nonetheless accurately detected the weak points of liberal and social democratic theories.

What is the cause of the crisis of the reformed capitalist system? From a Marxist point of view, reforms can mollify the contradictions of Western society or alter the specific form in which these contradictions are expressed by driving them deep down, but they cannot resolve them. Satan, banished in one manifestation, returns in another. It is like original sin. Society changes, but in the end it retains its fundamentals and stays the same. This is best exemplified by Marx's law of the tendency of the rate of profit to fall.

In 1958 Galbraith wrote that 'in this century, profits have shown no tendency to fall, and capital accumulation has continued apace.'[61] Moreover, in the years 1958 to 1965 the rate of profit in the USA grew rapidly. However, neither Galbraith nor anyone else has given a convincing explanation as to where Marx's error lay. For Marx never asserted that the rate of profit would fall uninterruptedly: 'it is always only in a very intricate and approximate way ... that the general law prevails as the dominant tendency.'[62] And as experience has shown this tendency still continues to exist. A Soviet economist writes that:

> In the epoch prior to monopoly capitalism, the indicator of the overall national rate of profit expressed the actual level of profitability of a majority of enterprises and branches, since the deviation from the average rate of profit was gradually eliminated by the effects of competition within and between branches. The transition from the capitalism of free competition to monopoly capitalism and then to state-monopoly capitalism modified the substance of the indicator of the average rate of profit. Thanks to the restriction of competition, the practice of monopolistic price-formation and the state's redistribution activity, modern major corporations gain not only an average profit on their capital but high and super profits while the

majority of enterprises in the non-monopoly sector of the economy has to be content with comparatively low profits. As a result of such a division, the overall national rate of profit has ceased to be the universal measure of profitability for a majority of the country's capitalist enterprises.

In a reformed capitalist system 'factors preventing a drop in the rate of profit have been significantly strengthened.'[63] And yet the rate of profit still continues to fall! In 1965 its highest ever level was recorded — 16.6 per cent. Then began a prolonged and steady fall. For the post-war period as a whole the value of the rate of profit declined by approximately a third, from 14.7 per cent in 1948–53 to 9.9 per cent in 1973–79.

The usual explanation given by most serious Marxists in both West and East is undoubtedly correct, if somewhat one-sided. The fact is that the crisis of the Keynesian economic model has been brought on not just by the aggravation, in a new form, of the old contradictions of capitalism, but by the appearance of a series of completely new problems inherent in the model itself. If, in the 1960s, we saw the virtues of reformed capitalism, then the 1970s showed us the reverse side of the coin.

Let us return to Galbraith. He emphasizes two features which are characteristic of the contemporary West (and not just the West). In the first place, the productive role, cost and time-span of scientific and technical research has increased. Second, there has been a rise in the standard of living. Consequently, 'high costs and the long period of gestation imposed by modern technology require greater certainty of markets.' If you begin scientific research the results of which have an impact ten years later, you have to be certain that in ten years the market conditions will be favourable for the introduction of these results: otherwise, you will simply decide not to run the risk of expensive scientific investigation. But, on the other hand, 'in a community of high well-being, spending and hence demand are less reliable than in a poor one.'[64] People's consumption is more diverse and demand less predictable. In this way the 'caprices' of the market, fluctuations in price and crisis cycles can spoil everything. The market must be placed under the control of the state or regulated by some other method. In other words, 'market behaviour must be modified by some measure of planning.'[65]

A Soviet specialist writes that:

Keynesians start out from the fact that the 'mature' capitalist economy does not possess the ability to overcome crisis situations independently through the actions of its own internal mechanisms. This leads to the conclusion of the need to utilize the state continually for all kinds of 'supportive' and 'corrective' measures to accelerate and stabilize the processes of economic development. They therefore indirectly recognize that the capitalist economic system is profoundly and inherently contradictory and historically doomed.[66]

In other words, for capitalism to be able to survive in the new conditions it must at least be supplemented by elements of socialism. True, new contradictions arise, but that is a matter of the particular.

Technocrats are ideologically predisposed towards planning. 'Technocrats assumed that anything unplanned was irrational', writes Akin. In their opinion, industry as a whole 'resembled a giant interconnected machine' while social production was 'a complex mechanical process.'[67] Moreover, society as a whole is viewed as a single great technical mechanism, 'one big factory', in which all questions are resolved through administrative–technical means. The only problem is to match these means with the requirements of technology (that such co-ordination is, at a certain stage, completely impossible in principle does not enter the technocrat's consciousness).

Consequently, what we have is not simply planning, but a very definite type of planning, counterposed to the 'vagaries' of the market mechanism and not dependent upon it. Plan and market are not combined in a single whole, and do not complement but confront each other.

In the USA, planning was implemented in the 1960s to a significant degree by the capitalist monopolies themselves, through 'vertical integration' (a firm gains control of sources of raw materials, creates its own sales network and scientific base and becomes less dependent on other firms). In a bureaucratic system, however, this leads to lamentable results. Here we encounter the dangers of super-centralization. It is curious to note that Soviet industrial ministries also travelled the route of 'vertical integration' in the 1960s and 1970s by creating a multiplicity of subsidiary producers which led to a general spread of 'departmentalism' (*vedomstvennost'*), the inefficient duplication of some ministries' functions by others, and so on. If the results of 'vertical integration' in the USA were less bad, this is probably because of its incompleteness. The essence of the matter is that such 'private planning', irrespective of who carries it out – the private firm or the state ministry –, affects the country's economy as a whole. As a result, such private planning, efficient as it is, can be extremely dangerous for the country if private or group interests become divorced from social ones. Because it conflicts with social goals, it inflicts more damage the more successfully it is carried through.

One can take an even more paradoxical example. In the 1930s Stalin implemented something like a policy of 'vertical integration' on a country-wide scale. Just as a monopoly strives to become independent of the internal market, so Stalin attempted to make the USSR economy absolutely independent of the world market and international division of labour. A Soviet economist writes:

> So for example, in 1928, 69.6 per cent of the country's consumption of mechanical engineering production was covered by our own output; in 1932 this proportion had risen to 87.3 per cent, in 1933 to 95.6 per cent, and in 1937 to 99.1 per cent. The net imported share of rubber consumption constituted 95.6 per cent in 1932 and 23.9 per cent in 1937; the corresponding figures for aluminium are 92.9 and 4.9 per cent, etc.[68]

The import of industrial components from abroad was considered to be, at best, an unavoidable evil. The course was proclaimed of 'freeing the national economy from importing commodities.'[69] No more, no less! And to some extent this task was actually accomplished by Stalin.

It is no accident that the period of maximum economic self-reliance and independence from the world market (the Soviet economy's almost absolute autarky was achieved by the end of the 1930s) coincided with the period of the cruellest internal repression and purges of the Party. These are two inseparable sides of Stalin's policy. While the country was 'closed' to the outside world he could do as he pleased. The sealed society of the 1930s was supported by a sealed economy. Fortunately, in the 1960s and especially the 1970s there occurred an opening up and important restructuring of the Soviet economy. The import of technology and export of raw materials began to play a major role in economic development. This can be considered Brezhnev's chief, if not only, undisputed achievement (although changes had already begun under Khrushchev). External trade grew steadily. This tendency proved to be irreversible even in the early 1980s when there was crisis in detente and a sharpening of the conflict between the Soviet Union and the United States. In December 1983 *The Times* reported that Soviet purchases of Western equipment 'continue to rise in spite of the cooler political atmosphere.'[70]

We should note another striking parallel between Stalin's practice in the thirties and technocratic theories (especially in their early forms). Akin writes that the founders of the technocratic 'movement' had a characteristic faith in 'the engineers' unique suitability for social leadership.'[71] Stalin reasoned in exactly the same way. G. Guroff, analysing Soviet cadre policy in the thirties, remarks that 'the decision to train the new political leadership as engineers with technical specialities was unprecedented.'[72] The Party's leading cadres under Stalin were in fact made up precisely of engineers. This novel cadre policy was, however, only the realization in practice of technocratic dogma. The resemblance between technocracy and Stalinism is here evident.

One of the forms of planning advocated by technocrats is control over demand. From this Galbraith draws the natural conclusion of the need for 'control of consumer demand'. Nor is this all: 'The purpose of demand management is to insure that people buy what is produced — that plans as to the amounts to be sold at the controlled prices are fulfilled in practice.'[73] Economic compulsion is reinforced. In the 'classical' capitalist system, a worker was obliged to work for an exploiter but was free, at any rate, as a consumer. Technocrats strive to take away even this last economic freedom. E. Ambartsumov calls this 'power over the consumer'. The definition is perfectly correct: 'Manipulating people like puppets spreads from the field of consumption to the political and spiritual sphere.'[74] Again, this was a task brilliantly accomplished by Stalin in the 1930s. It was achieved through the policy of planned shortage. Later, in the 1960s, some Soviet economists even spoke of a system of 'absolute shortage'. The fact is that, from the very beginning, a planned shortage of almost all types of production was contemplated, including raw materials and equipment and means of production as well as consumer goods. The population's needs were not completely satisfied even though production was one hundred per cent realized. From this derives the Stalinists' illusion that 'there is no problem of the market' in the Soviet system.[75] In a 1934 textbook we read that 'the category of value is quite inapplicable to the economy of the USSR'[76] — no more, no less. When, in the 1960s, Khrushchev and those who came to replace him tried to secure greater satisfaction of workers' needs they encountered a mass of problems bequeathed to them by Stalin and his 'successful' policy.

It should be remembered, however, that anti-democratic tendencies were inherent in technocratic thinking from its very inception. This is evident even without a comparison with Stalinism. Between the wars one of the founders of technocracy, Walter Rautenstrauch, insisted that parliamentary 'democracy accomplishes nothing and leads nowhere.'[77] Technocrats in the West later avoided such extremes, but such slips of the tongue were not accidental. Akin writes: 'While they claimed not to adopt police-state methods to maintain the new order, their passion for order led in that direction.'[78] And of course the slogan of planning has itself been used by various political parties of both Left and Right. President Franklin D. Roosevelt, creator of the American 'New Deal', said in 1933 that 'the problem of planning production and distributing the wealth that can be created by our great economic mechanism is of the utmost significance.'[79]

The problem is not, however, planning in itself, but its character. For totalitarian regimes, planning has always been a means not of achieving social justice, but of gaining political control over the economy. In a majority of cases the orientation towards economic autarky, towards a sealed economy cut off from the outside world, was linked to preparations for external aggression and internal terror. In Italy in the 1930s, for example, the fascist state sharply increased its intervention into the economy in preparation for war:

> The methods being utilized now, as in the past, are not only those of economic, but of political pressure. Thus, within the framework of a policy of autarky and militarization of the economy, special committees are convened to elaborate the general directives for a particular branch of industry and allocate raw materials and foreign currency between individual enterprises. In agriculture, within a system of centralized procurement of produce, a transition is made from voluntary to compulsory procurement.[80]

In Hitler's Germany an orientation to a closed economy was declared to 'maintain the "invulnerability" of the Reich in the event of economic blockade.'[81]

Keynes was also opposed, in his time, to the growing internationalization of economic relations, expressing his hope that 'commodity production will remain a country's internal affair.'[82] By this he assumed, quite justifiably, that successful national planning would prove impossible if it did not exercise control, in some form or other, over external trade. But he said not a word about creating a closed economic system and the compulsory restriction of consumer choice. History, however, posed these questions in the sharpest fashion. Control can only be exercised by flexible methods where there are democratic institutions, and cruel dictatorial measures where there are bureaucratic organizations. History shows that technocrats have gradually inclined towards the latter, more straightforward method. The technocracy has undergone a degeneration. 'The ruling elite is becoming more and more satisfied in its thinking with the bureaucratic model', wrote D. Schuman.[83] Thus a Soviet author is not so mistaken when he writes that, in both theory and practice, the technocrats' 'totalitarian outlines' have sometimes shown through.[84]

In any event, an economic strategy striving to turn the consumer into a slave of production is both anti-democratic and anti-humanitarian. If a state promotes such a strategy, it is bad. But if a capitalist monopoly does exactly the same thing then it is not much better.

Western European social democrats, as distinct from American liberals, are less inclined to entrust the business of planning to private corporations. In their view the running of the economy should be concentrated in the hands of state organs. Thus even parties on the right wing of the workers' movement have paid a great deal of attention to the state sector of the economy, which is supposed to control, to a greater or lesser degree, its 'commanding heights'. As is well known, this idea was advanced by Lenin back in the 1920s, although in a different context.

The classic country of social democratic power in Central Europe in the 1960s and 1970s was Austria, where the state had extensive economic positions at its disposal:

> Since 1946, ferrous and non-ferrous metallurgical enterprises, coal mines and shipping companies have been almost totally nationalized. The state owns a series of major enterprises in the electronics, chemical and machine-building industries. The major part of the credit apparatus is in the hands of the state: three of the most important banks have been nationalized. Each of these banks possesses industrial concerns, i.e. has a controlling interest at its disposal guaranteeing a majority or a qualified minority in the share capital of the industrial enterprises. In addition, since 1947, almost the whole of the electricity-generating industry has been nationalized, and the railways and post office, tobacco industry and salt production are owned by the state. Finally, there is a significant number of enterprises in which a large part of the share capital belongs to the state, provinces and communes. Around 30 per cent of all workers and employees, including public-service workers, are employed in the state sector.[85]

In analysing the Austrian experience, even Soviet economists with a critical attitude towards social democracy acknowledge that nationalized sectors 'have been less susceptible to crisis and recession and frequently

continue to develop at high rates even in periods of crisis.' Nationalization in Austria engendered a whole series of social changes and led in the
state sector to the creation of 'trades unions comprising 90 per cent of
the workforce in the mid-1970s, the formation of production councils,
an improvement in the system of self-provision, an increase in wages,
etc.'[86] Unemployment was maintained at the country's traditionally low
level.

In Britain virtually every Labour government has carried out
nationalization and even the Conservatives had to resort to this remedy
to save Rolls Royce:

> In the conditions of the scientific-technical revolution, the possibility of
> modernization and the introduction of scientific advances through the
> Treasury became a major factor in expanding the sphere of state enterprises.
> Thus, if the first wave of nationalization (1946-51) was basically limited to
> the capital-intensive branches of the productive infrastructure – ferrous
> metals, the Bank of England – then, as a result of the second wave (1971-
> 77), shipbuilding, aerospace industries and a series of monopolies in the car,
> machine-tool, electronics and other technological branches of manufactur-
> ing industry were, for the first time, included in the state sector of the
> economy.[87]

In Spain a strong state sector was created even under Franco's
dictatorship where the government took responsibility for the development of branches in which domestic private capital was unable to
operate efficiently. The bourgeoisie understood perfectly well the
advantages of such nationalization: when the Socialists came to power in
1982, the new Prime Minister, Felipe Gonzalez, recognized that the
government had to 'resist pressure from the private sector trying to
transfer enterprises they wished to get rid of into the public sector.'[88] For
its part, the Left began to speak of the need for strategic nationalization
of the most modern and advanced branches of production which
determined the development of the economy as a whole.

Finally, in the Federal Republic of Germany and Scandinavia, where
right-wing varieties of social democracy came to power, extensive
nationalizations were not carried through. However, state involvement
in the economy increased all the same through a series of measures. It is
possible that Left-centre governments in Germany and Scandinavia were
less inclined to nationalize because there the bourgeoisie displayed a
greater willingness to co-operate and greater discipline. British

communists wrote with regard to Germany that:

> The capitalist class, which in contrast to its British counterpart has excelled by its entrepreneurial vigour and expertise and its relative flexibility in the bargaining process with organised labour, has made a whole series of major and minor concessions ... which, taken together, give German workers a standard of living unparalleled elsewhere.[89]

Western European social democracy has not abolished and did not intend to abolish capitalism. The objective of nationalization was not to undermine the foundations of private enterprise. It could only extend the state's economic opportunities and create additional levers of planning. But it was precisely this that the mass of the proletariat desired. Even Soviet experts recognize that the measures introduced by Attlee's Labour Government in 1946–51 expressed the wishes of Britain's organized working class and

> not only went significantly beyond what the Conservatives were capable of (and they would also inevitably have had to carry out a series of measures in the sphere of state-ownership) but also transcended the immediate economic needs of the development of British capitalism.[90]

In the *Communist Manifesto*, Marx and Engels outlined the plan of a programme of preliminary reforms which must be carried out under capitalism. These reforms should prepare the ground for socialism and precede it 'in the most advanced countries.' It was stressed that, on coming to power, socialists cannot 'replace' the capitalist system immediately. Reforms must be implemented which

> in the beginning ... cannot be effected except by means of despotic inroads on the rights of property, and on the conditions of bourgeois production; by means of measures, therefore, which appear economically insufficient and untenable, but which, in the course of the movement, outstrip themselves, necessitate further inroads upon the old social order, and are unavoidable as a means of entirely revolutionizing the mode of production.[91]

Official Soviet textbooks stress that even if elements of capitalism developed within the framework of feudalism, elements of socialism cannot originate and develop within capitalism. Marx, however, asserted directly the opposite. His idea was that a workers' party initially takes power into its hands not to eliminate capitalism but only to create the preconditions for socialism within the old society and prepare the new one. Few people nowadays remember this brilliant idea from the *Communist Manifesto*. But what specific measures do Marx and Engels propose? 'Abolition of property in land', 'heavy progressive or graduated income tax', centralization of credit and transport in the hands of the state, 'extension of factories and instruments of production owned by the state', 'free education for all children in public schools', 'combination of agriculture with manufacturing industries', and so forth.[92] Clearly, this preliminary minimum programme has already been realized to a significant degree by social democracy in the West! Admittedly, of course, measures which Marxists regard as a minimum programme represent a maximum programme for Right social democrats. The trouble is not that the measures of social democratic reformism are insufficient for the transition to socialist society — nobody had expected that they would be sufficient — but that, in travelling the technocratic road, social democracy has lost its strategic perspective and got stuck halfway. Soviet political commentators have justifiably observed that 'the high level of technocratic elements in reformism has essentially neutralised it.'[93] Thus the Wilson Labour Government in the 1960s gradually altered a programme of social change into a programme of economic growth and modernization of Britain — which it also failed to carry out. Such an approach reduces all political and social tasks to organizational and technical ones.

Wherever social democracy looks to a technocratic course 'as an exhaustive means of implementing its programme of change, it turns out to be the same as wrapping it up. . . . Social-democratic politics and ideology are replaced by economic and organizational measures.'[94] Triumphant administrative illusions kill off the vestiges of social culture.

One way or another the mixed economy is now a reality in many Western countries. But the experience of social democracy, like that of the Soviet system and the Third World, has shown that nationalization, in expanding the opportunities for state intervention into the economy, creates new problems which must be tackled — and which on many occasions have been tackled unsuccessfully. One cannot reorganize a firm's work simply by changing its formal owner. Western sociologists have emphasized that

> the essence of property is not ownership and possession but is the *right* of participation and exertion. As such, the concept of property is extended as a share in political power to live a full life in the absence of extractive power. In essence, property is a right to the means of attaining a fully human life.[95]

Marx stressed that capitalist private property presupposes 'the non-existence of any property for the immense majority of society.'[96] But even if the capitalists have been expropriated and their property transferred into the hands of the state, this still does not signify that socialization has taken place in practice.

Marx showed that legal property relations merely express social relations between people in the production (and distribution) process. Simply to change the legal relations without reorganizing the whole system of the social relations of production by no means brings about a revolutionary overturn in the mode of production (something which vulgar 'Marxism' in either its Kautskyian or Stalinist versions could not comprehend). Formal socialization of the means of production still does not mean their socialization in reality. It is only the beginning.[97] Nationalization is not yet socialism, wrote A. Woodburn, a Scottish Left Labourite: 'Nationalization can be a method of administration under capitalism, under a dictatorship, under a democracy, or under social-ism.'[98] Genuine socialist property cannot exist if there is no broad demo-cratic workers' participation in economic decision-making at all levels. And a real restructuring of social relations requires, at the same time, a re-examination of formal legal property relations. In other words, the nationalization of enterprises is only a prerequisite of socialism, but without it socialism is impossible. The technocratic conception, accord-ing to which the structure of management is more important than the structure of property, therefore contains an inherent, irresoluble contradiction: the one cannot be divorced from the other.

The most right-wing social democrats derive from technocratic theory the conclusion that state intervention in the economy can be realized without nationalization. The managerial structure of production is subordinated to governmental organs although capitalist private property remains inviolable. In the final analysis this corresponds to Keynes's conceptions. And, in reality, if everything is reduced to the regulation of economic processes, nationalization is not an absolute necessity: 'It is not the ownership of the instruments of production which it is important for the State to assume.'[99]

This model has been implemented with the greatest success in Sweden. But the 'moderate' socialist government has had no wish to turn its attention to the fact that the structure of ownership is linked closely to social structure. The question of ownership in modern Western conditions is, in general, not only and not so much economic as social. The capitalist class retains all its privileges although the individual bourgeois becomes something of an involuntary parasite as managers and the state edge him out of control. And so that he does not 'grow fat' he is systematically squeezed with taxes. This is the origin of Sweden's celebrated 'redistributive socialism'.[100] As a result, an artificial state-'socialist' superstructure is built on top of the unchanged capitalist structure of society. The system proves to be highly complex and, more importantly, contradictory. The class struggle will continue until one of two things happens: either the bougeoisie overthrows the oppression of 'socialist' state institutions and re-establishes 'normal' organic capitalism, or the proletariat completes the construction of a socialist system from below by expropriating the capitalists.

The bourgeoisie retains definite means of impeding social democratic reforms even when it is not in a position to overturn a workers' government through political measures. It can resort to direct sabotage, an 'investment strike', the export of capital, and so on. In Chile such actions pushed the Left to take more revolutionary measures with regard to nationalization: this exacerbated an already tense situation and led, in 1973, to the downfall of the socialist government. In other cases things have not gone so far. But the danger is there. Keynes once called for 'the phenomenon known as the "flight of capital" to be brought under control.'[101] Not a single Left–reformist government, however, has been completely successful in coping with this task. Within the framework of the capitalist system, only partial successes are possible in this matter.

On the other hand, social democratic parties that remain faithful to the idea of nationalization encounter the problem of management at a new level. When British socialists brought a series of enterprises into state ownership in 1946 they still did not know, in Alec Nove's words, 'what criteria should govern their operation.'[102] Nationalized British firms began to operate according to the principle of 'neither profit nor loss'. There were no profits, but there were losses.... In the 1960s, management of the state sector was reorganized 'along the lines of private firms. Managers of state corporations strove to maintain their profitability, in the first instance by raising prices and tariffs on goods and services available to the broad layers of the population.' In the end efficiency and investment in the state sector proved to be higher than in some branches of the private sector. This led 'to a rise in labour productivity and a fall in production costs even in those branches, such as railways, transport, gas and coal, which were in decline.'[103] Nationalization also facilitated a 'radical structural and technical reorganization' in those branches where private capital was unable to cope with this task.[104] But at the same time, bureaucratization of the whole managerial system of nationalized industry was proceeding apace.

In an attempt to ease the conflict with the bourgeoisie, Labour rejected direct expropriation of capitalist enterprises, replacing it with a policy of 'creeping nationalization', or in other words with efforts to widen state involvement in private corporations. This led not so much to the weakening of the power of capital as to the bourgeoisification of the state itself, the unification of the ruling apparatus with the dominant class.

> There is therefore really no strong case for public ownership if the objectives to be pursued by nationalized industry are to be just as narrow, just as limited as those of capitalist production: profitability and nothing else. Herein lies the real danger to nationalization in Britain at the present time, not in any imagined inefficiency.[105]

Socialism must guarantee a 'more democratic and dignified system of industrial administration, a more humane employment of machinery, and a more intelligent utilisation of the fruits of human ingenuity and effort.'[105] Little by little the British Left came to the conclusion that 'nationalization alone does not solve the problem. It is necessary to work out a programme which includes points indicating what the state must do next.'[106]

The common programme of the Left forces in France in 1972, which later formed the basis of the actions of François Mitterrand's socialist government, acknowledged that an expansion of the state sector must be accompanied by the development within it of 'democratic forms of management'. The authors emphasized that 'political and economic democracy are indivisible' and that all workers must have the right to participate in those decisions which immediately affect them.[107] This was an important declaration, although the programme was not precise about exactly what forms of participation it had in mind.[108]

Engels criticized the socialists' naive belief that nationalization is a panacea for all of capitalism's ills: 'State ownership of the productive forces is not the solution of the conflict, but concealed within it are the technical conditions that form the elements of that solution.'[109] What has happened is that state firms either function in the same way as private ones (capitalism without capitalists) or become bureaucratic (the East European model). Bureaucratic and capitalist types of nationalization have not justified the hopes of the Left. But the choice is not limited to these two variants.

The best solution is, in my opinion, a third variety. State enterprises gain a certain autonomy which prevents their bureaucratization but they operate, as distinct from private firms, on the basis of an overall plan. This is what the French socialists' principle of 'managerial autonomy' ('*autonomie de gestion*') boils down to. However, the actions of Mitterrand's government are already transcending the bounds of the normal social democratic reformism which we are discussing: moreover (anticipating a little), it should be noted that defining the limits of 'autonomy' has not proved so easy in practice.

The nationalizations carried out in France back in the 1930s and again in the period of the Left course after the Germans had been driven out (1944–46) were highly effective. Even Giscard d'Estaing's government nationalized a series of enterprises in the late 1970s. By the mid-1970s the state provided jobs for 15.6 per cent of those employed in industry. A French economist has remarked that the state participates 'even in the production of cigarettes and matches.'[110] The comparative stability of prices on goods in the nationalized sector has helped to maintain market equilibrium.

When they came to power in 1981 the Socialists were able to utilize the experience of the past. The pattern of management in state enterprises had for a long time been the famous '*modèle "Renault"*'. Renault had been nationalized after the War and had remained fully competitive.[111] But by the beginning of the 1980s the '*modèle "Renault"*' had largely become a thing of the past. The company, which for years had contributed significant returns to the State Treasury, began to show a deficit. Renault cars became less popular in both domestic and world markets. Changes in technology in the conditions of capitalist crisis had inevitably led to mass unrest. The '*modèle*' had to be redeveloped 'on the move'.

In firms nationalized by Mitterrand, the process of reorganization was conducted extremely painfully. But gradually the policy of nationalization began to bear fruit, and public sector efficiency increased while some capitalist companies (for example, Creseau-Luard) found themselves in a calamitous position. Even the conservative London *Economist* was obliged to recognize this. The leaders of nationalized firms, the journal observed, 'were given as much autonomy as any manager can expect in France. The only fresh constraint was a law giving the workers a say in state-owned companies' policy decisions.'[112] Back in 1977,

Mitterrand had declared:

> It would be naive to divorce planning and market according to the character
> of the ownership of capital by proposing that public enterprises should be
> subject to the logic of planning and private firms to the logic of the
> market.[113]

Structural reform should have affected all sectors of the economy;
planning and the management of state companies should not have had
an anti-market character. But while they drew the right conclusion
about the inter-relationship between state and private sectors in a mixed
economy, the socialists underestimated the acuteness of the conflict
between them and the influence of private capital on nationalized firms.
Some managers took advantage of their autonomy to assist the bourgeoisie's policy by exporting capital and sabotaging the socialists' economic
policy. The leaders of nationalized firms (including Renault) also began
to invest abroad, striking a blow against employment in France.
Economic development proved intimately bound up with the course of
the class struggle. The socialists had clearly not foreseen this. It became
obvious that managerial autonomy must be supplemented by the
democratization of management.[114] In order to force managers to co-
operate with the economic aims of society while not subjecting them to
bureaucratic control, democratic control from below was essential. The
Communists stressed that 'managerial autonomy has a social aspect, full
implementation of the law on democratization and the creation of
consultative commissions in all nationalized enterprises employing more
than 200 workers.'[115]

Thus the involvement of the workers' collective in decision-making
proved an essential guarantee of social effectiveness, without which the
success of nationalization would have been in doubt. The policy of
industrial democracy, slowly and inconsistently implemented by the
French Socialists, was in any case the most radical element of their
programme. In his time Trotsky termed the struggle for extending
workers' participation in the management of capitalist production
'economic dual power.'[116] By affirming the rights of the collective to take
managerial decisions we are actually introducing elements of socialism
from below (both in the state and private sectors). But, as Trotsky
justifiably remarked, the question of participation in management
becomes a question of the class struggle: although these measures do not
themselves create a revolution, they must be implemented in a revolu-

tionary manner otherwise the programme of industrial democracy is doomed to defeat. By advancing the notion of a 'staggered break with capitalism', the French Socialists have once again linked reforms within the system with the anti-capitalist struggle, thus returning to the strategy propounded by Marx back in 1848. The government of the Left forces had to 'utilize political power in order to "realize the first stage of change" and place on the agenda the second: the transition to socialism.'[117]

The problem is that radical programmatic slogans do not necessarily lead to success. If a genuine revolutionary or revolutionary–reformist strategy is absent, they simply remain a self-deception. Meanwhile, with its very first steps, Mitterrand's government began to encounter numerous problems unforeseen by Socialist Party strategists. To tackle them, it was necessary to resort to 'improvisation'; and as a rule, at the base of this improvisation lay the usual, readily accessible prescriptions of technocratic reformism.

Statization of the economy is in any case accompanied by the danger of bureaucratization. This can only be fought on the basis of a consistent, socialist and democratic policy which goes beyond the 'usual' technocratic solutions. As we have seen, statization is not necessarily linked to nationalization. The key is that 'for all industrial planning … the control of prices is strategic.'[118] Control, however, must be flexible, and this is impossible if there is simply an attempt to ignore or suppress market price fluctuations through bureaucratic methods, as has happened in Eastern Europe.

Overall the problem of the market is, as experience has shown, the stumbling block for all advocates of technocratic planning. This is their weakest spot against which the attacks of conservative technocrats, who reject planning, are directed. Galbraith's critique of the market is extremely naive. As we have already observed, he starts out from the assumption of the technostructure's absolute competence which is, in itself, a utopia. But the main thing is that *planning in general can be neither competent nor effective in the absence of an objective control mechanism which can only be the market* (at any rate, no one has yet been able to suggest an alternative). If mistakes cannot be brought to light and corrected in the course of current actions, but can only be revealed at the end of a prolonged period (sometimes after twenty to thirty years, as happened with Stalin's industrialization strategy) then things are not made any easier. Just the opposite. In such conditions the long-term consequences of any incorrect decision inevitably prove extremely painful and even catastrophic.[119]

Stalin's decision to extort the means for industrialization from the countryside is a case in point. E. Kaganov writes that 'the redistribution of accumulation between industry and agriculture, between light and heavy industry, the redistribution of the country's national income between accumulation and consumption' had an incontrovertible effect initially, but led to the emergence of disproportions in the economy which, in turn, engendered the most difficult problems in the 1960s and 1970s.[120] Stalin's policy required the perpetual maintenance of agricultural prices at an artificially low level, which devalued labour power in the towns. As a result agriculture was unable to develop normally for decades. Right up to 1967 the level of agricultural production remained on the whole lower than in the pre-Stalin period. Stalin's heirs therefore came up against serious and almost insurmountable difficulties. They in their turn were forced to resort to a series of artificial measures to boost agriculture — and results were rather worse than expected. As Kaganov wrote, 'it is impossible not to take into account the needs of the market'.[121] The market takes its own revenge.

Unlike Stalinists, Keynesian technocrats favour planning in those conditions where a developed market system already exists. Nevertheless, the course towards creating some kind of planning independent of the market results in very serious consequences ... if it is to be successfully implemented in reality. If technocrats had been able to achieve their aims completely in the 1950s and 1960s, the consequences of the crisis in the 1970s and 1980s would probably have been even more terrible. This becomes quite clear if Galbraith's recommendations are carefully re-read today.

Galbraith proclaims not only a strategy of regulating the market with the aid of planning but also a strategy to 'eliminate the market'.[122] In his opinion, 'the market can be superseded'.[123] In reality such a policy, were it successfully implemented, would give rise to a system of administrative and bureaucratic control (in the twenties such a system in the Soviet Union was given the ironic name of *glavkism* or *glavkocracy* because of the omnipotence of the 'top managements' — '*glavnykh upravlenii*' — of various ministries). Galbraith concedes that, by itself, planning has 'no similar equilibrating mechanism' analogous to the market. In his opinion:

> The planner must deliberately insure that planned supply equals planned use. If he fails there will be surpluses or deficits. If the market mechanism is still not used — if prices are not lowered or raised — there will be a

disagreeable problem of storing or destroying the surplus or an unseemly scramble for the insufficient supply. These are common results of planning, commonly accompanied by a drastic slump in the reputation of the planner concerned.[124]

How this turned out in practice we shall see below. At present we are interested in how the technocrats try to avert such a situation. For Galbraith everything is reduced to error-free planning from the outset, but, for this, exact and exhaustive information must be received straight away. The idea is perfectly correct, but the point is that the objective source of information is precisely the market — which they are trying to abolish.

Planning must take into account the existence of market relations and be based on them. Social democracy's anti-market policy in the 1950s and 1960s gave rise to blatant contradictions, and the attempt to create some socialist institutions within the framework of the capitalist system, although it was to a certain extent successful, created new problems.

The policy of neo-capitalist reforms encountered the resistance of the right wing of the bourgeois class from the outset, but this resistance grew in proportion to the exacerbation of the system's structural crisis. The combination of socialist and capitalist elements in the West's economy means there is a continual struggle between them, in which the capitalist tendencies remain dominant and predetermine, to a significant degree, the ineffectiveness or inferiority of planning measures. On the other hand, the reinforced socialist 'subsystem', which appears up to a point to be a 'prop' for the old order, at the same time remains a continual threat to it.[125] If in the 1960s the opponents of Keynesianism, of a compromise solution, were few and had little influence, then by the late 1970s the picture was changing. As Joan Robinson has written, 'the bastard Keynesians' era is coming to an end in general disillusionment'.[126] By the beginning of the 1980s few could dispute such a pessimistic viewpoint. 'The socio-economic crisis of the 1970s itself signalled the total demise of technocratic doctrinairism', writes an official Soviet author.[127] One could only add that the technocratic models of the 1960s were, in the main 'worn out' but that this was due to a quirk of history. For even in those cases where things had gone well, the old solutions had become outmoded. The more successful the technocratic approach had been at first, the more quickly it discovered its limitations, contradictions and unidimensionality. The Keynesian compromise had exhausted itself, and, new ideas were becoming dominant. It was a case of returning to 'classical' capitalism or else continuing the policy of reforms which were already exceeding the limits of Keynesianism. Right-wing parties and governments — Ronald Reagan in America, Margaret Thatcher in Britain, the Christian Democrats in Germany — naturally adopted the first strategy as their main weapon. The second strategy was adopted by the Left — François Mitterrand in France and the Labour Party in Britain. Northern Europe saw a series of clear defeats for social democracy. In the countries of 'Romance Europe' the socialists everywhere came to power. In the late 1960s and early 1970s, alternating left- and right-wing cabinets, for example in Britain, implemented essentially the same kind of economic measures within the framework of the 'Keynesian compromise'. It was only a question of whether power would incline a little to the left or to the right of centre: the centrist orientation remained. But by the end of the 1970s, the picture was changing. Centrism was being defeated everywhere. The difficulties of Scandinavian social democracy and the weakening of its position during the 1979–83 crisis, and the electoral failures of 'model' social–liberal governments in West Germany and Austria, all testified to the end of the epoch of compromise.

From 1979 to 1982, Europe was outwardly split into two halves: the North, where an era of conservatism had begun, and the South, where the Left were triumphant. In fact, a common process of disintegration of the centrist bloc was occurring in both areas. In Northern countries, social democracy was the main proponent of a centrist course and proved to be the chief victim of the crisis. In the South, bourgeois parties had tried to implement a centrist policy under pressure from a quite radical proletariat. The breakdown of the centrist bloc in Britain led to a split in the Labour Party, but the ruling bourgeois Union of the Democratic Centre in Spain also collapsed. The West German coalition of Social Democrats and Liberals also fell apart — not because of the Liberal leaders' 'treachery', but because of the impossibility of continuing with a common platform when the mass base of one party was shifting to the left, and that of the other to the right. The political vacuum formed in such situations was always filled by the strongest opposition party. In the North, this role was played by conservatives and in the South, by socialists.

A new situation had arisen. Conservatives had previously opposed changes, now they began to implement them themselves. A Soviet author wrote of 'attempts at conservative reform' in the spheres of 'economics, social policy and ideology',[129] and the Western Left even talk about 'changing the system from the right'.[130] Unfortunately, social democrats did not meet this attack with any new ideas. Analysing the experience of the left-of-centre government in West Germany, the author of an article in a German Marxist journal writes that when the reformists ran into difficulties in the 1970s, they themselves swung to the right, favouring a return to the old economic methods: 'Social democracy proved itself the discoverer of but only a moderate vehicle for conservative policy.'[131] Sooner or later the social democrats would have to give way to those who implemented the same policy with greater determination and ideological consistency: the real conservatives. As a Soviet author has correctly observed, German social democracy 'was gradually approaching the line beyond which it would disappear as an independent political force, as an alternative to bourgeois reformism.'[132] In such circumstances defeat at the polls was seen, even by many of its supporters, as a salutary experience. Lev Kopelev wrote in 1983 that the SPD 'had become "worn out" as a ruling party and could only become politically and morally stronger in opposition.'[133]

If the collapse of the centrist bloc in West Germany led to the loss of a significant section of social democracy's support, then in France a significant section of the young generation of technocrats, on which the Right had placed its hopes, unexpectedly supported the Socialists. Many graduates of the privileged Higher Administrative School sided with Mitterrand's party, and frequently with its left wing. In 1978, when the Socialists were on the threshold of power, a Party leader remarked that 'offers of service are coming in from all directions'.[134] Disillusioned with centrism, the young generation of technocrats was becoming more and more interested in left-wing ideas.

The downfall of the centrist bloc revealed internal conflicts within the technostructure itself, so that it could no longer appear a unified whole. In many countries, junior managers began to join trades unions. Sociologists note that 'the identification of their interests with those of wage-workers' became the norm.[135] On the other hand, senior technocrats in the main supported the conservatives, recognizing their affinity with the traditional bourgeoisie. If the technostructure chiefs had previously tried to edge capitalists away from the levers of management, then both were now united against the lower social strata. Once the redistribution of power within ruling circles had been achieved by a mutually acceptable compromise, the dominant groups consolidated themselves. The technocrats lost interest in reforms.

The crisis of reformism led to whole parties — for example, the Free Democrats in Germany — and innumerable individuals 'deserting to the

Right'. Shchelkin writes that among neo-conservatives there are many former progressives who 'went over to conservative positions as a consequence of the insoluble contradictions in which liberal technocrats had entangled themselves.'[136] Despite this, however, a common techno-cratic and anti-humanitarian style of thinking was retained.

It cannot be said that neo-conservative ideas were in any sense novel. F.A. Hayek wrote *The Road to Serfdom*, which has become the Bible of contemporary reactionaries, back in the 1940s. This book argued, by pandering to banal and vulgar prejudices, that planning 'leads to dicta-torship' and that democracy is possible only in a society in which 'a competitive system based on free disposal over private property' is domi-nant.[137] Since the subsequent experience of social democratic planning, for all its technocratic limitations, gave no grounds for such categorical conclusions, more specific arguments were required, such as were later elaborated by Milton Friedman and the economists of the Chicago School.

This group led the Right's attack in the late 1970s. The 'Chicago Boys' focused their attention on the declining effectiveness of the Keynesian policy of regulation. The West had become inured to Keynesian measures. Market regulation had ceased to work and was exhausted. Society lived with 'inflationary expectations' as a result of which

> government measures aimed at 'pumping up demand' could only have an influence on employment in conditions of 'unforeseen' ('unanticipated') inflation, i.e. an increase in prices too high to be taken into account in drawing up collective agreements and long-term contracts.

But alas, this only has a temporary effect, for equilibrium re-establishes itself at a new and higher level: 'The new round of attempts to raise employment again leads to price increases and so on ad infinitum.'[138] Inflation is continually growing and the effectiveness of previous decisions declining.

Many left-wing theoreticians agree with this. As soon as inflation ceases to stimulate production, it can no longer be viewed as an acceptable method from a social standpoint for it turns, in the words of Michel Rocard, into an attempt 'to redistribute the national income to the advantage of the strong by creating new inequality in the country.'[139] Property-owners are the winners and wage-earners the losers.

The theoreticians of the 'Chicago School' counterpose to measures of state intervention their own 'monetarist' and 'neo-classical' doctrine, which can be reduced essentially to a reiteration of the truisms of

Western liberalism in the third decade of the nineteenth century. Government policy, they argue, only muddles development and complicates the normal course of the market. Friedman indicts 'the limited success of central planning or its outright failure to achieve stated objectives': if the economic and political results of the Keynesian era are calculated 'there can be little doubt that the record is dismal.'[140] Planning violates the 'natural cycle of correcting the economy through the mechanisms of competition and price-formation.'[141] To solve all problems, one need only abolish planning and re-establish the 'natural' course of events. Then the market and free competition will resolve all contradictions by themselves. The state's sole task is to maintain a stable currency in order to facilitate the normal functioning of the market mechanism.

This conception has its merits. The market really does resolve all problems in the end through spontaneous self-regulation. But the question is: at what price? If, for example, a sick child is not treated, it will eventually either die or recover of its own accord. In both cases the problem of the illness is resolved one way or the other through the spontaneous development of processes occurring in the organism.... But, alas, the social price which society must pay while it awaits a 'natural' solution is excessively high. Friedman is the same sort of technocrat as Galbraith, in the sense that he completely ignores the problem of the individual. And the individual does not wish to be made a mere victim of economic necessity. The individual protests and resists, frequently quite successfully. Marx came to the conclusion that violent revolution was probable precisely through an analysis of the system founded on the principles of classical liberalism to which the Friedmanites dream of returning. In *Notes from Underground*, Dostoevsky demonstrated the incompatibility between the interests of individuals and an 'objective' order foisted on them in the name of universal prosperity understood as universal satiety. Both prophesies are recalled forcibly to mind.

The more the West returns (or tries to return at a higher level) to the nineteenth-century model, the more there is the prospect of a social explosion. Under the Thatcher government, Britain has already experienced mass unrest the like of which the country has not seen since the time of Chartism — possibly since the enclosures. The long miners' strike, with its bitter clashes with the police, showed once again that the period of class peace was at an end. What had become of traditional British good nature, so much admired by foreigners? Newspaper reports from areas in the grip of the strike were reminiscent of summaries of military actions. The press recorded the numbers arrested and injured and even killed. It was impossible to estimate precisely the direct and indirect material cost to the two conflicting sides. Once the miners had been defeated journalists praised the government's firmness or the workers' heroism and steadfastness, but no one could bring themselves to ask: how was all this possible in the oldest democratic country, which had successfully carried through its revolution three hundred years before?

Government intervention in the economy has become unavoidable, but now it pursues quite different ends. Previously, expenditure had risen, now it is cut back; previously there was nationalization, now privatization; previously there had been a struggle with unemployment, now with the unemployed. Keeping inflation in check becomes the major goal, and in its name the workers must make any sacrifices demanded by the government. Friedman emphasizes that 'there is always a temporary trade-off between inflation and unemployment; there is no permanent trade-off.'[142] There follows from this the need for a complete repudiation of preceding policy and the abolition of all social institutions connected with it. The trades unions, naturally, become enemy number one. The government enters into direct, open and continual conflict with the organizations of the workers' movement. New slogans are advanced with a patently anti-worker character: 'The owners must be the bosses in the factories.'[143] The state's task is proclaimed as 'the defence of the owner from the unions' dictates.'[144] This state of affairs is reminiscent of the nineteenth century. But in twentieth-century conditions, the workers' movement is strong enough to impede the government's course and force wage-rises from the owners, thus fuelling the growth of inflation, and so on.

There has been large-scale selling off of state enterprises in Britain, Japan, West Germany and even a series of developing countries. Conservative technocrats have argued that this is essential to increase efficiency and have alluded to the bureaucratism and excessive centralization in the state sector. Unfortunately, big capitalist firms are not exempt from these evils. Even the conservative *Economist* has recognized that 'privatised monopolies are not necessarily more efficient than nationalised ones.'[145] Moreover, capitalists have been in no hurry to buy those nationalized firms being sold off and take upon themselves the associated problems. In December 1983, the *Times* reported that 'professional investors in the City turned their backs on a Government share sale for the second time in just over a year', although it was not a case of these being loss-making companies. The government was so struck by such 'improper' behaviour on the part of capitalists that an official representative candidly expressed his bewilderment: 'it was difficult to determine exactly why the issue had not been a success.'[146]

Since selling off state assets has proved a fairly complicated affair even from a purely commercial point of view, British conservatives concluded that firms being denationalized should be reorganized beforehand to make them profitable and highly efficient. In several cases the reorganization was a success, thus refuting the government's own thesis that state property and efficiency are incompatible. Thereafter the class essence of the policy being implemented became readily apparent: it was not a case of restoring the British economy's dynamism but of strengthening the position of the traditional bourgeoisie.

As the difficulties and contradictions of the neo-conservative course have increased, many slogans have gone by the board. By declaring themselves the heirs of classical nineteenth-century liberalism, neo-conservatives have laid claim to the role of defenders of democracy. But it has become gradually clear that it is precisely this element of the 'classical heritage' that interests them least of all. It was Hayek, again, who insisted: 'We have no intention, however, of making a fetish of democracy.' Nor does he rate political rights too highly:

> Democracy is essentially a means, a utilitarian device for safeguarding internal peace and individual freedom. As such it is by no means infallible or certain. Nor must we forget that there has often been much more cultural and spiritual freedom under an autocratic rule than under some democracies.[147]

The pupils have gone further than the teacher but not in the direction he had indicated. The American neo-conservative, Samuel Huntington, has written that 'a greater degree of moderation' is needed 'in democracy'.[148] It turns out that in Western society ... there are too many liberties. If the Right had previously criticized liberals for spreading bureaucratism and counterposed to this a model of capitalist decentralization, then the accent has subsequently been placed on powerful, centralized government, which they have found essential for the struggle with trades unions and the Left. In theory neo-conservatives are in favour of an absolutely open economy but, in practice, such a course runs counter to the interests of a series of national business organizations whose goods come up against very fierce foreign competition. The government therefore resorts to protectionism. Situations arise where, as Western experts have recognized, neo-conservative policies 'will cause more inflation instead of less.'[149] Thus expectations have not been justified.

Friedman has talked about the link between market capitalism and democracy, but his most faithful disciples have proved to be dictators. In Chile, Pinochet was able to achieve short-term economic successes by following the recipes of the 'Chicago Boys', but the end results of the military regime's rule have been miserable for a majority of the population and even for bourgeois strata. By the mid-1980s, the failures of Allende's left-wing government began to pale into insignificance in comparison with the dictatorship's economic bungling. After ten years of military rule the level of industrial production was 'lower than in 1972 when Salvador Allende's government was in power.'[150] Thirty per cent of the active population were unemployed and inflation, once again, began to increase rapidly; market mechanisms either did not work or worked with delays; the country could not pay so high a social price for 'spontaneous' development. Pinochet himself was forced to resort to nationalizing a series of companies to save the Chilean economy from bankruptcy. 'His economic policies are crumbling', stated the respectably conservative *Newsweek* in a matter-of-fact way.[151] The people took to the streets. Demonstrators clashed with the army and police. Even the bourgeoisie turned their backs on the regime. This was something more than a collapse of political line. In the words of the British journalist, Richard Gott, the whole accepted economic model had been 'totally discredited'.[152] The military governments of Argentina, Brazil and Uruguay preferred to cede power voluntarily in the face of a swelling popular movement.

In other cases the results of neo-conservative policies have been less deplorable only because right-wing figures have proved less consistent — or, in conditions of democracy, have simply lacked the unrestricted 'freedom to experiment' enjoyed by Pinochet in Chile.[153] A growth in unemployment and social tension has been observed everywhere that neo-conservative forces have found themselves in power. This has led a section of Friedman's followers to change their emphasis. No longer is it a question of the whole economy being remodelled along nineteenth-century lines, but only of the creation within it of a kind of free private enterprise zone unrestricted by any laws. An Italian right-wing techno-crat wrote that 'we do not believe that one fine day neo-liberalism will arrive and finish with state intervention. State intervention has become a constituent element of the Italian economy.'[154] Now the stakes have been placed on small and medium-sized firms standing in opposition to both the nationalized sector and private corporations more or less under government control. Soviet experts note that, in Italy,

> this group of enterprises is often not registered at all with official bodies and has not only 'liberated' itself from any sort of state regulatory influence, including the payment of taxes and social dues, but has no dealings with trade union organisations.'[155]

In the United States, small firms utilize the scientific and technical resources of much more successful large companies: 'According to a series of data, they introduce 17 times more innovations per dollar of expenditure compared to the major corporations (those employing more than ten thousand people).'[156] These 'youngsters' have no other option: the only way to survive is by taking risks, whereas for big companies, as Galbraith himself recognized, it is precisely the minimalization of risk that is law. The comparatively high level of efficiency of small and medium-sized firms is, however, not only related to this. In modern conditions, super-centralized bureaucratic systems are extremely clumsy (and in this sense American corporations suffer from the same ills as Soviet *glavki*). In the 1980s a vital shift towards decentralization of the entire economic mechanism has occurred in the West (incidentally, this has also been characteristic of several countries with 'communist' regimes: Hungary, Yugoslavia and China began such transformations even before the West). The strengthening of the role of small firms is only a reflection of this tendency.

Nevertheless, there is another side to the coin. Small firms, acting autonomously, are not in fact absolutely independent. Their 'unexpectedly high competitiveness', observed Yu. Korolev in the journal *Latinskaya Amerika*, 'is explained by a veiled protection on the part of powerful international concerns which are, properly speaking, their employers if not their bosses.'[157]

The spread of new technology has generated the illusion of a revival of free entrepreneurship, if only in the microcomputer industry and associated branches. Large firms, governed by the principle of risk minimalization, have let slip a whole series of opportunities in this field. It seemed that the time of the nineteenth century had indeed returned: 'heroic capitalism, the triumph of the individual determined to test his strength against the transnational giants, the victory of "I" over structure, of will over economic mechanisms.'[158] But it has all been an illusion. The process of capital concentration, characteristic of Western economies, is still in its first stages in new branches, but the more quickly production develops, the larger its scale will become and the more intensively will it proceed. As has already happened in other branches, a significant proportion of small firms either disappears or grows to the size of large and average companies (and this is already happening). A steady structural decentralization can be achieved only under socialism and a self-managing, planned, market economy.

The dream of reviving the conventions of capitalism's 'Golden Age' remains a utopia. Keynesianism gave rise to many problems but, as Willy Brandt has remarked, 'the primitive economic ideologies of the period of early capitalism … exacerbate but do not solve these problems.'[159]

The actual problem is, however, more complex than Brandt and other social democratic theoreticians suppose. The neo-conservative offensive, although presented by bourgeois ideologues as a return to the free market of the nineteenth century, has objectively pursued quite different goals. A return to the nineteenth century within the present structure of productive forces is simply impossible, and attempts of the kind carried out by the military in Latin America, with the naive straightforwardness of performing gorillas, were doomed to failure from the start. Matters have followed a similar course in Israel. But in the highly-developed industrial countries it is a different question. The modern economy cannot, in general, exist without planning. It is only a case of *who* plans and *how*. Neo-conservatives, hiding behind the slogan of a return to the market, strive, in reality, to replace planning by surrendering the control of democratic organs to the private planning of transnational corporations. This really is the road to serfdom.

The neo-conservatives' desire to limit the 'omnipotence' of the state has not only coexisted with their increasing authoritarianism but has been organically linked with their assault on workers' political liberties. The 'return to the nineteenth century' has meant a rejection of advanced democracy in favour of a liberal dictatorship of the bourgeoisie. For it is no accident that the epoch of 'free-market capitalism' was a time when a significant section of the population in the West had no right to vote and was unable to participate in political life (according to British sociologists, the lower classes were afforded fewer political opportunities at the beginning of the nineteenth century than on the eve of the overthrow of the Stuarts in 1642–48). The neo-conservatives' policy has its logic. The more the state's social and economic functions are restricted, the more the specific weight of its repressive functions will increase. Within the state apparatus a continual struggle is being waged between bureaucratic factions. Even if the military–police bureaucracy is not in itself strengthened, the weakening of competing structures reinforces its position and changes the alignment of forces to its advantage. In fact, of course, the military–police complex has grown not only comparatively but also absolutely, receiving additional resources at the expense of those institutions of the social state which are in decline. The more influential the military–repressive organs become, the greater are the chances of further attacks on workers' rights. The process acquires its own dynamic.

But the neo-conservatives' onslaught continually confronts the developing opposition of the democratic forces in society, and comes more and more into contradiction with the traditions of Western civilization. As Milton Friedman himself expressed it: 'the interwoven network of free institutions will withstand much.'[160] Right-wing governments have proven powerless completely to overcome the opposition they encounter. Each step of neo-conservative technocratic counter-reform engenders new difficulties.

It does not follow, however, that a return to the 'Keynesian compromise' is inevitable. Right-wing technocrats are, in any case, more consistent than social democratic politicians. The Right is in favour of 'pure capitalism' unadulterated by socialism. If capitalism is considered the 'sole normal' form of contemporary society, then their correctness must be acknowledged. Fortunately, this is not the case. An absolutely practical socialist alternative does exist, but the real difficulty consists in working out an effective strategic path to socialism in the conditions of modern industrial society. Technocratic solutions cannot help us approach this goal — all the more so since the technocrats have no such end in view.

Notes

1. For more detail, see Chapter 3.
2. Albert Einstein, *Why Socialism?*, Monthly Review Pamphlet Series, No. 1, New York 1960.
3. J.K. Galbraith, *The New Industrial State*, London 1972, p. 2.
4. See James Burnham, *The Managerial Revolution*, New York 1941.
5. Karl Marx and Friedrich Engels, *Capital*, vol. 3, London 1981, p. 568.
6. Ibid., vol. 20, p. 280.
7. Galbraith, *New Industrial State*, p. 49.

8. Ibid., p. 49.
9. *Sotsiologicheskie Issledovaniya*, no. 1, 1982, p. 82. In the USSR control functions are exercised by the Party apparatus.
10. M. Weber, *The Theory of Social and Economic Organisation*, Oxford 1947, p. 248.
11. *Sotsiologicheskie Issledovaniya*, no. 1, 1982, p. 79.
12. Ibid., p. 77.
13. Galbraith, *New Industrial State*, p. 59.
14. Ibid., p. 62.
15. *Literaturnaya Gazeta*, 14 April 1971, p. 14.
16. Galbraith, *New Industrial State*, p. 68.
17. Ibid., pp. 168–69.
18. One could say that, in this sense, contemporary 'cyberneticism' maintains the traditions of seventeenth-century Cartesian rationalism. It would be naive to think that there are no adherents of this mode of thinking in Russia. See, for example, V. Turchin's book *The Inertia of Fear*.
19. E.F. Schumacher, *Small is Beautiful*, London 1973, p. 60.
20. Hwa Yol Jung, *The Crisis of Political Understanding*, Pittsburgh 1979, pp. 118, 121.
21. M. Weiss, *Systems of Thinking*, New York 1978, p. 374.
22. Schumacher, *Small is Beautiful*, p. 78.
23. Alvin Toffler, *Future Shock*, London 1970, p. 400.
24. W.E. Akin, *Technocracy and the American Dream*, Los Angeles 1977, p. 133.
25. E. Mounier, *Le Personalisme*, Paris 1971, p. 27.
26. John Maynard Keynes, *The General Theory of Employment, Interest and Money, Collected Writings vol. 7*, Cambridge 1978, p. 33.
27. See *Problems of Economic Dynamics and Planning: In Honour of M. Kalecki*, Warsaw 1964, p. 340.
28. Quoted in L. Lekachman, *The Age of Keynes*, London 1967, p. 41.
29. J.M. Keynes, *The Economic Consequences of the Peace, Collected Works vol. 2*, London 1971, p. 186.
30. Ibid., pp. 186–187.
31. Lenin, CW, vol. 24, p. 403.
32. *New York Times*, 31 December 1933.
33. K. Marx, *Capital*, vol. 3, p. 569.
34. Keynes, *General Theory*, p. 247.
35. See V.I. Lenin, *What Is To Be Done?*, in CW, vol. 5. Some of the positions in this work have been justifiably criticized by Plekhanov and Luxemburg but, in this instance, we are interested only in his analysis of the two types of working-class behaviour.
36. N.I. Bukharin, *Economics of the Transformation Period*, New York 1971, p. 54.
37. Ibid., p. 214.
38. Jean Blondel, *Voters, Parties and Leaders*, p. 77.
39. Maurice Duverger, *Les Parties politiques*, Paris 1951, p. 381.
40. See Boris Kagarlitsky, *Dialektika Nadezhdi*, Part I. Some features have perhaps been set out too categorically, sharply and simply, but the question has at least been formulated. The term 'postponed revolution' has been borrowed from Trotsky. He used it to characterize the situation in Russia from 1907 to 1917. With certain

provisos, this term can be applied to the contemporary West. The problem has been partly presented in Marcuse's works although in different terms and, in my opinion, without satisfactory resolution.

41. *Problems of Economic Dynamics*, p. 338.
42. Ibid., p. 337.
43. *Sotsial-demokraticheskii i burzhuazny reformizm*, p. 5.
44. Ibid., p. 6. This truth has also been confirmed in the East (for example, in Poland).
45. Galbraith, *New Industrial State*, pp. 3, 9.
46. Keynes, *General Theory*, p. 129.
47. Ibid., p. 27.
48. Lekachman, *The Age of Keynes*, p. 89.
49. *Problemy mira i sotsializma*, no. 3, 1965, p. 18.
50. *Voprosy Ekonomiki*, no. 7, 1981, p. 106.
51. Ibid.
52. The author defines 'statocracy' as 'an organisation which, on seizing power, rapidly turns into the foundation of a new ruling class which exploits all of society through monopoly control over the nationalized sector of the economy and state institutions. The new set-up established in this way is termed "statocratic" by M. Cheshkov and its ruling class, the "statocracy". The system's specificity is in the "unbroken combination of base and superstructure", and the concentration of all state power and property "within a single social community". Power becomes "the decisive factor of reproduction"' (M. Cheshkov, 'Metodologicheskie problemy analiza gosuklada: tip obshchestvennogo vosproizvodstva i sotsial'nyi nosiltel'', in *Ekonomika razvivayushchikhsya stran: teorii i metody issledovaniya*, Moscow 1979, pp. 333–334). See also B. Kagarlitsky, *The Thinking Reed*, London 1988, pp. 80–85. (Translator's note).
53. Schumacher, *Small is Beautiful*, p. 26.
54. D. Goulet, *The Cruel Choice*, New York 1971, p. 330.
55. J.K. Galbraith, *The Affluent Society*, 3rd edn, London 1977, p. 58.
56. *Amerika*, no. 10, 1983, p. 19.
57. M. Fagg, 'When the Lights Go On Again', *Times Educational Supplement*, 7 April 1978, p. 20.
58. W. Brandt, B. Kreisky, O. Palme, *Briefe und Gespraeche, 1972 bis 1975*, Franfurt and Köln 1975, p. 80.
59. *SShA* [USA], no. 9, 1983, p. 25.
60. *Sotsial-demokratiya i sovremenny krizis kapitalizma*, Part I, Moscow 1983, p. 5.
61. Galbraith, *The Affluent Society*, p. 63.
62. K. Marx, *Capital*, vol. 3, p. 261.
63. *SShA*, no. 9, 1983, pp. 20–21.
64. Galbraith, *New Industrial State*, p. 6.
65. Ibid., p. 24.
66. *Voprosy Ekonomiki*, no. 7, 1981, p. 106.
67. W.E. Akin, pp. 147, 73.
68. E.D. Kaganov, *Sotsialisticheskoe Vosproizvodstvo i Rynok*, Moscow 1966, p. 40.
69. *Istoriya Sotsialisticheskoi Ekonomiki v SSSR*, vol. 3, Moscow 1977, pp. 298–9.
70. *The Times*, 14 December 1983, p. 13.

71. W.E. Akin, *Technocracy*, p. 26.
72. G. Guroff and F. Carstensen, *Entrepreneurship in Imperial Russia and the Soviet Union*, Princeton 1983, p. 202.
73. Galbraith, *Affluent Society*, pp. 201, 204.
74. *Literaturnaya Gazeta*, 14 April 1971, p. 14.
75. See Kaganov, p. 23.
76. *Ekonomika Sovietskoi Torgovli, Uchebnoe Posobie*, 1934, p. 383: quoted in A.G. Shchelkin, *V Plenu Novykh Illiuzii*, Moscow 1983, p. 17.
77. Akin, *Technocracy*, p. 52.
78. Ibid., p. 141.
79. Quoted in F. Freidel, *Rol' Gosudarstva v Ekonomicheskoi Zhizni Strany*, Moscow 1970, p. 11.
80. B.P. Lopukhov, *Istoriya Fashistskogo Rezhima v Italii*, Moscow 1977, p. 195.
81. A. Yudanov, *Teoriya 'Otkrytoi Ekonomiki': Doktriny i Deistvitel'nost*, Moscow 1983, p. 16.
82. *New Statesman and Nation*, 8 July 1933, p. 37.
83. David Schuman, *The Ideology of Form: The Influence of Organizations in America*, Lexington 1978, p. 17.
84. Shchelkin, p. 17.
85. *Problemy Mira i Sotializma*, no. 3, 1965, p. 16. On the Austrian economy in the 1980s see *Malye Strany Zapadnoi Evropy*, Moscow 1984, pp. 139–150 and elsewhere.
86. *Voprosy Ekonomiki*, no. 1, 1984, p. 114. Regarding the problem of employment: a brilliant article was published in *Marxism Today*, June 1985, by Göran Therborn: 'West on the Dole'.
87. *Velikobritaniya*, Moscow 1981, p. 108.
88. *El Pais*, 28 April 1984, p. 42.
89. *Marxism Today*, December 1980, p. 18.
90. *Sotsial-demokraticheskii i burzhuazny reformizm*, p. 391.
91. K. Marx and F. Engels, *The Manifesto of the Communist Party*, in *The Revolutions of 1848*, David Fernbach, ed., London 1973, p. 86.
92. Ibid., pp. 86–87.
93. *Sotsial-demokraticheskii i burzhuazny reformizm*, p. 76.
94. Ibid., p. 77.
95. Jung, p. 142.
96. Marx and Engels, *The Communist Manifesto*, p. 82.
97. See W. Brus, *Socialist Ownership and Political Systems*, Oxford, 1975.
98. Arthur Woodburn, *An Outline of Finance*, 4th edn, London 1947, p. 172.
99. Keynes, *General Theory*, p. 378.
100. What has been written here on 'Swedish socialism' might seem an exaggerated caricature but I have simply tried to draw the logical conclusions from the Swedish social democrats' programmatic aims. A theoretician of the French Socialist Party aptly defines their policy as an attempt to 'implant socialism in distribution into capitalism in production' (Y. Bernard, *La France vers le Socialisme*, Paris 1977, p. 77.)
101. *New Statesman and Nation*, 8 July 1933, p. 37.
102. Alec Nove, *The Economics of Feasible Socialism*, London 1983, p. 168.
103. *Velikobritaniya*, pp. 112, 113.

104. See ibid., pp. 113–114.

105. Schumacher, p. 242, p. 243.

106. *Rabochii Klass i ego Revolutsionnyi Avangard*, Prague 1983, p. 64.

107. *Programme Commune de Gouvernement du P.C.F. et du P.S.*, Paris 1972, p. 105.

108. Practice showed that it was a matter of forming democratic administrative councils in the enterprises. But many writers were already acknowledging in 1975 that this was insufficient: 'It is essential to organize the workers' active participation and responsibility for the taking and implementation of decisions at all levels and in all spheres of activity' (F. Chevallier, *Les Entreprises Publiques en France*, Paris 1975, p. 235).

109. F. Engels, *Anti-Dühring*, Moscow 1947, p. 320.

110. Chevallier, p. 9.

111. See *L'Etat Entrepreneur. Le Cas de la Régie Renault*, Paris 1971.

112. *Economist*, 16 February 1985, p. 70.

113. *Nouvelle Revue Socialiste*, no. 22, 1977, p. 10.

114. Even in Russia, where the self-management experiment of 1917–18 collapsed through the workers' councils' lack of power, there were striking examples of effective participation. One example was the 'Joint-Stock Company' in Voronezh (1918–25), an industrial co-operative which successfully endured War Communism and N.E.P. In 1925 it was expropriated by the state.

115. *Economie et Politique*, nos. 75–76, 1983, p. 5.

116. *Biulletin' Oppozitsii*, no. 24.

117. *Paese Sera*, 23 October 1983.

118. Galbraith, *Affluent Society*, p. 198.

119. It is not a question here of combining plan and market in the conditions of democratic socialism. This question has been elaborated well enough in the works of Wl. Brus, O. Sik, A. Nove, J. Attali and others. It is in any case clear that if planning cannot substitute for the market then the market cannot substitute for planning. Left-wing Spanish theoreticians note that socialist planning must, without eliminating the market, reject profit 'as the sole principle of economic activity' by orienting to a long-term strategy of development. The plan is needed as it predetermines 'changes in society' (*Economia y Socialismo*, Madrid 1978, p. 199). This position is more precisely formulated by J. Attali: 'the plan can propose and organise reforms in the structure of the market' (*Nouvelle Revue Socialiste*, no. 22, 1977, p. 10).

120. See Kaganov, p. 40.

121. Ibid., p. 27.

122. Galbraith, *Affluent Society*, p. 38.

123. Ibid., p. 27.

124. Ibid., p. 41. I would recommend that readers remember these general positions when they come to read Part II.

125. This situation can be compared to the ambiguous position of bourgeois structures in Tudor England or in France under the first Bourbons. Just as at a definite stage of history absolutism could not manage without the bourgeoisie and the corresponding forms of production, modern capitalism cannot survive without some elements of socialism. The threat to the old regime is that it might lose control of the new relations: what was subordinate might acquire a dominant

position. The struggle is conducted between capitalist and socialist structures and institutions and not only between bourgeois and proletarians. Capitalism cannot permit the socialist sub-system to grow beyond definite limits.

126. Joan Robinson, 'What has become of the Keynesian Revolution', in Milo Keynes, ed., *Essays on J.M. Keynes*, Cambridge 1975, p. 131.

127. Shchelkin, p. 9.

128. To avoid misunderstanding, the term 'social-liberal government', in my view, defines not only the coalition of social democrats and liberals in Germany but also the political course carried out by this government. In Austria, the social democrats implemented *exactly the same* course on their own, without the liberals' participation. In other words, both Kreisky and Schmidt were social liberals rather than social democrats. It is difficult to include them among the Left, even conditionally.

129. Shchelkin, p. 3.

130. *Sozialismus*, no. 4, 1983, pp. 2–3.

131. Ibid., p. 3.

132. L.I. Piyashcheva, *Mezhdunarodnaya Ekonomicheskaya Teoriya i Praktika Sotsial-Reformizma*, Moscow 1983, p. 205.

133. *Tribuna*, no. 2, April 1983, p. 13.

134. *Nouvel Observateur*, 27 November 1978, p. 31.

135. *Rabochii Klass v Mirovom Revoliutsionnom Protsesse*, Moscow 1983, p. 124.

136. Shchelkin, p. 4.

137. F.A. Hayek, *The Road to Serfdom*, London 1944, p. 52.

138. *Voprosy Ekonomiki*, no. 7, 1981, p. 111.

139. M. Rocard, *Parler Vrai*, Paris 1979, p. 100.

140. M. Friedman, *Capitalism and Freedom*, Chicago 1962, pp. 11, 199.

141. *Voprosy Ekonomiki*, no. 7, 1981, p. 107.

142. M. Friedman, *The Optimum Quantity of Money and Other Essays*, Chicago 1969, p. 104.

143. *Mondo Economico*, no. 32–33, 1981, p. 86.

144. *Il Giornale*, 18 April 1981.

145. *Economist*, 23 February 1985, p. 15.

146. *The Times*, 3 December 1985, p. 21.

147. Hayek, p. 52.

148. Samuel P. Huntington, 'The Democratic Distemper', in *The Public Interest*, no. 41, 1975, p. 36.

149. *Newsweek*, 15 June 1981, p. 42.

150. *Latinskaya Amerika*, no. 9, 1983, p. 29.

151. *Newsweek*, 22 August 1983, p. 21.

152. *Latinskaya Amerika*, no. 9, 1983, p. 35.

153. European neo-conservatives point to the comparative success of the rightward course in the USA. Indeed, after the severe crisis of 1979–82, the American economy was able to create a large number of new jobs and emerged from the depression faster than the European. But in achieving this, the growth of labour productivity in the USA lagged behind the European level, and unemployment benefits and wages for the new jobs were somewhat lower. In other words, the greater quantity of jobs in the USA compared to Europe was secured at the cost of

their lower quality (and the predominance of extensive over intensive factors). The 'boom' in the American economy was accompanied by accumulating unresolved structural problems (the increase in the budget and trade deficits, the weakening of the USA's role in the world market, excessive devaluation of the dollar). Thus the policies implemented by President Reagan to combat the crisis laid the foundations for a new crisis. America's technological leadership was also enfeebled. In 1984 in the USA there were on average twice as many robots for every ten thousand industrial workers as there were on average in Europe, but more than three times fewer than in Japan and more than four times fewer than in Sweden. It should be recalled also that in the period 1945–80 the standard of living in Western Europe grew at a faster rate than in the USA although after the Second World War the Americans were in all respects the leaders. The Japanese, for all their successes, have a lower standard of living, work longer hours and have shorter holidays than the Europeans. Consequently, the 'European model' of capitalism (and we are talking only about capitalist Europe) has a whole series of advantages over both the American and Japanese models.

154. *L'Espresso*, no. 28, 1979, p. 159.
155. *Voprosy Ekonomiki*, no. 4, 1983, p. 127.
156. *SShA*, no. 4, 1983, p. 89.
157. *Latinskaya Amerika*, no. 8, 1983, p. 29.
158. *L'Esprit*, no. 2, 1985, p. 10.
159. Quoted in *Latinskaya Amerika*, no. 8, 1983, p. 142.
160. Friedman, *Capitalism and Freedom*, p. 202. In any case the polemic against authors of Friedman's type must be constructive. While repudiating the neo-conservatives' arguments and carrying on a political struggle with them, the Left must simultaneously rethink its own positions. This was very precisely expressed in a Catalan Marxist journal. Defending nationalization is essential but 'we will not make a fetish of the public sector.' the task is, by defending it, to transform it through 'the masses' political intervention in the solution of the public enterprises' problems' (*Nous Horitzons*, no. 94, March–June 1985, p. 15).

3

Structural Reforms

The late 1970s and early 1980s were very trying times for the Western Left. The Right's ideological counter-offensive had everywhere been launched on an unprecedented scale. The conservatives' political positions in many countries had also been reinforced. It cannot be said that the Right achieved all its objectives. It was precisely from 1980 to 1982 that socialists successfully gained or returned to power in a whole series of countries. However, in a sense, this only intensified the Left's difficulties. Numerous new problems arose which had to be solved in a very short space of time and in a very unfavourable situation.[1]

Nevertheless, the major causes of the crisis of the Left were rooted neither in the bourgeoisie's developing aggressiveness nor in the economic recession but in the internal contradictions of the socialist movement itself. Old principles and schemas were clearly 'not working', and a re-examination of values became not only desirable but obligatory. This affected in equal measure social democrats, socialists, communists and various 'new left' tendencies. The situation was not, of course, the same for every country, but it is impossible not to notice that French Socialists, Italian Communists and British Labourites frequently encountered common problems and even arrived at analogous solutions.[2] The crisis affected everyone but it also provided an excellent opportunity for joint inquiries, strategic reorganization and reconsideration of the Left's role in society. It was precisely the Left's difficulties which provided hope for the gradual formation of a *new strategic bloc*. A united and renovated movement of the European Left must confront the general neo-conservative challenge.

The struggle for change may not be successful if nothing alters in the workers' parties themselves. The demand for new ideas and methods developed long ago and the crisis has only demonstrated the urgency of this question. A new political strategy can only be created through a blend of theory and practice. To date, this has been precisely the Left's weakest spot. A theoretician of the Spanish Socialist Party, Sotelo, has said that Western socialists suffer from an inherent ideological 'schizophrenia'.[3] Theoreticians have developed the Marxist concept of revolution while practitioners have busied themselves with their daily reformist labours. Revolutionary ideologues, communist parties and social democracy's left wing have accused the movement's right wing of opportunism and apostasy, but have, in fact, played the part of a kind of 'second eleven'. Their utterances have forced social democracy to be more consistent and decisive but, in the event of failure and return to opposition, they have proved to be its strategic reserve. In periods of opposition, social democracy has been able to make use of both ideas and people originating from radical groups to infuse its own political organism with a certain amount of fresh blood. Harold Wilson, a former left-winger, was able to re-establish Labour Party unity after a series of defeats. In the 1950s, numerous former communists joined the ranks of social democratic activists in many countries (especially in Britain). One way or another, revolutionary currents remained custodians of the socialist ideal, a fact of which reformists and pragmatists should be continually reminded; but this was the limit of their political role. Such a 'division of labour' proved acceptable to both sides but it was effective only while social democratic reformism remained dynamic and capable of assimilating external impulses, and while objective conditions were favourable to it. The gradual weakening of the reformist onslaught throughout the 1960s and 1970s, accompanied by the technocratization of party ideology, changed the situation. From reformists, the leaders of social democracy turned, in the expression of Western Marxists, 'into mere managers of capitalist society.'[4]

Adam Przeworski wrote in *New Left Review* that:

> Reformism always meant a gradual progression towards structural transformation; reformism was traditionally justified by the belief that reforms are cumulative, that they constitute steps, that they lead in some direction. The current policy of social-democrats by its very logic no longer permits the cumulation of reforms.[5]

Meanwhile the radical Left was not only unable to seize back the initiative but was even incapable of successfully projecting itself as a 'pressure group' on an enfeebled social democracy. Thus reformism's crisis, far from strengthening the position of the 'revolutionary currents', revealed their political inconsistency.

Eric Hobsbawm wrote in 1973 that

> the trouble about the revolutionary left in stable industrial societies is not that its opportunities never come, but that the normal conditions in which it must operate prevent it from developing the movements likely to seize the rare moments when they are called upon to behave as revolutionaries.... Being a revolutionary in countries such as ours just happens to be difficult.[6]

Simply stating this fact, however, does little to establish the real reasons for these difficulties and find a means of overcoming them.

In and of itself, Marxism is neither a 'revolutionary' nor an 'evolutionary' theory. As a *theory of practice* Marxism derives from the alternation of evolutionary and revolutionary stages in history and crucially from their organic interconnection. This latter feature has been completely overlooked by both Right social democrats and their left-wing critics.[7] It is also absent from Hobsbawm's discussion. Not only Marxist theory but the most elementary logic demands different responses in different situations. Further, the very concept of the *revolutionary situation*, elaborated by Lenin and accepted by a majority of other Marxists, assumes that revolutionary actions can be successful only under certain socio-economic and psychological conditions. The trouble is not that Marxists have adopted the idea of a revolutionary transformation of the world, but that they have made it an absolute by drawing the conclusion that 'genuine' changes are possible only on a revolutionary basis. There has arisen a particular moral doctrine according to which reformist politics merits disdain at best. This 'revolutionary ethic' came into being, of course, long before the appearance of Marxism. As we have seen, Marx himself never adopted such positions. But, by an irony of fate, it is precisely people who consider themselves his followers who, in the twentieth century, have become the heralds of such principles. The practice of 'opportunist reformists', which has indeed often been inclined towards compromise, has tended to confirm these ideas by reinforcing sterile 'revolutionism' on the Left, which has degenerated into insurrectionary phrase-mongering. The Paris students in 1968 had some grounds for declaring that 'All reformism is distinguished by utopianism in strategy and opportunism in tactics.'[8] It would appear that the daily experience of the workers' movement confirms this. For its part the Right has convincingly demonstrated that the Left, with its revolutionary slogans, has been completely incapable of achieving even minimal changes.

Radical theoreticians have either gone from abstract philosophy to minor political questions, like Sartre, or maintained the purity of their ideas by scorning political activity, like Adorno. It has, however, proved impossible to guarantee even the development of theory by such means. Many authors have justifiably observed that, despite Adorno's genius, his thought remains embedded in an infinite sequence of abstractions which, by being locked in an endless cycle of criticism and self-criticism, turns it into a 'negative dialectic'. Adorno's critics justifiably remark that 'in this way Adorno's Marxism dissolves itself into a "repudiation of practice".'[9] However profound his philosophical ideas were, their political significance and immediate influence on society proved negligible.

The effort to preserve the 'purity' of the revolutionary spirit at all costs in fact led to the erosion of this spirit and the disillusion and desertion of activists (former communists and leftists often become right-wingers). But the problem cannot be solved by a simple declaration of the necessity of reformism. An ideology and a psychological climate are needed in which both reformist and revolutionary actions would be possible. Ideological and moral principles must be worked out which permit a painless transition from reformist to revolutionary politics and vice versa, depending on the concrete situation.[10] This has not proved altogether simple to achieve.

It is clear that in the late 1950s and early 1960s, Right social democracy was still in the ascendant: despite the evident technocratization of reformism, it was impossible to counterpose any kind of radical alternative to it. The sole force in the workers' movement capable of opposing social democracy consisted of the Stalinist communist parties. Nevertheless, the embourgeoisement of the workers' parties' leaders and their loss of a socialist perspective were sufficiently obvious for a significant section of the Left intelligentsia to prefer collaboration with the communists. After the unsuccessful attempt to establish a Revolutionary–Democratic Association, standing between social democracy and the Stalinists, Sartre came to the conclusion that a rapprochement was needed with the Communist Party as the only means of 'guaranteeing the effective practice of joint actions.' This would enable Left intellectuals to criticize Stalinism while remaining 'on the side of the Party, but never within its ranks.'[11] In Sartre's opinion, they would play the role within the communist movement which in other instances would be played by an internal opposition. But for the most part, the Communist Party leaderships were not prepared for such collaboration. Only in Italy were intellectuals able to count on a degree of autonomy within the ranks of a common movement. In France, independent left-wing theoreticians found themselves hostages of the Party. When the existence of Stalin's 'corrective' camps became known in the West, between 1952 and 1954, they protested, but so indecisively and ambiguously that Albert Camus accused his friends of cowardice — they were prepared 'to rise up against anything, only not against the Communist Party and the state.'[12]

By exposing Stalin at the 20th Congress of the Soviet Communist Party, Khrushchev dealt a blow not only against the myth of Stalin but also against the world-view of the radical intelligentsia. In general the communist parties' position became more flexible, but the project of 'critical collaboration' came crashing down: its authors considered themselves involuntary accomplices of Stalin's crimes and forsook the communists. It was precisely because of this that the advocates of a revolutionary socialist alternative attempted, first of all, to 'go round' the communist movement 'to its left'. This route seemed most attractive for it afforded them an opportunity to create their own profile and distance themselves from Stalinism without making concessions to social democracy.

During his polemic with Sartre in 1951-52, Camus accused the communists of not believing in the 'freedom and spontaneity' of the workers' movement, of subjecting it to barrack discipline and of being prepared to sacrifice 'today's freedom in the name of freedom in the distant future.'[13] Since Marxism had, in his opinion, been usurped by the Stalinists, Camus called for a return to the traditions of 'non-Marxist socialism' and primarily to anarcho-syndicalism. Camus counterposed to Marx's theory the 'moral of historical risk.'[14] Sartre quite rightly reproached his former friend for criticizing Marxism when he evidently had no knowledge of it. Nor could Stalinism's practice be equated with Marx's theory. But for all its naivety, Camus's book *The Rebel*, in which he formulated his position, proved prophetic. It overtook events. In the 1950s his call was heard by no one, but ten years later, when Camus was already dead, the embryonic Left-radical movement, in search of a new revolutionary ideology, trod the same path.

In the 1960s, the socio-political situation had changed sufficiently for

the rise of a mass anti-capitalist movement autonomous of the communist parties. At the same time the intelligentsia had become more and
more a part of the proletariat and its numbers and significance in society
had grown. Social democracy, which had carried out important reforms,
was clearly a spent force and the communists were unable to overcome
the internal difficulties which followed in the aftermath of the 20th
Party Congress, the 1956 Hungarian Revolution and the Sino-Soviet
conflict. In the meantime, the new proletariat, inclined to greater
decisiveness, required its own political movement.[15]

Such a movement arose during the student revolts of 1967–69. This
time, unlike Camus, the ideologists of protest made no attempt to deny
Marxism, even finding support in the works of such Marxist philosophers as Sartre, Marcuse, Bloch and, occasionally, Althusser. But the New
Left more readily derived its practical activity from anarcho-syndicalist
traditions.

It is, of course, rather difficult to give a precise definition of the
ideology of student revolt, since it did not depend on some unified
theory. 'There is no revolutionary thought, only revolutionary action',
proclaimed one of the slogans on the walls of Nanterre University.[16] But
it was just this that showed up the return to dogmatic socialist traditions.
The most important tactical and organizational principle of the New
Left was spontaneity, and its strategic goal was self-management. These
two principles have proved inseparable and date back precisely to
anarcho-syndicalism. A spontaneous movement lays the foundations of a
self-managed society 'on the spur of the moment'. Self-managing
institutions consolidate and organize the freedom gained.

The idea of self-management was not, of course, the exclusive
property of anarcho-syndicalists; it can be found in Marx. Kautsky wrote
that socialism, in eliminating compulsory labour, must replace it with
proletarian self-discipline at work, and for this it was necessary 'to
organize production on democratic foundations'.[17] The British Labour
theoretician, G.D.H. Cole, devoted a number of works to the problems of
industrial self-management. For Gramsci the workers' councils, formed
during the strikes in Turin, were the prototype of the future organization of society. Finally, the Yugoslav communist reformists, in their
endeavours to counterpose their own socialist ideal to that of Stalinism,
have declared self-management an official slogan, and in Czechoslovakia
in 1968 the ideologists of reform began to speak of the link between self-
management and political freedom.

However, the New Left made self-management a central theme of its strategy for social change:

> For us the transition to a classless society is possible through self-management. When the workers return to work they are faced with the question: how and for whom to return? Can the factories be run without the bosses? To destroy capitalism self-management must be established.[18]

The student revolt really did provoke the mass strike in France, but this strike led neither to the downfall of capitalism nor to the triumph of self-management: the working class did not desire the overthrow of society, its revolution was postponed. As a result, students who had set out to transform society gained reforms in higher education. True, the May events in Paris showed that revolutionary actions can be an effective means in the struggle to realize reformist demands. In such an instance, revolutionary illusions 'work' objectively in favour of reformism, but the participants in the events did not themselves draw this conclusion.[19]

Although the immediate results of 1968 were insignificant, the long-term consequences have turned out to be very important. During the period between 1968 and 1972, the first crisis of social democratic reformism set in. This crisis was partially related to the student movement but was engendered by the internal dynamic of social democracy's development. In Britain, the Labour Party lost power after the collapse of its efforts to introduce technocratic 'socialism'. Hopes for renewal, raised at one time by Wilson's victory, proved groundless. In France the old socialist party, the SFIO, was initially dismissed from its participation in government by the Gaullists and then ideologically 'buried' by them. It suffered complete demise as a result of the 1968 events. Throughout this period bourgeois centrist parties everywhere attempted to regain the initiative from the social democrats by appropriating their slogans and methods. The creation of a system of social security and a mixed economy had been essentially accomplished everywhere and Western reformists had no further significant objectives. On the other hand, the 'Prague Spring' provided a graphic illustration of a different and genuinely radical reformism.

The appearance of a New Left led to a mass exodus of young activists from the Labour Party. In France, where the youth movement's assault was even more forceful, the SFIO actually fell apart and in December 1968 announced its disbandment. But the New Left was unable to fill the political vacuum and the communists themselves entered a severe crisis when Soviet tanks appeared on the streets of Prague. Most authors acknowledge that the success of radical groups among the youth was 'punishment for the opportunism of the leaderships of the social democratic parties',[20] but it was also retribution for the communists' dogmatism and 'revolutionary conservatism'. The leader of the Italian Communist Party, Luigi Longo, honestly confessed that they were 'isolated and confused'.[21] The communist students' union in France was plunged into crisis and lost its position. This disarray and disorientation on the Left allowed social democracy of the right-wing variety, at least in several countries, not only to ride out the crisis but to gain a second wind. In September 1969, the Social Democrats, in coalition with the Liberals, came to power in West Germany, largely by harnessing the social enthusiasm generated by the student unrest. Even Marxist authors concede that the new government at first attempted to conduct a 'dialogue with the critical young generation.'[22] In Sweden, social democracy, which had been headed since 1969 by Olaf Palme, strengthened its position. The new leadership entered into collaboration with the communists in parliament and attempted to implement a 'Left course' by speeding the introduction of reforms.[23] A new, more radical party programme was prepared. The leadership also changed in Austrian social democracy, with Bruno Kreisky becoming the first leader in the country's history to form a government without the participation of bourgeois politicians.

But no genuine renewal of social democracy took place. The degeneration of reformism and the drift of party leaders to the right was swiftly resumed. This generated an inevitable second and more profound crisis of social democratic politics. But this time it was threatened not by a noisy but ineffectual assault from the Left, but by crippling blows from the Right. The class struggle intensified and the politics of reform, based on compromise, became unworkable. Kreisky admitted that:

> In this situation the gap between the views of Social Democrats and Conservatives is widening. I don't deny that Social Democrats may temporarily lose strength under such conditions. But the process can very soon lead to new strength, since the problems cannot be solved by conservative economic policy.[24]

This time, however, it was obvious that something more than a simple renovation of reformism's traditional concepts was involved. Serious changes were taking place in the workers' parties themselves.

Until 1968, right-wing reformism seemed the sole force capable of ensuring, albeit within limits, society's democratic reorganization. The events of 1968–72 altered the situation. Longo noted with justification that 'the most varied strata of the Italian Left camp' had entered the political arena.[25] The same thing happened in other countries. In the 1970s a serious restructuring began to take place in the communist parties. The outcome of this was the phenomenon of 'Eurocommunism'. On the other hand, many participants in the New Left, convinced that their efforts to end the system through a single revolutionary assault had collapsed, came to the conclusion that serious political work was needed and began to treat reforms with more tolerance. They found co-thinkers among Left socialists dissatisfied with the course of the party leadership and among Marxist intellectuals estranged from official communist organizations. Thus a new political project arose almost everywhere. If in 1968 the movement had endeavoured to be more left-wing than the communists, now it was a question of occupying an intermediate position between social democracy and the communist parties. If the project of a 'third way', proposed by Sartre at the time of the Revolutionary–Democratic Association had, by his own evaluation, been at odds with 'political reality',[26] then by the end of the 1960s the situation had changed. Before 1968, Left socialist parties had sprung up in Italy, Spain and France, and even earlier in Norway and Denmark.[27] Founded as a rule by former social democrats (in Denmark, by former members of the Communist Party), they very quickly united around themselves proponents of radical reformism, and afterwards attracted many participants in the student movement. The New Left had been incapable of forming its own organization and making the transition to everyday activity. In France the Unified Socialist Party (PSU) which had existed since 1960 began to grow rapidly after the 'May revolution'. A Soviet researcher remarks that the New Left 'flocked into the PSU' which 'appeared to be its party'.[28] But the PSU's political programme was markedly different from the slogans of the student movement. The influx of young rebels into this party indicated the radicalization and growth of Left socialist forces, but also a recognition by revolutionaries of the need for reform.

The PSU has played a major role in the history of the Left in France and Western Europe. From its very inception this party succeeded in creating 'its own distinctive style'.[29] It was a party looking for ideas, a theoretical school. Many leading members of the French Socialist Party, ministers in Mitterrand's government, started out in the ranks of the PSU, among them Michel Rocard, Jules Martine, A. Savary and Pierre

Beregovoi. Nevertheless, the party itself was a total failure as a political organization and by the end of the 1970s was on the verge of disintegration. For this reason, Soviet political commentators maintain that the PSU did not fulfil the 'tasks it had set itself at the beginning' and proved unable 'to fully establish itself as an independent Left socialist party.'[30] In fact the PSU achieved rather more than this by elaborating the bases for a *strategy of revolutionary reformism*.

The search for a new road was not, of course, their monopoly. The same question was being posed at exactly the same time by the leaders of the Italian Communist Party (PCI). Palmiro Togliatti saw with exceptional clarity that the revolution in Western Europe had been delayed. But while social democrats might passively accommodate to this fact, communists must take another path.[31] In 1963, Togliatti declared:

> That the advance towards socialism and the building of a new society must be realized by other methods, and not as it has happened in the East and the colonial world, is now, in our opinion, completely self-evident. But woe betide us if this truth should be understood only as a simple call to repeat the catastrophic experience of social democracy or to justify that experience.[32]

Togliatti considered it essential, in not waiting for the revolution, to begin a struggle for the transformation of society's structures. It was a question of introducing some anti-capitalist measures in capitalist conditions. This enables the communists to act successfully even if they are not participating in government. This latter aspect was very important in Italian conditions, where one of the strongest parties cannot attain governmental status, in many people's opinion, only 'because it calls itself the communist party'.[33] The participation of communists in the process of change is therefore hampered, but it is nevertheless necessary and possible. The course chosen by Togliatti can be defined as *reformism from below*.

First, communists have exerted revolutionary pressure on the government, forcing it to introduce reforms. Second, having seized the organs of power in the localities, they have pursued a policy of change in the cities they control. Observers have noted that the activity of left-wing municipalities has become a part of 'the general strategy of the Italian communists'.[34]

The policy of 'municipal socialism' has been promoted in other countries than Italy where powerful anti-capitalist parties or groupings have existed. The *Financial Times* recognizes that communists in Bologna and socialists in Sheffield have been able to create an exemplary 'model of left-wing administration' distinguished by a 'pragmatic, effective implementation of socialist policy.'[35] Reformism from below has important advantages. First of all a socialist party that comes to power with even the most radical programme of reform is by no means proposing the revolutionary destruction of capitalism, and must take upon itself the responsibility for the management of capitalist society. It must manage well so as to demonstrate the Left's competence and retain power. One of Mitterrand's most popular ministers, Jacques Delors, declared that 'it is the Left's duty to show that they can manage, so that they can better prepare France's economy to solve the tasks of tomorrow.'[36] However, in doing this, the movement can lose its revolutionary spirit and become too closely tied to the system. A Left government must overcome the resistance of the bourgeoisie and, at the same time, take on the obligation of organizing the capitalist economy with all its inherent defects — which the socialists cannot answer for and which for the moment they are unable to eliminate. This may lead to a moral crisis, incompetence and even corruption in the ranks of the ruling party. At first glance reformism from below might seem to avert these dangers. But sometimes the revolutionary spirit fades even in an opposition party, and municipal employees are not immune from corruption. In Italy in 1984, 260 mayors and their officials were arrested for abuses of power. Most of them, 77 people, were Christian Democrats; 71 were socialists and 30 communists. In Bologna in 1985, 23 municipal employees were arrested, and although none of these had been elected to their position on the Communist Party slate, journalists considered this, not without foundation, as 'a blow to the Communists' pride'.[37]

The major problem, however, is not corruption, which is rare on the Left, but that the possibilities for reformism from below are limited. PCI leaders acknowledge that by the end of the 1970s their party was extremely close to power, but they could not seize it since the communist movement had no overall worked-out programme of transformation. One of the PCI's leading activists, L. Lama, notes that because of this, the party proved incapable of fulfilling 'its own role as a reformist force'.[38] After the death of Enrico Berlinguer, the recognized leader who had headed the PCI from 1972 to 1984, a bitter polemic began in the party between supporters of the social democratic line of 'improving capitalism' (the 'ameliorists') and the left wing who called for a break with capitalism (the 'rupturists'). Neither was able to propose a consistent strategic project. The reason for this was evidently the internal contradictoriness of the PCI's culture — that of a reformist party with no chance of taking power. The practice of reformism from below did not create favourable conditions for elaborating a strategy of governmental reforms. The 'ameliorists' hoped to solve the problem by removing the word 'communist' from the party's title, but in order to gain real success it was insufficient simply to change the sign. The social democratization of Eurocommunism led only to the loss of its own profile, while the relevant political space in the 1980s had already been filled in Italy by the Socialists.

Back in the 1960s, the Italian Socialist Party had rejected a radical course in favour of a rapprochement with centre forces. A Soviet researcher writes that:

> The basis of this strategy was a programme for carrying out a series of tightly connected socio-economic reforms stimulating a spontaneous process of successive changes. Each subsequent reform, by breaking the existing equilibrium, would have to take society to a new equilibrium at a higher level and engender new problems demanding in their turn the implementation of further reforms. This cumulative process of the consequences of reform would lead to a qualitative change in the system and to the transition to a socialist society.[39]

However, as a means of realizing this programme, the party leaders chose collaboration with the bourgeoisie. This was a very dangerous road. In the 1970s, the Communists also spoke of a 'historic compromise' with forces of the centre, hoping that the Left's participation in government would demonstrate its political competence: in other words, that it would play the same role as collaboration between the Social Democrats and the Christian Democrats in West Germany during the 'Grand Coalition' (1966–69). The 'Grand Coalition' was a transitional solution, as a result of which the Christian Democrats were edged out of power. Their Italian counterparts, learning from this experience, preferred not to allow the Communists to participate in running the country. The weaker Socialist Party, by collaborating with the Christian Democrats, found itself a hostage, notwithstanding the personal success of the Socialists' leader, Bettino Craxi, who proved to be one of the most effective and popular Italian Prime Ministers.[40] Craxi gained important successes in the struggle with the Mafia and raised Italy's international standing, but the Socialist Party had only the most limited influence on the government's policies, which were dependent on the more powerful partners in the coalition. The radical ideas of the PSI's Left theoreticians remained on paper and the course pursued by Craxi was more technocratic than reformist. Craxi's achievements were not so much political as administrative, and the growth of his personal popularity as a statesman in no sense meant the triumph of the Socialists' political project. Moreover, the Party itself was in a state of crisis. A leading Christian Democrat bluntly declared to the Socialists: 'you cannot remain in this coalition and talk about an alternative'.[41] The head of the Socialist parliamentary fraction, R. Formica, in his turn complained that, from the moment Craxi became Prime Minister, the PSI had turned into a 'party without a soul' and that its policy 'merely assisted the programmatic and strategic reorganisation' of the Christian Democrats.[42]

The theoreticians of the French Left close to the PSU provided a more profound strategic analysis. André Gorz wrote that revolutionary reformism could be distinguished from the social democratic variety by a whole series of signs:

(1) the presence or absence of organic links between the different reforms; (2) the rhythm and means of implementing the reforms; (3) the desire (or its absence) to utilize the disturbance of the equilibrium produced by the first changes for further steps.[43]

Revolutionary pressure, and not the search for compromise and mutual concessions, must become the tactic corresponding to these principles. Only in this instance could the final condition be fulfilled.

Contrary to the view of the 'orthodox Marxists', Kautsky and Plekhanov (and to some extent Lenin), the transition to socialism in Western societies began a long time before the revolution. Elements of socialism have arisen and developed within the capitalist system through the successes of the workers' movement. Revolution does not generate this process but completes it. The revolutionary principles of Gorz and other theoreticians around the PSU exactly corresponded to this state of affairs.

It must be understood that in such a situation the class struggle is not simply a conflict between bourgeoisie and proletariat (including, of course, all forms of wage labour), but a clash between socialized and capitalist institutions. It is a struggle between different structures within society, for these structures are themselves frequently far from homogeneous. Thus nationalization can be used to reinforce the state bureaucracy and have nothing in common with socialism, but it can also become the foundation for the development of a socialist sector of industry. This is precisely why it is necessary to fight for workers' self-management (or even industrial democracy and participation in decision-making) in state enterprises without waiting for the total transformation of the system. In other words, strategy must be directed at the creation and strengthening of 'islands of socialism' here and now. Social democracy's technocratic course spontaneously assists the growth of such 'islands' but it subjects them to the rules of the game, hindering their further development and allowing a rapid bourgeoisification of socialized institutions to take place. A more consistent and radical course is thus essential.

As the PSU theoreticians recognized, reforms cannot substitute for the transformation of society's foundations. 'The need for a revolution, i.e. the destruction of the structure as a whole' is therefore maintained: 'such changes make this destruction inevitable for the partially transformed structures do not correspond to the old social mechanism. They hasten the process of its reorganization.'[45] But here there arises a major problem which has become the stumbling block for theoreticians of revolutionary reformism elaborated as a particularly aggressive strategy. It is essential that, if these changes are to shatter capitalism's equilibrium, 'the concessions extorted are made irreversible and the positions captured are utilized for new offensives.'[46] But the closer the advocates of change get to the point which distinguishes revolution from reform, the more intense the social conflict becomes. Having upset the system's equilibrium, the changes destabilize the economy and jeopardize the government implementing them. The inadequacy of the reforms can be an argument in favour of new transformations, but can also be used by supporters of the old order. The right-wing counter-attack during the crisis of 1979–83 was a striking confirmation of this. In a revolutionary situation the masses choose to break with the system, but they remain sceptical of the ability of the Western Left to create a revolutionary situation purely through augmented reforms. For this to happen shifts on a global scale are required. Western Europe's integrated economy hampers any attempt to carry out a radical programme through the efforts of one state. Thus revolutionary reformism encounters the same problems as the social democratic variety. At a certain moment the reformists will have to come to a halt or even retreat, otherwise the Right will force them to do so.

The bourgeoisie's periodic and comparatively successful counter-attacks are inescapable and predetermined by the very nature of reformism. Under such conditions, old-style social democracy has tried to hold on to power at all costs in order to save the gains of the preceding period. But from that moment begins what Ralph Miliband has called 'a steady degeneration of purpose'.[47]

Social democrats have as a rule been unable to make the transition from the successful implementation of a short-term programme to that of a medium- or long-term one. But the same problem also confronts radical reformists. Even if it is successfully dealt with, there is inevitably a temporary weakening of the Left while its forces are regrouped and reorganized in accordance with the new tasks, and this moment will certainly be seized upon by reaction.

If periodic crises of reformism are unavoidable, then the call by Marxist theoreticians to make reforms irreversible takes on quite another meaning. *Not only an offensive but a defensive strategy is required*. Changes are needed that cannot be liquidated by the bourgeoisie even if the Left is removed from power. Self-management here becomes the key element of the programme. New procedures in a factory can make its denational-ization extremely difficult, even if they cannot completely exclude that possibility. However, by itself, self-management is insufficient.

The PSU in France posed the question of irreversible reforms without answering it. Another problem remained on the agenda: what sort of political force could carry through the revolutionary-reformist project? Hopes for a spontaneous development had not been justified in 1968 and they would not be justified in the future. In his analysis of the Left's prospects in the conditions of late capitalism, the radical philosopher, Jurgen Habermas, has correctly observed that 'the task is a very difficult one, for which an extraordinarily intelligent party is necessary.'[48]

The PSU's attempts to build a mass revolutionary-reformist party fell through. This does not mean, however, that it is impossible in general to create such an organization. The weakening of the PSU in the 1970s was brought about not by the bankruptcy of its strategy but, if this is not paradoxical, precisely by its success. The PSU's ideas were accepted to a large extent by the major Left parties — not only by Mitterrand's regenerated Socialist Party but also by the Communists. The slogan of self-management was incorporated into all party programmes. The Socialists spoke in favour of a system in which 'the workers themselves elect management and leadership at all levels.'[49] The Communists, who back in 1972 had proved that self-management leads to 'economic anarchy',[50] in 1977 declared themselves its consistent supporters. With the concept of structural reforms gaining widespread popularity, the

PSU's existence as a separate party lost all significance and the majority of its leaders and theoreticians joined Mitterrand's party.[51]

Thus the experience of the French Left demonstrates that a new socialist movement can be created neither 'to the left of the communists' nor 'to the left of social democracy', but in their place, in the same political space. It is not a question of founding a new political force but of transformation and renewal from within, the total political reorganization and ideological rearmament of *both* major tendencies on the Left.[52] That such a renewal is possible is evinced by the experience of the Italian Communists and the French Socialists. Both parties have changed in one and the same direction. Perhaps the traditions of Jaurès and Gramsci have had an effect. In any case, by the end of the 1970s these two parties began to resemble each other more than the comrades from 'fraternal' organizations in neighbouring countries.

The shifts that have occurred on the Italian Left have not been an exception. Similar processes have taken place in almost all Western European countries, although the work of internally transforming the Left has nowhere (not even in France or Italy) been completed.

In 1965, when French social democracy was in complete decline, a group of radical theoreticians, instead of abandoning the SFIO as the PSU activists had done, founded the Centre for Socialist Research (CERES). Their aim, they declared, was the regeneration of the Party: 'if nothing can be done without the Socialist Party, then neither can anything be done without its profound transformation.'[53] From the outset, the founders of CERES related changes in the Socialists' ranks to a simultaneous reorganization of the communist movement. Both parties would have to be transformed in the course of a common political struggle, in the first place through the development of 'joint activity at the point of production'.[54] This new practice requires an exceptional degree of ideological and organizational restructuring.

The Italian Communists were thinking along exactly the same lines. A. Rubbi, a leading member of the PCI, wrote that

> one cannot expect socialists, social democrats and progressive forces to overcome their contradictions in precisely the manner proposed by the Communists; a common platform is formed through joint efforts in which everyone retains their identity.[55]

In the end the leaders of the PCI came to the conclusion that a reexamination of its own positions on a series of questions was essential for the unity of progressive forces.

The SFIO's disintegration provided an opportunity for the activists and theoreticians of CERES to apply themselves to their task and ensure that the new organization would 'not come about simply by renovating social democracy' but would be a 'genuinely socialist party'.[56] On the whole they succeeded in imposing their conditions. Even official Soviet experts have been forced to acknowledge that 'obligations of a distinctly anti-capitalist nature' were included in the Party programme.[57] Its new leadership, many of whose members, like François Mitterrand, had never belonged to the SFIO, were aligned with the CERES political project. Even Michel Rocard who, after joining the regenerated Socialist Party from the PSU, headed its moderate wing, stressed that there could be no return to the experience of the SFIO which represented 'one of the worst varieties' of social democratic opportunism.[58] Mitterrand declared that 'the daily struggle for radical structural reforms is first and foremost a break', and that whoever thinks otherwise 'cannot be a member of the Socialist Party'.[59] Structural reforms must lead to a gradual rupture with the existing order and not rectify the 'individual consequences of capitalism'.[60] The strategy of change adopted by the French Socialists was designed to replace the very logic of society and not only its individual institutions.

In this case, radicalism did not mean a repudiation of realism. From the very beginning it was never intended that the proposed reforms would solve all problems. The taking of power by the Left did not signify the transition to socialism but only the 'transition to the transition'.[61] In this way *the Socialists' strategy corresponded to the real conditions of the postponed revolution*.

It is a well-known fact that ideas are no respecters of national boundaries. Left-wing currents advocating analogous projects very quickly came into being in most Western countries. Supporters of the new course proclaimed the need for a simultaneous struggle 'against the capitalist system which oppresses us' and against 'certain structures in our own organizations which threaten to render our activity pointless.'[62] Wherever radical restructuring of left-wing parties proved unavoidable, such a project was fairly easily incorporated into official party doctrine — although, as we shall see later, the actual extent of change varied from country to country.

The French experience influenced the Left in Italy, Belgium, Greece, Portugal and Spain. In a series of instances in Southern Europe, the old social democratic parties had been crushed by dictatorships, and the socialist movement had to be created practically from scratch.

The slogan of a 'break' with capitalism, the advancement of the model of 'self-managing socialism', the course towards possibly gaining power as part of a bloc of Left forces and further governmental collaboration between socialists and communists provided an inspiring example to Portuguese and Spanish socialists at the time their own parties were being formed. An example even more significant and attractive in that it came from socialists in an advanced capitalist country.[63]

There was a similar situation in Greece in 1974 after the fall of the Colonels, when the socialist party was established in literally an empty space.[64]

The bourgeoisie of these countries had been compromised by their support for the dictators, so it was already clear from the mid-1970s that in Southern Europe democratization would be inseparable from the success of the Left. As a result of this, the illusion that a victory for the socialists would inevitably provoke revolutionary shifts in society gained ground. Theoreticians and strategists in the workers' movement supposed that democratization would permit an immediate transition 'to the construction of a socialist society.'[65] The revolutionary character of the Left-wing parties was continually emphasized, and also in many cases, especially in Spain, their link with the Marxist revolutionary tradition. Many spoke of unity in action within the framework of a 'new class front' based on the 'unified bloc of wage labour'.[66] In the heat of the battle for democracy the 28th Congress of Spanish Socialists adopted a programme advocating a radical reorganization of the economy, the creation of a self-managing sector alongside state and private industry and the nationalization of key industrial branches and also private banks.[67] With this programme, the socialists gained second place in the elections to the Cortes in 1977. Party leader Felipe Gonzalez considered this a 'triumph' after which the Socialists would inevitably become the 'leading political force in Spain'.[68] In fact, however, the Left was a long way from reaching its strategic goals. Its radicalism assisted the recasting of the political system and the rapid liquidation of the Franco dictatorship. The Spanish sociologist, J.M. Maraval, has written that:

It is more than questionable that the policy of reform would have met with success against the resistance of Francoism's supporters if there had not existed pressure from below through which the entire process of democratization became a combination of reform and break.[69]

The Left's radical slogans frightened the bourgeoisie, forcing them to hasten the introduction of their own reforms. But when the process of democratization had gone far enough and the Socialists were able to move from putting pressure on the authorities to capturing power, they had to change their tactics. All commentators acknowledge that 'pretensions to being a governmental party have created a tendency towards greater moderation and caution.'[70] In this connection one Soviet expert has even declared that 'radical programmatic and ideological positions coupled with very moderate practical activity' have always characterized the Spanish socialists.[71] Coming to power only exposed this contradiction.

Matters were obviously quite different in reality. After the hopes for a transition to the socialist revolution had been dashed and it was explained that in Spain, as throughout Western Europe, genuine revolution had been delayed, the Left had to resort to reformism. However, its revolutionary illusions dating from the early 1970s were precisely what hampered the efforts of Spanish and other South European socialists to elaborate their own strategy of radical reforms. The new situation had condemned them to a return to social democratic methods, but here, unlike in France, the transition to reformism signified not only a rejection of revolutionary illusions but also a loss of strategic perspective. Electoral success and the taking of power only revealed the movement's internal crisis.

The vagueness of their strategic line and the need to review the party programme plunged the Spanish Socialists, already on the verge of power, into intense ideological and theoretical discussions. The leadership proposed that the word 'Marxism' be removed from the Party constitution as superfluous — for all supporters of socialism are convinced Marxists. How could it be demanded of the mass of Party activists, who incidentally included many believers, that they should all be experts in Marxist theory? A superficial assimilation of Marxism's platitudes leads to it becoming an ideology and, in the end, to the decline of theoretical culture. Apart from this the formula of a 'Marxist party' has frightened many people, and prevented full advantage being taken of socialist slogans. Roy Medvedev has written with justification about the enormous significance of 'tolerance and pluralism' of views for the Left.[72] The anti-capitalist positions of South European socialists were formed, to a large extent, under the influence of radical Christianity, personalist philosophy and 'social Catholicism deepened as far as Marxism'.[73] Thus the Party leadership's proposal to change the constitution was in itself a sensible one. But at a time when the movement was at a crossroads, left-wing activists saw in this a symptom of a return to social democracy. Even the most right-wing of Party ideologues, I. Sotelo, recognized the worries of many when he said 'let not the socialist perspective itself be tossed overboard with the rejection of the word "Marxism".'[74]

Only a few realized that the discussion on Marxism was a substitute for a more important debate.[75] The bitter struggle over the constitution resulted in defeat for the Left and their removal from leading bodies. Party leaders stressed that none of this meant a rejection of revolutionary ideals or a conversion to social democratic positions, for social democratic reformism 'does not correspond to the conditions of Spanish society.'[76] Indeed, the Spanish Socialists did not copy the strategy of the moderate North European Left, but neither did they work out their own. They came to power without a serious strategic project. They had not even reached the level of social democracy.

The Gonzalez government nationalized the 'Rumasa' concern, one of the country's largest monopolies, but did almost nothing to reorganize the state sector. Many enterprises proved unprofitable and had to be returned to private hands. A well thought out programme of inter-related reforms patently did not exist. The *Economist* noted with satisfaction that 'Mr. Gonzalez began shaking up Spanish industry and unions in a way no conservative government would have dared. His Socialist ministers defend their market-minded economic policies with apparently untroubled consciences.'[78] Although modernization of production was objectively necessary it was not accompanied by structural reforms, and followed the usual capitalist practices. Phrases about workers' participation in management did not lead to a rearrangement of organizational structures in the factories. The Socialists remained the major political force in the country (the Right was, in any case, unable to promote an alternative course), but a severe crisis arose within the ruling party and an overt struggle between currents and groupings began.

In Greece, things were even worse. The leader of the socialist movement, Andreas Papandreou, made such radical calls while in opposition that many mistakenly discerned a severe crisis. E.P. Thompson wrote that 'if he wins, Papandreou will become, like Allende before him, a candidate for destabilisation and will need all-European support.'[79] Reality proved to be rather different. Having captured power, Papandreou and his supporters made fiery speeches as before but undertook no serious attempts to alter the country's socio-political structure. The new government rushed to secure the dominant posts at all levels of the state apparatus for its party activists. The Pan-Hellenic

Socialist Movement (PASOK) was turned more and more into the personal instrument of power of Papandreou and his associates. Even Party congresses were not held. Many Socialists broke with the government, accusing it of incompetence and opportunism:

> It is being run by savages. Sixteen ministers and deputy ministers turned up from America. They do not even know the streets of Athens.... Only a few questions are considered by the Council of Ministers and its meetings are very brief. Reforms exist only on paper.[80]

In addition, Papandreou supported Jaruzelski's military coup which suppressed the workers' movement in Poland. He accused the Polish workers themselves of not operating 'in the context of existing historical possibilities'. Such declarations might not only explain the Greek leaders' repudiation of solidarity with the Polish workers, but also justify Papandreou's own opportunism in internal politics. References to 'objective difficulties' can, however, justify anything you like apart from lack of principle. *Le Monde* acknowledged that, instead of promised changes, Papandreou achieved only universal disillusionment. Everything remained the same: 'strikes just as before, economic crisis as always.'[81] Nevertheless, at the 1984 elections Papandreou's party won new success and held on to power: the Greeks recognized that a right-wing government would be *even worse*.[82] In Spain, Gonzalez staked everything on the same card: reformists without reform are still better than blatant reactionaries....

The experience of the Portuguese Socialists, who have moved steadily to the right through fear of the Communists, has proved no more inspiring. After the April Revolution of 1974 which overthrew the rightist authoritarian regime, the Portuguese Socialist Party was one of the most radical anti-capitalist forces in Europe, but by 1984 it was already clear that it belonged to the right wing of international social democracy. Supporters of revolutionary traditions left the Party and established the 'Union of Left Forces for Socialist Democracy', the programme of which was patently influenced by French ideas. In 1980, they succeeded in getting their own deputies elected to Parliament, although the general opinion was that they had achieved 'neither mass base nor influence'.[83] In the 1985 elections significant success was gained by the Party of Democratic Renewal which had been founded by supporters of the retired President, R. Eanes. This grouping, Left critics of the official Socialist party, expressed the growing desire of broad strata of Portuguese society for genuine changes. But, being a radical protest movement, the party was unable to propose to the people either a strategic project or a coherent programme. Having demonstrated the possibility of a radical alternative to the opportunist practice of the Socialists, it did not itself become that alternative.

If the Spanish Socialists adopted a technocratic course, at least they proved competent administrators — more than could be said for their Portuguese and Greek counterparts. Their terms in office were marked not so much by a failure of economic policy as by a general and complete absence of any sort of precisely formulated economic course. Strategy was replaced by accidental, uncoordinated and frequently contradictory decisions.

In the end the lessons of Portugal, Spain and Greece have once again affirmed the correctness of the ideas of the CERES theoreticians about the link between the renewal of the socialist parties and processes occurring within the ranks of the communists. It is quite obvious that this inter-relationship also exists in other countries even including West Germany and Britain, where the communists are extremely weak.

The inability of the Portuguese Communists to accept the democratic rules of the game, and their leaders' devotion to Stalinist dogma, strengthened the positions of the right wing of the socialist movement. The Socialist Party leader, Mario Soares, accepted that 'some of our alliances might seem strange but collaboration with the bourgeoisie is essential in order to maintain a free Portugal.'[84] In other instances the relations between communists and socialists turned out more favourably, but the Portuguese events forced a rethinking of everything. The fact is that in 1974–75 the Portuguese Communist Party formally recognized some Eurocommunist principles — respect for parliamentary democracy and elections, rejection of the term 'dictatorship of the proletariat' and so on.[85] Military leaders close to the Communists, for example the Prime Minister of the Provisional Government, V. Gonsalves, insisted that they 'did not wish to establish a people's democracy and one-party state in Portugal.'[86] Actually, the rejection of Stalinist slogans changed nothing in the policy of the Communist Party and its allies. The Party revealed itself, according to a majority of observers (including left-wing ones), to be 'totalitarian and intolerant of dissident opinion.' The discrepancy between the Portuguese Communists' word and deed

crystallized European fears that any communist party given the opportunity to come close to, or share, power would elbow out all opposition and, against the wishes of the public, install a regime of tightly controlled state capitalism.[87]

Processes occurring in other countries reinforced these apprehensions.

If in the early 1970s a reassessment of values and democratization within the communist movement happened almost everywhere, then by the late 1970s and during the 1980s Stalinist tendencies were once again beginning to be reinvigorated. There were splits in the Swedish, Spanish and British parties. From 1978, the French Communist leadership, which had assiduously propagandized Eurocommunism at the time of the PCF's 22nd Congress, changed course. In Finland, Stalinists and Euro-communists for a long time conducted an open struggle while remaining formally within a single party. Even among Italian communists, con-sidered a model by supporters of renewal and Left unity, there emerged a Stalinist current headed by Senator A. Cossuta.[88] In Greece, the Euro-communists were unable to gain the upper hand over the Stalinists at the polls, and were pushed into the political wilderness.[89]

Having recognized the value of civil liberties and reformist methods, Eurocommunists proved not only partners but also serious rivals to the socialists, encroaching on their ideological monopoly. Each party had henceforth to convince progressive voters that it was the only force capable of playing a leading role in the struggle for *democratic* socialism. On the whole, therefore, the Eurocommunist phenomenon reinforced radical tendencies in world social democracy. In practice, however, the interaction between two fundamentally left-wing parties led to different results in different countries. The process proved rather more com-plicated than the CERES theoreticians had assumed. In several instances the successful renewal of one of the parties hindered the struggle to transform the other. In Italy, for example, the Socialists were unable to keep pace with the much more attractive Communist Party, and conceded that the mass of left-wing voters who had been traditionally oriented to reformist politics 'had, over the past 20–25 years, gradually transferred to the PCI.'[90] In these circumstances, the Socialists' radical wing did not so much advance the Party's renewal with their propaganda as strengthen the Communists' position as the major force capable of implementing desired reforms. Their arguments only confirmed the correctness of the Communists' course. This situation generated mutual hostility between Communists and Socialists, which naturally bolstered the position of the Socialist Party's right wing.[91] By the mid 1980s, both leading parties of the Left in Italy were in crisis. In Spain, the success of the Socialists brought a mass influx of voters behind their banner and weakened the Communists. Eurocommunism's democratic slogans and reformist calls played into the hands of Gonzalez's party, which alone was capable of realizing these reforms in practice. The natural consequence was a crisis of Eurocommunism and the revival of Stalinist tendencies.

At first, the Stalinists assumed that Eurocommunism would be a short-lived fad. For their parts, the advocates of renewal were certain that, in the West, Stalinism contradicted both historical tradition and social conditions, and must inevitably die out. The Eurocommunists pointed to their electoral success, recalling that the Italian Communist Party

> alone constitutes almost 60 per cent of communists and 54 per cent of their voters in the whole of Western Europe. Three parties, the Italian, French and Spanish, form the base of the so-called 'Eurocommunist' tendency and have 86–87 per cent of voters and members.[92]

Reality confounded both these points of view. Eurocommunism has become an important fact in the political life of the West and many parties have travelled even further along this road. It is generally recognized that after their 16th Congress the Italian Communists experienced a 'very real genetic mutation' similar to that which had previously affected the French Socialists. As one Party activist declared, 'In Italy, we are Mitterrand.'[93] At the same time, as we have seen, Stalinism did not disappear, but at times strengthened its positions. After 1978 the French Communist Party became more and more restalinized, and even continual political failure and mass electoral desertion could not halt this process. It is clear that *Eurostalinism* has proved altogether viable, and consequently possesses a stable social base. To bring this point out, it is sufficient to compare the communist movements in France and Italy.

Although the communists in these countries have moved in opposite directions since 1978, opposition exists in both parties and they have both retained a serious presence in the unions even at times of political failure. Both parties operate in countries with democratic traditions and both possess stable support among significant sections of workers. Moreover, they have both undergone the experience of resistance, collaboration with the Socialists and participation in governments, and since 1968 have distanced themselves from Moscow. Why, therefore, have their paths diverged?

From the very beginning, of course, the two most powerful Western communist parties have been sharply differentiated from one another.

Jean-Paul Sartre said that the French Communist Party in the 1960s was already 'the biggest conservative party in France', while enjoying the 'confidence of the workers'. On the other hand their Italian comrades were distinguished by 'freedom of expression, vitality of thought and an easy self-irony which concealed neither their faith nor their resolution.' They quoted Marx infrequently, but often applied 'his principles and method' — for instance, in their critical analysis of events in Eastern Europe. Sartre explained this by reference to the particular qualities of the Italian national character, culture and history. 'The PCI was Italy', he concluded.[94] A more profound explanation is to be found in the reminiscences of Simone de Beauvoir. In Italy, she writes, resistance was directed not only against foreign occupation but against native fascism. It was more homogeneous than in France and, to a large extent, bore the character of a social movement. Thus, even after the collapse of the united anti-fascist front, its former participants retained many values in common. On the whole 'the PCI's position was more favourable than that of the PCF.'[95] The psychology of the besieged fortress, typical of the French communist movement at the time of the Cold War, was not characteristic of Italian Marxists. This, and also the traditions of Gramsci, allowed the PCI to embark comparatively early on the road of renewal.[96]

For all the differences between communists in France and Italy, the PCF's restalinization at the end of the 1970s cannot be explained purely by reference to the Party's history. The French Communists might have been slow in developing, but why did they travel backwards? To understand the real underlying state of affairs the social base of the communist movement in the West must be examined.

The official documents of all communist parties stress that they represent the interests of the working class, the proletariat, and, in the last analysis, all workers. Clearly neither the mass of workers nor the proletariat is homogeneous. In the nineteenth century the proletariat, that is the class of wage labourers, coincided with the working class as a whole, although Marx indicated that 'proletariat' is a broader concept than 'working class'. In the twentieth century massive detachments of labouring people, who were far from being workers in their way of life, jobs and traditions, have been subject to proletarianization. In France in the period 1961–81 the number of wage labourers increased from 62 to 82 per cent of the active population. Sociologists see this correctly as an 'experimental confirmation of the Marxist theory which envisaged the disappearance of small firms and the growth of the proletariat under the influence of the concentration of production.'[97] The remuneration of hired labour improved everywhere, but this did not at all change its social essence.[98] Thus the opportunity arose for left-wing parties to create a mass social base beyond the bounds of the traditional working class.

At the same time, the working class itself in capitalist society became less homogeneous. Some sociologists even assert that 'it is possible to speak of two working classes.'[99] New jobs have appeared alongside traditional workers' occupations, differing not only in the level of skill required but also in the specific nature of the work itself. New specialisms demand not only physical skills but also definite intellectual qualities. The old working class has been more interested in defending its rights through trade unions and in the preservation of jobs. It frequently supports nationalization not as part of a socialist project but as a means of maintaining employment (the implementation of mass redundancies in the state sector has proved extremely complicated). The new sections of the working class have a much greater striving for structural reforms and industrial self-management. Both old and new working class are in conflict with the bourgeoisie, but the old strata are more conservative. As a rule they are much more acutely aware of the contradiction between labour and capital, but at the same time they take a purely defensive posture. The British miners' strike against the right-wing government in 1984–85 showed that even the traditional working class's most resolute actions are distinguished by their narrow political vision and lack of dynamism.

The old and new working class are condemned to a prolonged co-existence, for the emergence of new technology does not exclude the old. Indeed, low wage-rates can sometimes mean that it remains more profit-able than the new. In those countries in which two powerful left-wing parties exist side by side, the old working class orientates as a rule to the communists, and the new working class to the socialists. Such a tendency has been recorded by French sociologists, but it is not only typical of France. In Finland, where 'a very high degree of correlation has been observed between the political orientation of the electorate and the class structure of society', it has been even more evident: 'The communists base themselves primarily on traditional groups within the working class, while the social democrats win over the new layers, particularly the youth.'[100] The orientation to old working-class strata reinforces the communists' inclination to limit struggle to defending the workers' economic interests, to the detriment of reformist activity. Thus in the West it is the communists who, contrary to Leninist traditions, emerge more and more often as a kind of political wing of the trade unions.[101]

In crisis conditions it is precisely the old working class which is the first to suffer from rising unemployment and falling living standards. Worst of all, the decline in jobs has an irreversible character. From 1930 to 1975, the number of miners in France fell by five times and the number of workers in textile manufacturing by seven times. The crisis of 1979–83 coincided with the beginnings of a new technological revolution. This meant inevitable social degradation for many sections of the old working class. The only way out is through retraining on a mass scale, but this is very difficult to implement in a crisis, the more so as entrepreneurs are not particularly concerned about this problem. The situation is complicated by the old working class's comparatively low level of education and the concentration of dying industries in 'depressed areas' where it is very hard to find work.

Even in France, where the Socialist government made serious efforts to organize retraining, it proved extremely difficult to solve all the problems because, as the Socialists themselves recognized, workers with old skills did not believe they could 'do anything else'. Lotharingian steel workers were ready to 'perish along with the steel industry.'[102] The Communist Party, taking its cue from its social base in these regions, was at first usually prepared to support this position, although it was undoubtedly a loser. The Party altered its approach to the problems only when it felt that its position would lead to a loss of support in other sections of the population (including many groups within the working class). Such vacillations reflect the duality of the Party itself. On the one hand it leans for support precisely upon the old working class, many strata of which are experiencing social decline; on the other, the PCF cannot survive as a mass national movement if it directs itself exclusively to them.

The Communists' situation in Italy is completely different. Over the course of the entire post-war period they have stood out, in the words of a Soviet expert, 'as the most powerful, authoritative and forward-looking force on the Left.'[103] Being the country's major left-wing party, the PCI has proved more capable than the others of fighting for the common interests of all workers. Italy is a Catholic country and this means that very backward sections of the workers inevitably lean towards Christian Democracy.[104] This weakens the Communists' position at elections, but increases the weight of advanced social strata within the Party. It could be said that by keeping the backward workers under its influence, the Italian bourgeoisie has assisted the PCI's renovation and undermined the social base of traditionalists and Stalinists within it. After 1968 the composition of the PCI's leading cadres and also its rank-and-file and electors were renewed. As researchers have acknowledged, new sections of the working class have occupied 'leading positions' within it.[105]

A comparison of French and Italian experience at first glance shows that the correlation between Eurocommunist and Stalinist tendencies depends on the ratio between new and old proletariat in the Party's social base. It does not follow, however, that the old working class has a 'primeval' inclination towards Stalinism. On the contrary, in the first half of the 1970s the French Communists were able to advance a critique of Stalinism without any change in their social base.

Stalinism in the West is different from Stalinism in Eastern Europe, both in its class base and its ideology. In the West, there is no party bureaucracy maintaining its privileges. Eurostalinism, like Eurocommunism, has been engendered by specific Western conditions. In essence it can be defined as the ideology of disappearing groups in the working class in the conditions of capitalist crisis. In other words it is not simply a question of the old proletariat but only of those strata devoid of the prospect of social development. Psychologically, this phenomenon is reminiscent of the 'reactionary socialism' of dying classes portrayed by Marx back in 1848. Here everything is turned inside out: under the guise of protesting against the capitalist form of technical progress a struggle is waged against progress in general, for no real alternatives are proposed. The French sociologist, Maurice Duverger, writes that

> to assert that it would be possible on a permanent basis to buy raw materials for industry and energy from abroad without paying for them with exports of equal value, that it would be possible to increase exports without lowering prices and improving quality, that it would be possible to achieve both of these without modernizing the productive apparatus, that it would be possible to carry out modernization without loss of jobs in the initial stages, that it would be possible to safeguard the coal industry, steel and shipbuilding with the aid of public subsidies, that it would be possible to satisfy workers' demands without considering the costs — all this is completely unserious.

If communist leaders utter such declarations it is only because they desire to destabilize the economy and thus provoke a 'revolution'.[106] In reality the PCF has no such revolutionary programme and its leaders are not mad. As opposed to Duverger they know full well that do not have sufficient means at their disposal to destabilize the economy even if such a stupid idea entered their heads. In fact the illogicality of their demands is explained much more simply: the Party's goal consists in fighting against technical progress. Revolutionary slogans conceal the conservative (if not reactionary) essence of this policy. At a moral level such anti-reformism 'from the Left' is more attractive than its right-wing analogue: in 1983–84, many voters in France transferred from the communists to the neo-fascist National Front, but all the same, anti-capitalist conservatism is more appealing to workers than any form of overtly right-wing ideology. This is not to assert that Stalinism is the sole possible form of 'reactionary socialism' in today's conditions, but in those countries with a developed communist tradition this is the most natural form of protest against technical progress.

The continuing technical revolution creates the conditions for the growth of such tendencies. For the ruling class, Eurostalinism is completely harmless. The rejection of reformist transformations, which can in no way be explained by revolutionary phraseology, means in the last analysis the rejection of change altogether for, in contemporary society, the road to revolution lies only through reforms.[107] The Eurostalinists have turned their backs on the capitalist system, but this suits the system very well. Towards the end of his life, Raymond Aron, the ideologist of right-wing liberalism, advised French bourgeois politicians to help strengthen the Communist Party in every way possible as their 'objective ally' in the struggle against socialist reformism.[108]

What Aron had let out of the bag had, however, become clear to the Socialists themselves from the late 1970s. And before the 1981 Presidential Elections the Communists themselves openly opposed the rest of the Left by channelling their efforts into maintaining a bourgeois government. Such a position provoked the displeasure of many of the Party's supporters and led to its crushing defeat, after which the Party agreed to enter a government of Left unity despite its unwillingness 'to be involved in regulating the capitalist crisis.' Then, in 1984, the Communists went into opposition precisely at a time when the right-wing assault had become particularly fierce. Attacks on the Socialists were even more vitriolic in the Communist than in the conservative press. In its policy the PCF essentially confirmed Aron's correctness, emerging in this period as the objective ally of reaction.

The anti-socialist utterances of the French Communist Party in 1984–86 should not be seen solely as an attempt to place narrow party interests above class interests, or simply as an inclination towards treachery. The

PCF's vacillations, switching from support for the Socialists to savage attacks on them, expressed the contradictoriness of its social base.[109] Small Stalinist parties in Switzerland and Spain could permit themselves greater consistency. It was a similar matter in comparatively backward countries like Greece and Portugal.

The problem of sections of the working class disappearing or going into decline also exists in those countries where no powerful communist movement exists. In this case it must be dealt with by socialists or social democrats. Obviously there can be no Stalinist factions in social democratic parties, but similar tendencies do still arise there. The experience of British Labourism is especially typical in this regard. After the right wing had left the Party, it could not achieve unity. The discussions which began among Labour Party members were strongly reminiscent of the polemic between Eurocommunists and Eurostalinists – as the participants in the disputes themselves recognized. In order to understand what happened we cannot simply refer to the higher level of theoretical knowledge enjoyed by communists (of both factions), thanks to which the battle of ideas in the small Communist Party had an influence on the whole of the British Left.[110] It is not just a question of this. It is not at all accidental that the Stalinist *Morning Star* received the support of the Labour weekly *Tribune*. In Britain, a country undergoing a severe structural crisis, such ideas readily find mass support.

The collapse of the centrist policies of Wilson and Callaghan, who had led the Party over the course of almost two decades, the crisis of the right wing, and the departure from the Party of its leading figures, made the Left the masters of the situation. At once, however, it became clear that they had no alternative strategy of any kind. 'Pragmatism may have failed, but it survived because nobody could agree on what philosophy to replace it with', observed a British journalist.[111] The Party declared its loyalty to revolutionary ideals, but in practice this only meant using more radical slogans. The Labour Left accused the Right of incon- sistency, correctly showing that disjointed and half-hearted reforms do not assist the transition to socialism. But when the Left took the future of the Party into its hands it could not at first propose anything but uncoordinated radical appeals. The economic programme, which had been worked out on the basis of old demands, was merely given a more radical form. Thus a new, genuinely alternative strategy did not emerge – only a renovated version of the old. All its essential inadequacies were retained, and indeed became even more apparent; for its previous inconsistency had at least been compensated by half-heartedness and had not been so noticeable. The 'hard Left' in the Party not only closed its eyes to this but plainly expressed its disdain for such questions. Tony Benn, leader of the 'hard Left', declared, with devious reasoning, that 'the real strengths of socialism lie in the non-economic values that we advocate, the rejection of economics even if we can manipulate them in our favour.'[112]

The chief idea of the 'hard Left' has been reduced to assuming a 'correct' anti-capitalist stance and waiting 'for the British people to agree'.[113] The sole concrete strategic proposition consisted in withdrawal from the European Economic Community. Such a demand was not only unrealistic but was contrary to the general direction of the Western Left.[114] While criticizing the Common Market in its present capitalist form, the Left in a majority of Western countries has been in favour of transforming its institutions. From the mid-1970s the Italian Communists have seen the Community as a 'necessary field of battle for social renewal.'[115] The French and Spanish Socialists had always adhered to a similar viewpoint.

The hostility of the Labour Left towards the Common Market has been understandable: capitalist integration complicates the task of national planning. The economic harmonization of the European countries is an objective necessity. The inadequacy of national planning places on the agenda the question of regional planning and here there is no other way than by transforming already existing European institutions. A French Socialist Party theoretician, Jacques Attali, has written that 'changing society means changing the process of reproduction.'[116] This task can only be achieved at a regional level since the economies of Western European countries have an open character and attempts to return to isolationism are fraught with catastrophe. Little by little the British Left has begun to understand that the only way a socialist government in Britain 'could survive would be by working with other left governments in Europe and the Third World. There is an enormous potential in Europe.'[117]

Defeat in the 1983 elections forced the Labour Party to begin a reassessment of its values. Anti-European prejudices were discarded. There was a consensus among ideologists and activists on the need for a consistent reformist strategy: 'Slogans won't do: the problems a future Labour Government will face will be far greater than in the 1960s or 1970s.'[118] Despite the resistance of the 'hard Left', British socialists began to orient to a policy of structural reforms like their comrades on the Continent. But progress along this road remained very difficult for them, as the major problem was created not by sectarian obstinacy but by the social crisis affecting many sections of the old working class. Britain's economic backwardness and the Conservatives' vicious anti-worker policies made this crisis more severe than anywhere else in Europe.

Britain's experience once again underlines the fact that what is needed is *a strategy of reform that takes into account in equal measure both the interests of scientific-technical progress and the problems of declining strata of the working class. Otherwise millions of people will have no other choice than 'reactionary socialism' in one guise or another*. The pragmatic technocratic utopia of the 1960s is dead. It can be replaced either by revolutionary reformism or by 'revolutionary conservatism' in the spirit of the old communist ideology. If the latter triumphs, the Left will be doomed to disaster. But there are reasons to suppose this will not happen.

The right-wing social democratic politicians of Northern Europe still cling to the old principles more than anyone else. But even Swedish social democracy has been forced to pose the question of a more radical course. Its economic strategy has come to include the creation of 'workers' funds', to which part of annual profits would be assigned. The collective fund thus formed must be turned into shares in the enterprise. Thus — and this has been acknowledged even by official Soviet researchers — 'the problems of ownership and power were at the core of the project.' For the first time in a long while, reforms with a 'system-changing character' have been pushed to the forefront.[119] In a period of crisis the choice was made not in favour of more radical slogans but in favour of more profound reforms. The left-wing current, while remaining a minority, proved capable of constructively influencing the policies of the social democratic party and fighting for its renewal.

A similar review of values also began in West German social democracy after the loss of power.[120] Here the crisis was not so acute as in Britain (possibly because of the reformists' prolonged period in power). The Communist Party remained openly Stalinist, although the social base for such an ideology was minimal. This led to the disappearance of communism as an important factor in the country's political arena. Throughout the 1970s, social democracy had no serious rival on its left. Having the East German police state as a neighbour also inevitably reinforced anti-communist tendencies in the workers' movement. The upshot of all this was that during their period in office, the social democrats moved steadily to the right. The crisis changed the situation. The coming to power of conservative forces in autumn 1982 was accompanied by the abrupt revival of left-wing tendencies.

Strictly speaking, these tendencies had long existed both inside and outside social democracy. The Party's youth organization, the Young Socialists, openly criticized the leadership while striving to reform the Party from within and turn it once again into an anti-capitalist force. The Young Socialists insisted on the need to formulate socialist principles 'aggressively and without looking to the right.'[121] In short, they hoped to turn German social democracy from a party of class collaboration into a party of class struggle. Many of them inclined toward the theoretical positions of Eurocommunism while some were disposed towards 'revolutionary conservatism'. The degeneration of the official reformist course and the collapse of attempts to shift the Party to the left led many of them to the idea of capitalism's unreformability:

> Any policy of reform initiated by the bourgeois state comes to a halt when it touches the fundamental interests of capital. Attempts to encroach upon these interests will lead to severe crisis, which could only be turned against capitalism rather than against the socialist government in rare instances and under the widest-ranging working class struggle.[122]

The theoreticians of the Young Socialists raised a very real problem, but instead of developing a flexible offensive strategy of reform, which *takes these dangers into consideration*, they have, as a rule, confined themselves to enumerating the difficulties.

The failure of the Young Socialists, and of the Communist Party's Stalinism, led to radical forces in West German society rallying around the Greens. The struggle against atomic weapons and environmental pollution had unexpectedly united social democrats disillusioned with their party, the growing New Left, and Eurocommunists unable to find a political haven. Various ecological and pacifist movements exist throughout Europe but when, under the influence of the German experience, they began to unite in Green parties, failure everywhere awaited them.[123] The secret of the German Greens' success was not only the strength of their ideas but also the weakness of social democracy.

The problems of the environment and the struggle for peace are very important but they do not obviate the necessity for a radical party to elaborate a comprehensive socio-economic programme. The Greens pushed the most pressing problems to the foreground, but these are not always the most crucial. Defence of nature requires profound structural reforms, and therefore the ecological movement is destined to come into conflict with the capitalist monopolies and state bureaucracy. But reformist strategy must be based on a comprehensive analysis, in which the ecological and military dangers are only a partial expression of more general contradictions. This has been noticed by several of the Party's supporters. 'The greater the Greens' success, the more sharply the question is posed as to what they really want', one of them recalled.[124] The strength of the Greens is in their ability to give a new expression to the struggle around partial questions. Although their demands were, in themselves, particularly reformist, the spirit of the movement was undoubtedly revolutionary. The Greens aimed to achieve stricter laws on preserving the environment and the elimination of American nuclear missiles. Neither of these demands affects capitalism's foundations, but meanwhile the Greens reiterate that the 'system is bankrupt', that capitalism is contrary to 'even the elementary needs of the broad mass of people' and that it is necessary to replace bourgeois democracy by 'socialism with a human face'.[125] These radical slogans at first served to unite reformists and revolutionaries, but when the Greens became a serious political force with their own press, organization, and deputies in the Bundestag, it became evident that such an approach was untenable. In the words of Green parliamentarians themselves, 'a "catalogue of wares" does not replace a strategy'.[126] It began to prove impossible to remain at once a protest movement and a parliamentary party without a major reorganization. Links with the working class were minimal; the Greens had become more and more clearly a party of the intelligentsia, defending the social interests of workers by brain. A Green author candidly conceded that the economic sections of their programme would allow them to preserve jobs only 'in one specific branch': research institutions.[127]

In 1985, the young politician, Oskar Lafontaine, united social democrats in the Saarland around a new Left–reformist programme, including some anti-war and ecological demands. He easily defeated both conservatives and Greens. At the same time, in West Berlin, G. Apel was unsuccessful when a significant portion of votes transferred to the 'Alternative List', a local Left–radical coalition. Lafontaine attracted votes by advocating structural reform, the nationalization of industrial sectors in crisis and workers' participation in management. While fighting for ecological principles, he attempted to relate them to a concrete programme of reform. A British journalist stated that 'Without the threat of the Greens as rivals, the Social Democrats would never have moved so quickly on either of these topics.'[128] But the Greens could also draw lessons from what had happened. *Without the renewal of old social democracy, a radical reformist initiative is impossible in Germany, as well as in other Western countries.* The activity of the Greens is only effective to the extent that they recognize this and assist such a renewal.

As we have seen, the voicing of radical slogans is no guarantee of genuine renewal. The Left needs a strategy, not slogans. Back in the 1960s, the Japanese Communists turned towards reformist activity designed to 'create more favourable conditions for revolution'.[129] Attempts to deflect the Party from this course provoked an acute crisis and ended in failure. Paradoxically, the Japanese Communists are among the most consistent Eurocommunist parties, and it is the Socialists who maintain a radical orientation.[130] Nevertheless, the projects for 'first-stage' changes proposed by the Left in the 1970s did not go beyond the bounds of a moderate social democratic course. Nationalization with subsequent democratization of management was projected only in power engineering. A Soviet author quite correctly remarked that the communist project in Japan envisaged changes 'within the framework of and not affecting the foundations of the existing system.'[131] The proposals of the socialists and social democrats were very similar.

Japan's prosperity greatly assisted the destalinization of the communist movement. It would be naive to assume that the working class there did not encounter the same problems during the technological revolution as in Europe; several occupations declined sharply in importance. But in a rapidly growing economy it is easier to secure reskilling, and the creation of new jobs and unemployment are easily dealt with. The system, employed by many companies, of hiring workers for life seems feudal to Europeans, but it ensures guaranteed jobs for millions of people and forces the capitalists themselves to concern themselves with retraining workers. In such conditions, technological restructuring does not lead to the social decline of broad strata of the proletariat. This situation is to the advantage not only of Japanese capitalism but also, to a certain extent, of the Left, which is distinguished by its high degree of organization and realism. Nevertheless, it has proved extremely difficult to formulate a strategy of radical reforms in the most dynamic capitalist country. General capitalist contradictions exist, of course, in Japan as in other countries, but on the whole the system 'works' better here than anywhere else. On the other hand, despite the country's massive economic success, the Japanese standard of living is still lower than that of Europe or America. They have the longest working week and the shortest holidays in the advanced capitalist world. The Japanese earn significantly less for their labour than Europeans (one reason for the cheapness and competitiveness of Japanese goods). In these conditions raising workers' living standards and income redistribution, rather than structural reforms, are a first priority. In other words, the path taken by Swedish social democracy — securing the redistribution of incomes without reorganizing successfully functioning economic structures — is the most attractive for the Japanese Left. Although Japanese Socialists and Communists often make reference to their anti-capitalist and Marxist principles, it is difficult not to notice the social democratic orientation of their practical proposals.

It is natural to expect radical changes not in the most prosperous countries, but in those where the problems are more acute than elsewhere. It is precisely because of this that comparatively backward countries can, at times, become the most advanced. On the other hand, the final success of the transformation depends not only on a crisis of the old order but also on the level of development already attained. The greatest opportunities for the Left are therefore opening up in those countries which occupy an intermediate position in capitalist competition without being either leaders or outsiders.

The technological revolution has significantly altered the character of the class struggle. This is especially noticeable in Western Europe. An article in the Belgian Communist paper argues:

> The workers' movement, having encountered problems new to it, must decide to what extent it should assist the speedy introduction of new technology into industry, whether it should be financed by the state and, in the event of a positive response, what forms of workers' control will be implemented.[132]

Of course, the real problem is not whether new technology will be introduced but *how and for what* it will be employed. Robots and microcomputers can be used to save people from the most alienating forms of labour (and from the division of labour), to extend individual liberty and shorten working time. They can create more favourable conditions for decentralization, self-management, workers' access to information, planning and the socialization of production in the course of its structural reformation. But they can also further enslave workers, weaken the role of trade unions, increase unemployment and deprive the working class of its gains. All new technology is 'two-faced' in its social relation, and it is precisely this which makes it an object of class struggle.

Radical reformism in the late twentieth century must be directed towards organizing technological restructuring, if not on the basis of socialist principles then at least by taking these principles into consideration. The objective need for structural economic reorganization increases the chances of simultaneously transforming society. In this sense the activity of Mitterrand's government in France is of great interest. His policy has been distinguished from the practice of other Left governments precisely because such questions have been seriously posed, if not always successfully resolved.

By the mid-1980s France remained the sole laboratory of revolutionary reformism in the Western world, regarded by all Europe 'with disquiet or with hope'.[133] In assessing the actions of the Socialist government from 1981 to 1986, most observers stress that it made a whole string of errors and that its practical achievements were fewer than expected by its supporters. Undoubtedly, not everything the Left did in this period met with success, and mistakes were unavoidable. But if the acuteness of the crisis, the fact that after twenty years in opposition the Socialists lacked practical experience of management, the unfavourable external situation and the novelty of their tasks are taken into account, it must be acknowledged that their mistakes were in fact very few — fewer than could have been assumed beforehand. What is even more important is that the French experiment helped to define the boundaries of the then new reformism's real possibilities, prospects and methods of overcoming the emerging difficulties. In this sense, Mitterrand's failures have been no less valuable than his successes.

The reforms in France were not directed at changing the system as a whole, but *in those areas where transformations were carried through, they were consistent and radical.* Coming to power during the most severe crisis in post-war history, the French Socialists were patently swimming 'against the stream'. Unlike right-wing governments which cut state expenditure and made the battle with inflation their objective, the French Left began to implement a policy stimulating economic growth. It was not successful in achieving the desired increase in production and employment, but France was still able to avoid a slump. In 1982, production fell in the USA by 1.7 per cent, in West Germany by 1.0 per cent and in Great Britain by 1.4 per cent, but in France the Gross National Product grew by 1.9 per cent. At the same time a large number of private banks and companies were nationalized, as a result of which the state sector encompassed 32 per cent of productive output, and one third of productive capacity and employment in industry. 85–90 per cent of the banking sector was nationalized. Of particular importance was the fact that not only were branches in crisis (such as steel) nationalized, but so too were leading enterprises on the development of which the economy's future depended. Nationalization allowed an agreed policy of technological renewal to be implemented and assisted the modernization of the steel industry with minimal losses for the workers, although the communist unions criticized the government's programme as 'unacceptable'.[134] The state sector had to be turned from an accidental conglomeration into an organic whole. After a painful and difficult reorganization, the nationalized companies began to make a profit.[135] Successful cooperation with the Japanese speeded the technological restructuring of French industry.

Nationalization was only one part of the Socialist government's reform programme, but cardinal importance was attached to it. The creation of a more powerful state sector was seen as the beach-head for further socialist transformations. While traditional social democratic reformism confined itself to changes in the sphere of distribution and indirect regulation of the economy, strategic revolutionary reforms inevitably had to *affect the spheres of property and organization of production*. Nationalization carried out a whole string of tasks. It created the conditions for the planning and democratization of production, undermined the position of monopolistic groups and thereby altered the relationship of class forces in the country. An effective model for running the state sector had to be elaborated which presupposed 'interaction between a revived market and democratic planning.'[136] The best forms of workers' involvement in management and the most humane methods of technological restructuring had to be found.

It was impossible to achieve quick success in resolving all of these complex tasks, and France's resources were limited. In a period of crisis, a policy of growth could be carried out only up to a certain limit. By the summer of 1982, 53–58 per cent of French people were in favour of a 'pause' in the implementation of the reforms. The centre of gravity of the government's activity shifted from technological modernization to anti-inflationary measures. Unemployment once again began to increase. The Socialists went over to a programme of economies, and many reformist projects were either cut back or shelved. An attempted reform of schools failed in the face of fierce resistance from the Right and the displeasure of the Church, which both defended private education. The government's obvious retreat provoked criticism not only from the communists but also from many of Mitterrand's supporters, who declared that the new line was contrary to the initial course towards a break with capitalism. Some party activists put their hopes in Michel Rocard, in whom they saw a person capable of putting the party back on the rails of moderate reformism without destroying its traditions and ideology. In many respects Rocard was the French version of Felipe Gonzalez — in the past a fighter against social democracy, now an advocate of moderation. He also gained considerable popularity through personal charm and his skilful combination of radical utterances and technocratic eclecticism. His lack of any kind of consistent theoretical or ideological programme at least rendered him free of dogmatism. In the period when Mitterrand's policies became less successful, there was naturally a sharp increase in the influence of Rocard and his followers within the party.

Both Left and Right spoke of the 'failure' of the radical experiment. Many even accused the Socialists of not being conscious of 'their real mission' and, instead of reconsidering their ideas, of 'preferring to postpone (or forget?) them.'[137] Some communists, quite in the old Trotskyist spirit, proposed radical measures to overcome the difficulties, forgetting that such a method can only succeed in time of revolution. Neither left- nor right-wing critics of Mitterrand could suggest any realistic alternatives. Meanwhile, by 1985 the economic situation began slowly but surely to improve. The unemployment problem became less acute, the franc was stabilized and exports increased.

The rejection of the initial policy at a certain stage was both logical and necessary. It was explained by the fact not that the first steps were mistaken, but that by the end of 1982 the possibilities of a radical course had been exhausted. Everything that could have been achieved through that policy in that situation had been achieved. Nothing like a revolution had occurred in France. The Socialists had had to manage the bourgeois state and had managed it well. Consequently, the interests of capital had been taken into consideration.[138] The responsibility for this situation lies not with the party leaders, but with the workers themselves: they had voted for the Left but not given them a mandate for a revolutionary transition to socialism. On the other hand, the radical measures of the first two years had laid the ground for the government's successes during the second stage, when a policy of modernization was implemented. If the reforms of 1981–82 had really fallen through, the subsequent progress would have been inconceivable.

The French experience has demonstrated not only that socialism in one country, as Trotsky correctly maintained, is impossible in principle, but also that the prospects for reform in one country are extremely limited. A minister in the Left government, Jacques Delors, conceded that external circumstances, particularly the crisis in Europe, had left him with 'no room to manoeuvre'.[139] Strategic reform should aim to engender analogous processes in other countries. The French Socialists' chief mistake, about which their left-wing critics simply kept quiet, was that they made no efforts to build a united front with other left-wing governments in the West and elaborate an international policy which would have reinforced reformist tendencies in neighbouring countries. This is a complex and perhaps difficult task, but it is essential to make every effort in this direction.

In the conditions of the postponed revolution, the limits of reformism become narrower. The success of reforms depends especially upon the continual possibility of their developing into revolution, for otherwise the Left's retreat and a ruling class counter-offensive are inevitable. Socialist forces must be prepared beforehand for this eventuality. *The strategic aim in such a situation is not only and not so much to hold onto power as to ensure the irreversibility of the reforms which have been implemented.*

For this to happen a mass movement is essential — one which extends beyond the bounds of political parties, is autonomous from their day-to-day leadership and is not subject to their tactical failures and petty mistakes (in this sense, the experience of the Polish workers' movement in 1980–81 is not without interest). The French Socialists' second serious error lay precisely in their underestimation of the masses' spontaneous support and in their desire to carry out everything 'from above' through the channels of Party and State. Government figures themselves recognized that 'having seized the fortress of power, the Left raised the drawbridge and locked themselves in.'[140]

Nevertheless, Mitterrand did a great deal to ensure the irreversibility of the reforms. As the right-wing press acknowledged, democratization of the state sector 'was related to a number of very "socialist" measures.'[141] The participation of workers' collectives in the management of nationalized enterprises has changed much at the very base of the relations of production. In this way, the Left can develop elements of a new social system, albeit within a confined social space, without entering immediately into conflict with the bourgeoisie.[142] Moreover, privatizing a company where there are factory councils and the workers participate in decision-making is not an easy matter. The workers' collective itself gains the opportunity not to allow such a turn of events. Social democrats usually set aside their own reform programmes during a crisis. In France the changes continued, primarily in the sphere of managing the state sector. Even the Party's right wing, the supporters of

Rocard, understood that the success of the reformist project as a whole depended upon this, and that democratization of the public enterprises must 'become the decisive factor for a successful movement forwards despite the difficulties of the current period.'[143]

The bourgeoisie's radicalization, which began in the 1980s, represents a threat not only to the gains of the working class but to society as a whole, for the Right's counter-reformism frequently assumes an anti-social character. The existence of the capitalist class has long since ceased to be an economic necessity, but its disappearance is impossible without a radical restructuring of society which, even to a majority of workers in the West, seems too risky a business at present. Thus while the revolution is delayed, the bourgeoisie is ever turning into a lumpen-bourgeoisie and its political representatives are becoming increasingly irresponsible. Paradoxically, in this situation it is right-wing forces which strive to destroy the existing order, 'the Western European model of development', which has taken shape over the course of forty post-war years. The success of such a policy has led at best to the economic dictatorship of transnational corporations freed from any responsibility to society, and at worst to social chaos. In opposing the bourgeoisie's extremist outpourings, the Left has found itself in the unlikely role of defender of the system. This makes it seem that socialist and communist parties are shifting towards the centre. But this does not signify a return to the safe and featureless centrism of the 1960s for this time reformism must ward off the radical threat from the right and simultaneously, by broadening its social base, begin the work of forming a new class bloc and lay the foundations of the future.[144]

The Left's defensive policy need not be passive and featureless. Neither moderation nor revolutionary slogans can be a substitute for strategy. A serious and profound search is required, which is only now beginning.

The efficacy of strategic defence determines the possibility of a new offensive and its tasks.[145] Each new onslaught by the Left provides hope in a final victory. Revolutionary reformism must turn this hope into a concrete strategy, a programme of consistent political and economic measures. But whether the next reformist offensive will be the beginning of revolutionary changes in society, or prove just as limited as its predecessors, depends on the world political situation. *The triumph of the Left in the West is inconceivable without changes in the developing countries and in Eastern Europe*, and the political struggle which is happening there is subject to the same general dialectic of reform and revolution.

Notes

1. 'In recent years in the Western world socialism, both as an intellectual current and in political practice, has appeared to be a declining force' (*British Book News*, December 1984, p. 722). Such is the unanimous opinion of political scientists. But as a rule they do not acknowledge that the crisis of socialism is the product of preceding successes of Left forces able to change much in the system but also linking themselves with it and thereby compromising themselves: they have to pay for the crisis of capitalism.

2. Where there is free exchange of information and ideas, ideological principles in the end inevitably assume a universal generalized form. We will investigate not a particular country or party, but these universal forms. As political scientists note: 'In the West, political forms and demands and ideologies are often more similar than the social structure or economic conditions in which they operate' (R. Grew, ed., *The Crisis of Political Development in Europe and the United States*, Princeton 1978, p. 9).

3. *El Sistema*, no. 15, October 1976, p. 9.

4. *El Socialista* (*especial XXVII Congresso*), no. 1, p. 4.

5. *New Left Review*, no. 122, July–August 1980, p. 54. So long as the reforms remained unimplemented, the class struggle was continually being resumed at a new level, for after each success it soon became necessary to engage in a new battle to preserve what had been gained. Social democratic reforms are *reversible* and whenever the workers' movement slackens its reformist onslaught they begin to be dismantled; and to halt this through purely defensive actions is very difficult, if not impossible. Nor is it possible to rely on the trade unions in this confrontation as the last stronghold of the workers. As a French commentator has rightly observed, for them 'everything is reduced in a crisis to the defence of jobs and the struggle cannot therefore be effective' (*L'Esprit*, no. 2, 1985, p. 2). Letting slip the strategic initiative in such a situation causes a chain reaction of failures and the loss of previously won positions. The 1984–85 miners' strike and the 1926 General Strike in Britain were both doomed to defeat because they were limited by defensive slogans. In both instances the unions were unable to provide society with an alternative plan of struggle for the transformation of the coal industry. Success would only have been possible if the degree of solidarity was such that other sections of workers had been prepared to risk their own jobs for the sake of the miners. For this to have happened other slogans would have been necessary. Nevertheless the miners' failure did not on the whole signal a catastrophe for the Left and the working class, but only the start of a new phase of struggle and of new strategic quests.

6. E. Hobsbawm, *Revolutionaries*, London 1973, pp. 14–15.

7. In the 1920s Right social democrats attempted to defend themselves against accusations of revisionism by referring to the fact that Marxism is itself a theory of 'social evolution' distorted by 'revolutionary appendages' (*Die Theorie des modernen Sozialismus*, ed. R. Abraham, Berlin 1923, pp. 112–13).

8. 'Les murs ont la parole', *Journal mural, Mai 1968*, Paris 1968, p. 23. A Paris student leader in 1968 declared that traditional forms of workers' movement had only given rise to 'reformists, more or less wise, more or less capable of implementing

some reforms, but incapable of calling in question the social structures' (*La révolte étudiante: Les animateurs parlent*, Paris 1968, p. 50).

9. *Présences d'Adorno. Revue d'Esthétique*, no. 1–2, Paris, 1975, p. 39.

10. Reformism is naturally more boring than revolution. For reformist zeal to arise, a programme of transformations is needed which is genuinely impressive and contains within it revolutionary features.

11. Jean-Paul Sartre, *Situations IV*, Paris 1964, pp. 155, 228.

12. *Les Temps Modernes*, no. 82, 1952, p. 328. The discussion on the camps in 1952 is of particular interest, but we are unable to devote sufficient space to it. The thought expressed by Sartre — that the greatness of the idea serves to atone for the camps — is horrific. But the position of the contemporary '*nouveaux philosophes*' who endeavour to justify any ugliness created in the capitalist world by reference to the Gulag is no less monstrous. See M. Contat and M. Rybalka, *Les écrits de Sartre*, Paris 1970; de Beauvoir, vol. 1; Sartre, *Situations IV*; A. Camus, *L'Homme révolté*, Paris 1951; H. Lottman, *Camus*, London 1979.

13. Camus, *L'Homme révolté*, p. 261.

14. *Les Temps Modernes*, no. 82, 1952, p. 327.

15. Official Soviet political commentators proclaimed the student movement 'petty-bourgeois'. This rather contradicted reality and provoked protests on the part of serious researchers even in censored publications. 'The depiction of student protest as a petty-bourgeois anti-social revolt', one of them wrote, 'serves openly reactionary ends' (*Levoe studencheskoe dvizhenie v stranakh kapitalizma*, Moscow 1976, p. 5). If the petty-bourgeoisie can be characterised as a 'dying' class then the intelligentsia can be characterised as the most rapidly growing section of workers.

16. 'Les murs ont la parole', p. 96.

17. K. Kautsky, *Na drugoi den' posle sotsial'noi revoliutsii*, Petrograd 1917, p. 23.

18. *La révolte étudiante*, p. 63.

19. At first anti-reformism and anti-parliamentarism were the twin banners of new Left activists. In West Germany they rejected participation in the 'electoral circus' from the very beginning (*Die Zeit*, 30 May 1968). In Italy they strove to turn the universities into a 'minefield against reformism'. Such a position was appropriate to the moment of revolutionary onslaught, but when the struggle became less hot some activists lost interest in politics or swung to the right, and the most persistent resorted to terror. Nevertheless, many participants in the movement later 'discovered' reformism for themselves by joining the socialist parties. In West Germany, where the social democrats were moving ever further to the right, such a path was unthinkable. Because of this there appeared a 'second edition' of the New Left in the shape of the Green party, both reformist and parliamentary. A conservative British journal was forced to acknowledge that activists among the Greens, 'coming from the "extra-parliamentary opposition" of the late Sixties, are learning to work with profit and even pleasure, through the parliamentary system.... They certainly make Bonn politics less dull' (*The Spectator*, 27 October 1984, p. 13).

20. *Levoe studencheskoe dvizhenie v strankh kapitalizma*, p. 25. In the USA there was yet another factor: the hopes associated with the coming to power of John F. Kennedy were not justified, but the striving for change that this aroused pushed the youth to the left.

21. *Rinascita*, no. 18, 3 May 1968, p. 14.

22. *Sozialismus*, vol. 4, 1983, p. 27.

23. Typically, in local elections in Sweden, on the question of economic policy and nationalization social democratic candidates in local elections 'were closer to the communists than to leaders of conservative parties' (Charles F. Andrain, *Politics and Economic Policy in Western Democracies*, North Scituate, 1980).

24. *New Hungarian Quarterly*, no. 83, 1981, p. 111: from *Nepszabadsag*, 22 March 1981.

25. *Rinascita*, no. 18, 3 May 1968, p. 15.

26. Contat and Rybalka, p. 192. Sartre's political project, even if premature, was in its way prophetic. In the 1970s its basic features were accepted by the Socialist and, in part, by the Communist Party. The discussion centred around the slogan of 'revolution in the conditions of freedom', radical changes without blood-letting and an attempt to overcome the 'weaknesses and waning of social democracy and the limitations of communism in its Stalinist form' (*Combat*, 27 February 1948).

27. In France, the Unified Socialist Party (formed 1958–60); in Italy, the Socialist Party of Proletarian Unity (formed in 1964); in Denmark, the Socialist People's Party (founded in 1959); in Norway, the Socialist People's Party (formed in 1961). The French PSU later split and the major part poured into Mitterrand's renovated Socialist Party. The SPPU joined the Communist Party. In Denmark and Norway the SPP essentially played the role of a Eurocommunist force. In the mid-1970s the Norwegian SPP united with Left social democrats to form the Left Socialist Party. In Spain there existed the Socialist People's Party of E. Tierno Galvan, which joined the Spanish Socialist Workers' Party (PSOE) after the fall of Francoism. The Pacifist Socialist Party of Holland (1957) and the Finnish Socialist Workers' Party (1973) also deserve mention. We will confine ourselves to an analysis of the French PSU.

28. *Razmezhivaniya i sdvigi v sotsial-reformizme*, Moscow 1983, p. 42.

29. *Critique socialiste*, no. 38–39, 1980, p. 102.

30. *Razmezhivaniya i sdvigi v sotsial-reformizme*, p. 57.

31. The PCI leaders did not as a rule discuss the postponed revolution, but they acknowledged it. All of their tactics were derived precisely from this, and they expounded their principles quite openly from the 1960s. The British Left began to debate the problem of the postponed revolution later than others — in the 1980s. See Stuart Hall in *Socialist Register 1982*, London 1982.

32. P. Togliatti, *Izbrannye staťi i rechi*, vol. 2, Moscow 1965, p. 897.

33. *Cambio 16*, no. 647, 23 March 1984, p. 67.

34. *Der Spiegel*, no. 13, 1975, p. 97.

35. *Financial Times*, 8 October 1983, p. 28.

36. *L'Esprit*, no. 12, 1984, p. 117.

37. *The Economist*, no. 7382, 23 February 1985, p. 60.

38. *L'Espresso*, no. 50, 16 December 1984, p. 14.

39. *Burzhuaznyi i sotsial-demokraticheskii reformizm*, pp. 174–175.

40. On leaving the PSI, the left socialists of the SPPU opposed the enforced collaboration of the official party with a radical call to 'break with parliamentarism' (see *Mirovaya ekonomika i mezhdunarodnye otnosheniya*, no. 3, 1969, p. 121). The Communists were critical of these views, declaring that such a course meant 'a repudiation of the positive actions that can be carried out within the state and in

all its institutions through which the alignment of forces can be altered and definite shifts in the power structure achieved' (*L'Unita*, 13 September 1962).

41. *L'Unita*, 16 January 1984.

42. *Panorama*, no. 1017, 13 October 1985, p. 55.

43. A. Gorz, *Socialisme difficile*, Paris 1967, p. 71.

44. The Belgian Young Socialists, under the strong influence of the French Left, wrote that, although self-management is 'a long-term socialist aim', 'it is possible and necessary' to move in this direction 'now by relying in part on continually extending workers' control over the taking of decisions which directly affect them.' It should be understood that 'socialism is not built only or mainly "from above" but primarily "from below"' (*Le Socialisme*, no. 126, 1974, p. 558).

45. S. Mallet, *La nouvelle classe ouvrière*, Paris 1963, p. 19.

46. *Razmezhivaniya i sdvigi v sotsial-reformizme*, p. 35.

47. R. Miliband, *Parliamentary Socialism*, 2nd edn, London 1972, p. 318. Ernest Mandel maintained, in his time as a member of the Belgian Socialist Party, that structural reforms initiate a 'period of dual power' and will either be liquidated or 'reinforced by the proletariat achieving power and the socialization of the means of production managed by the workers themselves on a democractic basis' (*La Gauche*, 30 April 1966). It would be possible to say the same thing about social democratic reforms. There is nothing revolutionary in such a conception of reform. Genuine revolutionary reformism must realise such changes as cannot be liquidated by the ruling class without threatening to destabilize the whole system. This is the main difference between new and old, liberal–technocratic reformism. Reforms must be irreversible.

48. *New Left Review*, no. 115, May–June 1979, p. 82.

49. *L'Unité*, no. 25, 1974, p. 25.

50. *Politique aujourd'hui*, no. 1–2, 1972, p. 14. Giscard d'Estaing was at one with the Communists in suggesting that self-management provokes 'disorder and impotence' (V. Giscard d'Estaing, *Démocratie française*, Paris 1976, p. 88).

51. A Soviet author writes that the PSU turned into the 'intellectual shadow' of the renovated PS by fulfilling the role 'of its perpetual critic and supplier of cadres and ideas' (A.M. Salmin, *Promyshlennye rabochie Frantsii*, Moscow 1984, p. 236).

52. G. Ruffolo, a theoretician on the left wing of the Italian Socialist Party, underlines the need to create a 'new political force' embodying the spirit of the 'new reformism' on the basis of the existing workers' parties (*L'Espresso*, no. 41, 13 October 1985, p. 139). In his opinion this is the only way to repulse the Right's offensive and go over to the counterattack. Many figures in the PCI argue along the same lines. It is interesting that, as a rule, Left socialist currents are not closer to the official Communist leadership but to the Left opposition within the Communist Party. The '*Tribune communiste* group, having left the PCF, participated in 1960 in the founding of the PSU. In Italy, the '*Il Manifesto*' group which split away from the PCI held fruitful discussions with Left socialists. A number of figures from '*Il Manifesto*' and PSUI joined the PCI and went into its left wing.

53. *Le Partie pour la gauche*, Paris 1965, p. 28.

54. M. Charzat and G. Toutain, *Le CERES: Un Combat pour le socialisme*, Paris 1975, p. 1.

55. A. Rubbi, *I partiti comunisti dell'Europa Occidentale*, Milan 1978, p. 23.

56. *CERES par lui-même*, Paris 1979, p. 55.

57. *Razmezhivaniya i sdvigi v sotsial-reformizme*, p. 70.

58. *Faire*, no. 41, 1979, p. 11.

59. *Mitterrand, l'homme, les idées*, pp. 78-9.

60. P. Joxe, *Parti socialiste*, Paris 1973, p. 10.

61. G. Defferre, *Si demain la gauche ... Réponses a P. Desgraupes*, Paris 1977, p. 77. Socialist strategy was directed towards a prolonged period — 10-20 years. In a democratic society 'such time does not seem extraordinary' (ibid.).

62. M. Pedro Caro, *Las escesiones del PSOE y las intentas de reunificacion*, Barcelona 1980, p. 62.

63. *Razmezhivaniya i sdvigi v sotsial-reformizme*, p. 117. The emigré leadership of PSOE, which had quite right-wing positions, lost its control over activists within the country and was later removed (1974) and left the party. The ideologues of the new PSOE said that work to reorganize the party in underground conditions was 'extremely complex' (*El Socialista*, no. 76, 1976). But in fact these conditions made the task easier, for the radical wing had no ideological-bureaucratic apparatus to cope with.

64. Before the military coup of 1967 Greek socialists operated within the 'United Democratic Party' (EDA). In the period of its greatest success in 1963 EDA received 14.3 per cent of the vote. The new socialist party (PASOK) received 13.58 per cent in 1974, 25.32 per cent in 1977, and 48.06 per cent in 1981, when they won an absolute majority of seats in parliament. PASOK's rapid rise occurred, therefore, in a country with feeble socialist traditions. The majority of its voters (unlike those in France) had no experience of participation in the socialist movement. This applies even to a significant section of PASOK activists.

65. *El Socialista*, no. 58, 1976, p. 2.

66. *El Sistema*, no. 15, October 1976, p. 58.

67. Among branches subject to nationalization were energy, steel, food and pharmaceuticals, etc.

68. *Cambio 16*, 1977, no. 289, p. 17.

69. *El Sistema*, no. 35, 1980, p. 10.

70. *Sovremennaya Ispaniya*, Moscow 1983, p. 130.

71. *Voprosy Istorii*, no. 4, 1983, p. 56.

72. Medvedev, *Leninism*. This did not, however, prevent PSOE leaders from declaring that Trotskyists who joined their organization 'had made a mistake' (*Cambio 16*, no. 391, 3 March 1979, p. 23).

73. E. Diaz, *Notas para historia del pensiamento espanol actual, 1939-1973*, Madrid 1974, p. 152.

74. *Vida y obra de Marx y Engels*, Madrid 1979, p. 40.

75. J.M. Maraval declared that 'we must think more about political strategy than about ideological principles' (*Cambio 16*, no. 392, 10 June 1979). Gonzalez himself acknowledged that the discussion on Marxism appeared to be 'a departure from decisions and real problems' (*El Socialista*, 27 February 1979). But as a Soviet writer correctly notes it was precisely the party leader who 'aroused passions around Marxism as a theoretical and ideological problem' (I.V. Danilevich, *Sotsialisticheskie partii Ispanii i Portugalii*, Moscow 1984, p. 203).

76. *El Socialista*, 28 October 1981.
77. The leader of the Spanish Eurocommunists, J. Iglesias, wrote that the politics of PSOE 'from the very start led to the betrayal of the hopes for change which had united the broad social bloc which had ensured the party's triumph at the elections of 28th October 1982' (*El Pais*, 17 May 1984). As Iglesias correctly observed, the entire Left had to pay for this. For its part, the Communist Party, rent by factional struggle, could not advance a concrete alternative. By 1985 there were twenty-four communist parties and organizations in Spain, of which at least three (the 'official' party, Gallego's party and Carrillo's group) claimed an important portion of Left electors who had previously voted for the Communists. A former leader of the Communist Party, R. Tamames, founded his own 'Progressive Federation' under the slogan 'a new left for future renewal and progress' (*Cambio 16*, no. 719, 9 September 1985). Although the official party retained its leading position despite the rivalry of the breakaway groups, it could not overcome the crisis. Its leaders honestly conceded that they had 'no precise programme' (*El Pais*, 21 December 1984).
78. *The Economist*, 27 October 1984, p. 23. In 1985 public opinion polls on the whole demonstrated PSOE's success; very many people chose at subsequent elections to vote for the party again. But for all this a majority of Spaniards was unhappy with the government's activity, emphasizing that the Socialists had done rather less than they could. Up to 39 per cent of voters surveyed assessed the results of Gonzalez's policies as neither bad nor good. His policies were featureless and, unlike Mitterrand's in France, encountered no serious failures, but neither were there any serious achievements to go down in the annals of socialist reformism. The preparedness of a significant section of Spaniards to vote again for PSOE 'is explained', wrote *Cambio 16* with justification, 'not so much by the government's successes as by the lack of another political party capable of generating more trust' (*Cambio 16*, no. 726, 28 October 1985, p. 43).
79. E.P. Thompson, *Zero Option*, London 1982, p. 116.
80. *Panorama*, no. 917, 14 November 1983, p. 105.
81. *Le Monde*, 23 March 1985.
82. The demise of Papandreou's government was just as inglorious as its entire period in office had been. In 1989 it was forced to go to the polls in an atmosphere of political scandal while unsuccessfully trying to defend itself against accusations of corruption. As was anticipated, the result was a defeat for PASOK. But even in this situation the Right was unable to gather a sufficient number of votes to govern the country on its own and had to form an administration with the Communists!
83. *Razmezhivaniya i sdvigi v sotsial-reformizme*, p. 141. In Portugal many did not even know of the existence of the 'Union of Left forces'. The possibility of forces to the left of the official Socialist Party attracting electors was meanwhile demonstrated by the success of the Party of Democratic Renewal, which drew 15.68 per cent of its votes from the Socialists and 2.3 per cent from the Communists. The main victors proved to be the social democrats, who gained almost 30 per cent of the poll. This party's success can be explained by the fact that, in essence, it promised to follow the same polices but more competently. Thus in Portugal, as distinct from Spain, there existed an attractive alternative to the Socialist Party which had

lost face. The combination of cowardly moderation and incompetence led to the socialists losing their dominant position in Portuguese politics. The Social Democrats counterposed overtly technocratic policies, mixed with a quota of moralizing, to the featurelessness of preceding governments. 'This summons to purity and modernization received the approval of the Portuguese and won over an important section of the electorate and broad strata of society' (*Tiempo*, 21 October 1985, p. 116).

84. *Le Monde*, 8 October 1975.

85. A few other Stalinists groupings inserted isolated Eurocommunist slogans into their programmes in the 1970s. The programme of the Austrian CP announced that 'any road to socialism, supposing it can be followed [!], can only be democratic' (*Sozialismus im Oesterreichs Farben: Programm der KPO*, Vienna 1982, p. 43). Here one senses a clear desire to build a bridge between Stalinism and Eurocommunism.

86. *Der Spiegel*, no. 15, 1975, p. 102.

87. Diana Smith, 'The Alternative: Portuguese Communism', in Paolo Filo della Torre and others, eds, *Eurocommunism: Myth or Reality*, London 1979, p. 189.

88. The only surprising thing, in the opinion of most observers, was that this faction's weight was so 'insignificant' (*L'Espresso*, no. 6, 12 February 1984, p. 47). It was nevertheless a genuine opposition. At the PCI Congress in 1983, Cossuta's supporters gained 9 per cent of the vote and an intermediate current received around 15 per cent.

89. In Britain the Stalinists grouped around the *Morning Star* newspaper and the Eurocommunists around *Marxism Today*. Although the newspaper was continually losing readers and the journal was increasing its circulation and began to enjoy wide popularity, the Stalinists succeeded in seriously complicating the party's work. In 1984 the newspaper's editor, Tony Chater, and his deputy D. Whitehead, were expelled from the CPGB. In Finland, the party leadership were also forced (in 1984–85) to take organizational measures against Stalinists. In several cases new organizations were formed. The Stalinists walked out of the Left Party (Swedish communists) to found the Workers' Party (Swedish communists) in 1977. A similar split occurred in Spain and this led, as has already been said, to the immediate appearance of three parties. Alongside Gallego's overtly Stalinist party, groups outside the old organization included the semi-Stalinist group of former PCE General Secretary, Santiago Carrillo. In France, on the other hand, the Eurocommunist minority was to a significant extent forced out of the party and its leaders, after unsuccessful attempts to establish their own organization, converged with the socialists. The fate of Eurocommunism in Greece turned out tragically. While Papandreou and the Stalinist leaders were sitting it out in exile, the Eurocommunists were engaged in an underground struggle. In 1968 they founded the 'Internal Communist Party of Greece', but after the downfall of the military dictatorship in 1974 were unable to compete successfully with the powerful apparatuses of the Stalinists and PASOK.

90. *Panorama*, 11 April 1978, p. 55.

91. In 1976 youth gave A. Petrini (the future Socialist president) a stormy ovation. When he thanked his audience they replied 'we applaud you for what you said but we will vote for the Communists' (*Paese Sera*, 9 July 1976). B. Craxi, who had

begun a struggle against the PCI, succeeded in winning back a section of the reform-minded electorate. From 9.6 per cent of the vote in elections in the 1970s, the PSI share rose to 12 per cent in the early 1980s, but the unity of the Left was sacrificed.

92. A. Rubbi, *Partiti Communisti*, p. 10.

93. *L'Espresso*, no. 9, 6 February 1983, p. 8.

94. J.-P. Sartre, *Situations IX*, Paris 1972, pp. 128, 137–8. It should be remembered that Gramsci's ideas always determined the PCI's strategy. The party's policy from Gramsci and Togliatti to Berlinguer and Natti has been distinguished, according to general opinion, by an 'invariable continuity' (*Panorama*, no. 981, 3 February 1985, p. 45).

95. S. de Beauvoir, *La force des choses*, vol. 1, Paris 1963, p. 147.

96. As regards the PCF, even in the destalinization period its leadership acted in the spirit of Stalin. The Party's 22nd Congress proclaimed renewal but as the British Communist journal acknowledged it 'functioned, paradoxically, in the purest "Soviet" manner' (*Marxism Today*, August 1978, p. 268).

97. *Français, qui êtes-vous. La Documentation française*, Paris 1981, p. 40.

98. The rise in workers' standards of living induced some communists to speak of the disappearance of the proletariat. This is illiterate. The value of labour power and proletarianization are different things. It is curious that the proletariat is now growing against a background of a comparatively declining working class (in the old sense).

99. *Français, qui êtes-vous*, p. 67.

100. *Problemy sotsial-demokratii v issledovaniyakh uchenykh sotsialisticheskikh stran. Vypusk I. Referativnyi sbornik*, Moscow 1984, pp. 150–1. In France the Communists are the 'youngest' party, but they lag behind the Socialists in the number of young voters. In Holland, as the journal *International Viewpoint* notes, the Communists 'are concentrated in the old industries, such as shipbuilding and steel, which have been hard hit by the crisis' (*International Viewpoint*, 11 February 1985, p. 21).

101. The Stalinists' position in the Spanish workers' commissions is typical. Lenin called for the unions to be politicized, but the Stalinists from Gallego's party are only prepared 'to hold discussions on the minimum wage' (*Cambio 16*, no. 641, 12 March 1984, p. 43). This is a conscious repudiation of offensive reformism.

102. *Le Monde*, 7 April 1984.

103. *Italiya*, Moscow 1983, p. 298.

104. According to figures in *L'Espresso* no. 50, 16 December 1984, among workers the Christian Democrats occupied third place in popularity (6.6 per cent) after the PCI (43.6 per cent) and the socialists (13.5 per cent). 18.8 per cent, however, did not know which party they preferred. According to data from the same journal (no. 41, 13 Ocober 1985), workers and peasants constituted 23.7 per cent of Christian Democrat voters and 35 per cent of PCI voters. Although there is an undoubted preponderance of workers among Communist voters (as there is a preponderance of pensioners among Christian Democrat voters), it cannot be said to be overwhelming.

105. S. Vasil'tsev, *Rabochii klass i obshchestvennoe soznanie*, Moscow 1983, p. 134.

106. *Le Monde*, 24 October 1984.

107. The British Eurocommunist journal justifiably remarked that in general Stalinist

parties have no 'detailed strategy for the advance to socialism' (*Marxism Today*, August 1978, p. 239).

108. R. Aron, *Le Spectateur Engagé*, Paris 1981, p. 338.

109. Despite its Stalinization, the PCF felt some lasting effects of Eurocommunism. The leadership's Stalinism encountered internal opposition, and not only on the part of intellectuals. In October 1983 a right-wing French journal established with amazement that 'the Communists are rather more divided than the Socialists' (*Le Point*, no. 585, 1983, p. 35).

110. See the article by Jon Bloomfield in *Marxism Today*, April 1984, pp. 25–9. The theme of Stalinism is frequently encountered in discussions among Labour Party members, and they accuse each other of precisely this. They sometimes try to defend Stalin. Thus the miners' leader, Arthur Scargill, has, in his time, carefully distanced himself from Eurocommunism. In an interview with John Mortimer he has declared that he 'objected to the moving of Stalin's body outside the Mausoleum and changing the name of Stalingrad' (J. Mortimer, *In Character*, London 1984, p. 66).

111. *The Listener*, 1 March 1984, p. 13.

112. *Marxism Today*, January 1985, p. 14.

113. *The Listener*, 1 March 1984, p. 14. Tony Benn, starting out from this logic, endeavoured to present the collapse of the Labour Party at the 1983 Elections as an 'outstanding achievement' since the Party had 'for the first time since 1945' come out with the correct slogans and, despite this, had still been able to poll several million votes (see *The Guardian*, 10 June 1983).

114. In their anti-European stance the 'hard Left' closed ranks with right-wing Conservatives. A reader of *Tribune* remarked that it had not even thought through 'the class and socialist consequences of its anti-European prejudices' (*Tribune*, 6 April 1984, p. 10).

115. *Socialismo reale e terza via*, Roma 1982, p. 25.

116. J. Attali, *La nouvelle économie française*, Paris 1978, p. 17.

117. *New Left Review*, no. 140, July–August 1983, p. 32.

118. *New Socialist*, November 1984, p. 41.

119. *Razmezhivaniya i sdvigi v sotsial-reformizme*, pp. 256–7.

120. In the 1970s, German social democracy underwent a fundamental but not total technocratization. The crisis of pragmatism therefore dealt it a severe but not fatal blow.

121. *Der Spiegel*, no. 35, 26 August 1974, p. 44.

122. *Razmezhivaniya i sdvigi v sotsial-reformizme*, p. 209.

123. Observing the congress of the Spanish Greens, journalists came to the conclusion that it all produced 'a very unserious impression' (*Mundo obrero*, 28 February 1985, p. 14). A similar picture could be drawn in Italy, France and Britain.

124. *Grünes Info*, no. 12, 1984, p. 9.

125. P. Kelly, *Fighting For Hope*, London 1983, pp. 11–14, 70, 56.

126. *Tribune*, 23 March 1984, p. 10.

127. *Grünes Info*, no. 12, 1984, p. 8. Rudolf Bahro declared in defence of his party's economic policy that it had a 'left social democratic programme' (R. Bahro, *From Red to Green*, London 1984, p. 171). But why is this necessary if there are already Left social democrats? In fact the documents of the Greens combine 'fundam-

entalist' radical slogans and moderate practical proposals, without any link between the two. Theoreticians like Bahro bear not a small part of the responsibility for this hopeless situation.

128. *Tribune*, 23 March 1984, p. 10.

129. *VIII s'ezd KPYa*, Moscow 1961, p. 294.

130. The Japanese CP was not only enunciating pluralistic principles back in 1970, declaring its readiness to co-exist with an opposition even after the victory of socialism, but it has been in conflict with Moscow since the 1960s over the question of sovereignty over the South Kurile Islands. Marxists exerted a strong influence in the Socialist Party. The 'Socialism Society' in the Socialist Party is a Japanese version of CERES.

131. I. Tsvetova, *Bor'ba demokraticheskikh sil Yaponii za formirovanie edinogo fronta*, Moscow 1984, p. 69.

132. *Cahiers marxistes*, no. 111, 1983, pp. 10–11. It is necessary to recall, with regard to the technological revolution, the discussion on the future of surplus value. Some authors assert that it will disappear with automation and profit, and capitalism along with it. Others insist that profit is not dependent on surplus value (see *New Left Review*, no. 151, 1985). In fact science, as Marx predicted, has become an indirect productive force. A significant portion of surplus value will be produced by scientific and engineering labour and then redistributed. The technological revolution, accompanied by the disappearance of entire professions, mass unemployment and the weakening of trade unions, has induced moods of panic and 'neo-Luddism' in a section of the Left. As a matter of fact mankind has already experienced an analogous process at the time of the great industrial revolution in the nineteenth century after the introduction of steam power. All the problems were very similar. It is no accident that the bourgeoisie in the period of the new technological revolution are striving to return to the methods of classical nineteenth-century capitalism. But now as then the proletariat, forced into temporary retreat, will regain control of the situation and re-establish its influence.

133. F. Borella, *Les parties politiques en Europe*, Paris 1984, p. 134.

134. See *Le Monde*, 7 April 1984. The French press later acknowledged that not one region of the country 'had received such help and support for industrial reorganization' as Lotharingia under the Socialists (*Le Monde*, 5 April 1985, p. 24). When discussing the problems of technological restructuring in France the European Community's technological project 'Eureka' should be recalled — a project promoted precisely by Mitterrand's government.

135. For figures see MEMO, *Ekonomicheskoe polozhenie kapitalisticheskikh i razvivaiush-chikhsya stran; prilozhenie. Obzor za 1982-83. Sotsial-demokratiya i sovremennyi krizis kapitalizma*, Moscow 1983, pt. 2, and also *The Economist*, 16 February 1985. Paradoxically, the success of nationalization disconcerted the Left socialists, who were afraid that profitable firms would be more easily denationalized. This is a clear case of defeatism.

136. *Nouvelle revue socialiste*, no. 22, 1977, p. 9.

137. *L'Esprit*, no. 12, 1984, pp. 93, 61. Compare *Le Monde*, 7 April 1984.

138. The principal question is: what measures can a Left government carry out to modernize capitalism that are not at the workers' expense?

139. *L'Esprit*, no. 12, 1984, p. 115.

140. *Le Monde*, 12 July 1983.

141. *Daily Telegraph*, 16 March 1984.

142. Jacques Delors calls this a 'new dynamic compromise' (*L'Esprit*, no. 12, 1984, p. 123).

143. *Le Monde*, 13 December 1984.

144. Mitterrand did not put an end to the polarization between Left and Right by introducing proportional representation, as his critics claim, but created a situation where a small majority at the polls was insufficient for radical change and the consent of at least two thirds of society were needed. This is an important guarantee against irresponsible counter-reformism from the Right. The Left will also run into this problem at a later date. Achieving changes will be more difficult, but it will also be more difficult to eliminate their consequences.

145. The Soviet political scientist, B.P. Kurashvili, considers a counter-offensive by reaction after every major success by the Left to be inevitable and sees in this a law of political struggle: alternating attack and defence. See B.P. Kurashvili, *Politicheskaya bor'ba i ee zakonomernosti Ezhegodnik Sovietskoi assosiatsii politicheskikh nauk*, Moscow 1979. The Scandinavian sociologist, Göran Therborn, notes that the Right's counterattack forces the Left to rate social democracy's achievements more highly. Contrary to the opinion of radical theoreticians in the 1960s, the redistribution of income and social legislation 'has not meant the final integration of the working class' into the capitalist system, and the bourgeoisie's attacks on this legislation are proof of this. 'The stakes in this battle are high and serious, but instead of whimpering at blows received, the Labour Left should be aware that it is being attacked in positions of strength' (G. Therborn, "Classes and States: Welfare State Developments, 1881-1981', in *Studies in Political Economy — A Socialist Review*, no. 14, Summer 1984, p. 36).

Poland: Reformist Revolution

It is evidently a universal historical law that the more conservative the rulers, the more decisive and aggressive the opposition. Prolonged periods of a conservative course lead to the accumulation of social tensions, which cannot usually be alleviated at a later date. Liberal half-measures implemented after a delay can no longer avert the explosion. De Tocqueville remarked that revolution occurs at the moment of untimely reform. The fact is that, in certain conditions, even reformist forces begin to act in a revolutionary manner, for they are left with no other way out. The events in Hungary in 1956 and Czechoslovakia in 1968 are striking examples of this.

On the whole the mass opposition movements in Eastern Europe have always assumed a revolutionary–reformist character in both ideology and political practice. Reform developed into revolution because revolutionary means were required for the successful implementation of reforms. But, in its turn, the mass movement suffered defeat when it went beyond its own historical tasks. Objective conditions in Eastern Europe render impossible the complete victory of democratic socialism in 'small countries' until such time as profound socio-political changes have occurred in the global centres. The 20th Congress of the CPSU created the illusion of such changes and assisted the rise of the liberation movement in Poland and Hungary. But on the whole, the character of the mutual relations and mutual dependence of the Eastern European countries has not changed sufficiently during the thirty years since then to allow a revolution to succeed in a single, isolated country. The real task has been the struggle for reforms. But in most cases, the extreme conservatism of the ruling statocratic groups has pushed reformists onto the road of revolutionary action. A vicious circle has been created; a truly tragic situation. Nevertheless, the working masses in Eastern Europe have sometimes managed to achieve substantial successes. Without the unsuccessful uprising in Hungary in 1956, Kadar's reformist course would not have been possible in the late 1960s and 1970s. The struggle was tragic but not useless.

This is almost unanimously acknowledged by specialists both in Hungary and abroad:

> The very intensity of the uprising and the loss of life that ensued served to bring the Hungarians together in a resolve that such a tragedy must never be allowed to occur in Hungary again. Somehow, a consensus was created and almost everyone agreed to limit their demands and accept a compromise.[1]

In order to strengthen the statocratic regime in Hungary, Kadar implemented some of the demands of the revolutionary programme of 1956, with the blessing of Khrushchev, Andropov and Brezhnev. In a sense, restoration proved a continuation of the revolution. This brings to mind Gramsci's words on 'passive revolutions' or 'revolutions–restorations' 'which in fact progressively modify the pre-existing composition of forces, and hence become the matrix of new changes.'[2] It was crucial in this case that the successful reforms received their initial impulse from the revolutionary events of 1956.

The most interesting case is not Hungary, however, but Poland. Poland has always been the model country of class struggle in Eastern Europe, as France has in the West. The 1980–81 revolution in Poland attracted the attention of the whole world, but the numerous appraisals and commentaries have often been superficial. It cannot be said that everything that happened in Poland in this period has been sufficiently well studied and understood. In order to analyse what occurred and draw the necessary historical lessons, the revolution's prehistory must be recalled. The events of 1980 were a long time in the making. The preparation began in 1956 for the explosion which was to rock all of Eastern Europe a quarter of a century later.

There is probably not a single country in this region where the order implanted after the Second World War met with such opposition as Poland. The armed struggle against the government was, in the words of the eminent Polish Marxist Wlodzimierz Brus, 'reminiscent of a civil war'.[3] The most serious resistance was encountered in the countryside where the peasants fought collectivization. Its consequences in Eastern

Europe were not so grave as in the Soviet Union, and the measures through which it was implemented not so rigid, but nevertheless, as the British Marxist Chris Harman emphasizes, 'everywhere the result was stagnation and even a fall in total agricultural output.[4] The sole and evident exception was Bulgaria, where collectivization not only encountered no serious opposition but even proved successful in a purely economic sense. In Poland, on the other hand, the peasants' unwillingness to subordinate themselves to government policy was so strong that by 1955 the state-cooperative sector encompassed all of 34 per cent of agriculture.

Nevertheless, the government of 'people's democracy' in Poland endeavoured with all its might to copy Stalin's policy of the 1930s, ignoring not just the protests of the people but objective socio-economic factors. Brus remarks that:

> The People's Democracies which were at a higher level of economic development, did not have to start from scratch and were consequently able, even in a period of accelerated industrialisation, to utilize more complete and effective methods of planning, implement a more balanced agrarian policy and attract experts not just on the basis of party.[5]

In practice, the Polish government contrived not only to repeat but to surpass many of Stalin's mistakes in the economic field. Some figures in the Polish United Workers' Party (PUWP) who favoured a 'national road to socialism' were accused of sympathizing with the Yugoslav revisionists and subjected to repression. Among the leaders dismissed and arrested was the Party's General Secretary, Wladislaw Gomulka, who had to spend three years in jail because of differences over the question of collectivization.

Although Poland remained one of the least developed Eastern European countries, it could not be called backward. As early as the 1930s Soviet specialists had placed it in the group of countries with 'an average level of capitalist development.' In 1937 the working class comprised 858,800 people, but the proletariat was concentrated in a few traditional industrial areas, where the continuity of the workers' movement was maintained. Before the Second World War, town-dwellers already comprised 30 per cent of all the state's inhabitants.

During the War Poland probably suffered more than any other country in Europe. But by way of compensation, it gained the highly developed regions of East Prussia, Silesia, East Pomerania and Gdansk.

This made the rapid growth of industry possible. By 1953, mechanical engineering production exceeded the pre-war level almost seven-fold, and the number of workers reached 2.5 million. By volume of industrial production, Poland was in fifth place in Europe.

But the standard of living remained extremely low, and economic inefficiency was staggering. Poland was distinguished among all the countries of the Eastern bloc, primarily by the grotesque incompetence of its bureaucracy, which had turned planning into a perfect farce. The cost of living rose swiftly. From 1950 to 1955, the prices of consumer goods rose on average by 80 per cent (in Hungary by 70 per cent, in Czechoslovakia by 20 per cent, in Romania by 17 per cent, etc.). Of course, price rises were in no way the cause of the crisis in Hungary and Poland in 1956, but social tension naturally increased particularly in precisely those countries where the government cared least for the workers' living standards. Moreover, inequality in Poland was more striking than in other countries. 'Closed' shops for party apparatchiks and other privileges of the statocracy were a particular source of indignation for workers called upon to tighten their belts. What is more, the Polish ruling circles, far from concealing their wealth, flaunted it.

After the 20th Congress of the CPSU, a sharp and open struggle flared up between Stalinists and reformists within the ruling group of the PUWP itself. The first steps along the path of liberalization were very timid. While the broad masses simply did not notice them, some hopes were aroused among the intelligentsia. Shifts began to occur in the middle strata, making them politically more active. The crisis became more acute. The workers, at first indifferent to the reforms and even mistrustful of them, were drawn into politics. The struggle among the groups at the top began to affect those at the bottom. In Poznan in the summer of 1956, there was an uprising, cruelly suppressed by the army and police. By autumn, virtually the whole country was in the grip of strikes. The split in the ruling statocracy became so acute that the Stalinists were prepared to resort to a military coup. Troops moved into Warsaw. For his part, Gomulka, released from imprisonment and heading the PUWP's reformist faction, threatened to distribute arms to the workers. It was like a civil war. The party–state apparatus was patently falling to pieces. In Moscow there was manifest disquiet. *Pravda* published articles about 'anti-socialist' agitation in Poland.

At the last moment, Gomulka succeeded in obtaining the Stalinists' capitulation. After some vacillation, Khrushchev supported the new Polish leadership. The strikes slowly abated and the government established total control over the situation. The working class was unorganized and its political consciousness weakly developed. In those years, comments K. Pomian, 'official ideology or, if you prefer, communist rhetoric, still seemed convincing.'[6] Social factors played a no less important role. The skilled working class was small in numbers and the majority of workers were from the countryside. Gomulka was able to conclude an agreement with the Catholic Episcopate. Western observers wrote with justification that the Church 'greatly contributed to the consolidation of his position among the people, if not within his Party.'[7] For its part, the government permitted the teaching of God's law in schools and authorized the building of 220 new churches after 1956. For those from the countryside who were accustomed to trust the words of the priest more than the newspaper or radio, this was a very persuasive argument.

In their turn, left-wing circles and the organs of the press — which in fact turned out to be under their control during this stormy period — conducted a fierce polemic against Catholicism. The youth journal *Po Prostu* simultaneously attacked both Stalinists and the Church and the ideologue of the 'October Left', Leszek Kolakowski, accused by the official organs of revisionism and other sins, was actively engaged in anti-religious propaganda. The Polish socialist theoretician, Adam Michnik, later acknowledged that 'a lack of understanding of the Church's functions in social life' and of 'the role of Catholicism in the national culture' was typical of the Left.[8] Even as Gomulka's reconciliation with the Church was strengthening his influence over the workers, the socialist opposition, imprisoned by its own dogmas, lost all contact with the masses.

Having gained the upper hand over his opponents on both Left and Right and repaired relations with the Church and Moscow, Gomulka and the reformist groups in the statocracy behind him were able to implement their programme. Real changes, however, proved extremely modest. At first Gomulka embarked on a whole series of steps in response to the spontaneous demands of the masses. Economic reform was initiated and in several enterprises workers' councils were established by way of an 'experiment'. In truth, these councils had in fact been organized by the workers themselves on the spur of the moment during the strikes, and Gomulka merely legalized them. As the government's position gained in strength, the powers of workers' self-management gradually diminished until the councils were reduced to a pure fiction.

Gomulka's most important reformist measure was the actual decollectivization of the countryside. When peasants gained the right to leave co-operatives, 90 per cent of collective agriculture collapsed. Additionally, the Party apparatus was purged of Stalinists. The liberal publicist, A. Werblan, even wrote later of the '1956 revolution in cadres'.[9] This all created the impression of real destalinization and reinforced Gomulka's position still further. Brus writes that 'by the end of 1956, Poland had become a country further removed from Stalinism than the others and, for some time, it seemed that it was travelling along a new road.'[10] It was not long before this illusion had to be abandoned. By 1957, the assault had already begun on the workers' gains. The journal *Po Prostu* noted with alarm that workers' councils were being subordinated 'to the central apparatus, which the working class is in no position to control.'[11] A little later it was the turn of the intelligentsia to come under attack. *Po Prostu* was closed down and the editorial board of *Nowa Kultura*, another stronghold of the 'October Left', was disbanded. By 1960–62 the press was once again totally subordinate to the apparatus.

The chief conclusion drawn by the Polish Left from the 1956 events was that the temporary victories of 'society's unorganized forces' over the state do not alter the situation if no 'continual, general and organized response' is directed against the government.[12] While such an assessment is certainly correct, many important questions remained unanswered. First, why in 1956 did a liberal wing come into being, within the ruling elite itself, which was prepared to take decisive action against the Stalinists? Second, why did these same liberals so easily reach an accord with the Stalinists once they had seized power? Finally, why did no such reconciliation happen in Hungary in 1956 and in Czechoslovakia in 1968?

It is clear that the ruling elite was not united. The structure of the ruling class community is sufficiently complex for each country to have its own peculiarities even if the basic model is the same. In one sense, the word statocracy denotes the aggregate of the privileged higher levels of the party–state apparatus: but contradictions exist within the apparatus itself, and the balance of forces between groups changes quite frequently. The whole history of Poland is testimony to this. Higher party functionaries have little responsibility but enjoy considerable rights, and this impels some strata of the economic bureaucracy to insist on a more equitible distribution of power. Moreover, within the party apparatus itself the central organs are more inclined towards reformism for, as was noted in one of the documents of the Polish opposition, they 'would not initially interpret these reforms as a restriction on the limits of their own power; on the contrary, the reforms would free them from the continual effort to supply the population with food and essential commodities.'[13] The central apparatus includes the most cultured and competent section of the bureaucracy and conflicts have therefore periodically arisen between the organs in Warsaw and the regional committees of the PUWP. One way or another, the centre must take national interests into account, but in the provinces perspectives are limited to local interests. Because of this the provincial bureaucracy, if it is united, defends only its corporate interests at a national level, opposing both the capital's politicians and society as a whole. It has its own people in the central apparatus, just as in the provinces there are isolated, 'renegade' reform-ists. The monolithism of the apparatus is an illusion. In reality it is a structure that combines disparate groups which, in a period of crisis, begin to fight among themselves.

Serious skirmishes cannot be kept within the confines of the apparatus, leaving the masses unaffected. The reformists, as the weaker side, are sooner or later forced to seek outside support, albeit at lower levels of the same apparatus. Even if the reformists are successful, as was the case in Poland in 1956, in seizing the key posts, the resistance of the provincial oligarchies is so great that it cannot be broken without bitter conflict. Moreover, reforms need an ideological foundation, and con-sequently the assistance of the intelligentsia is required. Broader and broader layers are drawn into the struggle. *In the final instance*, political events involve the working class.

Although the workers are the last to take the political stage, their appearance brings about sharp changes in the character of events. The struggle of factions becomes the struggle of classes. The movement becomes broader and more radical than its instigators wished. Not only the position of conservative groups, but the whole structure of class relations is threatened. Under these conditions many reformists fall into the arms of the conservatives. Yesterday's antagonists project a united front against the forces they themselves have awoken. But it is not so simple to stop the process once it has begun. The genie has been released from the bottle. A pebble thrown from a hilltop causes a gigantic landslide, an avalanche sweeping everything before it. A revolution begins. What is surprising is not that many are frightened, but that many reformists, like Imre Nagy, have the courage and honour to go even further with the people. Here we might recall Marx's idea that ruling class ideologists go over to the side of the proletariat, not out of mercenary motives, but because the logic of their own ideas pushes them to do so. In other words, if reformists defend the idea of 'perfecting socialism', and make reference one way or another to Marxism, people's democracy and socialist ideals, it is conceivable that they will, in the end, stand alongside those who do indeed fight for socialism and democracy (although denying the system the right to call itself a 'people's democracy' or 'socialist'). For an individual, personal honour may well prove a stronger stimulus than class egoism.

The particularity of the 1956 Polish October was that the bureaucracy was able, through its ideological hegemony, to prevent the revolutionary-reformist process from becoming an avalanche. But the crisis of 1956 was only the commencement of a whole series of shocks which followed one another with increasing frequency. Since the questions raised in 1956 were not resolved by compromise (as in Hungary), while conservative forces did not succeed in gaining a total victory (as in Czechoslovakia), periodic crises became inevitable.[14] Changes in political line were always agonizing. Werblan wrote that 'it was a characteristic feature that attempts to correct an outworn policy were each time undertaken with the greatest possible delay and, at the same time, with the least possible consistency.'[15] Becoming detached from real life is in general inevitable in large bureaucratic structures, in which extreme inertia is typical. Where there is no freedom of expression and of the press, it becomes impossible to pose and discuss painful questions at the proper time.

The Polish intelligentsia continued to try and vindicate the ideals of 1956, but found no common language with the masses. Continual failure provoked confusion and apathy among intellectuals. Many broke with the Left opposition, and Marxists became an insignificant minority. When the leaders of the Left, Kuron and Modzelewski, were prosecuted for their 'Open Letter to the Party', neither students nor university lecturers supported them. 'The views of Kuron and Modzelewski', remarked two participants in the events, 'were condemned on every hand.'[16]

The situation changed only in March 1968, under the influence of events in Czechoslovakia. The socialist historian, Adam Michnik, had become incredibly popular among students. When he was victimized, a four-thousand-strong demonstration was organized in protest. The students' programme borrowed its ideas from the 'October Left' and the 'Prague Spring'. Its basic point was 'a consistent transition to democratic socialism.'[17] No specific social and economic demands were advanced, however, and the everyday problems of the working class were simply a closed book to student activists.

Despite the repressions, demonstrations continued for about a week, gripping the cities of Lodz, Poznan, Wroclaw, Katowice and Cracow. Kuron and Modzelewski, who had just been released from prison, were re-arrested. In an attempt to provoke a quarrel between workers and the intelligentsia, the official press launched an anti-semitic campaign. The Party organ *Trybuna Ludu* published a list of Jewish 'instigators' to show that the protests were inspired by Zionists. Of the 25,000 Jews who remained at that time in Poland (0.01 per cent of the population), more than half were forced to emigrate to Israel in the summer of 1968.[18]

On the whole, Gomulka was successful once again. The student actions failed to gain the support of the workers and were suppressed. Differences which had arisen between workers and intellectuals had an impact over a prolonged period of time. All the same, things were certainly not going well for the government. Social tension was on the increase. Despite its name, the PUWP had never in reality been a workers' party, and had never enjoyed effective control over the working class. The smouldering conflict between the proletariat and 'its' party was never extinguished even during the 'quiet' years. Gomulka's only solution was to create 'complaints commissions' under the auspices of Party committees in order to ease discontent.

The economic situation was continually deteriorating. The capital-output coefficient for the period 1951–63 fell from 0.373 to 0.201. Although this problem confronted all the countries of Eastern Europe, including the Soviet Union, it was particularly acute in Poland. The general volume of investments had to be constantly increased (from 271 billion zloty in 1955–58 to 501 billion in 1959–63) to compensate for their continually decreasing effectiveness. Polish planning fell into the same trap as do all centralized bureaucratic systems at a definite historical stage. The only way to finance the swelling investment programme was through a drop in the living standards of the population. President Bierut had hoped, through intensified exploitation of the 'collectivized' countryside, to secure the resources both to create heavy industry and to maintain living standards in the cities. The repudiation of collectivization made such a policy unrealizable, but the creation of heavy industry remained a goal. Gomulka was left with no other alternative than to make the workers pay for his industrialization programme. The difficulty was that such a policy provoked a breakdown in workers' discipline, a standstill in labour productivity, and political discontent. As one researcher puts it, 'stabilization turned into stagnation'.[19] The five-year plan of 1966–70 ended in utter failure. Investment was insufficient, deficits were widening, exports were not growing and the volume of production was increasing extremely slowly. Between 1956 and 1964 real wages had grown on average by 2 per cent per annum, but by the end of the 1960s they had begun to fall. In order to limit workers' consumption the government froze wages while simultaneously raising prices (by 41 per cent over five years).

Agriculture was in lamentable shape. A specialist joked that in their agricultural policy the Polish rulers 'were able to combine the worst features of both socialism and capitalism.'[20] Private holdings remained under strict centralized control but nobody paid for the losses frequently engendered by errors in planning. All investments were earmarked for the extremely inefficient state enterprises and the peasant sector fell gradually into decline. The youth left the countryside for the city, which in turn aggravated the food problem. 'Bad harvests', writes a British historian, 'brought this imbalance, a recurrent plague of the Polish post-war economy, into crisis during 1970.'[21] The ruling group itself lost faith not only in its own ideas but also in its capacity to achieve any sort of real results. True, the country was silent after the suppression of the student demonstrations in 1968. But this was the calm before the storm.

On Saturday 12 December, 1970 food prices were raised by 20 per cent. As a form of 'compensation', prices on some very expensive goods were cut. A new system of wage-rates was simultaneously introduced in productive industry. Workers in Gdansk and neighbouring cities on the Baltic coast were the first to voice their disagreement with the government's measures. The following Monday they organized a protest meeting instead of working, and then marched to the local Party committee building. The police charged the demonstrators and a battle began on the streets.

The struggle lasted several days. The police used firearms. Crowds of workers in Szczecin, singing the 'Internationale', came out in a demonstration of solidarity with their Gdansk comrades. They were met with a hail of bullets. According to official figures, seventeen were killed. And still the resistance did not cease. Strikes began in Silesia, Nowa Huta and other places. In Warsaw the decision to strike from Monday 21 December was taken in many enterprises. But this was no longer necessary. Gomulka's government had fallen.

The dominant group had had to sacrifice Gomulka and his immediate circle to avoid taking overall responsibility. In this sense the reaction at the top was exactly the same as in 1956. However, this time the workers' movement was notable for its much greater breadth and, most importantly, its deeper class consciousness. Werblan acknowledges that in 1970 the 'repudiation of violence against the masses' was in the forefront of demands. The new leader of the PUWP, Edward Gierek — considered a liberal (like Gomulka in 1956), and dependent on the technocratic current in the Party — promised the workers he would meet their conditions. On assuming office he declared that:

> The iron law of our economic policy and of our policy in general must always be the taking into account of reality, broad consultation with the working class and intelligentsia, observation of the principles of collectivity and democracy in the life of the Party and in the actions of its leading organs.

He promised to find 'a common language with the workers.'[23]

After the fall of Gomulka the strikes temporarily subsided, but in January 1971 a new crisis arose. Gierek himself travelled to Gdansk, persuaded the workers to return to their benches, promised reforms and, in the end, got his own way. The rapid implementation of a reform of planning and management was announced, along with a 'financial–economic reform'.[24] The programme of these reforms was not entirely clear even to the government itself. The official newspapers wrote primarily of the need for 'an effective overhaul of the state machine so that it can serve the people more successfully' and of the need to study public opinion. One government publicist even declared: 'Truth is not a luxury. Speaking the truth is a social necessity.'[25]

Life in Poland undoubtedly became freer after 1970 (as it did after 1956). In a sense, each new Polish government was better than its predecessor. But liberalization remained extremely limited, and the government was chiefly concerned with containing the spontaneous process and re-establishing control over public life. It should be noted that despite its economic incompetence, the Polish ruling class displayed great political skill. By changing personnel and programme it always regained control when this was slipping away from it and it did so, to use Gramsci's words, 'with greater speed than is achieved by the subordinate classes.'[26] The workers' leaders reached agreement with Gierek on some of their demands, but as the workers possessed no independent organization, they were unable to consolidate their success. Gierek, for his part, did not perhaps consciously intend to deceive the workers; but he proved to be a hostage of his own class. His liberal declarations were irresponsible, for the technocrats on whom he depended were a very long way from genuine liberalism. The very structure of the apparatus is so inimical to democracy that in normal conditions it is practically impossible to carry out any sort of liberal action with its assistance.

Each new reformist programme brought the country closer to the line beyond which begins what Kolakowski has called 'the ruling class's partial expropriation.'[27] The apparatus will not allow itself to be deprived of its rights without a struggle, just as the bourgeoisie does not give up its property voluntarily. To take away these prerogatives is an extremely difficult task, but to expect the apparatus itself to carry it out is quite absurd. Naturally, then, as soon as the pressure from below began to slacken the reformist programmes ceased to be carried out in Poland.

Gierek really did want changes. As Brus has acknowledged, the quest for new economic methods 'became more assiduous' after 1970.[28] The new leader removed those opposed to reforms from the highest echelons of power, replacing ten out of nineteen provincial leaders and a third of the members of the Politburo, Central Committee and Sejm. Unfortunately, the people who replaced them were products of the same apparatus. 'Thus', wrote Werblan, 'a ruling elite came into being with populist inclinations and provincial horizons.'[29] In its efforts to continue industrialization, the new leadership did not wish to resort either to lowering the people's living standards or to radical reforms. Nor could it stray very far from the path chosen in Moscow by the Brezhnev group, whose goal was to stabilize social structures. Gierek therefore gambled on foreign credits. The Swiss Communist newspaper termed this 'a strategy of imported growth',[30] but the opposition protested against the fact that the leadership was trying to compensate for 'the inefficiency of the system and the ineffectiveness of economic policy' by resorting to aid from 'capitalist bankers'.[31] At first, meanwhile, everything seemed to be going brilliantly. Credit in the early 1970s was cheap. Gierek's programme, it seemed, would achieve great results without big sacrifices. The people's living standards could even rise.

Loans enabled the newest technology to be bought in the West. It was proposed to increase reserves of hard currency and pay off the debts through a subsequent expansion of the export of modern industrial goods. It seemed like an adventure from the very beginning, but an attractive adventure. Over eight years, national income rose by 60 per cent, the productivity of labour increased and two-thirds of industrial machinery was renewed. As Western experts acknowledged, 'such a situation was unprecedented in Europe.'[32] Moreover Gomulka's price increases were revoked and prices remained roughly at the 1967 level.

According to some estimates real wages increased by 40 per cent in the first years of Gierek's administration. The only problem was that workers' incomes were not matched by commodities. The volume of production rose appreciably more slowly than the purchasing power of the people. By 1980 consumer goods constituted 26 per cent of Gross National Product, which according to official economists was 'lower than at the beginning of the 1970s'.[33]

The opportunities for social manoeuvring by the government in such a situation were limited. A new rise in prices was essential, but it was postponed: as a Western Communist newspaper correctly observed, food prices in Eastern Europe are 'political prices'.[34] A sharp increase in agricultural production was also out of the question, for in the first place all investments had been swallowed up to re-equip industry, and secondly the system's inefficiency had told on this sector most of all. Inflation was temporarily held in check but the problem remained unsolved. Moreover, as Neal Ascherson notes, Western inflation was imported 'in the cost of each machine-tool from West Germany or Sweden.'[35]

Enterprises were being brought into the system behind schedule, and imports were growing faster than exports. Poland's indebtedness to the West was increasing at a catastrophic rate, exceeding $20 billion by 1980. The capitalist crisis hit Poland badly. Foreign markets contracted and imports and credit became much dearer. Goods produced by Polish plants with Western technology proved to be of unexpectedly poor quality. Because of industry's lack of competitiveness, hard currency had to be obtained by exporting foodstuffs, which further exacerbated the position on the internal market.[36]

Not all objective conditions were quite so bad. Poland's military expenditure was still lower than that of its neighbours, the Soviet Union and East Germany, and the import of raw materials from the USSR had allowed $3.5 billion to be saved over the years 1976–80. Khrushchev had granted Poland additional aid in the form of 'compensation for past injustices'.[37] Nevertheless, Gierek's administration was unable to cope with the growing difficulties. The top bureaucracy had lost faith in itself. The demoralization of the apparatus provoked general corruption, which reached such a scale that Gierek's system began to be called the 'kleptocracy'.

In the absence of the necessary structural reforms, Gierek's new course proved just as ineffectual as Gomulka's policy. True, some kinds of reform were implemented. In 1973, the partial decentralization of planning was carried out and a 'new economic and financial system' was announced. But these measures did not affect fundamental economic principles; they simply gave an opening for the arbitrary initiative of regional Party committees. The power vacuum formed in the process of decentralization was filled not by widening real opportunities for managers but by the arbitrariness of local Party bosses. In order to resolve this problem Gierek implemented an administrative reform, creating forty-nine small provinces in place of the seventeen large ones. But this only made the situation worse. Local interests in planning began to take clear precedence over national.

The attempt to expand the independence of production associations ended in the same failure. The new rights were insufficient for effective management but perfectly sufficient to bring about an unjustified rise in prices and increase in inflation. Prices in production no longer expressed the correlation of supply and demand in the market and the cost of production, but the alignment of forces between administrative-bureaucratic groups and the political authority of association leaders. As Brus remarks:

> The strategy of gradually implementing the reforms assisted their demise. First, gradual and partial change, it appeared, required less thoroughly organized and theoretical preparation so that the quality of decisions taken declined. Second, the absence of a link between the old and new regulations, which coexisted in the spheres of planning, distribution, incentives etc., inevitably manifested itself. Third, while the old system was not completely dismantled, the possibility remained of turning back at the first sign of difficulties, the more so as the regime's political problems were becoming exacerbated with the development of the reform.[38]

The attempt to cross the ravine in two jumps (generally typical of all reformism from above) ruined the whole business. In the end the half-hearted reforms only aided the economy's disorganization. A kind of *bureaucratic anarchy* set in. The conflict between the various sections of the apparatus, aggravated as a result of the reforms, became a constant source of disaster for the system, heralding not only economic but political defeat. The system's complexity and maladjustment increased until it became unmanageable.

The productive forces were outstripping the relations of production and attempts to smooth over this contradiction without a decisive restructuring of the very basis of the system inevitably resulted in failure.

In exactly the same way, the social structure of Polish society was becoming much more homogenous and mature, making it incompatible with the statocratic state machine. The absence of collectivization and a mass exodus from the countryside had hastened the formation of a nucleus of a hereditary urban proletariat. At the beginning of the 1960s, more than half of workers in industry had rural origins, but by the end of the decade

> the industrial centres already possessed stable traditions: those who come to the cities were primarily single people who had settled down to family life in the cities, selecting their partners from among the city-dwellers; the educational, professional and cultural level of the migrants had increased.[39]

In the 1970s, Poland developed incredibly dynamically. But the new social structures founded in the 1960s were not wrecked by this; on the contrary, their position was reinforced. By 1979–80 a new generation of workers, in which hereditary proletarians were clearly predominant, had entered working life. The more rapidly society developed the more rapidly the old state and its political methods were exhausted.[40]

So long as the state managed to maintain the existing level of consumption, it was able to avoid an open confrontation. But this task was becoming more and more complicated. The failure of the 1979 harvest acutely worsened food supplies to the cities. Instead of planned growth of 3 per cent, national income fell by 2 per cent. The plan for 1980 had to be seriously revised and, as a Polish economist acknowledges, this proved, in the end, to be 'the direct cause of the August political storm.'[41] Insofar as the amended version of the plan made sacrifices on the part of the population unavoidable, a situation was created where all the contradictions and conflicts accumulated over long years rose at once to the surface.

The events of 1980 in Poland proved an experimental refutation of Alexander Zinoviev's pyschological theory, which asserted that any system automatically produces the social type most conducive to its aims. In fact everything is just the opposite. *Statocracy's fundamental psychological contradiction* consists in the fact that it is to its political advantage to have passive, socially inert citizens, but such civil passivity is economically disadvantageous and even dangerous to the system. *Apathy is akin to sabotage.* The economy, particulary in periods of reform, needs enterprising and active citizens — who may prove politically unreliable. In conditions of terror this contradiction is destroyed by periodic purges and the extermination of that socially active section of society which had previously been moblized to carry out the latest state task. When mass terror is not employed, the contradiction becomes irresoluble.

All complex modern societies simultaneously reproduce several (and frequently highly varied) types of social character. The trouble for the statocracy is that at a certain stage (in the conditions of a settled industrial society), it becomes impossible to produce the social type corresponding to its needs. A generation of rebels grew up in Gierek's Poland. Having exhausted itself, the system *itself begins to produce people on a mass scale who are incompatible with it — its own gravediggers.*

In June 1976 Gierek made a first attempt to raise food prices. The workers responded with mass strikes. On 25 June, the whole of Warsaw province was in the grip of strikes. This time the movement's heart was at Radom, an industrial centre close to the capital. One day was enough to force the government to make concessions. In the words of a French newspaper, the Polish workers 'had gained the right of veto in the domain of economic policy.'[42] Moreover, the events of 1976 proved just how precarious was the position of the Party leadership. Gierek promised much and aroused great hopes among the workers. Now all of this was turned against him. Having confounded the hopes of the masses, he activated their political consciousness, thereby preparing the psychological grounds for a revolutionary situation. From the mid-1970s the state could only maintain an unstable equilibrium by offering economic rather than socio-political concessions, but this strategy increased present problems and prepared the future crisis. As purely economic concessions became impossible, the political equilibrium collapsed.

For some time the government had lacked the means to carry out its own promises. After the events of 1976 it resorted to repression against worker activists, arresting several hundred people. Those who were sacked numbered in the thousands. But it was precisely these repressions which created the grounds for re-establishing contacts between the industrial proletariat and the Left intelligensia. In September 1976 a group of progressive intellectuals, among them Kuron, Michnik and Modzelewski, and also E. Lipinski, a veteran of the socialist movement in Poland, founded the 'Workers' Defence Committee' (KOR) in order to resist the repressions. Later they began publication of an unofficial newspaper, *Robotnik* ('Worker'). Despite the efforts of the police, this paper began to find its way into enterprises and to be distributed among workers. KOR was granted observer status to the Socialist International, and gained the support of several communist parties. The French communist, J. Estager, acknowledged that the activists of KOR expressed what 'the majority of workers in Polish society' were thinking.[43]

The Italian Communist paper wrote that a 'socialist problematic' predominated in the Committee's programmatic and theoretical documents.[44] However, this did not prevent official propaganda from christening KOR an 'anti-socialist group'. In fact, KOR's political practice fitted quite well into the general picture of the European left movement in the 1970s. At the heart of KOR's strategy lay Kolakowski's idea of a new reformism: reformist pressure on the system forces the ruling circles to implement changes even against their will. If the starting point of the Polish Right was the 'irreformability of communism' and the view that any reformist activity only deflects attention from the need to 'overthrow the system', then the Left, clearly seeing the difficulties confronting them, hoped to achieve changes and alter the balance of class forces in Poland by uniting revolutionary and reformist actions.

The Hungarian sociologist, Janos Kiss, later wrote that the Polish opposition strove 'to achieve limited changes, but by depending on autonomous organizations and acting independently of the authorities.'[45] In practice this led to the appearance of 'flying universities' which combined in a fellowship of scientific courses. In April 1978 the first worker's committee for the founding of free trade unions sprang up. In both cases KOR's influence was decisive. Many worker activists became 'probationary' members of KOR, among them such prominent figures of the future revolution as Lech Walesa and Andrzej Gwiazda. By 1980, despite the repressions, committees of supporters of new trade unions were already active in several parts of the country. Workers arrested in 1976 were released.[46]

KOR's activity led inevitably to the establishment of unity between intelligentsia and workers. In December 1970 the intelligentsia had not supported the workers, and had kept disgracefully silent. Kuron and his close friends had been exceptions, but they had remained in a tiny minority. The rupture between workers and intellectuals, manifest in 1968 and 1970, was very deep. It was not easy to reach a mutual understanding. Even at the Solidarity Congress in Summer 1981, several worker delegates spoke out in an anti-intellectual fashion. The anti-semitic prejudices of the masses had their effect (there were comparatively more Jews among the Left). Thus the problem of 'people and intelligentsia' was posed even more sharply in Poland than in other countries. But experience had shown that unity was essential. Workers had strength but no programme or organization. The intellectuals had no real social strength, but significant political experience. The working class possessed its own distinctive 'right of veto' in economic questions, forcing the government through strikes to reject one or another particular solution, but it needed a positive programme so that the workers' strength could be turned into real power. KOR's success is explained by the fact that it was able to give workers what they really needed, to formulate precisely those ideas already spontaneously taking shape in the consciousness of the class itself. Otherwise its appeals to the masses would not have had such an outcome (as happened with several youth groups in the USSR in the 1960s). Lenin notwithstanding, social consciousness is not 'brought' into the working class by the revolutionary intelligentsia. The *fundamentals* of class consciousness are created by life itself. Intellectuals can only formulate correct answers to questions which spontaneously arise in the workers' movement. This is their historical task and responsibility. If the industrial proletariat is in need of organization, its programme and optimal structure cannot be elaborated without the intelligensia's participation. But if the conditions for founding a workers' organization have not ripened and the spontaneous movement is not yet mature enough for it, the very best of plans will remain on paper. At times intellectual consciousness 'runs ahead'. Thus heroes and martyrs appear, inspiring new generations of revolutionaries. At other times, disillusionment as to their own forces leads intellectuals to lag behind events and to fail in their own historical task. KOR's advantage lay precisely in the fact that its activity was opportune.

The ideological and psychological evolution of the intelligensia and working masses does not proceed synchronously, but at all events it is a parallel process: they both live in the one society. Ideas are not the exclusive property of intellectuals, although it is in the intellectual milieu that manifestations of spiritual life receive their most complete and precise expression. There is naturally an unavoidable discordance between ideological processes occurring in different social strata. Nevertheless, in periods when a social structure is reaching maturity, there develops a resonance between these processes.

The Polish experience once again shows that *ideas take hold of the masses and become a material force only when the masses themselves begin to experience the need for precisely such ideas.* New ideals were penetrating into the midst of the Polish workers even without any purposeful propaganda. It would be very interesting to study the original paths of this 'diffusion of ideas', but such a question does not lend itself to purely theoretical analysis. In any case it is evident that the activity of socialists is not a source of the proletariat's class consciousness, but a means of establishing stable links between workers and intellectuals. These links are even more essential in that official propaganda creates a spiritual vacuum which generates, for lack of anything better, various ideological surrogates. In Poland nationalist moods became widespread, and took hold to a certain extent among the workers. KOR's task was to put ideas to the workers which corresponded better to their real interests. By managing to do this, KOR pushed aside other opposition currents and achieved mass success. It does not follow from this, however, that the Left's ideology was assimilated by the masses in a 'pure form'. Nationalism, temporarily pushed to the ideological sideline, continued to be an important element of social consciousness, frequently interwoven with ideological and religious ideas. The Left intelligensia itself was far from free of nationalist illusions. Poland's history, which for the last 300 years has consisted exclusively of a struggle for independence, makes such a position natural. Even Engels wrote that the Poles 'are most of all international precisely when they are genuinely national' and that they 'have showed this on all the fields of revolutionary battle.'[47] The struggle for independence and social transformations have proved so closely interwoven in Eastern Europe that this has been inevitable. The danger of nationalism in Poland is not that it has neglected social questions but that it has pushed them into the background, distorting people's sense of the real proportions of social life. It has created idols and sometimes led people to forget the class character of political struggle and to underestimate their opponents who are, after all, 'Poles as well'. As Marx prophetically said, 'the Hungarian, the Pole, the Italian shall not be free as long as the worker remains a slave!'[48]

The crisis of official ideology was also reinforced by the position of the Catholic Church. Worker activists understood perfectly well that the moral values of Christianity could not, of themselves, take the place of a political programme. This was why they turned not to the Church authorities but to the KOR intellectuals, schooled in Marxism. Nevertheless, the considerable services of the Church to the Polish workers' movement cannot be denied.

In the West, the Catholic Church has long and stable traditions, but in Eastern Europe only Poland is a genuinely Catholic country. Catholicism continues to exist in neighbouring states but has absolutely no real historical influence over the fate of the nation. An American commentator has noted that 'in general one may claim that the Catholic Church exudes greater dynamism in Poland than in any other Catholic country in the world, not to speak of the other East European countries in the Soviet bloc.'[49] Russian Orthodoxy, which has inspired right-wing dissidents in the USSR, has completely different traditions:

> The Orthodox Church is both economically and politically more dependent upon the State and imperial favours than the Catholic Church, and has been more intimately linked economically to the centralized state system. The differences between Western and Eastern Churches in the sphere of political relations and the internal structures of church organizations can be clearly traced.... In feudally fragmented Europe, in the early and classical Middle Ages, it was precisely the Pope's throne which was the proclaimer of universal theocratic ideas, which strove to affirm the pre-eminence of the spiritual over the temporal realm and become the centre of the Catholic world, independent of the state and standing high above it. The Orthodox Church in Byzantium, which existed in the conditions of a centralized state, was not a repository of universalist tendencies but, on the contrary, advocated the unification of church and state.[50]

Catholicism resisted the state, Orthodoxy was indissolubly linked to it. In the Catholic world, the Church itself was centralized, but in Orthodox countries, the cathedrals stood above the patriarchs and each national church retained its autonomy. In the end, however, this led only to subordination to the secular power in each individual country. Orthodoxy was a more open system but this meant above all that it was 'open' primarily to government influence. The longstanding conflict between Church and State, having created some freedom for diverse forms of dissent which gained support first from one side, then from the other, was supplemented in Poland by the nationalist conflict. The Catholic Church was the prop of the popular struggle against the enslavers who were of other faiths. Poland's enemies were always Protestant Prussia and Orthodox Russia. In the twentieth century, after the gaining of independence, the Church leaders, by pursuing an extremely reactionary policy, significantly comprised themselves. But the Second World War, the German occupation of the country and Stalin's repressions helped to re-establish Catholicism's prestige. The Church remained the sole organization not under the control of the authorities, a last resort and support for opposition. When believers were executed, this only reinforced its authority.

After 1956, the Episcopate, while avoiding direct confrontations with the government, took every opportunity to voice its disagreement on questions of human rights. The Catholic intelligentsia received the

Church's support in its conflicts with the state. Believers could be found in all currents of the opposition. The integrity of Church figures contrasted favourably with the venality and dissoluteness of officials in the Gierek regime.

In Poland as elsewhere, there existed various political tendencies among Christians. The officially recognized religious–political group 'Pax' promoted extremely nationalistic and anti-semitic positions, professing, in Michnik's words, 'the totalitarian cult of the state.'[51] Left-wing Catholics were represented in the parliamentary group 'Znak' and among supporters of the journal *Wiaz*. Under conditions of censorship, the differences between these currents were not always overtly displayed, but every crisis instantly revealed them. Nationalistic Catholicism, as we have said, enjoyed a certain authority, but in the 1980 events a major role was actually played by the social-reformist traditions of Western Christianity, in which even Engels had seen 'points of contact with the workers' movement'.[52] The election of Cardinal Wojtyla of Cracow as Pope John Paul II greatly revived popular Catholicism in Poland. This was perceived as 'the beginning of a new time when the unthinkable becomes the possible.'[53]

The influence of the Left intelligentsia and the Catholic Church significantly determined the form in which the workers' demands were expressed at the first stage of the revolution. But these demands were themselves engendered first of all by the Polish proletariat's historical and social experience and the level of its class development. As Chris Harman rightly remarks, the revolutionary movements in Eastern Europe were neither the result of agitation nor a 'mere mechanical reflection of economic crisis'.[54] They took stock of a long historical period and (so to speak) summarized the accumulated experience. From the very beginning, the spontaneous movement itself discovered the correct slogans and tactical or organizational methods. The influence of various ideologies and political currents only proved important later on, when the question arose of the realignment of forces in the new political situation. In the first few months the workers' limited collaboration with the left-wing ideologues and the Church was quite adequate for the tasks in hand.

The next attempt by the government to raise prices, on 1 July 1980, set off the explosion. Strikes began among railway workers and then among industrial workers in Lublin province. From there they spread throughout the entire country. The scale of the movement was such that the authorities were clearly disoriented. For example, in Warsaw new prices were announced on 1 July; on 3 July, from 10 a.m. till noon, the old ones were reinstated, and between noon and 2 p.m., the new ones were reintroduced — and after 2 p.m. and throughout 4 July, the old ones were in force. Then, from the morning of 5 July, it was the new ones again. The same thing happened throughout Poland. The government was lacking in common logic as well as in political resolution. The crisis at the top was starkly revealed.

For their part, the lower social strata advanced diverse and at times contradictory demands. The slogan of free trade unions arose only in the course of the struggle, after the movement had gathered strength. At first, some demanded that wages be increased, others that prices be lowered — and one Warsaw factory demanded both at the same time. The strikes were organized by no one. In Lublin province, where the protest actions began, there was no trace of KOR's activity. The authorities, in their efforts to deal with the 'ringleaders', began to arrest workers who had been put forward as leaders during the strikes. This not only failed to halt the strikes, it politicized them. KOR called for 'self-organization in the enterprises' and the creation of strike committees empowered to conduct negotiations with the government. On 11 June, it proposed its own programme for a way out of the crisis. This mentioned economic reform and the easing of censorship but said nothing about free trade unions. Meanwhile the workers were becoming more radical with every passing day. KOR's programme was already too moderate for them. Events were happening in the country which would have seemed inconceivable not long ago even to the most advanced section of the intelligentsia which had done so much for the revolution.

The politicization of the working classes was leading to a situation where proposals were being advanced from below that were bolder than the dissidents — not to mention ruling class reformist groups — expected.[55] When the shipyards and other plants on the Baltic coast stopped work in mid-August, the strikers were already demanding the formation of free trade unions, the release of political prisoners and worker activists who had been subject to repression, and the democratization of the whole of public life. Such a programme, as its proposers knew, was unacceptable to the ruling elite. 'There are certain limits', declared Gierek, 'beyond which we cannot go.'[56] The leaders of KOR, on their own admission, also refused to believe that the workers could succeed. 'We were a long way from the idea that a free trade union would be born from these strikes', one of them declared. Polish socialists were in favour of free trade unions from the outset, but considered there to be a long road in front of them before this goal could be achieved. KOR's experts in the enterprises in August found themselves in an absurd position – if anything, they were holding the workers back: 'We did not even have sufficient time to influence the strikers in this sense. Even before we were able to declare our positions, they had already declared theirs. Quite independently. Success was born out of crisis.'[57]

The slogan of free trade unions was not the invention of opposition intellectuals. It summed up the entire historical and social experience of the Polish proletariat over the preceding 25 years. It was obvious to the workers that without an independent organization they would lose the fruits of their victories just as had happened in 1956, 1970 and 1976. At the same time, the idea of free trade unions was an integral part of the world socialist tradition and the experience of the international workers' movement. Even the official press did not, at first, dare to call the strikers' demands 'anti-socialist', but tried rather to demonstrate that 'most of the proposals, desires and slogans' of the Gdansk workers 'began life in the Party.'[58] Left-wing forces in the West, in their turn, saw a clear resemblance between their own struggle and the revolutionary movement in Poland. Leading social democratic, socialist and communist parties came out with declarations in its support.

The strikers had drawn important lessons from the bloody events of 1970. This time blood-letting was avoided in Gdansk, as the official press conceded, exclusively thanks to the restraint and discipline of the strikers. The Party newspaper, *Trybuna Ludu*, drew attention to the 'incredibly high level of organization of the spontaneous workers' actions and to their decisiveness and political maturity', through which it had been possible to 'maintain calm and order even at tense moments.'[59] This time there were no demonstrations. The strikers occupied their enterprises, turning up every day as if going to work. Since the official organs had actually lost control of the situation, strike committees assumed some of the functions of power and maintained normal life along the coast. There was almost a holiday atmosphere among the workers. The consumption of alcoholic drinks was banned by the strike committees, and this provoked not the slightest objection on the part of the strikers. Although communications had been disconnected along the coast, the workers set up an effective underground information system. Such organization and discipline were completely unexpected both to the authorities and to many foreign observers. *L'Express* wrote:

The classics of 'scientific socialism' must be read and re-read in the light of the Polish events. The famous dictatorship of the proletariat, of which Lenin had spoken, has assumed concrete forms in Gdansk. The only problem is that this dictatorship has been directed not against a capitalist regime but against a regime which calls itself socialist.[60]

In August 1980, the Polish proletariat, to use Marx's words, from a 'class in itself' became a 'class for itself'. The high level of the workers' social self-consciousness can have been engendered only by the highest and most 'comprehensive' forms of class struggle. Harman correctly remarks that different strata achieve consciousness of their class interests 'at different speeds, depending on their particular experience and traditions.'[61] Thanks to the events of 1956–76, Polish workers were no longer novices in politics. Thus the proletariat's most advanced detachment – the Gdansk shipyard workers – drew the majority of workers behind them with incredible ease. The working class continued to learn in the course of the struggle. The masses were creating history, but historical events in their turn were transforming the consciousness of the masses.

During the August struggle an independent workers' press arose. The circulation of *Robotnik* sharply increased, and the information bulletin, *Solidarity* was founded at the Lenin Shipyard in Gdansk. Its name was later adopted by the new trade unions. The workers had gained the opportunity, for the first time in many years, to express themselves. The strikers' twenty-one demands were published. They envisaged an organization of independent trade unions, the freeing of political prisoners, the lifting of censorship and economic reform. A few days later even the official press was constrained to publish the list of demands (the first paper to do so was *Sztandar Mlodych*). Attempts to split the strikers and conduct negotiations with them on an individual basis came to nought. On the last day of August 1980 the government signed an agreement with the workers. This was the beginning of a new era not only for Poland but for Europe as a whole.

Of course, the authorities were not prepared to fulfil their obligations. But it had now become impossible to deceive the workers. When the authorities tried to confine the points of the Gdansk agreement to the Baltic coast, a new wave of strikes rolled across the country. Workers' actions were especially widespread in Silesia, Gierek's birthplace. In autumn, despite the authorities' propaganda campaign and efforts to intimidate workers through the security organs, the formation of new trade unions began everywhere. They united in a cross-industry organization,

Solidarity, which was joined by around ten million people (up to 95 per cent of the country's industrial proletariat). At the head of Solidarity were the most popular workers' leaders — Lech Walesa, Andrzej Gwiazda, Bogdan Lis and others. Breakaway 'branch' unions, which remained extremely small, were created from the remnants of the official trade unions. These were chiefly joined by functionaries of the old professional organizations, party workers and bureaucrats, some old people afraid of losing their trade union record before retiring, and a section of workers in small enterprises (here, incidentally, we might recall Lenin's famous observation to the effect that workers in big factories display greater class consciousness).

In November, a new conflict arose when the government refused to recognize the new unions because there was no mention in their constitution of 'the leading role of the Party'. There followed the threat of a general strike. The Supreme Court accepted that the workers were in the right, and Solidarity was registered. Every position had to be taken by force like this. Nevertheless, by the end of 1980 the revolution's first battle had been won. 'Polish reality', writes the historian and opposition activist Jerzy Holzer, 'was characterized in November 1980 by the strength of Solidarity and weakness dissipating the Party's internal unity.'[62] The question of strategy and the direction of the revolution's future development was now becoming decisive. It was a question which, as we shall see below, was to prove fateful for Solidarity.

In any revolution, the first success is most easily won. As history shows, the state has always been taken by surprise by revolutionary events. The ruling class can be aware of the acuteness of social conflicts, but when such conflicts develop into a revolution it comes as something unexpected all the same. On the other hand, a revolution is inevitably linked with a crisis at the top, when the ruling groups are split and demoralized and have lost their capacity for firm and decisive action. They become the victims of their own preceding policy: previous failures and errors hang over them like fate. The fact that the government has formal control over the army and police changes little in such a situation, for the state is simply incapable of effectively using its opportunities and implementing its decisions. A revolution is a 'break in gradualness', a leap in development, a shock even to to those taking part in it. But the shock is more severe for the ruling groups.

In a centralized bureaucratic system it is virtually impossible in principle for a sober assessment of the political situation to be made 'from above'. As Marx wrote in this regard: 'The top entrusts the understanding of detail to the lower levels, whilst the lower levels credit the top with understanding of the general, and so all are mutually deceived.'[63] Moreover the outward form of events is often deceptive. In a revolutionary situation the explosion may happen because of comparatively 'minor' troubles, which in 'normal' times would not have proked a crisis. Lenin correctly noted that in such conditions even the most insignificant conflicts 'can be of the most serious importance.'[64] As the state can neither avoid such conflicts nor evaluate them correctly, it finds itself in a losing position.

The labouring classes may not always assess what is happening soberly. The first success generates dangerous illusions in the victors. In France in 1789, it was not so difficult to force the convocation of the States-General and seize the poorly defended Bastille. In 1905, Nicholas II's October Constitution was achieved quite swiftly by the Russian workers, without an armed struggle. In such conditions it seems that the triumph of revolution is guaranteed, but in fact the struggle is only just beginning. After a retreat, the ruling class begins to appraise the situation more seriously and regroup its forces. Reaction's counterattack inevitably follows. The Tuileries proved more difficult to seize than the Bastille. The Polish revolution developed according to the same laws.

By dismissing Gierek and replacing him with Stanislaw Kania, Polish ruling circles by no means intended to disavow the previous policy. Revolutionary euphoria reigned among the Polish workers. Mass consciousness viewed the victory that had been won as definitive and the movement's leaders to some extent shared the general illusions. Meanwhile, it was necessary to prepare for the new stage of political confrontation, resolve complex organizational tasks and elaborate the strategy, tactics and programme corresponding to the new conditions.

The methods effective in the summer of 1980 were already inappropriate by autumn, when the situation had qualitatively changed. Solidarity, at once a trade union and a social movement, had to find new forms of activity. The revolution of 1980–81 demonstrated the massive and previously underestimated political possibilities which exist for a trade union. It provided a model of trade union struggle qualitatively different from both British trade unionism and the communist model. Both Marxists and social democrats had seen the union primarily as an organization for pursuing the economic struggle while leaving the 'higher' tasks to a party. The Polish revolution showed that a trade union can become an organization uniting the *whole* class on the basis of its most general interests, both economic and political. This is its advantage over parties. It is not restricted by ideological purposes and a specific programme. It sets itself the most general of class goals and provides more space for the spontaneous initiative of the masses themselves. This was achieved by Solidarity, 'one of the most significant revolutionary movements in the history of post-war Europe.'[65]

Solidarity was born out of spontaneous workers' actions. Both social democratic and Leninist traditions have underestimated the role of spontaneity. Emphasis has been placed on movements organized and directed by parties (the difference between communists and social democrats has been concerned more with the Party's structure and principles than with its role in relation to the working class). The experience of Poland has shown that, at certain stages of the revolution, the spontaneous workers' movement is itself capable of selecting the most correct path and best means of struggle.

The events of 1980 bring to mind the ideas of Rosa Luxemburg, which counterposed to Kautsky and Lenin's centralism the theory of the masses' spontaneous self-organization in the course of a revolutionary general strike. Since the Polish workers' actions were genuinely improvised, the strikers themselves knew nothing of this theory and acted according to their class instincts. J. Taylor was amazed at the indifference of Solidarity activists to questions of theory: 'they were unaware' of contemporary social thought in the West.[66] When Walesa was asked about Rosa Luxemburg he replied that it was not worth 'wasting time' on such conversations.[67] But it is precisely because of the Polish worker activists' lack of preparation that their activity is of considerable interest to theoreticians. The example of Solidarity allows us to study spontaneous workers' actions in a 'laboratory pure form'. The experience of eighteen months of the Polish revolution gives us the opportunity to see both the strong and the weak sides of spontaneity, its reformist and revolutionary potential.

From September to November 1980, Solidarity turned into an organization with its own constitution and leading organs. But it continued, to a large extent, to operate under the influence of the spontaneous moods of rank-and-file workers. This was how its structure took shape in the course of a general strike. The workers rejected the old principle of specialized trade unions, uniting workers according to their occupation, and founded an inter-industry trade union on a class basis. They were unable to make any distinctions between political and economic struggle so they rejected the heritage of British trade unionism and, this may seem paradoxical, followed precisely the road indicated

by revolutionary Marxists (including the Bolsheviks): from an organization defending common occupational interests they turned the union
into an organization struggling for the most general class interests in all
spheres of life.[68]

Having shown the enormous possibilities of trade unions and the
masses' spontaneous self-organization, Solidarity also demonstrated the
limits of these possibilities. The weak aspects of the movement quite
quickly became apparent. The enthusiasm of the first weeks was
insufficient. Maintaining co-ordination and unity in action proved
extremely difficult. Moreover, the new organization had no national
organ. Hundreds of local bulletins and factory news-sheets were no
substitute, the more so as they were not always totally under the control
of Solidarity committees. J. Olszewski complained, in working out the
union's constitution, that 'the situation may become pathological.'[69]

People did not wish to return to the old centralized bureaucratic
system. They hoped to replace it by direct democracy. Thus J. Knap, a
prominent activist in Warsaw Solidarity, declared that all decisions must
be taken by the rank-and-file and not the leaders. Achieving this proved
very difficult and 'unfortunately, some decisions still had to be taken at
the top.'[70] Such an interpretation of democracy differs little from anarchy
and the role of leading organs becomes ambiguous at best. Democracy
cannot manage without a central leadership — one which is accountable
to the rank-and-file and expresses its interests. The masses must control
their leaders, but this only means anything in a situation where the
leaders themselves are invested with real powers. Direct democracy can
augment representative democracy but it cannot replace it.

The Solidarity leadership found itself in a tricky situation. Local
organs were often not subordinate to it. Gwiazda complained that 'we
calm, we explain' and in the meantime 'wildcat strikes still do not
cease.'[71] It was difficult to harmonize sectional interests with those of
regional and national organization. The middle tier of the union's
apparatus was poorly developed. The leaders could issue calls to the
masses and, by using the union's authority, get essential decisions taken.
But the union was incapable of undertaking normal everyday work, and
in practice it was impossible to ensure that an adopted line was carried
out. Polish gentry anarchism became more and more apparent in the
workers' movement. Solidarity was destroyed by the same thing that
destroyed 'Rzeczpospolita' in the eighteenth century. Polish love of
freedom is exhilarating but it has cost the country dear. The weaknesses
of a great people do not cease to be weaknesses.

The chief result of the situation that had arisen was that Solidarity was incapable of political manoeuvring. This is not very important in moments of revolutionary onslaught but it is a different matter in the transition to reformist work. Polish conditions, the country's geo-political position and the situation at the beginning of the 1980s demanded restraint and caution. Moreover, there are stages in any revolution when a regrouping of forces and breathing space are essential. Solidarity's organizational structure made it impossible to carry out such tasks successfully.

The experience of the Polish revolution shows that, at a definite stage of the struggle, spontaneity must give way to organization. It is impossible to manage without a 'workers' bureaucracy'. It remains true, of course, that the apparatus of trade unions or workers' parties should be under the control of democratic organs, that the organization should not totally exclude elements of spontaneity, that it should not be too rigid, and finally that it should be founded *on a class and not an ideological basis.* But the apparatus must always be in a position to obtain the effective and concerted actions of all tiers of the organization, the implementation of the will of the majority. This does not exclude disagreements on specific questions or strategic discussions, but actions must be united.

The lessons which can be drawn from the Polish events by the workers' movement throughout the world cannot be reduced to some sort of magic formula. The optimum correlation between centralism and spontaneity can only be found in practice in accordance with the specific circumstances of each individual country. The Poles' misfortune lay in the fact that they demonstrated the significance of this problem in the best possible way but were unable to resolve it. From this flow many of Solidarity's other weaknesses, which, in the last analysis, predetermined the defeat of the workers.

The popular movement's inability to manoeuvre flexibly was engendered not only by the frailty of organizational structures but by the unpreparedness of the workers' political leadership to resolve the revolution's theoretical and strategic questions. To them the whole, very rich historical experience of global revolutionary struggle was a 'closed book'. Analysis of concrete situations remained at an extremely low level although the specific conditions of Eastern Europe required a particularly careful and flexible approach to a whole range of problems.

These days any revolution must take external factors into consideration, but Poland's geo-political situation, as the second country in size and significance in the Eastern bloc, made these factors particularly important. Contrary to the assumptions (and hopes) of many Western observers, the Soviet Union did not intervene in Poland, despite the fact that in autumn 1980 and summer 1981 the Western press was not only guessing the date of intervention but even published its supposed plan.[72] But in any event, the government in Moscow could not watch with indifference as the situation destabilized in an allied — and neighbouring — country. It made it clear that there was a limit to its patience.

Solidarity and KOR were faced with the question of elaborating a revolutionary strategy which took Polish conditions into account. Lenin had said that the major question of any revolution is the question of power. In the Polish situation this question was in principle irresoluble: the patience of 'Big Brother' was not unlimited, as Brezhnev repeatedly made plain. In October 1980, Kuron quite correctly remarked that, were it not for external circumstances, 'we would have abolished this system a long time ago and we would now have free elections. This is as true as twice two is four.'[73] But external circumstances were not about to disappear. The KOR theoretician, A. Smolar, spoke of a 'limited revolution'. The revolutionary movement would have to be satisfied with reforms, if it desired to achieve anything at all. The Left intelligentsia had to assume a difficult role. Kuron reiterated: 'We cannot stop the movement, but we can make sure it does not attack the political foundations of the system. We hope that this will satisfy "Big Brother" which, in its turn, also has no interest in armed intervention.'[74] Michnik said that the opposition must learn 'to coexist with the state'.[75]

In other circumstances such words would be evidence of hopeless opportunism, but in this situation they simply expressed a high degree of revolutionary responsibility. Behind them lies not time-serving and a striving for 'social peace', but a sober grasp of the tragic lessons of the class struggle. Eastern European revolutionary movements have perished one after another by going too far. Democratic socialism in Poland is impossible while the global historical process does not create the appropriate conditions (in this sense the limitations encountered by the revolutions in both Poland and Nicaragua are, in their own way, alike despite the radical differences between them). The Soviet researcher, G. Vodolazov, wrote in 1975:

If revolutionaries are not conscious that their major immediate task is the resolution not of narrow national problems but of problems connected with the functioning of that broad economic and political system of which their country is a part, if they have not grasped this, if they have decided to seal themselves within their own national framework and give up on any neighbour, as they say, as a bad job — You can live how you like, just let us live how we want to — if they start out from this narrow national point of view, the cause of their revolution is lost. *They will not be allowed to live how they want to.*[76]

Walesa, most Solidarity leaders, Michnik and Kuron were conscious of the significance of global factors. But it is one thing to talk about a limited revolution and another to work out a corresponding strategy. Truth, as is well known, is concrete. One must know one's potential and the limits of one's potential. As Confucius said, he who truly understands where is the beginning and where is the end stands close to the truth.

All things considered, the Solidarity leaders lacked such an understanding. Michnik conceded that KOR also had no precise strategy. The new questions which arose after August 1980 took them unawares. 'I don't know the answer,' he said, 'and I don't think anyone in KOR knows it.'[77] At the same time the mass movement was living according to its own logic. The successes of August and November 1980 had inspired the people. The workers demanded all the more. Since the Solidarity leadership was unable to advance a specific programme of actions and was not in a position altogether to control the rank-and-file organizations, the masses were actually left to their own devices. The movement's leaders were subsumed by the revolutionary wave and swept along by the current of events over which they had no influence. At best they could ease confrontations, but they could not prevent them.

A limited revolution could achieve success only in the event that, at a definite stage, the popular movement passed over to reformist defence. Grasping this fact, Walesa strove to hold back the masses by using his considerable authority. But such an approach was doomed to failure. *Without a reformist strategy the calls to moderation and caution achieved nothing. The moderate workers' leaders understood perfectly well what not to do but they did not know how to inspire the masses.* Blatant disagreements arose between the masses and the reformist leadership. This complicated day-to-day work still further and weakened Solidarity in the face of its adversary.

By the end of 1980, even the official press recorded the 'strengthening of radicalism among the workers.'[78] It was already impossible to halt the escalation of demands. The Solidarity leadership could only induce labour collectives not to resort to strikes and promise that the union would show 'the effectiveness of its strategy of negotiations.'[79] In reality there was no such strategy. Not even its own relations with the state had been determined. Walesa hoped to establish relations with the government according to the principle 'conflict-cooperation'. The trouble was that the disorganization of the state apparatus in fact made it impossible to establish stable, reciprocal links. As Kuron remarked, 'the system of centralized government had already been destroyed and nothing new had arisen in its place.'[80] Even where the government was honestly trying to fulfil the obligations it had taken upon itself, it was not always able to do so. The local party apparatus took no account of the concessions to which the central leadership had agreed and resorted to any means to wreck every attempt at compromise. The violence against Solidarity activists in Bydgoszcz was only one of numerous such provocations. In turn the central apparatus was completely unprepared for a dialogue with the masses.

Jerzy Holzer correctly notes that in conditions where the ruling circles prove incapable of rational compromise and have desired only the liquidation of the workers' gains, 'only one path remains open to the revolutionary process — radicalization.'[81] To consolidate existing changes, new changes were demanded. Agreements were successfully concluded thanks only to powerful pressure on the government, and each time this required the maintenance of an alignment of political forces in the country more favourable to Solidarity.

Holzer stresses that the goal of the workers' movement in Poland was 'to realize irreversible shifts in the system.' In this sense Solidarity's revolutionary reformism is clearly reminiscent of the radical versions of socialist reformism in France and Latin America. On the whole, contrary to the illusions of the Poles who considered the events happening in their country to be quite exceptional, such analogies suggest themselves at every turn. But as opposed to the theoreticians on the left wing of the French Socialist Party who had chosen as their motto the phrase 'Neither treachery nor death', Holzer emphasizes that Solidarity was faced with a tragic choice from the very outset: 'capitulation or defeat'.[82] In other words death was, in his opinion, the only way of avoiding treachery (here, a comparison suggests itself with the final months of the Chilean revolution, which was confronted with the same alternative).

It is most probable, however, that Holzer is mistaken. The aim of the revolution, as he himself admits, was not simply compromise but structural reform guaranteeing the introduction of elements of the masses' democratic participation into the system of government, and elements of pluralism into political life, while retaining fundamental state principles — primarily 'the leading role of the Party'. It was clear that Solidarity would have to retreat from many of the positions it had gained, but it does not follow that such a structural reform was in principle impossible. The key was to be aware of precisely which institutions are susceptible to transformation within a chosen strategy, and to what extent. Having achieved a definite political space, Solidarity was quite capable of utilizing it at the next stage of the struggle when it was essential to go on to the defensive. But Solidarity was unable to secure the transition from an offensive war of manoeuvre to a war of position (in Gramsci's expression), chiefly because of the weaknesses of its organizational structures and the absence of a precise programme of action.

In the conditions of a limited revolution, the free trades unions should have focused their attention on a number of realizable demands and decisively insisted upon them. Other demands could have been sacrificed. In the event, Solidarity leaders were prepared on the one hand to defend in equal measure the whole complex of demands which had spontaneously arisen among the workers, and to enter into compromise at every specific instance. The local Solidarity organs displayed no greater respect for agreements than the local Party apparatus. Many activists accused Walesa, with some justification, of having a 'defensive' policy.[83] The leadership passively reacted to changing external circumstances and rank-and-file initiative without advancing its own ideas.

It would be interesting to compare the Polish revolution with the Nicaraguan. For all their dissimilarities, one is immediately struck by the fact that in both cases fundamental difficulties arose precisely when the revolution had to limit itself and turn into reform. However while in Nicaragua the Sandinista leaders were unable to expand the scope for spontaneous working class initiative, in Poland the Solidarity leadership proved wholly dependent upon such initiative. Paradoxically, the outcome turned out to be largely the same — a loss of political flexibility.

Restraining the masses in revolutionary conditions is possible only by acting offensively against the government while simultaneously restricting the struggle to achievable demands. The fundamental strategic questions must be revealed and all forces brought to bear on them so as to achieve their acceptable resolution. It is impossible to attack along an entire front in such conditions, but attempting to halt the workers' upsurge is inconceivable and even harmful. The unwillingness of the powers that be to enter into compromise and the passivity of the workers' leadership gave rise to a new current in the opposition — the young radicals (Jurczik, Rulewksi and, to an extent, Bujak) to whom Walesa and his supporters seemed to be compromisers. The radicals expressed the spontaneous mood of the rank-and-file, the dissatisfaction of many workers with their leaders' activity. Month by month the radicals' position became stronger. Nevertheless, they too failed to advance their own programme or strategy and did not even attempt to do so.

Among most radicals, disdain for theory was united with hostility towards the intelligentsia and sometimes even anti-semitism (here one recalls Kautsky's thought that there are inevitably reactionary tendencies in any mass democratic movement). Sociologists who have studied Solidarity emphasize that a characteristic of the radical current was its confidence that working-class problems can only be solved by the workers themselves, and its 'mistrust of leaders and especially of experts who are not from the working class. They even somehow suspected KOR activists, who had played a decisive role prior to 1980, and even threatened them.'[84] Most rank-and-file workers were also infected with such prejudices and suggested that belonging to the working class was the chief guarantee of loyalty to its interests. For its part, the Left intelligentsia, which had been unable to work out ideas to mobilize the masses in the new conditions and to answer the proletariat's new questions, actually retreated in the face of the onslaught by the young representatives of the new radicalism.

If the radicals had little interest in theory, they could still utilize Kuron's ideas from the 1960s. At that time the future leader of KOR had been in favour of a permanent revolution in Eastern Europe, dreaming of such a development of the revolution as would change the situation in neighbouring countries — Czechoslovakia, East Germany and Hungary. It was quite obvious that such a course, if it had been adopted by the Polish workers' movement, would have sharply increased the risk without guaranteeing success. Moreover, the radicals, even in those rare moments when they attempted to formulate the principals of a revolutionary strategy, confined themselves to generalities without specifying how such goals could be achieved.

American journalists correctly noted that 'if the workers' revolt in Poland has a lasting effect elsewhere in Eastern Europe, it will not be because it was an uprising against the Soviet Union, but because it achieved a measure of freedom within the system.'[85] Even a revolutionary approach can be effective in such a situation only through the success of reformism.

Revolutionary flare-ups in a single country are never of themselves sufficient to 'set fire' to another country, even one in a state of crisis (in Romania, for example, economic difficulties made the workers more receptive to the ideas of Solidarity). Workers need to be shown the actual, consolidated results of a revolution, but in the Polish case only a reformist compromise could consolidate the gains of revolutionary struggle. In the long-term perspective only such an outcome of the Polish crisis could influence the alignment of class forces in other countries and create new possibilities for revolutionary struggle in Poland itself.[86]

The problem was that not only did the state not desire a compromise, it was incapable of it. The state granted concessions only when it had no other alternative. Continual political defeats led to the collapse of the bureaucratic apparatus. The workers' organizations filled the power vacuum which had been formed. General Jaruzelski later declared that the official state structures had in fact ceased to operate and that the organization of an 'anti-state' had commenced in the country.[87] Prominent government figures were forced to acknowledge the existence of dual power. Such a situation is generally typical of any revolution but it is not at all favourable to a reformist compromise. As Kuron put it, 'each periodic conflict, which is unavoidable in present conditions, threatens an explosion. The danger therefore arises of the state being inadvertently overthrown.'[88]

The only way out was to force the terms of a compromise upon the ruling class. To this end, Solidarity could have acted decisively but carefully by defining precisely its tasks and possibilities and by maintaining unity and discipline at all levels of the organization. But instead of being concerned with resolving these problems, the union's leaders were engaged in sterile arguments over specific questions. Meanwhile, the situation in the country continued to deteriorate. The economy was collapsing to the point where it was appropriate to speak no longer of a crisis, but of a catastrophe. 'Comparisons with the war became commonplace', wrote *L'Alternative*.[89] Inflation led to a precipitous decline in living standards. The official press conceded that at this time in Poland there were no less than three million people in receipt of less than the minimum wage (2,400 zloty). The petty-bourgeoisie and shopkeepers were enriching themselves through speculation at the same time as the burden of the crisis was placed upon the shoulders of the workers. The masses' irritation was growing. The wage increases achieved in August were losing their value at once. The authorities acknowledged in autumn

1981 that 'every third zloty spent in Poland cannot be met by goods.'[90] There were fewer head of cattle than in 1974, and food was short. A transition to a system of rationing was agreed, but when, after great delay, ration cards were introduced there were insufficient goods for them to purchase. Petrol and motor oil began to disappear from sale, along with food. Cigarettes and matches also became a rarity.

There is nothing surprising in the fact that the government, engaged in the struggle against the revolution, lacked strength to care about solving economic problems. A way out of the crisis depended exclusively on the workers themselves. In many instances, they displayed incredible awareness. During the whole of 1980 just twenty-four hours of working time were lost through strikes, despite the very broad sweep of the struggle: significantly more was lost as a result of stoppages which were the fault of management. The official newspaper *Zycie Warszawy* acknowledged that 'Chaos reigns in the country because the influence of the workers is missing.'[91]

At the same time, the Solidarity leadership was slow to develop its own economic programme. While correctly demanding that the unions be granted the opportunity to participate in the taking of economic decisions, the leaders of the workers' movement were unable to promote their own ideas. 'Above all we want them to consult us,' said Bogdan Lis.[92] In such circumstances economic reform inevitably proved subordinate to government strategy. The ruling class, with no possibility of preventing changes, sought to link them with its own general counter-revolutionary and anti-worker course. Stanislaw Kania's policy contemplated widening the role of the private sector and the rights of the economic administration, while simultaneously lowering workers' living standards. Such methods of implementing reform were to lay the ground for the formation of a new, anti-worker social bloc encompassing intermediate strata, the technocracy, petty and middle bourgeoisie. In brief, the government of the 'workers'' party was prepared to enter into compromises with any social layer in order to isolate its prime adversary — the industrial proletariat.

Kania's government was ultimately intended to present the economic reform as a substitute for genuine democratization. It is interesting that even right-wing Western commentators stressed that 'political freedoms are likely to work against Poland's present economic priorities.'[93] Since the ruling circles sought to begin the restructuring of the economy with a weakening of the working class's position, price increases and a further lowering of workers' living standards (since, that is, they hoped to make the lower orders pay for the collapse of the rulers' previous policy), political freedoms were a serious obstacle to that restructuring: here the Polish statocracy was encountering the same problems as neo-conservatives in the West. But in a long-term perspective any serious reform of the economic mechanism (as the experience of Czechoslovakia in 1968 and Hungary in 1968–72 has shown) presupposed at least a certain degree of political liberalization, and it was simply impossible to combine it with 'tightening the screw'. Thus from the outset, the strategy of the ruling circles contained irresoluble contradictions.

The elite's social policy proved just as ineffective. The creation of an anti-worker bloc was rendered impossible for the same reason that the government's economic plans were unrealizable. While making concessions to the peasantry (especially the kulaks) and intermediate strata, the government was simultaneously striving with all its might to prevent their self-organization and the growth of their political influence. The middle tier of the Party apparatus in the localities, which feared the total loss of its social significance, was especially strongly opposed to this. The government refused to recognize the peasant organization, 'Rural Solidarity', but it was not even able to take advantage of the presence of several warring tendencies within this organization. The result was a sharp conflict with the peasantry, who found support from the working class. Actual social development upset the counter-revolution's plans. Instead of an anti-worker bloc a broad anti-bureaucratic front had been formed.

On the other hand, a significant section of the apparatus, including the economic sector, thought that the attempts at reform from above were too radical. Managers, unable to lead enterprises successfully in the new conditions, were by no means rushing to gain additional rights and responsibilities. They resisted. 'In a certain sense it's obstruction', complained a contributor to the liberal newspaper *Polityka*. 'They are anti-reform'.[94] The managers of advanced enterprises demanded more decisive steps forward, while backward ones insisted on a swift turning back.

Both the government and Solidarity were constrained in this situation to define their position more precisely on the question of economic reform. If before 1980 it had been a question of whether the reform would be implemented at all, then in 1981 it was clear even to the Party leadership that, despite the opposition of reactionary bureaucratic circles, the reform had to be carried out. The question was what sort of reform it would be. The technocrats united around S. Olszewksi, who was in favour of a limited restructuring of the managerial system. Proponents of more radical measures sought the support of Solidarity. Thus, irrespective of its original intentions, the union leadership was drawn into the work of preparing an economic programme by the very course of events.

Difficulties relating to the reform were engendered, not by a shortage of theoretical endeavour, but by the political situation. As Alec Nove noted, 'Poland had the good fortune to possess three distinguished socialist economists: Lange, Kalecki and Lipinski.'[95] All more or less agreed that it was necessary to utilize market factors, decentralize planning and widen enterprise autonomy. But a transitional model was lacking. It was not understood at all how to implement the changes and what specific measures should be undertaken and in what order. The government chose the path of little steps, announcing the beginning of a 'mini-reform' and promising a 'big reform' some time in the future. The 'normed net product' (NNP) indicator was introduced in place of gross output (val). Central planning ceased to interfere in questions specific to enterprises, confining itself to fixing the volume of production of basic forms of raw material and goods and also to tasks relating to exports. In a sense this represented a return to the method of the first years of the Gierek administration, which Gierek was later forced to revoke under pressure from the bureaucracy. At the next stage, it would be necessary to regulate the new production relations and make them more stable. By spring 1981 discussion on this theme involved both the official and the Solidarity press. It was essential to prepare a price reform and elaborate new policies on income distribution, regulation of employment and investment. It was necessary to define precisely the rights and resources of state enterprises and restore genuine autonomy to co-operatives. The specifically Polish problem of small peasant holdings occupied a special place.

The proposals advanced by the economists — including the official economists — were quite consistent. Many recalled the ideas of the 'Prague Spring'. Experts attempted to devise a model of a market-planned economy along the lines of Hungary while also utilizing the experience of Yugoslav workers' self-management. The difficulty lay in the fact that for all the evident merits of such plans, it was not easy to turn them into laws. The logic of economic reform was too blatantly contradictory to the statocracy's class interests. The Polish specialist W. Kuczynski wrote that the country needed 'an economy of use to consumers and not to bureaucrats.'[96] Precisely because of this, a project based on such principles was bound to remain on paper.

Apart from this, a serious danger to the official economists' project lay at those points where they preferred to abstain from clear and definitive formulations. The most important of these 'obscure passages' was the section on the formation of enterprise councils. The council was to be composed of representatives of the work collective, suppliers, consumers and 'collaborative enterprises and organizations'. At the head of the council stood the director. In the draft it was left completely incomprehensible as to whether the director would be elected or appointed, and the council's powers and the procedure for its formation also remained unclear. But the further development of social relations depended precisely on the resolution of these questions. Who would be the master of production: the manager–bureaucrats or workers' self-management?

Initially, the authorities themselves advanced the slogan of workers' democracy in production. Back in August 1980 Gierek had proposed self-management within enterprises *as a substitute for free trade unions.* The aim of this was obvious. Wherever a united class organization is absent, and political and supreme economic power is concentrated in the bureaucracy's hands, self-management by labour collectives only divides the workers. Yugoslav experience has shown that factory councils are no substitute for free trade unions, for they cannot resolve questions which emerge at a national level. Moreover, the slogan of self-management had been discredited in Poland. In 1956 and 1970 organs of 'workers' democracy' had been created in the enterprises but each time they were gradually reduced to the level of an appendage of the bureaucratic administration. Such 'democracy' allowed the responsibility for decisions not taken by the workers to be shifted onto them.

In August 1980 Brus remarked that 'if in 1956 the formation of workers' councils had been the major demand of the workers' movement, then in 1980 not a word was heard about councils.'[97] He predicted, however, that sooner or later this demand would be raised. And after Solidarity had won its first battles, there was indeed a spontaneous revival of interest among workers in industrial democracy. While not replacing the national workers' organizations, factory councils can materially broaden the sphere of social freedoms. Self-management allows workers' interests at the level of the enterprise to be taken into consideration in the planning process and is a guarantee against bureaucratization of the administrative apparatus and social institutions as a whole. Roger Garaudy has written with justification that self-management became 'a nightmare both for capitalists in the West and for technocrats in the East.'[98] This is one of the key socialist demands directly linked with the socialization of ownership. Without it, Marx's 'association of free men, working with the means of production held in common' is inconceivable.[99]

Self-management cannot, of course, reach its full potential without political democracy (as the Yugoslav experience from the 1960s to the 1980s confirms). It must be part of a broad democratic system. But socialist democracy, in turn, needs self-management of production as its starting point for 'the existence of a factory council is essential for the appearance of a new type of parliament capable of seriously participating in economic planning.'[100] The logic of proletarian revolution must inevitably push the question of self-management to the forefront. A survey of workers in Warsaw showed that new organs of industrial democracy had begun to be formed in 68 per cent of enterprises and that in 18 per cent of cases they were even supported by the pro-government branch unions. In these conditions the authorities' primary goal was to maintain the old system of appointing directors. This question has remained decisive to this day. If the old methods of appointment are kept in force, the organs of workers' representation rapidly lose their influence and become an appendage of the administration for, as sociologists have observed, 'leaders will always pay attention to how an association or ministry, but not their own collective, assesses them, and the monitoring functions of self-management ... will retain a purely formal character.' In the event of a conflict with the labour collective, the director inevitably emerged 'as the representative of the political system (organs of state power and the party) appointed to oversee the enterprise's activity.'[101]

The experience of 1956–7 destroyed many of the Polish proletariat's illusions. Then the question of self-management became a question of control over production, of the class nature of the administration. The government attempted to reduce this to purely technical problems by arguing that extending industrial democracy is contradictory to the 'principle of one-man management' (*edinonachalie*), without which effective management is impossible. In fact, however, the authorities themselves undermined the principle of '*edinonachalie*' by requiring that workers' representatives coexist with bureaucratic administration. If the director and top industrial management were elected, the principle of '*edinonachalie*' would be more fully maintained.

The greater the interest displayed by the workers in self-management, the less prepared the government was to meet them half-way. Since the Solidarity leadership was not concerned at that time with preparing a corresponding scheme, most proposals emanated from among the workers themselves. In May 1981 steelworkers at Nowa Huta approved 'thirteen points on workers' self-management.' Then workers in Warsaw formulated 'ten conditions for the renewal of worker representation.' In both documents it was pointed out unequivocally that self-management should become the chief element of the proposed economic reform. Unless general planning conditions were altered, discussions about industrial democracy were meaningless.

Under pressure from below, the Solidarity leadership made self-management its own programmatic demand. Then the free trade unions declared that the key to reform was the 'three S's': 'self-management, self-determination, self-financing.'[102] The new workers' councils must become democratic, elected organs independent both of party and Solidarity. This meant the downfall of the *nomenklatura* principle of selecting cadres, which ensures that memebers of the ruling bureaucracy need have no worry about their jobs, at any rate so long as they do not come into overt conflict with the Party's supreme organs. Such demands provoked natural indignation among the ruling class.

Workers' councils without rights, counterposed to the Party's total power, would have worked out very well for the apparatchiks. But independent workers' councils in association with a united national class organization of workers, Solidarity, would have undermined the very foundations of the system. The apparatchiks' resistance was therefore unyielding — but unsuccessful. Solidarity threatened strikes and the holding of a referendum in the enterprises on the question of self-management. The second threat appeared more terrible to the government than the first, for in the course of the referendum members of the branch unions and even some of their individual lower tiers would be able to support Solidarity's demands. For the apparatchiks, who had put their efforts into splitting the workers' movement, such a turn of events would be extremely dangerous. Feeling itself driven into a corner, the government agreed to a compromise.

The government-prepared law on self-management envisaged the election of directors in most branches of industry. On the whole Solidarity had got its way. Nonetheless, many of its activists were not satisfied. The rank-and-file organizations were inclined to be still more radical. As always happens in such cases, the bosses' belated concessions provoked an escalation of demands. When Walesa submitted a resolution in support of the compromise to Solidarity's Presidium, he was backed by only three people (with one against and seven abstentions). Western journalists wrote that on that day 'King Lech tasted his first humiliation.'[103]

It would be very easy to accuse Walesa of opportunism or of being 'divorced from the masses'. In fact, the Solidarity leadership was combative and determined in achieving the fulfilment of workers' demands. Its prime misfortune was that the leaders did not promote their own initiatives and did not lead the masses, but trailed the spontaneous movement. Thus it not only had no influence over the course of events but continually lagged behind them and put off slogans until tomorrow. Even in the heat of the struggle for self-management the Solidarity leadership did not advance its own project, and in the end it was doomed to support the amended and improved official law.

The leaders' political incompetence inevitably led to a crisis in Solidarity. As Tamara Deutscher remarks, the lack of a 'theoretical base' prevented the leadership of the workers' movement from preparing a programme of reform at an earlier stage. As a result,

> all questions were decided spontaneously under the influence of circum-
> stances. Naturally, a union can be born without 'heavy ideological baggage',
> but some amount of such baggage is needed for those who strive to establish
> genuine socialism in a country which, for the first time in its history, has
> gained such an opportunity.[104]

It may have been possible to manage without theory at the first stage of the struggle, but the events of 1981 revealed, in Gramsci's phrase, the opposition's inadequate level of strategic preparation. Many of the revolution's figures began to speak at this time of the need to elaborate a new ideology. The 'discussion theses' prepared on the eve of Solidarity's congress stressed that this should be based on 'the best traditions of the people, the ethical principles of Christianity and the political principles of democracy and socialist thought.'[105] But such quests for an ideology could not, of course, replace theoretical investigation. In the modern world any attempt to work out a new ideology without a more or less profound theoretical foundation is hopeless. Questions of revolutionary strategy could not possibly be resolved without serious analysis of society, its contradictions and tendencies of development.

Such theoretical labour cannot, in general, be the affair of a trade union. The ideology of such an organization, uniting workers on a class basis, must be as broad as possible. The programme of trade-union struggle, therefore, must inevitably be concerned only with the most general of questions. But actual practice continually pushed problems to the forefront which required additional analysis. It was evident that for the successful development of the revolution, the broad popular movement ought to be linked with a narrower organization possessing a precise, strategic programme. Lenin was absolutely correct when he said that 'the role of vanguard fighter can be fulfilled only by a party that is guided by the most advanced theory.'[106] Recognition of this fact in no way presupposes a repudiation of democratic principles. Any socialist must be conscious of the necessity for unity of theory and political practice, even if they reject Lenin's theory of party organization and favour political pluralism.

The formation of political parties in Polish conditions was impossible. At most one might speak of groupings and currents. In the revolution's initial stages it would have been a question of new social associations, 'pre-parties' of a kind. There is evidence in the formation of KOR that this process had already begun. The combination of spontaneous movement and organized political struggle was the only road to success, but in 1980–81 no new steps were taken in this direction. As Denis MacShane, a British trade unionist resident in Poland at the time of the revolution, remarked, up to the last days of its legal existence Solidarity remained 'a union with all the limitations that unionism entails.'[107]

Solidarity's lack of structural development, and the absence of political groups capable of assuming the strategic initiative and heading the movement, led to the 'personality cult' of the leader becoming the organizing principle. A charismatic leader was essential to mobilize the masses and maintain unity. Lech Walesa coped with this role well, but from the very beginning the extraordinary authority of one individual represented a danger to the revolution. Poles said that Walesa was 'a kind of symbol, and such movements, especially in Poland, need a symbol.'[108] Walesa, however, had little real power, and his position stemmed from his enormous personal authority. Many radical workers demanded from the beginning that the leader's powers be restricted still further. When, in autumn 1981, Walesa's authority began to waver because of disagreements over the question of self-management, there was clear disorder in Solidarity and the union's capacity for united, decisive action was cut to a minimum. The revolution's enemies inevitably exploited this.

Polish socialists talked of founding a party, but took no real steps in this direction. Moreover KOR, the chief organizational and ideological centre for the country's Left, declared its own disbandment since, as its leaders averred, Solidarity had already adopted all the main ideas KOR had advocated between 1977 and 1980. Litynski, clarifying KOR's position, emphasized that the political currents in Poland could not turn into parties for 'not one of them possesses a definite programme' (although the socialists had not even attempted to elaborate one), and Kuron complained about the Poles' 'terrible impatience', declaring that, since free elections were out of the question, the time for founding parties 'had still not arrived.'[109]

Such statements are very indicative. The organizational and programmatic weaknesses of the Polish Left were directly related to a lack of theory and strategy. To see political parties as purely pre-electoral associations is completely to ignore their real tasks. Kuron, Michnik, Modzelewski and others were familiar with the experience of the Western Left and with Marxist theory. Nevertheless, as Ascherson correctly notes, KOR 'was not a Marxist group, and it avoided any definite ideology just as it avoided any formal structure.'[110] On the one hand, Polish revolutionaries were not generally interested in theory and ideology, stressing that they had no time 'to think about the distant future'; and on the other hand, Marxism and socialist terminology were compromised in Poland as part of official jargon.[111] If it had stressed its Marxist traditions, the Left might have alienated itself from the Catholics. Finally, an exaggeration of Poland's national originality led to an underestimation of general theories, as if they had little to offer in local conditions.

In reality the Polish crisis once again demonstrated the necessity of Marxist analysis. The events of the revolution affirmed the correctness of Marx's idea about proletarian liberation being the work of the proletariat itself. The political process developed in accordance with the schemas of 'classical Marxism' (which is a most rare phenomenon in the twentieth century). Poland's uniqueness was manifest precisely in the fact that here the class struggle unfolded according to the traditional rules, well understood by Marx, Engels and their followers back in the nineteenth century. The Polish revolutionaries only acknowledged this themselves after the proletariat had suffered defeat. In the heat of the revolution no one even attempted to subject events to serious theoretical analysis.

Clearly, people engaged in practical struggle often just do not have the opportunity to busy themselves with theory. That is why an analysis of the alignment of class forces and the prospects for the revolution's development (and also the possibilities of reformist changes) should have been carried out on the eve of the workers' actions by supporters of KOR. They themselves had acknowledged the necessity of this, for the inevitability of a crisis was already evident to Kuron and his friends in

1976. Why was KOR unable to cope with this undertaking?

The leading representatives of the progressive opposition in Poland were the ideological heirs of the 1956 'October Left'. Although the government called the October Left 'revisionists', they were actually inspired by a return to the original principles of Marxism. After the failure of the student actions in 1968, however, most participants in the movement, while maintaining their loyalty to socialist ideals, lost interest in theory. 'Revisionism', writes an Italian researcher, 'derives from the notion of a thoroughly ideologized society.' This corresponded to the situation in the 1950s, 'but Poland in the 1970s is a country where ideology is dead and ideological conflict provokes not the slightest interest among the masses (in contrast to 1956).'[112] The opposition ceased to inflict serious damage on the state by finding it guilty of departing from socialist principles. Under Gierek the state was the ultimate beneficiary of the de-ideologization of both rulers and ruled. The Polish Left's lack of original theoretical ideas after 1968 was intimately connected with the general spiritual crisis of Polish society.

Polish experience confirms Gramsci's words that 'in reality it is easier to form an army than to form generals.'[113] Solidarity proved to be an army of selfless fighters, but lacked seasoned tacticians and strategists. The collapse of reformist revolution is explained in the last analysis by the absence of a revolutionary–reformist project. If the workers' movement in Poland could have developed in a geopolitical vacuum, if the revolution could have been divorced from what was happening in the outside world, if other countries had had no influence on Polish events, the workers' movement could have spontaneously worked out a new social project. But in the twentieth century, no such conditions exist anywhere. From the very beginning, the Polish revolution could survive only as a limited revolution. And it was not simply the workers' demands which would have had to remain limited, but also the time-scale within which the revolutionary process could develop unhindered (in 1981, East Germany and Czechoslovakia had already made the Moscow government aware that their patience was running out). Such conditions made life extremely difficult. Solidarity's actions were like a mechanical reflection of the unfolding internal situation.

It is quite understandable that the Polish Left had no desire to follow Stalin's doctrine of the leading party, and were inordinately afraid of 'overorganizing' the mass movement and so rendering it lifeless. But it was impossible to do completely without a strategic vanguard. The intelligentsia failed to fulfil its mission in the revolution.[114]

It should be remembered that where the authorities forbid normal exchange of ideas and free theoretical discussion, the political culture of the opposition is formed under the influence of a comparatively small circle of ideologues (for example, KOR's overall membership in its initial stages was just 33 people). This only increases the responsibility of these people to the whole of society. Not only personal self-sacrifice and conviction are demanded of them, but professionalism and profound theoretical knowledge — which can be some compensation for the lack of essential scientific freedom.

The activists of the Polish Left showed themselves to be courageous fighters but feeble theoreticians. Convictions are no substitute for strategy. In the de-ideologized society of Poland, the socialist intelligentsia can either sacrifice the ideological aspect of Marxism and opt for its scientific content, or reject any attempt at theoretical interpretation of existing reality and turn to solving routine political questions. KOR activists chose the second option, sacrificing science along with ideology. This proved costly in 1981, when it became impossible to orientate to the rapidly changing situation without a grasp of deep-seated social processes.

The Left intelligentsia saw the events primarily as a struggle between society and the state, and considered itself an expression of society's interests. But it was impossible, meanwhile, not to notice that a class conflict was occurring in the country, that society itself was divided and that the state was defending definite social interests. Sociologists investigating the formation and development of Solidarity have written that this organization had from the beginning, as it were, 'two faces': one was 'the workers' movement born in the factories' and the other was 'a national movement struggling for the democratization of society.'[115] In other words Solidarity simultaneously emerged as representative of the working class and as embodiment of the developing forces of civil society liberating itself from despotic power. Such duality is altogether natural, and analogous situations have arisen in almost all great revolutions.

The changing structure of society entered into contradiction with the immovable structure of state power, and at the same time exacerbated the traditional contradiction between exploiters and exploited. The duality of the revolutionary process was natural and unavoidable. The only trouble was that the leaders of the Left, who also figured as Solidarity's chief experts, did not draw the necessary political conclusions. At best they established that the interests of the working class coincided with those of the majority of society, at a time when a more profound and precise analysis was required. Because it assessed events primarily from the point of view of the opposition between society and state, the Polish Left achieved an oversimplified and unidimensional grasp of what was happening, and this made the elaboration of a flexible political line inconceivable. This was rather like an inversion of the old Comintern doctrine: whereas in the 1930s communists reduced every social movement to class struggle, Solidarity's experts interpreted the class struggle for the most part as a social movement, not giving a moment's thought to the actual dialectic between the one and the other.

The problem could only have been resolved if political parties or even emerging groupuscules had existed alongside the spontaneous mass movement. In such conditions all the opportunities might have been seized. What could not be realized by a trade union could have been achieved by a more narrowly political organization. Only such an organization is capable of ensuring collective analysis of the situation and a concerted search for the best solutions. By the end of 1981, an attempt had been undertaken to found a political wing of Solidarity – the Polish Party of Labour, constructed, as Holzer observes, 'according to the prototype of the British Labour Party.'[116] Typically, the initiators of the new party were close to the circles of young radicals and not to the traditional leaders of the Left. The British Labour Party was hardly a good model in the Polish situation.

A party, remarked Gramsci, is founded for the struggle for power but it only becomes historically necessary at the moment when the socio-political conditions for victory in that struggle 'are at least in the process of formation, and allow their future evolution – all things going normally – to be foreseen.' The political organization must rally activists, theoreticians and leaders of the socialist movement into a single whole and prepare them for new tasks. 'Since defeat in the struggle must always be envisaged, the preparation of one's own successors is as important as what one does for victory.' If these conditions are fulfilled, the party 'cannot be eliminated by the usual means.'[117]

Kuron and his friends felt the need for political organization but did not know what to do. They hoped to substitute workers' councils for the party. Such plans were patently utopian. Councils are an important form of the democratic self-organization of the working class but, as Harman rightly remarks in regard to the 1956 Hungarian Revolution,

> not just the workers' councils were needed, but also an organization, a 'party', that stood for the councils taking power. Like the old parties, such an

organization would have had to propagate its ideas, contrasting its position with the others; unlike them it would, of necessity, have had to have been a genuinely democratic organization.[118]

The Polish Revolution of 1980–81 turned out the direct opposite of Latin American revolutions. In the latter case 'vanguard' political groups subordinated the spontaneous mass movement to themselves and, to a large extent, deprived it of its life force; in the former case, the revolution was deadlocked through the absence of a political vanguard. Behind the apparent differences there lies a common problem. It was necessary to find organic forms for combining the masses' initiative with the actions of revolutionary elites. It is impossible to realize social change in a dependent country while this problem remains unresolved.

As the Polish socialists had let slip the strategic initiative, only the reformist wing of the PUWP could lay claim to the political leadership of the process of 'social renewal'. The crisis engendered a stratification in the ruling elite. Since the statocratic class apparatus does not have its own social structure, the collapse of the apparatus and weakening of bureaucratic ties has always amounted to the rulers becoming declassed on a mass scale. The *déclassé* bureaucracy divides into numerous warring factions, and in such situations several representatives of the ruling groups inevitably cross over to the side of the revolution. So it was in Hungary in 1956 and in Czechoslovakia in 1968. But it takes time for the ruling class to disintegrate. By the summer of 1980 this process had not yet gone particularly far. The party–state apparatus, still retaining much of its former cohesion, proved a match for the working class which appeared a united and threatening force. The opposition was simple: for the revolution or against it. There were no intermediate possibilities. In such conditions the reformist bureaucrats preferred to stand on the side of their class and oppose the revolution. Premature mass pressure from below, especially in spring 1981, assisted the consolidation of the statocracy. The whole *nomenklatura* united around its conservative wing. More flexible tactics on the part of the revolutionary forces might have prevented this but Solidarity was incapable of political flexibility. From the very beginning it gave the liberals no chance, depriving them of even faint hopes of gaining power. Mieczeslaw Rakowski, who had achieved considerable popularity under Gierek in his capacity as editor of the Warsaw newspaper *Polityka* and who was the acknowledged leader of the liberal bureaucrats, openly called for the revolution's suppression in autumn 1981, stressing that 'no further grounds for a dialogue exist.'[119]

The reform-minded intelligentsia who preferred to work 'within the system' were, prior to 1980, united around the 'Experience and Future' group (DiP). This group was a sort of legal analogue of KOR. It was originally organized to carry out sociological analysis of the basic problems of Polish society and propose recommendations which could be acted upon by the ruling circles. It soon became clear, however, that the experts' conclusions were too radical. As Holzer remarks, after the August events the supporters of DiP strove 'to find a compromise solution, to build bridges between Solidarity and the government and at the same time to secure profound changes in the system.'[120] Although they initially expressed certain hopes in the liberal wing of the party hierarchy, the logic of events drew them ever closer to the working class. In October 1980 DiP's most prominent figure, S. Bratkowski, became editor of the popular newspaper *Zycie Warszawy* and leader of the Union of Journalists. But his activity in these posts invoked the displeasure of the authorities and in the end he was expelled from the PUWP.

The collapse of bureaucratic liberalism did not signify the total disappearance of reformist moods within the ruling party. But their exponents turned out not to be enlightened representatives of the leadership but of the party rank-and-file itself.

The official party in Poland manifested itself as a complex vertical structure, uniting in one organization both oppressors and oppressed, exploiters and exploited. With its aid the former could, in normal times, successfully manipulate the latter, creating the appearance of popular support for the regime and thereby deceiving both public opinion and itself. But in a period of crisis the vertical fissures 'horizontally', and the rank-and-file emerges from its subjection. Created as a tool for the subordination of the bottom to the top, the party in Poland turned into an instrument with which the rank-and-file attempted to exert influence over the government. French Communists who were then in Poland remarked that 'the same contradictions that existed in society were being displayed in the party.'[121] The apparatus lost control over the masses. In spring 1981 the class struggle was transported into the party. This was a predictable and logical outcome of the revolutionary crisis.

Gramsci wrote in *Prison Notebooks* that:

In those regimes which call themselves totalitarian, the traditional function of the institution of the Crown is in fact taken over by the particular party in question, which indeed is totalitarian precisely in that it fulfils this function.

The mass following serves here simply for 'manoeuvre' and 'is kept happy by means of moralising sermons, emotional stimuli, and messianic myths of an awaited golden age, in which all present contradictions and miseries will be automatically resolved and made well.' Since in reality there is nothing to unite the rank-and-file members and leaders of such an organization, 'the party ends up by becoming anachronistic and at moments of acute crisis it is voided of its social content and left as though suspended in mid-air.'[122] This is what happened in Poland.

Sixty per cent of worker-communists joined Solidarity. 'In July and August', conceded *Trybuna Ludu*, 'they were on strike together with their non-party comrades.' They joined the new trade unions 'of their own volition, of their own conviction and, most importantly, of their own need for active trade union work.'[123] Among the strikers there was even one member of the PUWP Central Committee, E. Pustelniak. Around a third of delegates to the inter-factory strike committee in Gdansk and Sczecin were in the Party, and at one enterprise the Party Committee secretary even headed a strike.

In its time the Gierek government had hoped, by beginning to admit the most dynamic and educated workers into the Party on a mass scale, to tame them, tempt them with career prospects and draw them onto the side of the regime. Nothing came of this. At the critical moment the Party workers found themselves on the side of their class. Gierek's policy only created the preconditions for a severe intra-party conflict. In summer 1980 the worker-communists not only joined the strikers but frequently headed them, using, as J. Litynski observed, 'the organiz-ational experience they acquired in the Party.'[124] Rank-and-file members of the PUWP could now remind the leaders of their existence. This did not happen only in factories or where the majority of the party organization consisted of workers. 'People who for years fell asleep at party meetings', wrote an American correspondent, 'are now sitting up — and, more important, talking.'[125] In Kuron's words, 'the revolution had reached the Party and was now going on within the Party.'[126]

The conflict became especially acute in the preparations for the extraordinary congress of the PUWP. At first workers simply refused to be elected as congress delegates. The official newspaper *Zycie Warszawy* acknowledged that 'they do not believe the situation will be put right and they do not want to be accused by others of being unable to do anything concrete for the country.' They all recalled very well how policies which were essentially anti-worker had more than once been carried out in the name of the working class: 'The workers are afraid that no attention will be paid to what they say and that everything will remain the same.'[127] Fifty per cent of party members questioned declared that the leadership took no notice of them and only 39 per cent of party workers said the opposite. The same survey noted 'a marked unwillingness on the part of workers to join the party apparatus.'[128]

As the day of the congress approached the political activity of the party rank-and-file increased. Conservative figures were everywhere rejected by internal party gatherings. At pre-congress regional conferences delegates demanded changes to the rules and structure of the PUWP. 'Horizontal links' spontaneously emerged between lower party organizations, and were condemned by the leadership. This movement was clearly aimed against the apparatus.

In Torun in April 1981, the communist opposition founded an All-Poland Forum for the Party's reorganization. The movement's leader, Z. Iwanow, had been expelled from the Party but this did not prevent workers from electing him delegate to the congress. The British Communist paper, welcoming the Torun Forum, wrote that this was the 'first such measure organized from below without the influence of the Party apparatus.' Delegates condemned the Party leadership for the rift between its declarations and its deeds: 'We are fighting for an idea, but the leadership for its jobs.'[129] The Torun Forum worked out a revolutionary, anti-bureaucratic platform somewhat reminiscent of the programme of the Western New Left in the 1960s. To members of KOR such undertakings seemed too radical. 'It would be better if the party remains undemocratic', declared Litynski.[130] The slogans of the intra-party opposition were rather closer to the calls of Solidarity's radicals than to the moderate wishes of bureaucratic reformers. KOR's leaders were afraid that a victory of the anti-bureaucratic faction in the PUWP could provoke an international crisis and foreign intervention.

In turn the Stalinists convened their own forum in Katowice, where the government was charged with indulging the strikers. The Party was patently divided. Rank-and-file party organizations in the enterprises were quicker to act in the spirit of the decisions of the Torun Forum than in accordance with instructions from the PUWP's central organs. Meanwhile the apparatus, which clearly represented no one, acted as before as a cohesive social group fighting for its privileges independently of, alongside and frequently against the Party, thereby demonstrating its class essence.

The Torun Forum showed the decisiveness of rank-and-file worker communists in fighting for their rights and ideals both in and outside the

Party. Nevertheless, the intra-party opposition was unable to attain a single one of its stated aims. Without support 'from above' the party ranks could not succeed. Only by collaborating with the liberals and isolating the conservative groups in the apparatus could the advocates of party renovation gain real changes in the PUWP. On encountering a united front of apparatchiks, they proved incapable of influencing congress decisions even though they were backed by a majority in the lower organizations. The leadership successfully ran the congress according to its own script, despite a whole sequence of annoying setbacks in its preparation.

'Horizontal structures' turned out to be an insufficiently effective means for struggling with the apparatus. Lacking the necessary support from Solidarity and the Left intelligentsia, this movement gradually came to nought. Shortly after the PUWP congress, Bratkowski and his supporters mounted their final attempt to revive the intra-party opposition by creating the 'Renaissance' society. In Holzer's words, Bratkowski's idea consisted in 'preserving an organizational framework for collaboration with party functionaries disaffected with the leadership and other left-wing circles.'[131] 'Renaissance' united the intra-party opposition with communist reformists already expelled from the Party. Apart from this, Bratkowski and his friends hoped to attract representatives of all socialist and left-wing currents. 'Renaissance' stressed its links with the traditions of the pre-war Polish Socialist Party (PPS) and Left Catholicism, and also with the 'October Left'. One of the society's founders was R. Turski, an editor of the legendary journal Po Prostu.

Essentially, 'Renaissance' endeavoured to carry out the organizational, political, ideological and theoretical work with which KOR could not cope. The orientation towards co-operation between the party opposition and democratic Left was undoubtedly very effective, but time was already slipping by. The party opposition had already lost its battle before the foundation of 'Renaissance' and collaboration with activists of the democratic movement at this stage could only weaken the position of those who hoped to remain within the Party by incurring charges of factionalism and anti-Party activity. Thus only at the end of the revolution was the Polish progressive intelligentsia able to create a more or less suitable instrument for its struggle. Unfortunately, in certain circumstances nothing can compensate for lost time. 'Better never, than late.'

Having no possibility of controlling the apparatus, workers either left the PUWP or, while retaining their formal membership of the Party, pinned their hopes exclusively on Solidarity (at the congress of the new trade union 9.4 per cent of delegates were members of the PUWP and 7.1 per cent had recently left the Party). After the PUWP's June Congress, there was a mass exodus of workers from the Party. Between May 1980 and May 1981 the Party lost 306,000 people (of which 180,000 were workers) and, according to official figures, half a million from July to December.

The Party's crisis and even its actual disintegration did little to weaken the position of the apparatus, although it did call in question the legitimacy of its existence. By autumn 1981 the class struggle in Poland was evidently deadlocked. The government could retreat no further and the leaders of Solidarity could not extract new concessions from the ruling class and simultaneously restrain the masses who were demanding a decisive offensive against the government. As is well known, the crucial question of any revolution is the question of power. In this case it could not be resolved. Even if Solidarity could have toppled the government without fear of external policy difficulties, it is unclear how it could have coped with its new tasks. Power is taken by a party or coalition but not by a trade union or spontaneous mass movement. The state was reeling but there was no alternative to it. The crisis of the system augmented the crisis of Solidarity, which was very evident during the trade union's congress in October 1981. Delegates elected in Gdansk had to make a difficult choice. The future of free trade unions in Poland depended on them. However, questions of strategy were not even discussed at the congress. Instead, various currents held sharp discussions on particular questions, but without coming to any general conclusions. Supporters of KOR wrestled with followers of the well-known historian L. Moczulski, organizer of the nationalist 'Confederation for an Independent Poland' (KPN), and with other national democratic groups. S. Kurowski, an economist with a rightish bent, spoke of the advantages of a market economy on nineteenth-century lines (although without demanding a return to private ownership), and a representative of the Left, R. Bugai, disputed this theory and argued for a socialist, planned market economy. On the whole Walesa associated himself with KOR while simultaneously attempting to maintain his position as a popular leader standing above factions. Delegates enthusiastically supported the speech of E. Lipinski, a participant in the socialist movement since 1906, in which he demonstrated that Poland's ruling regime is both 'counter-revolutionary and anti-socialist.'[132]

Solidarity's programme, adopted by the congress, at bottom repeated the demands laid down in 1968 in the 'Action Programme' of the Czech reform communists. Solidarity promised to fight for the democratization of the various spheres of public life, the abolition of censorship, a planned market economy and self-management of production. The *nomenklatura* principle of forming leading cadres was subjected to sharp criticism. Besides this, the programme contained no overt demands for political pluralism and free elections. The word 'socialism' was not employed once in the document, although it spoke of the socialization of production and the main points of the programme coincided with the principles of Western European socialists (here the leaders of Solidarity preferred to avoid the compromised pseudo-Marxist official language). In the final analysis the programme was totally in accord with KOR's wishes and they could view the congress as a success.[133]

Most delegates, however, were interested not so much in ideological confrontations on programmatic questions between the socialists and nationalists as in the tactical discussions between Lech Walesa and the radicals who were demanding a more active struggle with the state. In the elections for leader Walesa received just 55 per cent of the vote. Although he was victorious in the first round, his influence was clearly waning. From now on, the leader could be openly criticized.

Walesa's 'personality cult' was a major organizational factor. The protests of many workers against this cult were proof of their growing social consciousness, but they led to a weakening of unity. By reducing the role of the apparatus in Solidarity's structure to a minimum, its founders had increased the role of the individual who headed the movement to a maximum, and the weakening of this individual's position threatened the disintegration of the whole organization. No one and nothing could replace Walesa. His personal failures testified to Solidarity's crisis.

Walesa called in vain for the congress delegates 'to make less noise and concentrate more on the business', and insisted on 'more centralized direction of the organization.'[134] He was elected leader but the radicals won all of the basic tactical resolutions. It was they who now constituted a majority in the union's leading bodies and who determined Solidarity's policy. They dominated both the commissions drawing up the resolutions and the speakers' rostrum. They demanded free elections, a re-examination of Poland's foreign policy and a rejection of compromises. The revolution had ceased to be limited. It had reached the summit of its ascent, but was simultaneously undermining its own initial achievements. By rejecting reformism Solidarity doomed itself to failure.

The radicals' success reflected shifts in the consciousness of the Polish proletariat. Paradoxically, in the period of the revolution's greatest successes — the summer and autumn of 1980 — the masses remained convinced of the reformist character of their actions, but once reformist retreat offered the sole practical way out the proletariat finally realized that what was going on was a revolution and was filled with revolutionary illusions.

Walesa suggested that following the congress disorder would reign in the union for at least two to three months, after which he would succeed in re-establishing control over the situation. Unfortunately, time was running out for Solidarity. Although two months after the congress the reformist leaders had once again reinforced their positions and had even been able to establish relative control over the local union organizations, it was already too late: the possibilities of a peaceful solution were past. On 8 November 1981 the conservatives' newspaper *Reality* called openly for 'crossing the frightening Rubicon' and 'suppressing the revolt'.[135] The only question was from which side the blow against the workers' movement would be delivered.

During its congress, Solidarity was not only unable to reinforce its unity, it was unable to resolve a single urgent question. The revolutionary forces had become fragmented, had no precise perspectives, no effective organization and no political strategy. A stalemate had arisen. The revolution had come — in the expression of Z. Geisler, a Czech emigré comparing the Polish experience with that of his own country — 'to a full stop', and the question of 'who wins?' (*kto kogo?*) had to be resolved one way or another.[136] On the one hand, the ruling class was presented with a favourable opportunity to counterattack — and if this opportunity was let slip Solidarity might eventually re-establish its unity and become stronger. On the other hand, the apparatus itself was in crisis and was in no position to put down the workers' movement by normal means. A third force was required, and such a force was found. It was the Army.

The Army's intervention in Polish politics cannot be explained simply by the fact that the ruling class decided to employ armed forces against the people to re-establish its dominance. Neither in August nor in November 1980, when the party apparatus suffered crushing defeats, was it possible to use the Army against the workers. The successful application of military might to suppress the revolution only became a genuine prospect after a socio-political situation conducive to such solutions had been created.

A military coup was the ruling circles' last chance. They prepared for it long and painstakingly. In the end they gambled on General Jaruzelski who — unlike the other candidate, General Moczar — had not compromised himself in previous years by open association with reactionary bureaucratic tendencies. Like Pinochet in Chile, Jaruzelski had a reputation as a conscientious regular soldier uninvolved in politics. First Kania was dismissed, and Jaruzelski took personal control of three key posts: PUWP First Secretary, Prime Minister and Minister of Defence. Then rehearsals of mass repressions were staged through the dispersal of Solidarity activists for alleged breaches of public order (in Chile the same role was played by the military disarming the workers on the eve of the coup). On the whole, Jaruzelski's road to power is strongly reminiscent of his predecessor, Louis Bonaparte. The methods used in preparing to carry out the 'revolution from above' were just the same.

It is curious that Solidarity activists completely failed to notice the coup preparations. As commentators have observed, 'all the union activists' attention was riveted on the "hard" elements in the Party and not on the Army, whose neutrality they did not doubt.'[137] This illusion, bolstered by the army's non-interference in the class struggle at earlier stages in the revolution, proved fateful. When, on 13 December 1981, troops came onto the streets, Solidarity's resistance was desperate but ineffective.

Constitutional guarantees were abrogated, trade union activity forbidden, and thousands of activists and most Solidarity leaders thrown behind bars. The strikes which gripped the whole country after the coup were swiftly and successfully put down. According to Polish newspaper reports, on 15 December there were still 180 enterprises on strike in nineteen of the forty-nine provinces. The following day, according to official figures, nine people were killed and 45,000 arrested. By 17 December the number of striking enterprises had already fallen to forty-nine in five provinces. The Generals were triumphant.

In itself, the fact of a military coup in such circumstances should be no surprise to anyone. The ruling class had played out a classic scenario. The question is: why did the coup prove so successful?

The British communist, Monty Johnstone, recalls that Poland had already 'experienced the Bonapartist rule established by Marshal Pilsudski's coup in 1926.'[138] This makes the blindness of the Polish revolutionaries even harder to understand. To all appearances, the faith of progressive forces in the Army is explained primarily by the special role which it played both in Polish society and in the class struggle. Here we must turn once again to Gramsci's *Prison Notebooks*:

Caesarism can be said to express a situation in which the forces in conflict balance each other in a catastrophic manner; that is to say, they balance each other in such a way that a continuation of the conflict can only terminate in their reciprocal destruction. When the progressive force A struggles with the reactionary force B, not only may A defeat B or B defeat A, but it may happen that neither A nor B defeats the other — that they bleed each other mutually and then a third force C intervenes from outside, subjugating what is left of both A and B.... Caesarism — although it always expresses the particular solution in which a great personality is entrusted with the task of 'arbitration' over a historico-political situation characterised by an equilibrium of forces heading towards catastrophe — does not in all cases have the same historical significance. There can be both progressive and reactionary forms of Caesarism; the exact significance of each form can, in the last analysis, be reconstructed only through concrete history, and not by means of any sociological rule of thumb.'[139]

Caesarism or Bonapartism was the natural outcome of the situation in Poland. This is why there are such striking parallels between Jaruzelski's coup and that of Louis Bonaparte, which was consequent upon the impasse reached in the 1848 French revolution. This also explains the analogy with Chile. Poland's specificity consisted however in the fact that the future character of the military regime remained unclear at first even to its opponents. Many continued to hope for a progressive Caesarism.

From the masses' point of view it was quite natural that the Polish army aspired to the role of 'arbitrator' or third force standing above the contending classes. Jaruzelski's regime defended the interests of the Party apparatchiks, but they were themselves forced out of power. In saving the Party *nomenklatura* as a social entity, Jaruzelski expropriated it politically. In his first speech, the dictator made just one mention of the Party, and then only in passing. The military occupied the key posts involving the levers of political authority, and the PUWP was reduced to a purely decorative role. In the first months after the coup, virtually nothing was reported even in the official Polish press about the activity of leading Party organs. As a group of French sociologists has remarked, Poland was subject to 'absolute power, but more counter-revolutionary than totalitarian. From this point of view one can recall, probably, Franco and Pinochet and not Hitler and Stalin.'[140] The events of 1980–81 had engendered profound structural shifts in Polish society which could not be eradicated by the general's injunctions. Even Jerzy Urban, one of the leading figures in Jaruzelski's regime, acknowledged that these processes were 'irreversible'.[141]

Jaruzelski, for his part, distanced himself from the former rulers. 'The errors and guilt of the ruling groups are clear,' he declared. It was even promised that prominent figures in the pre-revolutionary regime (including Gierek) would be put on trial. Of course this promise was not kept, but in the first days of the military regime it helped to bolster the prestige of the new power. Jaruzelski stressed that:

> The Army is not and will not be a defensive armour for those who, either through ill-intention or incompetence, had a hand in the current crisis, who have learned nothing from this stern lesson and who wish to act in the old way.[142]

The armed forces had to intervene as the pace of events 'was leading to an unavoidable catastrophe'.[143] The General appealed to national democratic traditions and spoke in the language of a liberation movement (thus in the end compromising this language in the same way as the language of Marxism had been compromised). With regard to the Party itself, Jaruzelski projected himself as 'a man from the sidelines', a national leader, standing above bureaucratic factions. Although all representatives of the top were united in their class hatred of the workers, it was almost impossible for the various groupings to reach agreement among themselves. Jaruzelski attempted to establish unity in the Party from outside by forcing all factions into compromise. This task could not in fact be carried out, because the General reduced the Party apparatus to too insignificant a role in political life: the Party's departmental heads, kept away from serious matters, began to squabble among themselves with still greater bitterness since they now had simply nothing else to do. Even internal party affairs were in reality removed from their control. After 13th December the collapse of the PUWP's organizations quickened. By mid-1984 the official organs reported joyously that 'the number of workers leaving the Party is falling.'[144] We can infer that even two years after the coup, workers were continuing to leave the Party, albeit in smaller numbers.

The specificity of the Polish situation lay in the fact that the Caesarist regime could not reconcile the classes in conflict or even force a compromise upon them. Jaruzelski's regime proved to lack the strength to carry out a single one of the tasks confronting it. Engels had written about Bonapartist rule in France that 'under the cloak of the state of siege by military despotism which now veils France, the struggle of the different classes of society is going on as fiercely as ever.'[145] The same could be said about Poland in the ninth decade of the twentieth century.

The regime's inability to overcome the social crisis predetermined (as with Louis Bonaparte) a coup on the part of reaction.

General Jaruzelski's 'third force' had to compel the workers' movement to enter a compromise with the Party bureaucracy, having created conditions favourable to the latter. But the people, having passed through a revolution, could not easily be brought to accept such a solution.

Military domination had to be maintained through periodic repressions.[146] Since a highly developed industrial society, which Poland had been since the mid-1970s, cannot function normally in conditions of constant terror, a partial liberalization followed each wave of repression but quickly changed into fresh purges and arrests. Political and social life in the country became extremely unstable. The regime was in a fever. It was in no position to implement any sort of consistent long-term strategy. Acute economic crisis, workers' resistance to whatever the authorities attempted, managerial confusion and incompetence, the lack of a clear-cut programme from the military administration itself – all led to the collapse of the economic reform on which the General had staked so much. The military hoped that successes in the economy would raise the standard of living and stabilize the political situation. Jaruzelski hoped in this respect to repeat the experience of Janos Kadar's progressive Caesarism in Hungary. Alas, the Polish situation was quite different. As Brus notes, at the moment when Kadar came to implement the reform 'a political compromise had already been achieved and the government enjoyed a quite high reputation.'[147]

In Poland the apparatus had suffered a serious defeat but not a catastrophe. It did not wish to make concessions. The economic conjuncture was also significantly worse than in Hungary in the 1960s. Since reorganizing the state sector remained an extremely difficult and politically dangerous affair (given that Solidarity retained a firm position in the factories), the military gambled on giving incentives to small and medium-sized private enterprise. The major consequence of this course was a growth in social inequality. By the mid-1980s the average standard of living had fallen by 26 per cent by comparison with 1978, but for the well-off it had risen. In 1985, 30 per cent of the population owned 70 per cent of the savings. The nouveaux riches, unlike the working class, posed no problem for the regime. As a Western journalist noted, 'they are not concerned with politics, they use the laws and decrees, economic disorder and corruption, necessity and virtue, to become even richer.'[148] The neo-bourgeoisie became a prop for the regime but could not solve its economic problems because of its historical immaturity.

The blockage of the reforms turned the Army from an 'arbitrator' into the instrument of a conservative pseudo-reformism. Such an evolution of the Polish military's political role was entirely natural. True, back in November 1981 both soldiers and even many Solidarity activists hoped that events would take a different course. Most Western experts, in full agreement with opposition figures, considered that in the event of foreign intervention the Polish Army would fight on the side of the people. This was an army less subordinate to the Party and closer to the Western model than any other in Eastern Europe. In Warsaw there was a special army church where banners were blessed. National Catholic traditions were very strong and Party organizations weakly developed. Because of all this, as Brus observes, the Polish Army had, from the mid-1950s, 'provoked particular suspicion among the Soviet leadership.'[149]

Evidently, it was precisely the apoliticism and independence from the Party which Solidarity activists so admired that allowed the Army to become the PUWP's saviour in 1981. If the Army had been more closely tied to the Party it would have cracked and even split along with it. In fact the crisis in the Party apparatus and the disintegration of the PUWP's lower organizations had no reverberations of any kind within the Army. The failure of official ideology also did not affect it, as the Army had its own ideological traditions. Moreover, these traditions were in the main related to those to which Solidarity appealed. In such conditions the unity of the Army was even reinforced.

Many soldiers, no less than the workers, believed in the Army's neutrality. This was what allowed them to seize power with a clear conscience in the name of 'saving the nation'. Even after the coup, many opposition figures insisted on this interpretation of the December events. Michnik stressed that if power had been seized by out-and-out Stalinists it would have been still worse for the Poles. In actual fact the PUWP's Stalinist faction did not have the strength to seize power, let alone to hold onto it. Herein lies the crux of the matter: a counter-revolutionary coup could only be successful on the basis of a Caesarist policy which Michnik declared to be the lesser evil. In his analysis of the events of 1981, Michnik spoke of the struggle between 'the system' and 'organized society' without a thought for the actual alignment of class forces in the country. In his conception beautiful formulae replaced concrete sociological investigation. It is not surprising that such an approach led to the wrong conclusions.[150]

Solidarity was taken unawares and defeated, but it was not routed. A significant section of activists went underground. Workers' demonstrations periodically threw down a challenge to the government. Illegal literature continued to be distributed in huge quantities. New forms of protest appeared: for example, a boycott of public transport. A sizeable part of the priesthood, despite the conciliatory position of the Episcopate, retained a close association with underground workers' organizations, assisting them in every way possible. The effectiveness of mass resistance was one of the reasons for the collapse of the Caesarist compromise. The split in the ranks of the ruling class-apparatus continued to deepen. Jaruzelski's inability to 'introduce order' and completely re-establish the pre-revolutionary situation provoked increasing disquiet among sections of the leadership and repressive apparatus. After the murder in October 1984 of the worker-priest, Jerzy Popieluszko, by state security agents, an open political crisis broke out in the country. Jaruzelski was forced to put the murderers on trial. Thousands of people again came onto the streets. Nevertheless, Solidarity could not make use of the opportunities opening up for it. The union's leaders did not know what to do and activists had no distinct programme and no clear grasp of the new conditions.

Immediately after the coup, an intense discussion began in the underground about the character of the military regime and methods of fighting it. In the last analysis it was a question of radically reorganizing the workers' movement itself and creating new organizational and political forms. Gradually doubts began to surface about the validity of the principles which had guided revolutionaries in the period of Solidarity's legal activity. Most of the resistance leaders defended the concept of an 'underground society'. In and of itself, this term remained extremely vague and politically indeterminate. Bujak, who headed Solidarity while Walesa was under house arrest, spoke a great deal about the 'underground society' but was unable to clarify the term. It was a matter of creating informal structures in all spheres of life independent of the state. This process had been developing naturally in Poland since 1968. The existence of the 'underground society' undoubtedly undermines the position of the ruling class but, as a political alternative, it cannot be taken seriously. Solidarity's shortcomings are reproduced in a heightened form in the 'underground society'.

Kuron, who had assimilated the lessons of 1981 rather better, suggested another solution. He argued in favour of founding a centralized revolutionary organization capable of carrying on a consistent and effective political struggle. In a sense, this represented a return to Lenin's revolutionary strategy: but Kuron did not acknowledge this and did not elaborate what sort of programme, ideology and structure the proposed organization would have.

The weaknesses of the proposals being advanced by the leaders became more and more obvious to rank-and-file activists. As one of them remarked, the Solidarity leadership talks about 'a long road' but 'a road must have an end.'[151] An interest in theory was reawakened among those in the underground. Many remembered the existence of the works of Marx and Rosa Luxemburg. Left-wing activists united in the organiz-ation 'Fighting Solidarity'. Underground journals — *Robotnik, Front Robotniczy, Wolny Robotnik* — began a discussion on re-establishing the Polish Socialist Party, and the main arguments were not about whether a party is necessary in general (as they had been in 1981), but about what sort of structure and programme it would have. *Robotnik* fought for a social democratic orientation whereas several other groups under the strong influence of Trotskyism hoped to see a socialist movement in Poland that was implacably revolutionary and Marxist.

Experience shows that in the contemporary world no socialist organization striving to gain mass support and realize genuinely radical changes can manage without reformist politics.

In 1988–89 Jaruzelski's regime entered a new crisis which brought an end to all of the 'gains' of martial law. Once again, as in 1980, there were strikes and demonstrations; once again, Solidarity was operating openly. For the first time in the post-war period the authorities were forced not only to recognize the legal status of independent trade unions, but to hold semi-free elections. In accordance with the agreement with the government, Solidarity gained the opportunity to contest 35 per cent of seats in the Sejm and all the seats in the Senate. The outcome was that Solidarity won ALL of the seats it contested. It is hard to imagine a more catastrophic electoral result for the regime, which still endeavoured to call itself popular. But, in this difficult situation, Jaruzelski received assistance from an unexpected quarter: Solidarity's leaders in fact supported the government's course, thereby helping it to stay afloat.

This time there was no question of a threatened Soviet intervention. Solidarity's leadership emerged from its clandestine existence with its authority intact and a greater degree of professionalism; but it had, to a significant extent, lost contact with those who had supported and sustained it. Opposition technocrats were able to counterpose only one demand to those of government technocrats: give us the positions and we'll do exactly the same, only better.

Preparations for cutting back unprofitable branches of the economy — which were, at the same time, Solidarity's social base — and for linking Poland to the West's economy as one of the most prosperous and competitive Third World countries had taken Solidarity's leaders by surprise. However, the government was not able to carry out such a course — which would have ensured the definitive ruin and social degradation of the majority of Poles — without encountering the sharp resistance of working people. It was precisely this resistance which led to the crisis of 1988–89. But from that moment the Solidarity leadership, with all its moral authority, was called upon to ease the government's thankless task. Adam Michnik utilized all his considerable influence to assure his fellow citizens that there was 'no alternative' to the adopted course. This essential phrase of Mrs Thatcher's had now become popular even in Poland. Of course, the traditional cliché about the 'leaders' betraying the 'masses' explains very little. The Solidarity leadership's lagging behind events and its inability to advance its own alternative to the authorities' technocratic and monetarist course is related to Solidarity's general ideological weakness.

It is quite clear that the formation of a democratic alternative, which envisages the creation of democratic planning mechanisms or, most probably, the municipalization of a section of state enterprises in order to create on this basis a modern economy of 'small firms', and the gradual retraining of workers made redundant by obsolete enterprises alongside the creation of new jobs, could only successfully be realized as a conse- quence of the serious transformation of Polish society. The elaboration of a democratic strategy for a way out of the crisis was not an easy affair — there could be no guarantee of automatic success. But the fact is that the question of a democratic alternative was not even posed in Solidarity's leading circles. Its leaders, following the official experts, continued mechanically to repeat meaningless generalities about the need for a 'free market'. Even those elements of an alternative strategy which were directed at self-management and were in Solidarity's 1980 programme were either safely forgotten or pushed into the background.

One could say that, in a certain sense, the opportunism of 1989 was retribution for the spontaneity of 1980. With neither their own strategy nor theory, Solidarity's leaders found themselves hostages of the ruling caste with whom they had struggled their entire lives! One could scarcely find a better example to confirm the old thesis about the relationship between theory and practice. The democratic movement, striving for genuine renewal in Eastern Europe, cannot do without either Marxist theory or a revolutionary strategy. Otherwise, any of our victories may turn into infamous defeats.

Notes

1. Marshall I. Goldman, *U.S.S.R. in Crisis: The Failure of an Economic System*, New York 1983, p. 175.
2. Gramsci, *Prison Notebooks*, p. 109.
3. Wl. Brus, *Storia economica dell'Europa orientale: 1950–80*, Rome 1983, p. 12.
4. Chris Harman, *Bureaucracy and Revolution in Eastern Europe*, London 1974, p. 63.
5. Brus, p. 29.
6. *Pologne. Le Dossier de Solidarité. Par L'Alternative*, Paris 1982, p. 7.
7. *The World Today*, August 1957, p. 347.
8. Adam Michnik, *Pol'skii Dialog: Tserkov' – Levye*, London 1980, p. 76.

   In February 1957, Gomulka organized elections in which the number of officially sanctioned candidates exceeded the number of deputies' places. These semi-free elections received the blessing of the Church. The Episcopate called upon believers 'to carry out their duty' and take part in them. An Italian commentator correctly notes that this 'was equivalent to ordering Catholics to vote for the National Front list', i.e. for the government (F. Bertone, *L'Anomalia Polacca*, Rome 1981, p. 207). As a result of the elections, the Catholic group 'Znak' was formed in the Sejm. Its relations with the Episcopate remained, however, quite complex, for there were a number of left-wing Catholics among the 'Znak' deputies. The Primate of the Polish Church, Cardinal Wyszinski, declared that 'the Church does not need politics but confessors and defenders' (A. Micewski, *Wspolrzadic czy nie klamac*, Paris 1978, p. 493).
9. *Zycie Warszawy*, 13 January 1981.
10. Brus, p. 75. The tragic outcome of the Hungarian Revolution reinforced Gomulka's reputation as a moderate realist who knew the limits of what he could do.
11. *Po Prostu*, 6 January 1957.
12. *Poly'sha 1980: 'Solidarnosti' god pervyi*, London 1981, p. 19. (Hereafter *Poly'sha 1980*.)
13. Ibid., p. 27.
14. It is true that at first the illusion was created of a reconciliation between the contending classes. The extreme right-wing Polish emigré, J. Mackiewicz, concedes that Gomulka had gained 'a level of solidarity with the Party among broad layers of the population that had not been achieved, probably, by a single other Communist leader' (J. Mackiewicz, *Pobeda Provokatsii*, London (Canada) 1983, p. 164).
15. *Zycie Warszawy*, 13 January 1981.
16. N. Karsov and S. Szechter, *Monuments are not Loved*, London 1970, p. 285. In the West, however, Kuron and Modzelewski's 'Letter' became celebrated and was translated into several languages. In the eyes of the western Left, Kuron became 'a theoretician of the revolutionary movement and one of its major inspirations', an originator 'of the strategy of struggle for self-managing socialism' (Y. Craipeau). In actual fact, Kuron and Modzelewski's 'Letter' only repeated the notion of the

state–capitalist character of the system, widely disseminated in samizdat at that time. Kuron and Modzelewski's negative attitude towards parliamentarism at this time is proof of their extremely simplified approach to the problem of democraćy. The appeal to the Polish Left to implement an independent line and not rest content with supporting official reformism is suspended in mid-air, for it is unclear how this could be concretely expressed. The authors of the 'Letter' had already reviewed their ideas by 1968-70. Thus Fernando Claudin is patently in error when he writes that Kuron and Modzelewski's essay represented a major contribution to Marxist analysis of the societies of the East (F. Claudin, *La oposicion en el 'socialismo real'*, Madrid 1981, p. 294.)

17. *Le Monde*, 16 March 1968.
18. The organizer of the anti-semitic campaign was General Moczar, who in 1981 aspired to the role of pacifier, but was pushed aside by the younger pretender, General Jaruzelski. The anti-semitic campaign did not bring any glory to Gomulka. In the eyes of the West, he had lost his reputation as a liberal. In the words of Neal Ascherson, 'the world watched the "anti-Zionist" campaign with incredulous horror' (Neal Ascherson, *The Polish August: What Has Happened in Poland*, London 1981, p. 91). The reputation of the Catholic Church also suffered, as it chose to remain silent. A series of Polish Catholic writers had earlier attempted to justify the Episcopate's position (for example, Kisilewski), but it is still a fact that only Archbishop Wojtyla of Cracow supported the youth. 'The Church', remarks Bertone, 'did not even publish a document in protest, although it had done so for less important reasons' (Bertone, p. 237).
19. Bertone, p. 235.
20. *Problemy Vostochnoi Evropy*, no. 11/12. 1985, p. 166.
21. Ascherson, p. 97.
22. *Zycie Warszawy*, 31 December 1981.
23. *Pol'skoe Obozrenie*, 22 December 1970, p. 3.
24. Ibid., pp. 7-8.
25. *Zycie Warszawy*, 22 December 1970.
26. Gramsci, *Prison Notebooks*, p. 210.
27. L. Kolakowski, *Pokhvala Neposledovatelnosti*, Florence 1974.
28. Brus, p. 196.
29. *Zycie Warszawy*, 31 January 1981.
30. *Vorwärts*, Basle, 18 December 1980, p. 10.
31. *Kierunki dzialania zwiazku w obecnej sytuacji kraju. Texy do dyskusji*, Solidarnosc, 17 April 1981.
32. *Cahiers du communisme*, 1980, no. 10, p. 92.
33. *Zycie Gospodarcze*, 24 August 1980.
34. *Vorwärts*, Basle, 31 July 1980, p. 8.
35. Ascherson, p. 109. The increasing cost of imports was linked to the low rates of construction in Poland itself which created the need for additional expenditure.
36. Exporting enterprises were at first granted supplementary rights, but the shortage of hard currency led to this situation being changed. The interest of producers in the results of their labour was thereby diminished.
37. Brus, p. 113.
38. Ibid., p. 270.

39. R. Chernotsova, 'Osobennosti demograficheskoi situatsii v evropeiskikh stranakh – chlenov SEV', in *Regional'nye osobennosti vosproizvodstva i migrastii naseleniya v SSSR*, Moscow 1981, p. 113.

40. The Italian Communist, A. Guerra, has justifiably written that such a contradiction is typical 'not only of Poland' (*L'Unità*, 23 August 1980).

41. W. Kuczynski, *La seconda Polonia*, Rome 1981, p. 199.

42. *Le Monde Diplomatique*, July 1977.

43. J. Dimet and J. Estager, *Pologne: une révolution dans le socialisme?*, Paris 1981, p. 69.

44. *L'Unità*, 23 August 1980. Kuron and Michnik entered political life as left-wing socialists, and from the very beginning KOR united the most progressive section of the Polish intelligentsia. It was no accident that KOR's organ was called *Robotnik* (the same name as that of the old socialist party liquidated by the Stalinists). On the other hand, it should be remembered that by the 1970s Kuron and Michnik's views had changed in many respects compared to the 1966–68 period. Kuron said in the late 1970s: 'I remain true to the fundamental values that I have striven to realise but I have altered my opinion as to the methods through which they can be achieved' (*Praxis: Una rivista politica per una nuova sinistra*, no. 13, 1977, p. 15).

45. *Pologne*, p. 117.

46. Gierek's 'liberal' regime, which displayed some tolerance toward well-known dissidents, dealt very cruelly with anonymous worker and student activists. Unpunished police despotism in the localities was a logical part of bureaucratic decentralization. KOR's struggle to free 'rank-and-file' activists from the workers' movement was in these conditions a political and moral necessity for the intelligentsia. When those arrested had been released, KOR renamed itself the 'Committee for Social Self-Defence' (KOS), but the old title was so familiar that people continued to use it. The organization began to be called KOR-KOS or simply KOR. Curiously, official newspapers in some Eastern European countries wrote in 1980–81 that TsRU had organised the fusion of two underground groups – KOR and KOS.... Incidentally on TsRU: in 1978 the Polish Procurator's Office was forced to drop its case against the leaders of KOR for 'the investigation has not received full proof which confirms a direct link between those under investigation and foreign organizations hostile to Poland' (*Pol'sha 1980*, p. 206).

47. Marx and Engels, *Sochineniya*, vol. 35, p. 222.

48. Marx, *The Class Struggles in France*, p. 61.

49. *Problems of Communism*, January–February 1982, pp. 3–4.

50. *Vizantiiskie ocherki*, Moscow 1977, p. 54.

51. Michnik, p. 18.

52. Marx and Engels, *Sochineniya*, vo. 22, p. 467.

53. *Pologne*, p. 9. Wojtyla considered himself an expression of the social tendencies in Catholicism, differentiating himself from the more conservative Primate of the Polish Church, Cardinal Wyszynski. In 1968 Wojtyla spoke out in defence of rebellious youth and against anti-semitism. On becoming Pope, however, Wojtyla acquired a reputation in the West as a conservative. His polemic with liberation theology, which had become the banner of left-wing Christians in Latin America, while not devoid of some positive features, placed the Vatican

in the position of a clearly conservative force. This is explained, in my view, not only by the traditionalist approach of the former Cardinal of Cracow to questions of faith but also by a somewhat provincial outlook on the world. Despite a brilliant knowledge of languages, Wojtyla remained first and foremost a 'Polish Pope' and he assessed events in Latin America through the prism of his own Polish experience.

54. Harman, p. 255.
55. Official reformists afterwards tried to justify themselves by the fact that the Party leadership 'did not take heed of the realistic appraisals and demands coming from below to turn off from a mistaken path' (*Trybuna Ludu*, 11 December 1980).
56. *U.S. News and World Report*, September 1, 1980, p. 17.
57. *Pologne*, p. 51.
58. *Trybuna Ludu*, 11 December 1980. The Swiss Communist paper wrote: 'The Polish workers are not fighting to give their yards back to the previous owners but for socialist reforms' (*Vorwärts* (Basle), 4 September 1980, p. 8). It was precisely this that made the Gdansk strikes so dangerous for the Party.
59. *Trybuna Ludu*, 11 December 1980. The actions of the Gdansk strikers in 1980 were a 'model' in all respects. One Western observer accurately noted that the Polish workers' movement 'is acting as if it had come directly from the pages of Marx's book' (quoted in Claudin, p. 368).
60. *L'Express*, no. 4522, 1980, p. 50. The transfer of the functions of real power in the localities into the hands of the strikers (a typical sign of the revolutionary dictatorship of the proletariat) was recognized by the Party organs themselves on the Baltic Coast. See *Solidarnosc*, SBI, no. 4, 25 August 1980. Alongside the class factor an important role was played by the common Slavic tradition of self-organization. Those who were in Moscow on 16 October 1941 recall the surprising degree of order in the city, where there was no longer any government or security forces. In this respect Slavs are surprisingly different from, for example, Germans.
61. Harman, p. 113.
62. J. Holzer, *Solidarität*, Munich 1985, p. 162.
63. Marx and Engels, *Collected Works*, vol. 3, pp. 46–7.
64. Lenin, CW, vol. 15, p. 276.
65. *Pologne*, p. 195.
66. J. Taylor, *Five Months with 'Solidarity'*, London 1981, p. 36.
67. *Pol'sha 1980*, p. 234.
68. Soviet official researchers have always criticized the structure of British trade unions, stressing that the branch principle makes the creation of 'genuinely combative unions' more difficult (N. Matkovskii, *Kratkii ocherk profsoyuznogo dvizheniya v Anglii*, Moscow 1954, p. 15).
69. *Pologne*, p. 131.
70. Ibid., p. 92.
71. Ibid., p. 83.
72. Andrew Cockburn has written about the acute struggle within the Soviet leadership on the question of Poland. In his opinion there were moments when advocates of intervention gained the upper hand (see A. Cockburn, *The Threat: Inside the Soviet Military Machine*, London 1983, pp. 8, 109).
73. *Pologne*, p. 54.

74. Ibid., p. 55.
75. Ibid., p. 65. See also *Problemy Vostochnoi Evropy*, no. 2, 1981, p 41.
76. Vodolazov, p. 43.
77. *Pologne*, p. 71.
78. *Literatura*, 1 January 1981. The West German *Süddeutsche Zeitung* (7 October 1981) wrote that, in the opinion of many, the workers had become the 'actual ruling class' in Poland. This was a patent illusion.
79. *Pologne*, p. 82.
80. *Robotnik*, no. 68/69, 23 November 1980.
81. Holzer, p. 213. The authorities' concessions were always late in coming. When Lublin railway centre workers demanded new factory councils they were promised a freeze in meat prices for a year. When the Baltic Coast demanded free trade unions Gierek promised them new elections to the factory councils.
82. Ibid., pp. 213, 214.
83. *Osteuropa-Info*, no. 3, 1981, p. 76.
84. A. Touraine and others, *Solidarnosć*, Milan 1982, p. 81.
85. *Newsweek*, 8 September 1980, p. 11.
86. The Polish events had the biggest impact on the most prosperous country in the Eastern bloc — Hungary. They accelerated the process of internal reform and Hungarian reformists even hoped to find a strategic ally in the shape of Solidarity, although the latter was not ready for this. S. Gaspar, the leader of the official Hungarian unions, established relations with Solidarity. In December 1980 he declared 'we cannot speak about independence. Autonomy — yes' (*Weg und Ziel*, no. 12, 1980, p. 436.
87. *Izvestia*, 26 February 1982. See also *Pravda*, 14 December 1981.
88. *Robotnik*, no. 68–69, 23 November 1980.
89. *Pologne*, p. 61.
90. *Sovremennaya Pol'sha*, 1981, no. 21.
91. *Zycie Warszawy*, 29 October 1980.
92. *Pologne*, p. 75.
93. *Newsweek*, 15 September 1980, p. 14.
94. *Osteuropa-Info*, no. 3, 1981, pp. 55–6.
95. A. Nove, *Economics of Feasible Socialism*, p. 145.
96. Kuczynski, p. 56. For an account of the project prepared by official experts see *Sovremennaya Pol'sha*, no. 3, 1981. The final version has been correctly assessed by Western observers as 'a defeat for the economic "conservatives"' (*Problems of Communism*, no. 2, 1982, p. 8). Nevertheless, the project had important inadequacies. Complete clarity is lacking on the question of enterprise profit or income and agricultural problems do not receive a serious solution. Here, the project is of interest to us not as a theoretical document but as a political fact.
97. Wl. Brus, 'Prefazione', in Kuczynski, p. 16. See also *Marxism Today*, November 1980.
98. R. Garaudy, *L'Alternative*, Paris 1972, p. 231.
99. Marx, *Capital*, vol. 1, p. 171.
100. P. Ingrao, *Masses et pouvoir*, Paris 1980, p. 154.
101. *Sovremennaya Pol'sha*, no. 19, 1981, p. 2.
102. *L'URSS et L'Europe de l'Est en 1981–82*, Paris, 22 June 1982, p. 180.

103. *Le Soir*, 4–5 October 1981, p. 3.
104. *Marxism Today*, February 1982, p. 37.
105. *Kierunki dzialania zwiazku w obecnej sytuacji kraju, I.* Solidarity's actual ideology appeared a mixture of Christian socialism, populism and anti-communism.
106. Lenin, CW, vol. 5 p. 370.
107. *Socialist Register*, 1982, p. 106.
108. *Osteuropa-Info*, no. 3, 1981, p. 76.
109. *Pologne*, pp. 166, 168.
110. Ascherson, p. 138.
111. K. Pomian said bitterly that 'the Communists have killed Socialism in Poland' (*Tribuna*, no. 2, 1983, p. 15).
112. *Il fronte del dissenso polacco*, Milan 1979, p. 14.
113. Gramsci, *Prison Notebooks*, p. 153.
114. When we are discussing the intelligentsia in the conditions of revolution this concept should not be reduced to the sociological definition of 'persons engaged in intellectual labour.' The working class also has its intelligentsia. This was another of the problems examined by Gramsci. The Argentinian Marxist, E. Agosti, says that the revolutionary party of the working class is its 'collective intellectual' (Agosti, p. 358). In my view the 'collective intellectual' should not always be organized into a formal political party — there exist other possibilities. On the eve of the great French Revolution the 'collective intellectual' was a social circle formed thanks to the activity of Diderot and the Encyclopaedists. The trouble in Poland was that the 'collective intellectual' took the form of KOR and DiP, which were not conscious of their historical tasks.
115. Touraine and others, pp. 94, 38.
116. Holzer, p. 353.
117. Gramsci, *Prison Notebooks*, pp. 152, 153.
118. Harman, p. 187. Neil Ascherson (p. 245) comes to a similar conclusion from his analysis of the Polish events of 1981.
119. *Süddeutsche Zeitung*, 7 October 1981, p. 11.
120. Holzer, p. 171.
121. Dimet and Estager, p. 205.
122. Gramsci, *Prison Notebooks*, pp. 147–8, 150, 211.
123. *Trybuna Ludu*, 11 December 1980.
124. *Labour Focus on Eastern Europe*, November 1979–January 1980, p. 12.
125. *Newsweek*, 8 September 1980, p. 7.
126. Quoted in *New Left Review*, May–June 1983, p. 37.
127. *Zycie Warszawy*, 3 June 1981.
128. *Rinascita*, no. 25, 1981, p. 21.
129. *Morning Star*, 16 April 1981.
130. Quoted in Taylor, p. 77.
131. Holzer, p. 175.
132. *Pologne*, p. 173.
133. Marxist terminology was usurped by the ruling class and the need for a change of language was completely understandable. The trouble was that KOR did not even attempt to fight the PUWP for a part of its ideological space and show the difference between bureaucratic pseudo-socialism and democratic socialism.

Because of this, General Jaruzelski was able to depict himself as a defender of socialist principles. It should be remembered that among Solidarity's supporters there were in reality only a few people who held anti-socialist opinions. Kautsky's observation that there are reactionary elements in any mass movement should be recalled here. The question is who prevails.

134. *Le Soir*, 4–5 October 1981.

135. *Rzeczywistnost*, 8 November 1981.

136. *Problemy Vostochnoi Evropy*, no. 7/8, 1983, p. 142.

137. *L'URSS et L'Europe de l'Est en 1981–82. Notes et Etudes documentaires*, no. 4673–4674. *La Documentation français*, Paris, 22 June 1982, p. 12.

138. *Marxism Today*, February 1982, p. 14.

139. Gramsci, *Prison Notebooks*, p. 219.

140. Touraine and others, p. 235. Brus stresses that under Jaruzelski the military seized all key posts not only in the government but also in the localities, and the Party apparatus was pushed 'into a secondary role' (*Problemy Vostochnoi Evropy*, no. 9/10, 1984, p. 169).

141. *Pojedynek, Wtorkowe konferencje rzecznika prasowego rzadu, 1981–85*, Warsaw 1985, p. 35.

142. *Izvestia*, 2 January 1982.

143. *Pravda*, 14 December 1981.

144. *Prolemy Mira i Sotsializma*, no. 6, 1984, p. 57. The social processes occurring in Poland at the end of the revolutionary period and during Jaruzelski's 'normalization' (1981–6) have been analysed in great detail by participants in the 'Crises in Soviet-type systems' research project under Z. Mlynar. See *The Crisis – Problems in Poland. Parts I–II*, Cologne 1986.

145. Marx and Engels, *Collected Works*, vol. 11, pp. 215–16.

146. In cases where the police have killed workers, the official press has placed the responsibility for what happened on the workers themselves: 'Human life is of too much value for the inspirers of tension and disorder to be allowed to threaten it through actions that are irresponsible and inconsistent with martial law' (*Izvestia*, 19 December 1981). Such cannibalistic humanism!

147. *Problemy Vostochnoi Evropy*, no. 9/10, 1984, p. 173.

148. *Panorama*, 22 September 1985, p. 118.

149. Brus, p. 26. It is curious that among the causes of the 1973 coup in Chile, Soviet specialists name the 'apolitical character of the Chilean Army' (see *Komsomol' skaya Pravada*, 7 September 1983).

150. See *Eros*, 16 December 1983, p. 45.

151. *Inprecor*, no. 200, 1985, p. 16.

5

Stability instead of Reform: Brezhnevism and Technocracy

As history shows, reforms from above rarely prove sufficient to resolve society's basic contradictions, but they are at least evidence of the fact that the ruling class is conscious of the depth of the problems confronting the country. A repudiation of reform is, as a rule, proof of the opposite. In many countries the obstinacy of conservative ruling groups unwilling to make timely concessions has led to catastrophe. Sometimes the crisis has been successfully overcome (one has only to recall Alexander II's abolition of serfdom in Russia). In any case, however, prolonged periods of conservative rule have been paid for by both ruling circles and the country as a whole.

In the 1950s the Soviet leadership displayed considerable flexibility and ability to react in time to the changing social situation. The limited transformations carried out by Nikita Khrushchev in 1953–57 entirely corresponded to the country's level of development. In the USSR an industrial society had arisen for which Stalin's techniques were already an anachronism. After 1953 the new leadership began, without much hesitation and meeting no serious resistance, to implement changes not only in the methods of administering the state but in the whole way of life of the Soviet people. Although opposition from reactionary groups in the bureaucracy increased as the reforms bit deeper, reaching a climax in 1957 when a significant section of Stalin's 'old guard' opposed Khrushchev, such conflicts could not prevent the success of destalinization. As a result, at the end of the 1950s, our country was able to enter the epoch of the scientific-technical revolution in competition with the industrial democracies of the West. For a long time Soviet space technology was the most advanced, and in many other fields our country was also regarded as among the leaders. But in the 1960s new tasks began to face the country which demanded recurrent changes of course.

Under Stalin, Russia was turned into an industrial power. In the post-Stalin period the question arose of transition from 'primary' industrialization to higher forms of industrial production, from extensive to intensive development, from the first stage of the scientific-technological revolution, connected with the exploitation of new technological principles, to the renovation of the country's entire productive apparatus. This required, first of all, the creation of a dynamic, flexible system of economic management capable of self-regulation and self-development.

Khrushchev was evidently aware of the significance of these problems. His chosen path envisaged a partial decentralization of economic management by establishing territorial Economic Councils (Sovnarkhozy). At the same time, from 1962 onwards the policy of 'delimiting the spheres of activity' of city and rural Party organizations began to be implemented, and many viewed this as preparation for a two-party system. The uncompromising criticism of Stalin, begun at the 20th and continued at the 22nd Party Congress, also exceeded the limits initially set for it: not only Stalin was condemned, but Stalinism as well. The course chosen by Khrushchev led inevitably to ideological and political reform.

The Party apparatus was plainly unprepared for such radical changes. In the 1950s, when the consequences of Stalin's 'personality cult' were being overcome, Khrushchev successfully rallied the overwhelming majority of the Party leadership around him. The first stages of political modernization, implemented in 1953–57, won the support of a majority of Party functionaries tired of Stalin's purges and sensing the need for change. When, after the repeated condemnation of Stalin at the 22nd Congress, the question arose of the country's further development, the broad coalition on which Khrushchev depended began to break up. Conservative, reformist and technocratic tendencies could be picked out in the bureaucratic milieu. The cessation of Stalin's purges, which had destabilized the apparatus (while imparting to it a certain dynamism), reinforced social ties within the ruling groups, made them conscious of their specific interests and united them around those leaders capable of defending such interests. In this way Khrushchev's policy of destalinization itself prepared the conditions which later led to his fall.

Within the bureaucracy, the conservatives leant for support primarily upon provincial Party workers, whose main interest was in the stability of their own positions. Stopping the terror suited them down to the ground, for Stalin's purges had claimed the lives of many in their milieu; but socio-economic, and still more political, reforms did not enter their plans. Khrushchev eventually lost the backing of this social stratum when he demanded the renewal of cadres at all levels of the Party hierarchy. From that moment they saw him not as Party leader but as a subversive element.

The technocratic group arose on the basis of the central Party apparatus and officials in the economic and state system of management. If workers in the Party regional committees (*obkoms*) found their leaders in the persons of Leonid Brezhnev and Mikhail Suslov, then the technocrats were clearly sympathetic to Aleksei Kosygin. The reformist current proved to be the weakest. It was represented chiefly by experts and ideologists who had made their careers in the conditions of Khrushchev's thaw. It had no solid support in the apparatus. In these circumstances Khrushchev, who pinned his political career on the continuance of radical reforms, was doomed.

Khrushchev's ouster in October 1964 was the result of the combined efforts of conservative and technocratic groups. It is precisely this which explains the collective character of the leadership elected at the October Plenum. Having gained the position of Party General Secretary, Brezhnev was not elected to any of the leading posts in the state. The post of Chairman of the Council of Ministers was taken by Kosygin. Thus, from the very beginning, the policy of the new administration was determined by a compromise between the two currents (and the balance of forces between them). Both groups were interested in putting a stop to Khrushchev's experiments, which they found extremely radical and eccentric. At the Plenum, the conservative local bureaucracy succeeded in having the policy of 'stability of cadres' proclaimed, which ensured that Party apparatchiks need no longer fear for their positions. The technocrats for their part wanted the policy of change to continue, but understood by this something quite different from the reformists. For them changes meant perfecting the system of management. It was a question of regulating social structures, not of their transformation.

The 1965 economic reform, which was at once popularly christened the 'Kosygin' reform, was the technocracy's brainchild. The starting point for the authors of the reformist project was the need to supplement the political modernization of the Khrushchev decade with economic modernization. They certainly did not wish to go too far with this. From the very start, the limits of the reform were clearly defined. Instead of Khrushchev's experiments, they proposed precisely planned measures, all subordinated to a single end: simplifying the process of economic management. The reform had no other purposes. Although the course toward decentralization was retained, Khrushchev's idea of territorial *Sovnarkhozy* was buried. The path chosen by Khrushchev might have led to the formation of local socio-political centres independent of Moscow. Kosygin's technocratic faction, based precisely on the Moscow party-state apparatus, had no interest in such a solution. Its task was to lighten the economic load on this apparatus and increase its efficiency — but under no circumstances to undermine its power.

Stalin's system of planning was tailored to the conditions of a backward country. It was easier to conduct the process of industrialization from a single centre. This allowed resources to be concentrated and utilized in the most important areas. An industrial society's more complex economy requires other methods. The centre cannot solve all questions; it cannot differentiate between what is of primary importance and what is secondary. The planning apparatus proves to be in no position to cope with the increasing flow of information from all sides. Conditions arise in which a certain widening of the powers of local economic organs seems essential to lighten the workload of the central apparatus itself.[1]

In the late 1940s, a perspective plan for 15 years was worked out. 1965 was chosen as the end point. When Brezhnev and his colleagues came to compare actual results with the plan targets, a singular picture emerged. On the whole plan, figures were exceeded by 30 per cent; for the production of oil, by 100 per cent; for electricity, by 56 per cent; for gas, by 48 per cent — and so on. At the same time, agricultural production was underfulfilled by 38 per cent and the productivity of labour in the countryside was only 67 per cent of the target. Light industry also failed to meet the planned figures. Not one indicator was 100 per cent fulfilled — targets were either overfulfilled or underfulfilled, and in both cases the differences proved enormous. Analysis of the fifteen-year plan revealed the ineffectiveness of Stalin's system of planning. We can say in anticipation that subsequent long-term plans, elaborated far too thoroughly, proved no more successful than the first (the only difference being that long-term plans in the 1960s were as a rule underfulfilled, whereas Stalin's plan was, on the whole, overfulfilled). But failures of planning caused greater disturbance in 1965 than in subsequent years when they had become tolerated. Wide criticism of Stalin's methods of economic management began in the press. Many writers stressed that centralized planning had arisen 'in circumstances of a lack of experience of socialist construction and of a breach of democratic norms in state and party life.'[2] On the other hand, the difficulties and problems associated with decentralization were as yet unknown. The economic reform was therefore supported initially by all Party leaders, although not to an equal degree.

The preparation for changes once again revived reformist moods. Many experts began openly to criticize existing arrangements, expressing quite radical ideas. It was said everywhere that the system by which enterprises were assessed according to their level of plan fulfillment gave an advantage to those receiving less intensive tasks, thus furthering the fall in the economy's rates of growth. It was essential to give the enterprise more interest in the end product, to obviate the need for the centre to resolve petty, secondary questions, and to encourage initiative in the localities.[3]

Later, a series of writers underlined the fact that the measures which had been taken were obviously inadequate. Victor Zaslavsky wrote that the cause of subsequent failures was 'lack of independence, inefficiency and the conservative character of the reform itself.'[4] The collaboration of technocrats and conservatives in drawing up the draft reform could not but have an effect on the end result. But it should be remembered that the 1965 decisions were only intended as a first step. It was envisaged that the reform would find its own dynamic and create the opportunities for further steps. Reality, however, refuted such expectations. The middle tier of the economic apparatus and local Party bureaucracy displayed rather less interest in the reform than the central organs. In fact the middle tier sabotaged the new policy. Broadening the rights of enterprise directors clearly encroached upon their interests. What was devised as a purely organizational restructuring threatened to become a socio-political problem.

Under the influence of provincial apparatchiks, Brezhnev and other conservative figures began to take a more restrained attitude to the reform. The alignment of forces within the bloc of conservatives and technocrats had clearly altered to the latter's disadvantage. As Roy Medvedev has remarked, 'the reactionary tendency' had gained the upper hand in the apparatus.[5]

The countries of Eastern Europe, where from the beginning of the 1960s reforms had also been implemented, frequently surpassed the Soviet Union in their level of development, and were rich in democratic traditions. Here the development of reform provoked profound social conflicts and in Poland and Czechoslovakia gave rise to mass movements for political change. From the very beginning there was an obvious link between the reform programme and political demands. The 1968

Manifesto of Czech Youth stated that: 'One of the most important and pressing problems is to abolish the system whereby all decisions are taken anonymously and it is not known who bears the responsibility for them.' Such formulations were also used in the 'Action Programme of the Central Committee of the Czechoslovak Communist Party' adopted in the heat of the 'Prague Spring'. The reformists insisted that economic transformations could not be accomplished successfully without simultaneous political democratization.

After the reformist movements in Poland and Czechoslovakia had been suppressed, the reasons for the disquiet of Brezhnev and his colleagues still remained. The fact that political demands were closely tied to economic processes launched from above was especially disagreeable. True, the experience of Hungary had shown that political liberalization, unavoidably connected with economic reform, could in a series of cases be kept within previously stipulated boundaries. The 'Prague Spring' was only made possible because ruling groups soon lost control of the development of reform. This was assisted, in particular, by the dogged resistance of the conservative–bureaucratic faction which did not wish to compromise with the technocrats. As a result there was, on the one hand, the formation of a reformist–technocratic bloc which strove to implement measures more radical than those approved by the Moscow leadership, and on the other, an overt and bitter struggle unfolded between the bureaucratic factions. Intermediate layers and the working class were eventually drawn into this struggle and the reform began to turn into something like a revolution. In Hungary, where the opposition of the conservatives was extremely feeble (the Stalinists had suffered defeat back in 1956), nothing of the sort happened. Broadening the rights of managers did not increase the proletariat's participation in public life. A West German correspondent remarked in 1975 that:

> Those who have been the winners from the Hungarian reform are the successful managers and technocrats, the peasants and small traders — those who control production, trade and pricing. Only one class has lost — the very one in whose name the party and state have promised to build socialism — the workers.[6]

As the reform progressed it began to yield still greater benefits to various social strata. In the early 1970s, workers treated it with mistrust and in places went on strike, but by the end of the decade their standard of living had also risen significantly. Political liberalization was an ongoing but controlled and slow process. Timely concessions, the extension of the role of trade unions and of workers' rights in production, enabled acute social conflicts to be avoided in the 1980s despite the emergence of economic difficulties because of the world crisis.

In theory the 'Hungarian model' was adopted for the Soviet Union. Given the level of development of the working class in our country in the 1960s, there was no need to fear any sort of serious mass disturbances in the reform process. Control over the transformations would undoubtedly remain in the hands of the top Party leadership. But for the reform to be carried out, not only did it have to be objectively possible, but the political will was needed too. Brezhnev did not have and could not have such a political will. In 1964 it was the conservative provincial apparatchiks who were the decisive force which enabled him to achieve power. They remained his chief prop throughout the eighteen years of his rule. This was the social stratum most decisively against the reform. The 'Hungarian model' might have been attractive to economists but the ideologues saw in it a suspicious resemblance to the 'Prague Spring'. For some it was heresy, for others a threat to their own positions. Under the influence of technocratic moods in the ruling elite, Brezhnev and his administration displayed tolerance towards the changes occurring in Hungary, but it was clear that they had no intention of realizing similar changes at home.

Over the course of Brezhnevism's eighteen years, the influence of technocratic tendencies on economic policy grew steadily less and patriarchal–conservative principles were triumphant. Thus the terms of the compromise were constantly under review, although at the beginning of the 1970s the technocrats were still in a position to influence the taking of strategic decisions. They therefore bear a share of the responsibility for everything that subsequently took place.

The repudiation of economic reform assumed the existence of some sort of alternative strategy. Initially there was no such strategy, but by the start of the 1970s it began to take shape. This time the programme's technocratic elements were totally subordinate to conservative and protective aims. At the same time Brezhnev became sole leader, pushing Kosygin and other colleagues into the background. In the field of ideology the slogan of stability was advanced. Naturally this did not mean the rejection of revolutionary terminology, but the theme of stability little by little came to dominate. In precisely the same way, argues Zaslavsky, communism is mentioned less frequently in official speeches under Brezhnev than the 'Soviet way of life.'[7]

The rejection of an overall economic reform led to the re-establishment of the fundamental principles of the old system of planning, for example, 'the gross output plan' ('val') was now renamed 'the sales' plan'. The Brezhnev leadership endeavoured to secure the development of society's productive forces without altering the relations of production. The task was evidently unrealizable, since it is impossible to resolve questions engendered by new conditions on the basis of old methods. For anyone who has the slightest acquaintance with Marx this has to be a truism. But it is a fact that for a 'practical politician' such a task, while unachievable in principle, can be broken down into a multitude of individual tasks, each of which, in isolation, is completely feasible. As the Hungarian economist, J. Berend, has observed, such a policy will be accompanied 'by partial successes and at the same time an exacerbation of the contradictions.'[8] With this method the existence of isolated successes is taken as proof of the correctness of the general line, and problems are attributed to the incompetence of particular agents. All failures are explained either by individual error or by local conditions, but they do not cast doubt on the validity of the chosen course. True, it becomes obvious little by little that the cause of failure is the 'partial character', 'incompleteness' and lack of co-ordination of the adopted measures. At first glance this seems the beginning of a reassessment of values but it then becomes clear that it is not a question of reviewing strategy (which remained unaltered right up to Brezhnev's death) but of creating composite 'all-embracing programmes'. The contradictions, as Berend predicted, accumulate and become more complicated and involved. The feeling is created of a dead-end situation, of 'hopelessness'. The government finds itself in an equivocal position. On the one hand it is striving to develop production, raise the population's standard of living and improve the quality of production. On the other, it has itself taken decisions which are not only conducive to this but have led to directly opposite results. Similar situations have repeatedly arisen in history.

Engels once wrote that the state can either assist or hinder economic development, 'it can place barriers to economic development in certain directions and push it in other directions.' In this way, he continues, 'political power can occasion the greatest harm to economic development and cause the loss of forces and material on a huge scale.'[9] In the final analysis, in Engel's opinion, the social strata responsible for all this must pay with their positions.

The repudiation of reform does not always mean a repudiation of change. Herzen emphasized that Russian bureaucratism is by no means hostile to every innovation. The Brezhnev leadership was merely intending to replace reform by some measures of a general character.

The highest significance was given to the import of advanced technology. The insufficiently flexible organization of scientific research may have begun to cause us to fall behind in many branches of industry, but new equipment could be acquired from abroad. This principle of 'reform-replacing imports' stimulated the growth of trading relations with the West and the lessening of international tension, and this must be regarded as a positive factor. True, it soon became apparent that western technology was too expensive. Demand grew for the import of the raw materials and semi-manufactures essential to it. At first all imports of advanced technology were earmarked for a few sectors, but the practice soon became widespread. As a consequence, there was a six-fold growth in the volume of Soviet trade with developed capitalist countries between 1970 and 1980 (and it has continued to rise rapidly). At the same time, the trade deficit and foreign debt increased. Between 1970 and 1977 the debt grew from $1.9 billion to $11.23 billion.[10] Moreover after 1978 relations between East and West once again began to deteriorate. The war in Afghanistan and the siting of American missiles in Europe aggravated the crisis of detente in the last years of Brezhnev's rule. After 1980, obtaining Western technology became rather more complicated. In the first half of the 1980s our country was on the whole successful in solving the problem of the trade deficit and indebtedness (although the situation again became difficult after 1985), but the problem of technological renovation remained.

The worst of it was that even when new technology had been successfully acquired, it did not have the necessary effect because appropriate relations of production did not exist. An important aspect of Brezhnev's strategy was computerization. Through this, it was hoped to raise the quality of centralized decision-making. Alas, computers only solve those questions placed before them by people and the latter, in their turn, pursue their own departmental aims. The effectiveness of employing computers is connected to the reliability of information — which, in the Soviet context, as economists have remarked, 'is not easily given to control.'[11] By the mid-1980s the introduction of computers had not in most cases produced the intended results, being in some cases 'only a quarter or a fifth as effective as had been hoped.'[12] In such circumstances computerization sometimes even proved loss-making. It became clear that in itself the technological and organizational moderni-zation of production not only does not solve problems of efficiency or quality but may sometimes exacerbate them.

Brezhnev and his colleagues placed great hopes on the training of more competent cadres. To this end, an Institute of Management was specially founded in Moscow and numerous measures were carried out to allow Soviet managers to compare experiences and increase their skills. Much attention was paid to studying Western managerial culture although, as a British specialist stressed, 'it is less clear whether these techniques can be applied within such a different kind of society.'[13] The work of the new managers was often worse than that of the old ones since they had no experience of real leadership and had had no opportunity to put their learning into practice.

The development of backward industries was meant to be facilitated by additional investment. In the 1970s transport and agriculture, and later the coal industry, atomic energy and oil extraction, became such super-capital-intensive branches. The effectiveness of capital investments fell in proportion to their growth. A low capital–output ratio has been characteristic of our economy in the postwar period, but during the Brezhnev group's ascendancy not only did it not rise, it actually suffered an uninterrupted decline. According to official figures the capital–output ratio for the tenth Five-Year Plan alone had fallen by 14 per cent in terms of material production. If the ninth Five-Year Plan is taken as the base, then the picture is even worse: in 1981, *Voprosy Ekonomiki* reported:

> For every rouble of basic capital there is now 28 per cent less national income. If the capital–output ratio had been maintained at the 1970 level then, in 1980, it would have been possible to utilize an additional 166 bn. roubles of national income on consumption and accumulation, which exceeds the total sum of capital investments in that year by 24 per cent.[14]

As a result even massive injections of capital directed at the backward sectors proved inadequate. Additional investments were demanded — but these too failed to produce the desired effect.... The increase in production for every rouble invested fell uninterruptedly from 1959 to 1982, and the worst of it was that it declined at a faster rate than the planners expected.

The most important aspect of Brezhnev's economic course was the attempt to perfect the system of indicators and organizational structures. Without altering the principles themselves of bureaucratic planning, the leadership hoped to raise its efficiency through various corrections and improvements. A variety of 'quality indicators' was introduced. This policy gave rise to the appearance of additional book-keeping items and an increase in bureaucratic paperwork. While partial improvements were achieved in a series of cases, the strategic objectives were not met.

It was precisely the failure of attempts to improve planning which in the last analysis pre-determined the rest of the difficulties. The concentration of all forces and attention on a few key branches was normal under Stalin's system of management. This was how the 'economy of priorities' came into being. It was considered necessary to find the decisive link through which it would be possible to extend the whole chain. At times this genuinely did lead to success. But under Brezhnev, when the centre was already unable to cope with the running of an expanding economy, such methods no longer worked. It was impossible to define which branch was the most important. Basic resources were devoted to developing backward sectors (as a rule, precisely those branches considered secondary by Stalin). Meanwhile, other branches, which were not receiving the necessary aid, fell into decline and themselves began to require additional means. They could not deal independently with their own difficulties because of the inordinate centralization of management and investment processes.

So long as there was an abundance of resources, even those branches considered of secondary importance could hope for some sort of real support. In the 1970s the situation plainly deteriorated, and by the early 1980s it was clear that, because of limited resources, the 'economy of priorities' could not guarantee the needs of a whole range of productive industry even where it was a question of the most elementary items. 'The most prioritized sectors were given everything, the next — a fair amount, and the rest — what was left or nothing at all.'[15]

Those sectors which were not, in the planners' opinion, among the leaders (for example the coal industry) found themselves in a state of stagnation and chronic difficulty. By the mid-1970s their backwardness began to act as a brake on the development of the whole economy. By the end of the decade all efforts had to be focused on them. In turn, those who had previously not been doing too badly could no longer count on special attention, and they swiftly found themselves left behind. At the end of the 1970s investments were redistributed in favour of extractive industries. The outcome was a drop in the production of metals, some types of machinery and building materials. An endless cycle was emerging. And this was only one of Brezhnevism's dead ends. For in life one dead end is, as a rule, enough, but in politics it is possible to come to several dead ends simultaneously.

An American economist has called Brezhnev's investment policy 'unimaginative and contradictory'.[16] Some of the steps Brezhnev took in this field do indeed seem crazy; but there was a method in his madness. First of all it was quite clear that, although the distribution of investments between branches was far from optimal, the failures were not caused by this but by the inability of managers to utilize effectively the resources at their disposal. From the end of the 1970s the volume of capital investment in the Soviet economy was approximately equal to that in the American. Given that we have a smaller scale economy, then, by this indicator, we have clearly left the United States behind. Thus the resources at the state's disposal were sufficient to develop *all* sectors. If this has not happened, an incorrect distribution of means cannot be the sole reason.

The figures in Table 1 seem quite impressive, but as Yuri Andropov observed on coming to power, capital investments were not giving 'the necessary return'.[17] The rates of growth of the Gross National Product fell uninterruptedly from 1959. An average annual growth of 4.7 per cent was envisaged in the 1976–80 plan. This level was surpassed in 1978, but overall the plan figures proved too high. In 1979 growth was a mere 2.6 per cent instead of the planned 4.3 per cent. Moreover, the planned increase in industrial production was not achieved once throughout the

Table 1

The Growth of Capital Investments in the Soviet Economy

	1961–65	1966–70	1971–75	1976–80	1981–85
In billions of roubles	243.5	347.9	493	643.1	842
In comparative prices (1961–65 = 100%)	100	143.2	202.5	264.1	345.7
Growth (%) compared to previous FYP	—	43.2	41.7	30.4	17

Sources: Politicheskoe Samoobrazovanie, no. 1, 1982, p. 64; Report of N.I. Ryzhkov to the 27th Congress of the CPSU (*Izvestia,* 4 March 1986)

entire five-year plan. By the end of the Brezhnev era growth of 2–3 per cent was considered satisfactory.

As the emigré economist, Igor Birman, has remarked, by Western standards an annual growth rate of 2–3 per cent is not so bad, but it should be remembered that 'almost all the problems of the Soviet economy have been significantly diminished and eased as a result of its growth.'[18] The decline in rates of growth means, according to the most varied indicators, a corresponding increase in the economy's disequilibrium, the appearance of new difficulties, and in the end, a new decrease in rates of growth, as shown in Table 2.[19] By the end of the decade the evident ineffectiveness of Brezhnev's investment policy had reactivated technocratic tendencies. More attention began to be paid to questions of organization and management. 1976–80 was declared 'the Five-Year Plan of efficiency and quality.'[20] Primary emphasis was placed on the introduction of new, more scientific, indicators and the formation of specialized 'All-Union Industrial Associations' (VPO).

As soon as such associations began to be established, this was seen in the West as a symptom of a transition from bureaucratic to technocratic methods. 'Managers are taking power into their hands', declared *Der Spiegel* in 1973.[21] Indeed, the technocrats pinned definite hopes on the creation of VPOs. The new organization strengthened the middle tier of the industrial management apparatus, but the technocratic bureaucracy in the central organs had no desire whatsoever to cede their powers to them. Very little scope was accorded for the VPOs to take autonomous decisions: from the point of view of the enterprise, yet another super-

Table 2

The Rates of Growth of the Soviet Economy

	1957–60	1961–70	1971–80	1981–85
Average annual growth of National Income (%)	10.2	7.1	4.9	3.1
Average annual growth of industrial production (%)	11.8	8.5	5.9	3.7

Sources: K.I. Mikul'skii, Eknomicheskii rost, p. 379; Report of N.I. Ryzhkov to the 27th Congress of the CPSU (*Izvestia,* 4 March 1986)

visory body had appeared. Western observers remarked that enterprise autonomy even decreased, for the controlling authorities 'were closer'.[22] Soviet commentators on the whole concurred with this. As R.G. Karagedov observed, 'unless the general model of management, its fundamental and not just its organizational outlines are altered, there can be no essential increase in the overall impact of management.'[23]

Efforts to perfect the system of indicators continued throughout the Brehznev period, but they did not bear any fruit. Back in the 1950s, Janos Kornai had shown that it was impossible in principle to create 'good' indicators. Any subject is at once integral and multi-faceted. Its component parts and characteristics exist only in unity. The subject's different facets reflect different indicators, but each indicator remains individual and unidimensional. The sum of unidimensional indicators cannot be identical to the whole.[24] The planners hoped that the indicators would supplement each other, but this only increased the muddle. The Soviet economist, Otto Latsis, wrote: 'The plethora of indicators helps unscrupulous leaders to manoeuvre so that some particular indicators look all right at the expense of other indicators which may sometimes be more important for the state.'[25] The growth in the number of indicators automatically complicated the managerial process. In 1981 an economic planner complained in *Ekonomicheskaya Gazeta* that he had to prepare six volumes of technical documentation for re-approval and collect three hundred signatures and official stamps. The paper's editors justifiably commented that he had nothing to complain about: another association 'compiled in 1981 not six but forty-nine volumes in total ... and collected not three hundred but nine hundred (!) signatures and official stamps.'[26]

During the epoch of industrialization, when it was necessary to increase production of coal, steel and simple machines, quantitative indicators allowed more or less reliable control to be maintained over the production process. The complex economy of a developed industrial society does not permit this. Economists with reformist leanings compared theoreticians pursuing the quest for 'optimal indicators' with people inventing perpetual motion. As Alec Nove has said:

If the measure is tonnes, this rewards weight and penalizes economy of materials. If the measure is gross value in roubles there is benefit to be derived from making expensive goods, using expensive materials. Tonne-kilometres incite transport undertakings to carry heavy goods over long distances. Examples of wasteful or otherwise irrational practices designed to fulfil plans ... could fill several bound volumes, all the examples being taken from Soviet publications.[27]

Since gross output ('val') remained the primary indicator, it became advantageous when building to increase capital–intensivity. This meant that on farms, for example, the cost of one 'cattle stall' increased three- or fourfold between 1968 and 1978 as 'up to 8 cubic metres of concrete is needed for a cow, and up to 400kg of metal for a calf'.[28] The poor animals had become victims of 'val'.

Moreover, it paid better to begin building work than to complete it, since more expensive materials are consumed in the initial stages. As a result, unfinished construction was continually on the increase. By 1979 the volume of unfinished jobs amounted to 106.4 billion roubles (equivalent to 91 per cent of the volume of capital investment for that year).[29]

Efforts to curb this insidious indicator were repeatedly made. In the last years of Brezhnev's rule it was decided to replace 'val' with 'normative net output' (NNO). Henceforth enterprises were to be assessed not according to the aggregate price of articles sold but by the magnitude of newly produced value. At an experimental level the indicator 'worked' well enough, but it seemed strikingly clear that NNO was only a new variety of 'val'. Traditional 'val' encouraged expensive, heavy, material–intensive production. NNO encouraged labour–intensive jobs, and did nothing to encourage economies in tools and materials. It soon became clear that enterprises evaluated in terms of NNO had no interest in the growth of labour productivity – for greater labour productivity reduces the value of work carried out and the volume of 'net output' falls. Apart from this Western economists prophetically observed that the new indicator

seems to add to the system's already excessive information burden, both at the central planning (USSR Gosplan and Gossnab) and at the branch ministry levels. For this reason the inconsistencies that so often arise between output and supply plans for enterprises are more likely to be exacerbated than reduced.[30]

Even in the initial stages of NNO's introduction both planners and experts were stressing that the new indicator was 'causing many new problems.'[31] They soon stopped referring to NNO's positive aspects, and by the mid 1980s it was generally recognized that it had failed to displace 'val'. Attempts to stimulate the efficiency of production by focusing on 'net' output had not been justified.

The same fate befell the 'quality mark', 'mark N' (for new products), and a host of other measures to encourage quality. Some indicators had the opposite effect to that intended. For example, costs increased when the indicator intended to decrease production costs was introduced: it paid to raise the costs at the design stage, so as to lower them painlessly later on, thus easily fulfilling the plan. The same happened with the attempt to lower material consumption and limit energy usage on the basis of plan targets. Where the indicator proved more successful, it encouraged better solutions to various individual questions but simultaneously hindered success in other directions.

Only the consumer can give an objective assessment of quality. Such an assessment cannot be ensured in conditions where it is impossible to arrange normal market relations between consumer and producer. Marx wrote that commodities

> must stand the test as use-values before they can be realized as values. For the labour expended on them only counts in so far as it is expended in a form which is useful for others. However, only the act of exchange can prove whether that labour is useful for others, and its product consequently capable of satisfying the needs of others.[32]

Clearly this does not apply only to capitalism. Every commodity under any political system must possess use value, the utility of which, as Soviet economists acknowledge, 'only the market can verify'.[33] The misfortune is that in the 1970s the Soviet planning system did not and could not have any such mechanism for testing efficiency. Experts stress that the economy was governed by the principle of 'compulsory exchange' which functioned particularly strictly because of the universal shortage. Under these conditions, as commentators have observed, 'the problem of improving the quality of production becomes irresoluble.'[34] The growth of production did not assist its resolution; indeed, it brought the additional problem of overstocking. The difficulties in realizing some forms of production could be related entirely to the shortage of other products: the quality in both cases left a lot to be desired. An indignant reader wrote to *Literaturnaya Gazeta* (18 September 1985) that industry was putting out a growing quantity of useless items — drawing pens with which it was impossible to draw, locks which could not be locked, jugs which did not pour, handles which were only good for scrap, clothing condemned to lie in warehouses until the end of the century and vacuum cleaners which kill anyone who touches them. Yuri Andropov spoke repeatedly on the same subject.

A significant portion of productive effort was spent in the form of *socially useless labour*. One political economist noted in this regard that 'an item of production not utilized by society is not, strictly speaking, a product in a socio-economic sense.'[35] In other words, in such cases one should speak not of the production of commodities but of the destruction of raw materials, the waste of energy, and so on. Ordinary citizens could refrain from buying useless goods, but enterprises, as a rule, had no such choice: they had to 'take what was given'. This was all paid for by a fall in quality on a society-wide scale and an increase in prices. Back in the 1960s, reform-minded economists had warned that 'it is impossible not to take the needs of the market into consideration.'[36] Objective laws took their own vengeance.

Engels wrote:

> Whoever in a society of commodity producers, exchanging their commodities, wishes to establish the determination of value through labour time while forbidding competition to realize this determination by means of influencing prices, i.e., the sole means by which this can, on the whole, be achieved, only demonstrates that, at least in this sphere, he has acquired the contempt, common to all utopians, for economic laws.

Fluctuation in prices, Engels stressed, is essential in order to understand 'what, and in what quantity, society needs.' If the system of fixed prices excludes such a possibility, there can be no question of proportionality and efficiency in the economy, not to mention satisfaction of the needs of society. One recalls Engel's prophetic comment that 'we shall not go hungry in regard to corn and meat while we are … drowned in potato spirit.'[37]

Our country's experience has shown the correctness of Engel's thinking. As Soviet commentators have rightly remarked, the economic systems of East and West, despite all their dissimilarities, have one principal feature in common: 'the producers, while differing in their social nature, have one quality the same: they are all producers of commodities.'[38] Consequently, market relations are as essential to the normal development of the Soviet economy as they are to any other.

Under Stalin, there was an absolute shortage: there was literally too little of everything. But administrative control was of the utmost stringency, and market factors could sometimes be ignored. In the post-Stalin period the situation changed. Pavel Bunich, a leading ideologist of reformism, noted that 'the domination of the supplier over the consumer' and even 'the supplier's monopoly' was preserved in the country, but that consumers gained the chance to defend themselves and 'strive with all their might to free themselves from such dependence.'[39] The most effective form of defence was hoarding. Acting 'according to the hamster principle', enterprises accumulated the raw materials and equipment they needed for future use (private individuals created similar reserves too). Every department, association and enterprise strove to become as independent as possible from the deliveries of other departments.

In this way even an enterprise which did not receive the necessary resources in time would still be able to fulfil the plan thanks to its own 'hidden reserves'. If there were insufficient raw materials, components and equipment in the warehouse it was always possible to obtain them through barter (for this purpose there existed 'suppliers' or, more precisely, pushers — *tolkachi* — whose job it was to carry out such operations). Barter is rather odd from a theoretical point of view. It is possible to swap 'value for value' or alternatively, as one Tbilisi pusher put it to me, 'truck for truck'. The latter is absurd from the standpoint of political economy but it should be remembered that pushers act according to the laws not of the market but of shortage. The informal and unorganized process of exchange cannot be 'correct', orderly and according to the rules. Relations between enterprises remain disjointed and no single market is in the process of formation. Consequently the wildest combinations are possible during the exchange of surpluses. We have here millions of individual cases which cannot be reduced to a general rule. Informal barter between enterprises remains at a primitive, pre-market level and cannot compensate for the shortcomings of the economic mechanism. In turn, the pushers, who constituted the most colourful social group in Brezhnev's society, could not become genuine technocrats or managers in the Western sense.

Informal barter, far from solving the fundamental problems of production, complicated them by encouraging the formation of additional reserves. This in turn led to an exacerbation of shortages. At the end of the Brezhnev era experts established that '80 per cent of aggregate reserves are in the hands of the consumer.'[40] Attempts to combat this achieved nothing. Newspapers returned repeatedly to this theme. It was said that in Kemerovo region alone, up to 15,000 check-ups and inspections of every kind were held each year, and that inspectors were present in the enterprises for between one hundred and fifty and two hundred days a year, but that successes 'were rarely heard of'.[41]

Since the hamster principle did not always work and it was far from possible to achieve everything through informal links, enterprise leaders strove to produce everything possible themselves. Consequently, on the one hand, superfluous production lay pointlessly in warehouses and frequently simply vanished (which demanded additional premises and workers), while the same production had to be turned out again by semi-handicraft methods (once again keeping spare workers busy, squandering resources and energy, making inefficient use of equipment, and so on). This can be called, paraphrasing Marx, the *expanded reproduction of disorder*. Problems gather in one link of the economic mechanism and are gradually transferred to other links causing a chain reaction of difficult-ies throughout the system. Shortage has led to the weakening of formal connections within the official structure and the strengthening of informal relations. As the system becomes increasingly complex, 'it becomes more and more expensive: reserves grow, the supply of enterprises becomes more vulnerable and achieving regular work and production is more difficult.'[42]

The twin phenomena termed 'departmentalism' and 'localism' in the official press must be recognized as the natural outcome of this kind of situation. The content of these concepts is not, as a rule, deciphered but it will be carefully analysed here. Each department has its own plan. In the same way, each region (*oblast*) must report regularly on its successes. There are no incentives through which the workers in one department could have an interest in contributing to the fulfilment of the plan in another organization. There is not one region in which the local leadership would agree to damage its own plan for the sake of saving a neighbour. Whose production is of more importance to the country is of no consequence. Bureaucratic institutions operate according to the principle of 'everyone for themselves'. In distributing their products, all are governed by the principle of 'your own first'. This leads to the famous 'counter-transportation' where a factory sends its production not to its immediate neighbour but to the other end of the country — because that is where there is an enterprise from the same department, while the neighbour belongs to another one. Different ministries create production of the same type within their own system just so they do not have to depend on each other. A train transporting production from Brest to Vladivostok is quite likely to meet another on the way carrying the same sort of product in the opposite direction. The newspapers complain that enterprises are 'divided by numerous departmental fences.'[43] As specialists acknowledge, in the last analysis this 'leaves its mark on the structure of the country's production.'[44] The need arises not only for additional transportation but also for additional investments, which are frequently ineffective. By 1981 there were more machine tools in the USSR than in the USA, Japan and West Germany put together but this was not reflected in the quantity and quality of production. Forming regional economic structures has proved to be an extremely difficult business: different enterprises have been successfully integrated into a unified complex at the departmental or regional level, but not beyond.

At the time óf Stalin's industrialization, departmentalism could not be a serious problem since there were few central institutions. As the economy became more complicated the centre ceased to be able to cope with the increasing flow of information. It had already become impossible for a single body to take all the decisions. After the 1965 Reform folded, it was impossible to talk about transferring even a portion of the authority 'down' to the enterprises and associations. As a result the idea of 'specialization' came about. Brezhnev gambled on creating several parallel central institutions each of which would be concerned only with their own problem area. Unfortunately each of these bodies in turn soon encountered the problem of an excess of information and had to split up again into several autonomous units. Moreover specialization was not successfully realized in practice, for as they strove to protect themselves against each other all the ministries and departments created the most varied forms of production to service their own basic enterprises, and they began not to be concerned with their own business. The *departmental natural economy* which had sprung up totally excluded any possibility of genuine specialization: each followed its own plan. But things were becoming still worse. The indicators which had been drawn up were aimed 'principally at realizing departmental interests',[45] and the number of departments began to rise as though leavened with yeast. For example, in Kalinin *oblast* alone, construction organizations were subject to thirty ministries and departments in 1983! Horizontal links between enterprises were destroyed. Factory directors were more interested in collaborating with their superior bodies than with their colleagues.

Localism means the appearance of analogous relations at the *oblast* level. The point here is that Party *obkoms* and the state organs subordinate to them have actively defended local interests without taking into account the position of central institutions. Enterprise leaders, on the books of the local Party organizations, had to pay attention to how the *obkom* assessed them and had to carry out all its instructions. On the other hand, the activity of the *obkoms* did sometimes help overcome departmental barriers (in exactly the same way as ministerial activity overcame local ones). As Western commentators have remarked:

> A very considerable part of the local Party committee's job is assisting in the procurement of material supplies from outside the given region or district, and the redirection of materials, labor, and equipment within the given area.

Consequently, the *obkom* secretary not only 'substitutes for the market mechanism' (!) but is both 'manager and entrepreneur'.[46]

The activity of *obkoms* has indeed been very important. It has reinforced the significance of local interests in the economy, although the sum of local interests is not equivalent to that of the entire state. Where they have diverged, conflicts have arisen — resulting, as a rule, in the victory of localism.

What is this related to? Above all, the local bureaucracy remained the Brezhnev group's major prop. Stalin was continually shooting a portion of the Party leadership in the localities and Khrushchev shuffled Party cadres around from one part of the country to another, often demoting or removing people from Party work. But under Brezhnev, the 'policy of stability of cadres' was triumphant. The *nomenklatura* principle assumed that, if transferred, apparatchiks would not be given a position lower in rank than the one they already occupied. Brezhnev not only made the *nomenklatura* principle an unbreakable law, he went even further, rejecting any reshuffling of cadres at all. Leaders of the Party apparatus in the regions sat in their places for many years. Over this time their links with the lower tiers of the *oblast* bureaucracy were consolidated and stable interest groups came into being. In this context localism clearly became a crucial economic factor.

Moreover, departmentalism and localism also became social factors. Since the planners' firmest links were formed not with their colleagues but with the ministry's central apparatus and Party *obkoms*, the technocracy was unable to stabilize itself as a special group with common interests. It remained disparate. The lower and middle tiers of the administrative–economic apparatus were disorganized. As a result, the technocratic group at the top had no such stable and conscious support within the lower tiers of the bureaucracy, which is what Brezhnev intended. Further, the alignment of forces gradually changed still more to the conservatives' advantage. As the policy of 'stability of cadres' was implemented the technocrats' social support decreased and the technocratic tendency in the country's leadership became less and less distinct. For its part, the conservative grouping became increasingly patriarchal. The growth of localism engendered the feudalization of relations between apparatchiks supported by Brezhnev (it is no coincidence that the word 'localism' — *mestnichestvo* — is taken from the vocabulary of feudal Rus'). Personal links were interwoven with administrative on the basis of local, departmental or informal group (often kinship) interests. Stable informal stuctures arose which determined the actual functioning of power in the localities.

This feudal policy of Brezhnev's, pursued in the conditions of a modern industrial society, led inevitably to corruption. The middle tier of economic leadership, which was involved in non-market exchange and unofficial relations with Party and departmental patrons, and demoralized by its own ineffectualness, proved to be rather unsteady in the face of temptation. The moral factor played a considerable role here. Economic failures were evident; they had begun to write about them in the official press. The journal of Gosplan USSR stated plainly that 'the principles of the branch system did not work in the Tenth Five-Year Plan.'[47] Managers keenly felt their lack of rights and complained about the curtailment of their initiative, but at the same time they were closely linked to the very bodies which were curtailing this initiative and which were riddled with local and departmental interests. In this position they not only lacked the opportunity to alter the situation, they did not even feel a real need to. The managers' demoralization was one of the sources of corruption, which then began to spread both 'at the top' and 'at the bottom'. Brezhnev, with his policy of 'stability of cadres', found himself in a shady business which he himself had set up: he had not had the opportunity to act in time to cut out the negative tendencies. The central Party organs only intervened when the situation was becoming critical; in all other cases they had to rely on the purity and unselfishness of the local bureaucratic groups.

Meanwhile even honest and disinterested officials frequently became entangled in corrupt goings-on. The British commentator, Nicholas Lampert, who has studied Soviet corruption for a long time, has very precisely explained the reason for this phenomenon: the desire to fulfil the plan at any price.

Many forms of management illegality are means to that end. Sending gifts or bribes (what's the difference?) to suppliers, setting aside scarce goods or materials for people who will be useful to the enterprise in the future, engaging in some illicit wage payments, favouring certain employees in the distribution of bonuses, hiring private contractors to do building work – all these may be seen as different ways of establishing the conditions under which the enterprise can succeed.[48]

As the problems caused by Brezhnev's policy were exacerbated it became more and more difficult to fulfil the plan by 'normal' methods, without resorting to the assistance of pushers, bribes, gifts, illegal payments to workers and the *pripiska* – a report exaggerating the extent to which the plan has been fulfilled. This has been noted in the official literature. The eminent Soviet sociologist, Tatyana Zaslavskaya, has stressed that towards the end of the 1970s there arose 'a tendency for the scale of the "shadow" economy to increase and for individual links of the "official" to be corroded by elements of the "shadow".' In the final analysis, 'this testifies to the declining degree of manageability of the economy.'[49]

Interestingly, the same process was occurring on the eve of the 1965 economic reform. Then it was successfully cut out through active repression and simultaneous changes in the managerial system. A similar path was chosen later when Andropov came to power. But this time things had gone rather further than at the beginning of the 1960s. The 'shadow' economy and corruption had developed appreciably. In the Brezhnev epoch, as sociologists have correctly emphasized, these became more and more 'structural' factors.

Lampert has written:

> Soviet executives are clearly faced with a Catch-22. If they put themselves 'above the law' in the course of their duties, they open themselves, at least as a possibility, to unpleasantness from law enforcement agents. But the higher law is to make a success of the job, to fulfil the plan. No manager if she wants to succeed, can put herself 'above the plan'. . . . But from the standpoint of Soviet managers, the trouble is that to meet 'the interests of the state as a whole', i.e. to fulfil the plan, they must pursue the interests of 'their' institution and break numerous rules and regulations, and often the criminal law in the process. It is a question of choosing the smaller evil and the smaller crime.[50]

The trouble was that despite the large number of measures taken against corruption the volume of recorded economic crimes continued to rise and they became all the more severe. Each new stage in the development of Brezhnevism was accompanied by an intensification of corruption. The most widespread and 'inoffensive' form of economic crime remained the *pripiska*. As Lampert remarks, the entire planning system, which requires accurate information, is a victim here. Not only is there the decline in 'the manageability of the economy' noted by Zaslavskaya, but new links of corruption arise between those who add on the non-existent production and those who cover up for them. In 1985 it became clear that thousands of tonnes of non-existent cotton were regularly added to the harvest in Uzbekistan. All of this cotton was sold. The state paid the price for it and also paid out bonuses for fulfilling and overfulfilling the plan. Naturally, such a swindle could not have happened without the participation of a large number of public servants at all levels of the managerial apparatus. They were all linked by a collective guarantee and received a variety of benefits from breaking the law.

It proved very easy to proceed from the *pripiska* to more severe crimes. It was necessary to bribe those prepared to shut their eyes to minor errors in book-keeping, and create a 'black cash-box' — a fund for the purchase of various kinds of presents and bribes for higher officials. In order to create such a fund it was necessary either to take bribes oneself, resort to misappropriating state resources, or sell a part of production on the black market (*nalevo*) at higher prices (usually all three methods were resorted to at the same time). The planner who was breaking all these laws could remain confident in his own moral purity since he had not put a single kopeck into his own pocket (I met two such people in Lefortovo Prison in 1982–83).

The seriousness of the situation was acknowledged in the official press. *Izvestia* wrote that 'directors, while displaying enterprise in the state's interests, nevertheless come into conflict with existing economic norms and often find themselves liable to penalty.'[51] There is a striking similarity between the diagnosis presented by British sovietologists and Soviet journalists. The picture is absolutely clear.

But one point still remains to be clarified. First, it is obvious that, sooner or later, the transition from innocuous breaches of the law in the name of fulfilling the plan to nefarious dealings for one's own purposes becomes unavoidable. If an individual continually takes risks, transgressing the law for the success of the enterprise, he will sooner or later do exactly the same for his own enrichment. In most cases corrupt planners have attempted to follow both aims simultaneously (the more so as successful plan fulfilment can itself serve as a defence). The question inevitably arises of how it is possible to assess corruption and the 'shadow' economy if they are both so closely connected with the official economy.

Many people have emphasized that the 'shadow' economy allows existing contradictions to be eased and enables shortages to be eliminated and is, consequently, a stabilizing factor. Corruption, in this view, is nothing more than a necessary evil to which one must resign oneself. One person quoted in Lampert's book defended just such a standpoint, stressing that the results of the 'shadow' economy are 'not so bad for the inhabitants' and this means it is better not 'to rock the boat'.[52] It is possible that Brezhnev himself or people in his circle held such an opinion. Similar appraisals have at times penetrated the official press albeit in a watered-down form. It has been emphasized that illegal private business helps demand to be satisfied and that factory directors who do not act according to the rules cope better with plan tasks. This is a favourite theme of emigré literature. Vladimir Bukovsky has referred to the numerous occasions on which factory directors have set up underground, 'unofficial' (*levye*) workshops for the manufacture of unregistered production; in his view, this is a sign of the rebirth of capitalism. The efficiency of the 'shadow' economy has been contrasted to the inefficiency of the official, the successes of one to the failures of the other.

The reality is altogether different. A. Zlobin has quite correctly remarked that illegal private business has arisen at the heart of the official system, is an organic part of it and 'can only exist because of it.' Through illegal removal of state resources superprofits are made of which a capitalist could only dream: the private sector is 'subsidized' from state funds, only this 'subsidy' is gained through theft! 'The private sector', Zlobin continues, 'is a parasite on the state sector. This embezzlement of state property is not in the form of manufactured articles or raw materials, but in the form of the usage of premises, heat, electricity and means of transport.' (One might add that manufactured articles and raw materials are also, as a rule, appropriated by underground capital free of charge.) From this Zlobin draws the correct conclusion that 'the fund of public misappropriation' is used extremely ineffectively. If private traders had to pay full price for everything their manufactures would be even more expensive than the state's and the quality would leave even more to be desired.[53]

Other forms of 'shadow' economy are also far from efficient. Pushers help to obtain materials in short supply and equipment, but they do not solve the problem of the shortage. Bribes enable the plan to be fulfilled, but meanwhile someone else, who has refrained from breaking the law, is left on the rocks: it is not good enough that the choice is the same for everyone! Moreover, when corruption reaches a certain 'critical magnitude' it inevitably begins to destroy the formal structures of management, paralysing their activity. And the 'shadow' economy and corruption are, as we have seen, indivisible.

In other words, the 'shadow' economy helped to solve some problems and compensated for individual shortcomings in the economic mechanism during the Brezhnev period, but at the same time it gave rise to new problems, created new sources of inefficiency and waste of resources, redistributed goods in short supply (frequently only aggravating their shortage in particular parts of the system), and so on. It was at once a stabilizing and a destabilizing factor. And the development of relations of corruption was a major obstacle to the growth of reformist moods among the planners.

Andropov's group recognized this even during Brezhnev's lifetime. It was moreover clear at the beginning of the 1980s that the further growth of corruption might make the economy unmanageable and the power of the central apparatus nominal. The struggle against corruption became a question of principle. In the winter of 1981 investigations began into numerous affairs. Simultaneously the idea began to be expressed in the press that it was in general better not to fulfil the plan than to fulfil it at the price of breaking the law. In this situation reformist tendencies again began to be strengthened: if success cannot be gained by acting according to the rules and breaking the rules is risky, the idea of re-examining the rules appears.

A certain section of the ruling circles was also growing anxious about the influence of corruption on the Party apparatus. As we have already said, the source of corruption lay outside this apparatus, but local Party functionaries were in constant contact with corrupted planners and they sometimes proved vulnerable to the same infection. The population could not but notice this. The upshot was increasing discontent which gradually began to come out into the open.

Defenders of the 'shadow' economy and corrupt links would stress that this situation suited everyone (this is very precisely recorded in Lampert's book). Workers often received illegal payments. Petty theft was so widespread in production that it was no longer considered a crime — people did not steal but 'took away' the objects that they needed. Workers were only following the example of their superiors, and the latter had to close their eyes to the misdemeanours of their subordinates for they did not have clean hands themselves. In production, 'a kind of "shadow law" — a peculiar code of unwritten rules and customs' began to take shape.[54] The fundamental principle of the 'shadow law' was that of mutual concessions between workers and management, in other words mutual connivance. In breaking the law the management took upon itself 'secret obligations to the workers.' The 'shadow law' consequently spread to almost all questions of labour relations and production discipline: 'Since they forgive the workers their "sins", then the workers, in their turn, occasionally turn a blind eye to the intolerable conditions in which they have to work.'[55]

This compromise was more or less satisfactory to everyone while appreciable economic growth continued. When, in the second half of the 1970s, the growth rate of the Soviet economy began rapidly to decline and this was reflected in the population's living standards, workers began to take a more critical stance towards the norms of the 'shadow law'. It was quite plain that the bureaucrats gained more from these mutual concessions than the workers. Dissatisfaction with corruption and law-breaking grew as the injustice became ever more obvious. Corrupt officials who had lost touch with reality openly flaunted their wealth and the masses became increasingly estranged from those who had assumed the role of controllers of their destiny.

This dissatisfaction was initially expressed in the writing of letters to the higher Party organs. In 1972 the CPSU Central Committee received 352,500 letters, but in 1980 it received 671,600, with an annual average of 401,660 during the Ninth Five-Year Plan rising to 630,368 during the Tenth. The number of letters to newspapers also increased. Journalists recognized that the criticism in the letters 'is distinguished by its directness and even a certain sharpness of expression.'[56] More serious was the attempt made in 1977 to set up a free trade union. All the participants in this organization began by writing the customary letters to the papers but gradually came round to the idea of taking more decisive action. Naturally, their effort was suppressed, but the fact itself was noted — especially as in Poland it was precisely the growth of corruption at the top which was a catalyst of protest.

The struggle against corruption in the higher echelons of power, begun by Andropov in 1981, was conducted so decisively and uncompromisingly that a blow was struck against Brezhnev's own family. His daughter, Galina, was mixed up in a scandal which came to light during an investigation into bribery in the apparatus of the State Circus

Administration. Western journalists wrote about 'Moscow's circusgate', by analogy with the Watergate scandal.[57] Brezhnev kept his position, of course. But all these events demonstrated the serious failure of his policy and the appearance of new disagreements within the leadership.

By dealing with the corrupt elements, Andropov hoped to calm the population. To a large extent he got his own way, achieving considerable personal popularity in the process. Corruption, however, was far from being the only source of discontent. Most Soviet citizens were exasperated with the growing disorder in industry and the food shortage. The latter was particularly important.

The difficulties with food were not accidental. They were the logical outcome of Stalin's agricultural policy and the measures taken by Khrushchev and Brezhnev to try and correct the situation. In a speech to the May Plenum of the CPSU Central Committee in 1982, Brezhnev declared that 'the Soviet citizen's food ration corresponds to physiological norms.'[58] Experts, however, disagreed. They insisted that actual consumption 'remains below recommended norms.'[59] One way or another, by the end of his rule Brezhnev was forced to recognize the seriousness of the food problem and announce that the country was in

Table 3

Consumption of Basic Food Products per Head of Population

	Scientifically based norm (kg)	Consumption (kg)		% of norm
		1979	*1980*	
Meat and meat products	83	57	58	68.7–69.8
Milk and dairy products	430	321	314	73.0–74.6
Vegetables and melons	290	230	239	79.3–82.4
Fruit and berries	113	41	38	33.6–36.3

Sources: Prodovol'stvennaya Programma SSSR, p. 11; EKO, no. 10, 1981, p. 117.

need of a special 'Food Programme'. Typically, however, the goals stated in this programme were more than modest.

The results of the first years of the Food Programme, shown in Table 4, proved that these goals could not successfully be achieved. Grain production throughout the whole period of 1979–84 stayed markedly below the level of 1976, varying between 160 and 200 million tonnes. What was the cause of so serious a situation? Even Western experts consider that Soviet agriculture would be quite capable of feeding between three and four hundred million people. Our country has already surpassed the United States in numbers of tractors and their total capacity. In the volume of capital investment in agriculture the Soviet Union and USA were at the same level in the mid-1970s and the USSR took the lead after 1977. At the same time productivity of labour remained excessively low. In Europe, farms producing less than 3,000 kilos of grain per hectare would be considered loss making. In Hungary, where natural conditions are little different from those in Russia, more than 4,000 kilos are harvested per hectare. And in our country we could not reach 2,000 kilos for the whole of the Brezhnev epoch! The well-known commentator, Y. Chernichenko, remarks that 'in the most successful year of 1978, milled flour reached an average of 1,800 kilos.'[60]

Bad harvests are usually blamed on the weather. The vagaries of nature do have a serious influence on the level of production, but the very fact

Table 4

Planned Consumption by the Year 1990 According to the Food Programme

	(kg)	% of norm
Meat and meat products	70	84.3
Milk and dairy products	330	76.7
Eggs	260	89.6
Vegetables and melons	126	86.3
Fruit and berries	66	58.4

Sources: Prodovol'stvennaya Programma SSSR, p. 11; *EKO*, no. 10, 1981, p. 117.

that our agriculture is so 'vulnerable' is extremely indicative. A highly developed country must aim at ensuring that the harvest depends as little as possible on the weather. This aim was established back in the 1960s but has not yet been achieved: indeed, as specialists concede, at the end of the 1970s 'the opposite was beginning to take place.'[61] Variations in the volume of national income produced in agriculture were constantly increasing! If net income is taken, then they grew from 16.8 per cent in 1959–69 to 31 per cent in 1970–80, i.e. they almost doubled.

The policy of 'pulling up backward sectors through additional investment', which began under Khrushchev and which later became the main plank of Brezhnevite economics, was least effective in agriculture as shown in Table 5.

It is well known that the root cause of all the difficulties lies in Stalin's course of the 1930s. Official economic history speaks in vague terms of 'errors and excesses' which were 'condemned by the Party and government' and then 'swiftly rectified'.[62] Stalin's agrarian policy was seriously criticized (especially in the 1960s) by many official experts and even public figures, but unfortunately it proved extremely difficult to repair the consequences. The measures undertaken by Khrushchev and Brezhnev were in any case plainly inadequate.

For many years, not only all the surplus value but also part of the subsistence value has been extracted from the countryside. This was how Stalin forced the peasantry to finance industrialization. As a result,

Table 5
The Effectiveness of Investment in Agriculture

	1966–70	1970–75	1975–80
Increase in investment as % of previous FYP	57.9	65.9	29.6
% increase in labour productivity	30	22	15
% increase in production	21.2	13.2	8.7

Sources: Problemy truda v sel'skom khozyaistve, pp. 6, 9; SSSR v tsifrakh v 1979g., p. 116; EKO no. 10, 1981, p. 133.

agriculture itself began to experience severe shortages in resources, the standard of living in the countryside was significantly lower than in the towns, and the peasant's legal position was ambiguous. Young people began to leave for the cities, and this was accompanied by the break-up of traditional social ties in the countryside. This process, which was restrained under Stalin by administrative measures, became irrepressible when the peasants finally gained legal equality with city-dwellers. Something had to be done quickly. Massive funds for re-equipping industry and raising the standard of living were then directed into agriculture. For the entire period from 1918 to 1982, 556 billion roubles were spent on developing the agricultural sector, of which 171 billion roubles were in the Tenth Five-Year Plan alone. In the years 1976–80, the Brezhnev administration invested in agriculture more than 30 per cent of all the resources devoted to this sector since the Revolution. In 1961–65, 23.4 per cent of investments went to agriculture (substantially above the level of Stalin's time), and from 1976–85 its share constituted 27 per cent. Unfortunately, after everything that had happened under Stalin, our agriculture was in no fit state to 'digest' such an influx of investment. The American economist Marshall Goldman has cruelly joked that 'investing more later is not enough to compensate for the inadequate investment of the earlier period. It is like starving a baby and then overfeeding him in adulthood in order to compensate for the initial neglect.'[63]

In essence it was as if all the economic contradictions of the Brezhnev epoch were concentrated in agriculture. The massive resources aimed at boosting that sector could not be effectively used within the framework of an outmoded organizational structure. At first, as the newspapers acknowledged, rural bureaucrats 'excessively increased the construction of major complexes without knowing how to take advantage of them.'[64] Later the money was divided between a whole range of the most varied programmes – not one of which had been properly thought out – and this led to a dissipation of resources without any special results. The powerful machinery supplied to the collective farms proved far from perfect (difficulties in industry and the inadequate incentive to scientific and technical progress had a telling effect). In 1982, *Pravda's* economic columnist wrote: 'Total agricultural machinery includes a quite high proportion of obsolete, underproductive tractors. At the start of the current year they accounted for about 44 per cent of the total number of machines.'[65] The assessment of the State Committee on Science and Technology was that out of 272 types of vehicle then in production, 131 needed modernization and 40 were generally no good for anything. Meanwhile the Ministry of Agricultural Machine-building proposed to replace twelve machines in 1983 and another five in the following year. So severe a reorganization threatened to disrupt the plan, but the producers' monopoly position saved them from any problems with obsolete machines.

Rural enterprises were not themselves ready to use the technology effectively. There was a problem with engineers, people with technical abilities continued to leave for the towns, and the new equipment was operating at a loss because of excessive running and repair costs although it was very easy for an enterprise to obtain. The enterprise did not face ruin: the losses were shifted onto the state. The eminent economist, G.G. Lisichkin, compared the tractor to a luxurious limousine given to beggars who were forbidden to resell it: taxes, petrol, garaging and repair prove beyond the owners' means.... It is best if the machine simply does not work.

The efforts of producers to fulfil the plan according to gross output have resulted in exceptionally powerful technology. Where they could have managed with a small horse they have had to use a tractor of sixty horse power. For many years, new, cheaper tractors developed by Soviet designers did not reach the production line (this happened with the Lipets LT3-145 tractor and the Kharkov T-150). The same occurred with other agricultural technology. Yu. Chernichenko wrote sadly that the low quality of our combines dooms them to perish while 'still young' and that 'the million combines produced in the 1970s have passed into oblivion ahead of schedule.'[66]

The departure of young people from the countryside created new problems for Brezhnev's agrarian policy. The efforts of the authorities to hold back social change in the villages by means of additional capital investment led only to growing contradictions. The peasantry's standard of living grew rapidly (by the end of the 1960s, villagers' savings bank deposits were approaching city levels, and in 1984 the average deposit in the countryside was 12 per cent higher), but people continued to leave for the towns. The socio-demographic equilibrium of the countryside was disturbed, and the growth of labourers' incomes, far from helping to restore it, actually accelerated the process. Sociologists have argued that the cultural question came to the forefront. It was assumed that making radio and television available to the vast majority of peasants would help resolve the problems of cultural deprivation, but it only aggravated them by demonstrating the advantages of city life. The thousands of clubs built in the villages every year did not help: the number of buildings increased, but the needs of the population remained unfulfilled. More arduous labour and obviously ineffectual job organization alienated people from village life. Excessive centralization made a successful social and demographic policy impossible, for different regions sometimes demanded qualitatively different solutions. Experts admitted that the unified social policy led 'to the village losing a whole series of unique features.'[67]

There were occasional moves towards a partial review of priorities in agrarian policy. Under the influence of technocratic elements, Brezhnev twice attempted to gain improvements in agriculture through incentives to the individual sector — the 'private subsidiary plots'. The first such attempt took place during the 1965 Reform and was part of the revision of Khrushchev's course towards the complete elimination of the 'private trader'. By 1 January 1965, Khrushchev had reduced by 4.1 million the number of head of horned cattle in the individual sector, and the volume of gross production had fallen by 8 per cent compared to 1958. The sale of products on the collective farm markets in turn declined by 16 per cent over this same period 1961–63. The population was not ecstatic about such 'successes' and the first step taken by the Brezhnev group was to review the policy with regard to private plots. Henceforth, production on these plots was to be encouraged by a whole range of state measures. Nevertheless, the decline of the private sector continued, although its tempo was successfully slowed.

In 1982, the second attempt was made. Measures aimed at stimulating private plots had some results but they proved short-lived. From 1982 to 1984, the number of head of cattle and production on private plots increased a little, but then began to fall again, remaining on average at the level of 1979. Even less meat and milk were produced than in 1979, not to mention 1975.[68]

The failure of attempts to stimulate the private sector was related to its subordinate position in the structure of agriculture. The private sector does not exist independently from the state sector and the people working on private plots are not farmers but workers and peasants employed by state and semi-state enterprises. In the last analysis, their behaviour is determined by precisely this latter fact. They have neither the time nor the legal opportunities to increase production on the private plots, and to turn them into autonomous commercial enterprises working for the market. The term 'subsidiary plot' is perfectly accurate. The conduct of Soviet 'private traders' is sometimes diametrically opposed to that of the Western variety. When prices rise they are inclined not to increase but to reduce production as they receive the same income for less labour and simultaneously gain free time, often at a premium in the countryside. Since market prices continually went up because of a shortage of foodstuffs, there was no incentive to raise production on the private plots. Furthermore, the departure of people from the countryside was accompanied by a decline in the private sector which is basically dependent upon the number of working hands. While the problems of state agriculture remain intractable nothing can help the 'private trader'.

At the end of his life, Brezhnev made one more effort to alter the situation. The 1982 Food Programme should have been a turning point. It envisaged a new wave of capital investment and additional deliveries of chemical fertilizers and technology. There was a sharp increase in the purchase prices of food which should have cost the state an extra 16 billion roubles per year. 9.7 billion roubles of collective farm debt was written off and the payment of 11 billion roubles was deferred. The salaries of rural management and specialists were raised by 30 per cent and it was proposed at the same time to carry out a reorganization of some tiers of management. This was evidence of increasing technocratic influence on economic policy, but even here the compromise between technocrats and conservatives did not lead to success.

The technocracy gambled on the creation of regional agro–industrial associations (RAPOs). The idea, which originated in Estonia, was not in itself a bad one. Technocratic circles were upholding the Estonian experience as a model even before Brezhnev announced his basic official course. It was suggested that numerous enterprises, belonging to various departments and each fulfilling their own plan, could be successfully drawn together if they were all placed 'under one roof'. The RAPO was to become this 'common roof'. In other words, it was a question of attempting to overcome departmentalism 'from below'.

The trouble was that the technocratic reformers placed too many hopes on purely organizational measures. Since the rights of basic enterprises remained limited, the hands of RAPO leaderships were tied. Superior bodies declared openly that they had no intention 'of letting them do anything they want'.[69] In many cases RAPOs were not even able to obtain their own funds. In such instances, as the newspapers acknowledged, their Presidents proved 'as poor as church mice — they did not have a rouble or a nail to their name.'[70] The activity of such 'associations' was limited to scribbling. Wherever it was able to achieve more, the RAPO leadership came into conflict with higher bodies, since at all subsequent levels the management was again 'splintered' between departments. Mutual understanding and closer collaboration between partners could not be achieved. B. Yarushin, the director of a leading state farm, declared in an interview with *Sovietskaya Rossiya* that after reorganization 'nothing changed, everything stayed as before, there was no single boss in the regional team.'[71] The point must be made that in this case, the technocrats could not even stand up for a very moderate proposal which was far from inconsistent with traditional methods.

The Food Programme helped to raise the volume of production a little in 1982–83, but the beneficial effect of the measures adopted had already begun to die away by 1984–85. In 1986, specialists noted that the situation 'is not improving and has even deteriorated in comparison with 1980.'[72] Brezhnev's measures always turned out like that: at first the situation began to get a little better but then it fell back to the old level. And in any event, the results did not justify the expense of resources.

Alongside the agricultural problems traditional in our country, the Soviet economy began to encounter a whole series of new problems by the mid 1970s. The Brezhnev group was plainly in no position to resolve these. First, a shortage arose of all kinds of resources, for the first time in Russian history. Energy and raw materials became more expensive and there was insufficient labour power. All this was not, of course, fatally unavoidable. Despite the burgeoning difficulties, our country remained one of the world's richest in resources. The problem was that enterprises had no incentives to economize. 'Val' forced them to strive for just the opposite. While there was a surplus of resources (and this was how things stood under Stalin and Khrushchev) it was possible to pursue 'val' without a thought for the future. When the position became rather more complicated, a severe shortage instantly arose. It came to light that valuable raw materials were being used extravagantly. The senseless waste of increasingly expensive oil was exposed. Questions were repeatedly asked about difficulties in the coal industry. The introduction of new indicators to encourage savings was mooted (the most important was NNO, the fate of which has already been mentioned). None of this could be effective without radical changes in the economic mechanism. But changes in the economy were feared because they inevitably threatened Brezhnevite stability by demanding at least a new alignment of forces in the ruling elite.

In order to compensate for the shortage of resources without deviating from accepted policy, new sources of raw materials and energy were constantly required. And this essentially only covered the losses which inevitably resulted from wastefulness. The extractive sectors swallowed up to 40 per cent of investment and their capital–output ratio fell by 4.9 per cent in the Tenth Five-Year Plan (the average in industry was 2.9 per cent). Labour productivity in a series of sectors also began to decline, and this then affected the volume of production. Extravagance reached such a pitch that specialists have acknowledged that, using the same quantity of raw materials and energy, the country could have produced 1.3 to 1.5 times more in finished production.

The position with regard to labour resources was no better. 'Exaggerated' demand for labour power led to the situation where, at the beginning of the 1980s, around two million 'superfluous' jobs had been created. In conditions of a clear shortage of labour, there were always more people to be found employed in enterprises than were necessary to fulfil the plan. Economists disagreed how far the numbers working in each industry could be reduced without altering the technology or cutting back on plan targets; some said by 12 per cent, others by 20 per cent, and one author even by a third.[73]

How did this paradoxical situation come about? Economic planners were clearly more interested in attracting the maximum numbers of workers than in raising labour productivity or decreasing the number of jobs. Managers' rights in hiring labour power were certainly extremely limited. Any reduction in the workforce led to an immediate cut in the wage fund and even, at times, to the enterprise being transferred to a lower category (with a corresponding loss of scope for the director). Irregularities in production, causing various 'disturbances' in the economic mechanism, forced management to aim at creating not only material reserves but also supplementary labour resources. At the end of each month, quarter or year, all available labour was mobilized so that the plan could be completed even in comparatively unfavourable circumstances. With a more normal organization of labour it would have been possible to manage with fewer workers, but in the actual conditions there was simply no other alternative. Here as elsewhere, quantity had to substitute for quality. Specialists have calculated that 'up to three-quarters of output is produced in some enterprises in the second half of the month. This means that in such enterprises labour power is under-utilized by at least a third.'[74] Moroever, factory workers are dispatched to the countryside by way of 'aid' (disgruntled Soviet managers call this *barshchina* − corvée − and the term has percolated through even to serious publications) to bring in the harvest. This has created an additional interest in having a surplus of bodies in the factory. All this logically resulted in an exaggerated demand for labour power. The enterprise director would attempt, at every opportunity, to 'play down' the number of additional jobs. The ministry would resist but, under the pressure of numerous fully documented requests, would finally give way — if not in every case, then in some.

The existing economic mechanism pre-ordained the failure of a whole series of technocratic undertakings relating to the questions of labour and wages. Attempt after attempt was made to regulate labour relations and create additional incentives to the growth of labour productivity — for at an experimental level, the results were always satisfactory. After 1978 the ruling circles showed more interest in innovations, and technocratic groups gained the opportunity to realize some of their ideas. The best known of these were the 'Shchekino experiment' and the 'brigade contract'. In the first case, the enterprise gained the right to cut back the number of its workers without any alteration in the wage fund. The money released was spent in various ways. A worker who assumed part of another's obligations received a bonus. Two then did what had previously been done by three, and they were paid accordingly. Unfortunately, it all proved more complicated in practice. There was a heightened risk of failing to fulfil the plan, and no one abolished the *barshchina*. Most crucially, the ministries decided to appropriate the resources gained by adopting the Shchekino system. *Izvestia* reported that 'savings on the wage fund not utilized by the end of the year began to be removed from the enterprises.'[75] Both workers and management felt they had been cheated. Interest in the experiment dwindled. 'The impression is created', wrote *EKO* 'that someone deliberately wanted to weaken the desire for the Shchekino method, and they had no little success in this.'[76] The reformist journal is here alluding to the absolutely real struggle of the conservative bureaucracy against any changes, even those sanctioned from above. However, the main cause of failure was still the objective rules by which the economic mechanism functioned.

The brigade contract fared no better. It was proposed that workers' brigades be given some autonomy. Western commentators rightly characterized this as an attempt 'to combine grass-roots autonomy with the maintenance of a fairly traditional planning system at higher levels.'[77] Brigade members could divide the work among themselves and share the wages 'at their own discretion and without management interference.'[78] The more radical 'Kaluga variant' of the brigade contract had already clearly gone beyond the limits of technocratic reorganization. The experiment was implemented in the Kaluga turbine factory in a way that enabled workers to elect their brigade leaders independently, and a council of brigade leaders under the director was given broad rights: real workers' participation in the management of production. The 'Kaluga variant' became for some time the flagship of most supporters of the reformist current, although the technocrats regarded it without enthusiasm. The left wing of the reformists saw the brigade contract as linked to hopes for the democratization of production, whereas the technocrats saw it only as a new and more efficient way of organizing labour. Since the technocratic version of the brigade contract was victorious, the democratic principles of the 'Kaluga variant' were either forgotten in other enterprises or reduced to an empty formality. There was a corresponding reaction on the part of workers. According to Soviet sociologists, 'many workers consider that the administration has no interest in granting the workers real rights in management.'[79] Only 8.7 per cent of workers surveyed confirmed that the management always took the brigade's opinion into account. On the whole the new method could only 'exacerbate existing contradictions'.[80] In the event of conflicts between brigade and management, the position of brigade leader was subject to re-election'. N. Maksimova, who studied the situation in a number of factories, came to the conclusion that workers were increasingly dissatisfied with the 'brigade method'.

> The management endeavours to make the brigades into purely a 'battering-ram' for fulfilling the plan, to smooth out all the rough edges of the strong characters and the desire to decide independently some of the questions of collective existence. But administrative pressure gives rise to protest. While some are broken, others hold their heads up, ask audacious questions, think about tomorrow and seek a way out of the moral labyrinths.[81]

The brigade system to some degree raised both workers' social activity and the level of conflict in production. More could not be achieved through this means. Similarly poor results had attended the other half-hearted organizational measures undertaken on the technocrats' initiative, for example the 1979 'mini-reform', which envisaged an insignificant extension of the rights of directors and regulation of relations between enterprises. Many points of the 1979 decree were not as a rule carried out, because of the position occupied by the bureaucrats in the branch ministries and the local authorities.

As a rule the technocratic measures had the same short-term effect. As time went on, their results became less and less impressive. It is quite obvious that the same thing happened to the 1965 Reform, the Food Programme, the brigade contract and the Shchekino method. The reformist impulse gradually died out and the effectiveness of the measures adopted declined along with it. The inability of the ruling group over the course of twenty years to secure the promised transition from an extensive, labour- and material-intensive economy to an intensive, science-intensive and dynamic economy revealed the inconsistency of the conservative-technocratic approach itself. The situation was becoming ever more tangled. The old contradictions were not being resolved: on the contrary, they were becoming more complicated, intertwining with the new contradictions. The British Communist, Monty Johnstone, has commented that under Brezhnev 'stability turned into immobility.'[82] In fact both society and the economy continued to develop — by no means always in the optimum direction. Brezhnev succeeded in ensuring stability at quite a high price. Unresolved problems left their mark on the structure and functioning of the economy. One writer commented in *Literaturnaya Gazeta*: 'Bad management is a specific, even highly regulated and sensible form of economic activity.'[83] The essence of the situation was that such pseudo-order, the logic of bad management, became more and more the norm for thousands of workers in the managerial apparatus. In such circumstances half-measures not only failed to produce the expected results, they were doomed from the very start, because they were totally divorced from reality. The central organs started from the workable order envisaged in resolutions, but another order — or to be more precise, anti-order — had arisen in actual economic practice.

It was the consumer who had to pay for all this.

The government's social programmes, aimed at raising the living standards of the population, and the shortage of labour power were two factors contributing to the sizeable growth of workers' money income. Since social programmes were fulfilled better than production programmes and enterprise directors endeavoured to increase wages at every opportunity (this was the only way of attracting additional workers), the situation arose where 'mechanical increases in wages are not being accompanied by growth in labour productivity.'[84] This resulted in the appearance of a distinct disproportion between incomes and commodities. Material incentive proved ineffective in such circumstances. A *Pravda* columnist remarked that labour productivity cannot seriously improve 'while there are more roubles in circulation than good commodities and services. People already see less value in money.'[85]

Table 6
The Growth of Labour Productivity and the Average Wage in the Tenth Five-Year Plan (average annual increase in %)

	Average productivity of labour	Average wage
Industry	3.4	2.2
Agriculture	3.0	3.12
Construction	2.2	2.4
Railways	0.1	2.2

Sources: *SSSR v tsifrakh v 1979*, pp. 172-3; *Voprosy Ekonomiki*, no. 2, 1982, p. 6.

Apart from this, the orientation towards quantitative indicators required that 'labour be compensated while producing nothing of benefit to society.'[86] The absence of criteria for assessing the social utility of labour meant that many had to work 'according to the Sisyphus principle.' It is no accident that this hero of ancient legend became a constant character in satirical newspaper articles. Payment for labour depended not on the result but on the taking part. Useful goods were for the most part disappearing because of this. It is true that on the whole the population's income did not increase so dramatically. The biggest rise in wages was observed in the period of economic reform. From 1965 to 1970 there was a sharp upturn in the standard of living. The population's income continued to increase after that date, but rates of growth (shown in Table 7) began to fall back at roughly the same pace as they had previously risen (a similar tendency is revealed in analysis of the rates of growth of social consumption funds).

In Hungary the rise in the average wage for the period 1976–80 was 43 per cent, in Bulgaria 24 per cent and in Czechoslovakia 15 per cent. By this indicator the Soviet Union occupied last place in Eastern Europe. The minimum wage in East Germany for the same period was 400 marks, which is 133.3 roubles at the official rate — not much lower than the average Soviet wage and with a better supply of goods.

People were irritated, however, not so much by the reduction in the growth of wages (money incomes still continued to rise) as by the

Table 7
Rates of Growth of the Average Wage of Workers and Employees

	1950–55	1955–60	1960–65	1965–70	1970–75	1975–80
% increase compared to previous FYP	11.8	12.2	19.7	26.4	19.5	15.9
Increase in roubles	6.4	8.8	15.9	27.5	23.8	23.7

Sources: *SSSR v tsifrakh v 1979* p. 171; *SSSR v tsifrakh v 1984 godu*, p. 191.

increasing disproportion between the volume of money and its commodity guarantee. Since the prices on basic essentials remained stable and the whole system of price-formation lacked dynamism, the gulf could not but widen. Moreover, sectors producing consumer goods clearly lagged behind the heavy or defence industries.

In these circumstances workers began to accumulate money, as it was extremely difficult to spend. Economists called this 'deferred demand' giving rise to 'compulsory saving'. The seriousness of the problem is shown by the fact that by the beginning of the 1980s real incomes per head of population had risen by 95 per cent in comparison with 1960, but there had been a more than seven-fold increase in savings bank deposits over the same period. In the Ninth Five-Year Plan, for every rouble increase in wages 61 kopecks had been saved; in the Tenth Five-Year Plan it was 90 kopecks. Consequently wage rises led to no increase in demand. By the end of 1983 there were 186.9 billion roubles in savings bank deposits. Experts calculated that this corresponded to 'almost seven months' volume of commodity circulation.'[87] In 1984, the sum of deposits reached 202.1 billion roubles, an increase of 7.5 per cent, and an increase of all of 3.1 per cent over retail commodity circulation. To this could be added the no less than 60 billion roubles which, according to the estimates of western specialists, were piled up in the hands of Soviet citizens ('in money-boxes') at the end of the 1970s. And this figure may even be too low.

The existence of deferred demand played into the hands of speculators. Official authors remarked that it was precisely the latter who were, in the last analysis, accumulating a large portion of the money unsecured by goods from the state sector: 'People working honestly do not usually have excess money. "Easy money" can be seen in the hands of those who have unearned incomes, who speculate and who cunningly take advantage of shortages.'[88] Spontaneous redistribution commenced. In the early 1980s, Soviet sociologists agreed that there was a marked extension in the activity 'of the sphere of unorganised income redistribution' and that this was leading to increasing inequality between different social groups.[89] Victor Zaslavsky, a Soviet sociologist who has worked in Canada since the mid-1970s, also stresses that in the Brezhnev years 'the number of privileged groups and strata has comparatively increased but, at the same time, the gap has widened between privileged and unprivileged.'[90] The result of an examination conducted in 1982 of savings banks in Latvia corroborates this: 'about 3 per cent of the overall number of deposits hold half the total sum of deposits.'[91] While the average depositor in the USSR received twenty-five roubles in 1982 in interest on the sum invested (in Georgia it was forty roubles), the aforementioned 3 per cent received five hundred roubles, or twenty times more.

How is this 3 per cent made up? Apart from apparatchiks, high-ranking military officers, famous artistes and eminent scholars, there are representatives of the commercial pseudo-bourgeoisie, a significant part of the intermediate strata. It is a fact that in the 1970s some social groups could manage without the services of speculators, or needed to resort to them on extremely rare occasions. Different people had different opportunities to gain 'legal' access to scarce goods. This allowed a certain section of citizens to retain their incomes (including those which were completely legal and earned) without taking part in 'unorganized redistribution'. It was precisely these groups which gained the most from wage increases in this period.

Speculators could not, of course, take all the 'excess' money from the population. Moreover, they in their turn had to buy something with their unearned income. Consequently a sizeable part of the surplus volume of money returned to the state sector, although by a quite peculiar route. Sociologists note the origin in the second half of the 1970s of a whole series of 'consumer psychoses'. People 'who had no opportunity to use their money on rational needs, spend it on expensive luxury items, and so on.'[92] Consumer psychoses arose around carpets, jewellery, cut glass and leather jackets. The massive queues for these goods, the preparedness of many comparatively poor people to part with the shirt off their backs just to acquire a 'prestige commodity', the clear desire of the purchaser to get it 'at any price' — all these well-known facts had an influence on the policy being implemented at the end of the decade. Not wanting to raise the prices of basic essentials, the Brezhnev government opted for selective price increases. Prices had to go up primarily on those goods which had become the objects of consumer psychosis. In the opinion of those who devised them such methods would help reduce the disproportion between incomes and commodities without provoking mass discontent and without affecting the interests of the poorest layers of the population. At first the chosen path seemed effective. Despite the price increases, demand for 'prestige commodities' was maintained. Alcoholic drinks similarly became more expensive. Then cigarettes went up in price. All this, it seemed, had no effect on consumption and consequently gave the treasury additional resources without causing social problems. However, the possibilities for selective price increases were soon exhausted. In the early 1980s, prices on 'prestige commodities' reached a ceiling, and demand for them rapidly began to fall. The market mechanism had worked, albeit with a delay: the consumer psychoses had been resolved. Carpets had to come down in price. Cut-glass vases stood peacefully on the shelves. Drinking people chose cheaper drinks. Some people gave up smoking. The state had to lower prices in order to sell off the massive stocks of yesterday's scarce goods that had accumulated in the warehouses. The population's deposits in savings banks continued to grow, crossing the 200 billion rouble mark by 1984 (an increase of 33.2 per cent compared to 1979 when the policy of selective price increases was at its height, and more than double what it was in 1975 when this policy began to be widely put into practice). Curiously, the number of deposits increased rather more slowly (by 22 per cent compared to 1979) — which means that a large part of the additional savings belonged to quite narrow strata and the gulf between the 'successful' and those 'being left behind' was widening noticeably.

Between 1975 and 1982, state retail prices on all goods increased by 8.3 per cent and on foodstuffs by 8 per cent. Researchers also noted that throughout the 1970s there was 'a tendency for prices to rise' on the free market.[94] According to the estimates of official experts, prices of vegetables in the private sector increased by 8 per cent; fruit was 6 per cent and potatoes 1 per cent dearer just over the period 1981–85 (the period when the Food Programme was operative). Apart from this, there was a sharp rise in wholesale prices on a number of kinds of industrial production, and in 1983 on agricultural purchase prices. Raw materials became more expensive: coal by 42 per cent, oil by 230 per cent and gas by 33 per cent (for industrial consumption, by 45 per cent). Wholesale prices on ferrous metals rose on average by 20 per cent. Prices also increased in other sectors.[95] On the whole, the Brezhnev leadership succeeded in avoiding open inflation and maintaining social stability. But the problems, far from being resolved, had in fact been substantially aggravated. Experience had shown that the old economic mechanism was in no state to resolve the contradictions between value and use value, quantity and quality. It was unable to reconcile the interests of the producer (for whom value and quantity are important) and the consumer (for whom use value and quality are important). All of these contradictions can only be resolved in a dynamic fashion by the market. But the market, which presupposes the autonomy of participants in economic relations, seemed politically dangerous. The expansion of enterprise autonomy meant a reallocation of power within the ruling groups — and in the last analysis such a process might begin to deepen, engendering entirely new demands as happened in Kadar's Hungary. In the conditions of Brezhnevite stability, that could not be permitted.

Social stability should have been sustained within the framework of the chosen model by economic growth. This would have enabled the bottom to be satisfied without affecting the interests of the top. But the policy that was carried out led to a steady decline in rates of growth. In 1980–81 the situation suddenly worsened. Growth proved to be minimal.[96] Disproportions were exaggerated. Marshall Goldman wrote:

> The Soviet economy in 1980 reflected one of the most dismal performances in years. Not only was the harvest about 15 per cent below planned output, but production of such important items as steel, coal, meat and potatoes was actually lower in 1980 than in 1979.[97]

At the same time the conservatives adopted an even harder position. The American political scientist, Stephen Cohen, remarks that:

> By the early 1980s, this neoconservative philosophy, which gained strength from the anti-reformist spirit and growing Russian state nationalism of the Brezhnev government, had spread throughout the official Soviet press, becoming the editorial outlook of a number of important newspapers and journals, and even into uncensored samizdat literature.[98]

Cohen's explanation for this lies in the growing conservatism of Soviet society, and even of shopfloor workers. In fact the neo-conservative wave was evidence of the increasing isolation of Brezhnev's supporters who had lost contact with reality, openly defending ideas which were unacceptable to even moderate supporters of the system.

As the patriarchal–conservative group pushed the technocrats away from positions of power, the compromise became ever more unstable. After the economic failures of 1980–81 and the nonsensical propaganda campaign which accompanied them, the compromise no longer appeared viable. The crisis in Poland and events in Afghanistan were additional destabilizing factors. This all hastened the division in the ruling circles. There was a rapprochement between technocratic groups, which had undergone a notable revival in Brezhnevism's last years, and reformists, thus creating a new political bloc. The conservatives now found themselves isolated, just as the reformists had been in 1964. The Brezhnev faction was able to put up serious and sometimes successful resistance to the new bloc, but in the end the forces were unequal. The epoch of compromise was at an end.

Notes

1. The difficulties of the Soviet economy between the 1960s and the 1980s are often linked to the shortage of resources, but, as many economists remark this is 'true neither in a theoretical nor in a practical sense' (*Voprosy Ekonomiki*, no. 2, 1982, p. 4). The deficit of resources in such a rich country as ours can only arise artificially out of particular methods of management. Alec Nove remarks that Khrushchev 'half understood the need and even the required direction of change, and often spoke of managerial autonomy in industry and agriculture, economic criteria, rational investment policy.' Nevertheless, Nove argues that the methods pursued by Khrushchev were unsuccessful and 'traditional' (A. Nove, *An Economic History of the USSR*, London 1980, p. 368). It is difficult to disagree, though Khrushchev's measures were rather more innovative and decisive than Brezhnev's.

2. *Voprosy Ekonomiki*, no. 10, 1966, p. 131. Back in the 1950s Sartre emphasized the link between Stalinist planning and authoritarian–bureaucratic thinking: 'The planning carried out by a bureaucracy which does not wish to recognize its mistakes, turns into violence against reality as the future of nations and production is determined in offices.' It is, moreover 'absolute idealism: from the beginning people and things are subject to ideas, experience which refutes these ideas is declared erroneous' (J.-P. Sartre, *Critique de la raison dialectique*, vol. 1, Paris 1960, p. 25).

3. I have already written in more detail about the preparation and implementation of the 1965 reform in 'Dialektika Nadezhdi' and 'Myslyashchii trostnik' (*The Thinking Reed*). There is a large volume of literature on the subject. For an impression of the ideas of the radical reformists at that time, one should start with G. Lisichkin's book, *Plan i rynok*, Moscow 1966. This work is at once profound and popular. Interestingly, it was published in Czechoslovakia on the eve of the 'Prague Spring'.

4. V. Zaslavsky, *Il consenso organizzato*, Bologna 1981, p. 32.

5. R. Medvedev, *Kniga o sotsialisticheskoi demokratii*, Amsterdam–Paris 1972, p. 294.

6. *Der Spiegel*, no. 10, 1975, p. 108.

7. Zaslavsky, p. 97. On 9 June 1974 *Pravda* published a routine programmatic article in which it was stated that the major advantage of the Soviet system is that it 'guarantees social progress in the conditions of political stability'.

8. *Vengerskie novosti*, no. 9, 1983, p. 10. Similar utterances can be encountered from Soviet economists. K.I. Mikul'skii, for example, writes of the harm caused by substituting 'economic targets' for economic strategy and the loss of 'general orientation of economic development' (K. Mikul'skii, *Eknomicheskii rost pri sotsializme*, Moscow 1983, p. 13).

9. Marx and Engels, *Sochineniya*, vol. 33, p. 417.

10. See *SSSR v tsifrakh v 1979 godu*, Moscow 1980; *SSSR v tsifrakh v 1984 godu*, Moscow 1985.

11. *EKO*, no. 8, 1980, p. 99.

12. *EKO*, no. 8, 1985, p. 131.

13. R. Hutchings, *Soviet Economic Development*, Oxford 1982, p. 153.

14. *Voprosy Ekonomiki*, no. 8, 1981, p. 20. Brezhnev and his supporters criticized Khrushchev for voluntarism and for posing unrealistic objectives for the Soviet economy. But in the mid 1970s they themselves asserted that their strategy 'ensures big economic growth in the future, and will take the USSR into first place in the world by volume of production and then also by level of consumption per head of population' (*Voprosy eknomicheskogo rosta v SSSR*, Moscow 1974. Edition prepared by Acad. T.S. Khachaturov). Khrushchev promised the same thing. The extent to which the prognoses of Brezhnev's economic strategists contradicted reality is evidenced, for example, by the fact that in 1974 they promised that in 1976–80 the capital–output ratio would 'stabilize and in isolated branches there will be some growth.' Thus for that Five-Year Plan 'an increase in the capital–output ratio' would be typical (ibid., p. 148). Instead, the capital–output ratio fell by 14 per cent....

15. I. Birman, *Ekonomika nedostach*, New York 1983, p. 34.

16. *Problems of Communism*, no. 5, 1982, p. 68.

17. Yu V. Andropov, *Uchenis Karla Marksa i nekotorye voprosy sotsialisticheskogo stroitel'stva v SSSR*, Moscow 1983, p. 10.

18. Birman, p. 201.

19. Mikul'skii, p. 63.

20. L.I. Brezhnev, *Otchet TsK KPSS XXIV s'ezdu*, Moscow 1976, p. 53.

21. *Der Spiegel*, no. 15, 1973, p. 102.

22. *L'URSS et l'Europe de l'Est en 1982–83*, p. 31.

23. *EKO*, no. 8, 1983, p. 61.

24. See J. Kornai, *Over-centralisation in Economic Management*, Budapest 1957.

25. *Literaturnaya Gazeta*, 3 August 1983, p. 13.

26. *Ekonomischeskaya Gazeta*, no. 45, 1981, p. 24.

27. Alec Nove, *The Economics of Feasible Socialism*, p. 73.

28. *Voprosy Ekonomiki*, no. 2, 1982, p. 18. *Kommunist*, no. 10, 1978, p. 38.

29. For more detail see *Voprosky Ekonomiki*, no. 2, 1982, p. 10.

30. P. Hanson, in *Soviet Studies*, vol. 35, no. 1, January 1983, p. 4.

31. *EKO*, no. 2, 1982, p. 75.

32. Marx, *Capital*, vol. 1, pp. 179–80.
33. *Voprosy Ekonomiki*, no. 12, 1982, p. 86.
34. *EKO*, no. 2, 1982, p. 75.
35. *Voprosy filosofii*, no. 11, 1980, p. 53. As Marx observed, 'spinning that is not used for weaving and knitting is spoiled cotton' (Marx and Engels, *Sochineniya*, vol. 23, p. 294). For an assessment of the real position in the Soviet economy it is essential to compare data on the growth in production with data for the sale of consumer goods. The 'scissors' [divergence] obtained as a result are a criterion of efficiency or inefficiency.
36. Kaganov, p. 41.
37. Engels's introduction to Marx, *The Poverty of Philosophy*, Moscow 1956, p. 21.
38. *SShA*, no. 12, 1983, p. 15.
39. *Literaturnaya Gazeta*, 2 December 1981, p. 11.
40. *EKO*, no. 1, 1983, p. 41.
41. *Izvestia*, 11 May 1983.
42. *EKO*, no. 1, 1983, p. 42.
43. *Pravda*, 27 May 1983.
44. *EKO*, no. 8, 1983, p. 58. The eminent economist S. Kheinman notes that in our country 'three forms of machine-building' have in fact arisen. Of these, only one is genuine. The second type of machine-building is factories belonging to non-machine-building ministries and the third is repair and maintenance workshops of enterprises in other branches (see *Voprosy Ekonomiki*, no. 8, 1981, pp. 26–7).
45. *Problemy truda v sel'skom khozyaistve*, Moscow 1982, p. 35. The gigantomania of our planners was directly linked with departmental centralism. Ministries could more easily supervise the building of one large factory than five average ones (although, according to economists, the latter alternative would have been more appropriate).
46. G. Grossman, 'The Party as Manager and Entrepreneur', in Guroff and Carstensen, p. 297.
47. *Planovoye khozyaistvo*, no. 6, 1983, p. 44.
48. Nicholas Lampert, 'The whistleblowers: corruption and citizens' complaints in the USSR', in M. Clarke, ed., *Corruption*, London 1983, p. 279.
49. *EKO*, no. 10, 1983, p. 42.
50. Nicholas Lampert, *Whistleblowing in the Soviet Union: Complaints and Abuses under State Socialism*, London 1985, pp. 25–6.
51. *Izvestia*, 12 July 1983.
52. Lampert, pp. 182, 188.
53. *Literaturnaya Gazeta*, 31 July 1985, p. 11.
54. *EKO*, no. 7, 1984, p. 72 (L.V. Nikitinskii). The law lives when it is observed.
55. *Sovietskaya Kul'tura*, 6 July 1985.
56. *Pravda*, 7 July 1985. For figures on the number of letters see *Spravochnik partiinogo rabotnika*, no. 21, Moscow 1981.
57. *Newsweek*, 8 March 1982.
58. *Prodovol'stvennaya programma SSSR na period do 1990g. i mery po ee realizatsii. Materialy maiskogo Plenuma TsK KPSS 1982g.*, Moscow 1982, p. 8.
59. *Sotsiologicheskie Issledovaniya*, no. 1, 1983, p. 46.
60. *Novyi Mir*, no. 3, 1983, p. 171 (Yu. Chernichenko). The combine both mows and

threshes. Soviet official propagandists always take for comparison the United States, where the climate is significantly better than ours, and demonstrate that, with our weather, we should not expect better results than what we have now. Meanwhile individual farms in our country refute such theories. In Estonia in 1982, the 'Edasi' collective farm harvested 4,950 kilos of grain per hectare from comparatively poor soil and in quite difficult weather conditions. At 'Edasi' in 1983 the average milk yield per cow was 5316 kg: the average for the country was 2258 kg. (see *'Edasi' kolhoos*, Tallinn 1984).

61. *Voprosy Ekonomiki*, no. 1, 1984, p. 75.

62. *Istoriya sotsialisticheskoi ekonomiki v SSSR*, vol. 3, p. 374.

63. Goldman, p. 78.

64. *Sovietskaya Rossiya*, 27 January 1984.

65. *Stroki, rozhdennye poiskom. Sotsial'no-eknomicheskie obozreniya 'Pravdy'*, no. 2, Moscow 1984, pp. 197–8.

66. *Novyi Mir*, no. 3, 1983, p. 173.

67. *Voprosy Ekonomiki*, no. 8, 1984, p. 93.

68. Even the American Sovietologist, Richard Pipes, who holds to quite right-wing views and pins all his hopes for political or economic change in the USSR on the development of the private sector, has been forced to concede that 'the private sector in agriculture has no great prospects, so that even if the authorities grant it greater freedom of action it cannot have significant results. Reports exist which suggest that over the last decade the productivity of private plots has not increased but fallen' (R. Pipes, *Vyzhit' nedostatochno*, New York, p. 166). It is true that Pipes cannot be called a well-informed author. For example, he writes of 'pitiful conditions of existence and low wages' in the modern Soviet countryside (see p. 142). This does not simply contradict reality but is also evidence of Pipes's lack of understanding of the actual economic process: it was precisely an unjustified rise in peasant incomes in the state sector which undermined the private supplementary plots thus rendering them less necessary. Paradoxically, the Russian peasantry worked rather better during the terrible poverty of the 1940s than in the period of comparative material prosperity which began under Brezhnev.

69. *Sovietskaya Rossiya*, 27 January 1984.

70. *Izvestia*, 31 July 1983.

71. *Sovietskaya Rossiya*, 22 March 1983.

72. *Izvestia*, 21 February 1986.

73. For more detail see *Osnovy planirovaniya i sotsial'nogo razvitiya SSSR*, Moscow 1983, pp. 61–63; Mikul'skii, p. 196; *EKO*, no 2, 1982, p. 76; *Voprosy ekonomiki*, no. 2, 1982, p. 51. On the over-consumption of resources see *EKO*, no. 1, 1984, p. 4.

74. *EKO*, no. 2, 1982, p. 76.

75. *Izvestia*, 25 October 1983.

76. *EKO*, no. 8, 1981, p. 122. Western researchers have written candidly of the opposition of the Ministries' apparatus to the Shchekino experiment. Gertrude Schroeder notes that one way to neutralize the experiment was to issue numerous confused and contradictory instructions regulating its conduct. The rules foisted by Ministries 'are so complex as to almost defy description' (G. Schroeder, 'The Soviet Economy on a Treadmill of "Reforms"', in *The Soviet Economy in a Time of Change*, Washington 1979, vol. 1, p. 334).

77. Leonard Schapiro and Joseph Godson, eds., *The Soviet Worker — Illusions and Realities*, London 1982, p. 59.
78. A. Levikov, *Kaluzhskii variant*, Moscow 1982, p. 65.
79. L.A. Gordon, A.K. Nazimova, *Rabochii klass SSSR: tendentsii i perspektivy sotsial'no-ekonomicheskogo razvitiya*, Moscow 1985, p. 155.
80. *Sotsiologicheskie Issledovaniya*, no. 3, 1982, p. 114.
81. *EKO*, no. 8, 1985, p. 179.
82. *Marxism Today*, March 1985, p. 14.
83. *Literaturnaya Gazeta*, 2 February 1983, p. 13.
84. *Pravda*, 2 September 1983.
85. *Stroki, rozhdenie poiskom*, p. 177.
86. *Literaturnaya Gazeta*, 11 August 1982, p. 11.
87. *EKO*, no. 1, 1985, p. 33. See also *SSSR v tsifrakh v 1984g.*, pp. 215, 224; Birman, pp. 70–72.
88. *Stroki, rozhdenie poiskom*, p. 177.
89. See *Sotsiologicheskie Issledovaniya*, no. 1, 1982, p. 11.
90. Zaslavsky, p. 89.
91. *EKO*, no. 6, 1982, p. 122. It is interesting that in 1979 the samizdat journal *Levyi Povorot*, edited by myself and P. Kudiukin, pointed out that 4 per cent of deposit-holders owned 40 per cent of deposits. We were later accused of 'making the figures up', told that this was a slander, etc. I acknowledge that we really did make a mistake. Judging by official figures, the situation was *much worse* than we had depicted it.
92. *Sotsiologicheskie Issledovaniya*, no. 1, 1982, p. 11.
93. The active population, including those employed in the economy, students and pensioners, by 1984–85 comprised about 189 million people. Even if we assume that each deposit-holder has only one deposit, we discover that more than 15 per cent of the active population do not in general make deposits. In actual fact this figure must be significantly greater, since many people have several deposits at the same time. The totals of the deposits are also different.
94. *Izvestia*, 21 February 1986.
95. See *EKO*, no. 9, 1982, pp. 20–21, and also *EKO*, no. 1, 1985.
96. Precise figures are unknown because of the peculiarities of Soviet statistics. The Swiss Communist paper wrote that the growth of the USSR's Gross National Product in this period amounted to 'all of about 0.1 per cent' (*Vorwärts*, Basle, 7 July 1983, p. 8). I think this is an exaggeration. A more realistic assessment is that growth was not less than 2 per cent. For more detail on the processes occurring in 1980–81 see J. Kosta and F. Levcik, *Wirtshaftskrise in den Osteuiropaeischen RGW-Laendern*, Munich 1985, *Forshungsprojekt "Krisen in den Systemen Sowjetischen Typs". Studie No. 8.*
97. Goldman, p. 11.
98. Stephen F. Cohen, *Rethinking the Soviet Experience: Politics and History since 1917*, New York and Oxford 1985, p. 140.

6

From Stability to Reform: The Social Consequences of Brezhnevism

In one of his first speeches after coming to power, Yuri Andropov remarked that we still know little about the society in which we live. The declaration was quite clear: over the course of almost seventy years, official sociological science had been concerned with individual questions while avoiding serious theoretical analysis of society as a whole. This is not surprising. What is surprising is that samizdat had also devoted very little attention to the problems of social development. The same is also true of a majority of sovietologists, who have concentrated their attention on political, cultural and national problems but not on social ones. Thus there was not simply a lacuna in the research: the whole picture was distorted.

Robert Kaiser, the former Moscow correspondent of the *Washington Post*, complains that Americans writing about our country have not devoted 'sufficient attention to the actual character of Soviet society.'[1] Alas, in trying to correct this regrettable situation, Kaiser himself did not even attempt a serious analysis of the basic features of our way of life, our problems and perspectives. The social structure of society did not arouse the slightest interest in him. He confined himself to retelling Muscovite anecdotes, which he himself did not fully understand. His colleague, A. Nagorski, having promised finally to write a book in which all of the weaknesses of Western journalistic prose about the Soviet Union would be overcome, published a work full of traditional clichés and minor inaccuracies, and — most importantly — displayed an amazing inability to distinguish the important from the secondary, the incidental from the material. It is even more lamentable to listen to intellectuals taking information about their own country from books such as Kaiser's (it is no accident that this book was published in the West in Russian).

Official sociology had, in any case, collected sufficient concrete material in the 1970s to permit a serious discussion about the fundamental tendencies of society's development. If that discussion did not take place at the appropriate time, this was the fault not of the sociologists but of political circumstance.

The Brezhnev era is usually viewed by Western observers and by dissidents as a time of political standstill and economic stagnation. The weakness of the theoretical research of that period is naturally linked to political stability, which did not permit manifestations of bold thinking in the censored press. But in saying this we are only telling half the truth. The 1970s were a period of major social and socio-psychological shifts which will have far-reaching consequences for Soviet history. The processes which have occurred can only be compared in their significance with the social changes which occurred in Russia at the time of the 'tranquil' reign of Alexander III and which prefigured the 1905 Revolution.

Some authors in the West, recognizing the existence of new tendencies in our society in the 1970s, insist that this is a question of purely quantitative changes and that, qualitatively, nothing is changing. L. Sokhor even wrote that 'the law of dialectics on the transformation of quantitative into qualitative changes has ceased to operate' and that social relations 'remain quite static'.[2] The political stability of the Brezhnev epoch had genuinely created the illusion that all life in the country had died and that anything new simply could not arise in such conditions. Analysis of concrete factors, however, does indeed show that this was all an illusion. Society carried on living and developing in preparation for a new stage in its history.

In the 1970s an industrial society was definitively formed in our country, the process of urbanization was completed and a new generation grew up, shaped by the conditions of Europeanized city life.

Mass resettlement from the countryside to the town was characteristic of the whole period which followed collectivization. Demographers observed at the start of the 1980s that 'over 50 years (1927-76) the urban population of the USSR increased more than six-fold and today constitutes 62 per cent of the total population of the country.' The social significance and consequences of this process were different in different periods of Soviet history. In the 1970s, the ratio of labour resources between town and country had qualitatively changed in favour of the former: 'Important changes have occurred in the distribution of employment between town and village. In 1959 more than half the total population lived in rural areas, but in 1970 it was around 40 per cent.'[3] This is of historical significance; there had been a qualitative change in the whole social structure of society and way of life. The town began to prevail over the countryside in all respects. The Soviet Union entered the ranks of urbanized countries. The overall conditions of life for a majority of people approached those of the 'average European' — and so did their psychology.[4]

Another feature seems perhaps still more important. Prior to 1959, growth as a result of migration from the villages was more than three times higher than the natural growth of the urban population. In the course of the following twelve years (1959–70) the ratio between the natural increase in town–dwellers and growth as a result of resettlement from the countryside changed quite markedly in favour of the former, although growth as a result of migration still surpassed the natural increase by 20 per cent. In the first half of the 1960s a large mass of village youth resettled in cities but they retained their rural customs, way of thinking and behaviour. To a certain extent this even assisted urbanization: peasants were more inclined to have large families. Initially there was a sharp increase in the birth rate in the towns.

> The share of the natural increase of city dwellers was highest in 1961–65; in the subsequent Five-Year Plan it declined substantially, giving way to growth as a result of migration from the villages. In later years the significance of the natural increase in city-dwellers again became decisive and reached a maximum in 1976, approaching 47 per cent. In the future, it seems to us that this will become the main factor and that the component of population migration from the countryside into the cities will drop into the background.[5]

The rural population has, in turn, acquired urban norms of living. There has been a reduction in the natural increase of the rural population and the number of people resettling in towns has begun to fall regularly. 'The drama of transition from rural to urban, from peasant to industrial society is largely over', observed a Western writer.[6] What conclusions should be drawn from this?

For the first time in Russian history the urban population is predominant over the rural and, especially important, within the urban population itself the dominant role is played by hereditary city-dwellers. Contrary to Sokhor's view, quantity is here transformed into quality. The character of society is altering.[7]

Moscow remained the exception in the 1970s, its social development being vitally complicated by a mass influx of people from all corners of the country. The situation was constantly deteriorating. By the mid-1980s the authorities recognized that the city was beginning to turn into 'an ungovernable agglomeration'.[8] Nevertheless the same social processes were occurring in Moscow as in other places, though with a certain delay.

In the 1960s, most people who had come from the countryside into the town turned very slowly into 'real' town-dwellers. Their cultural level remained extraordinarily low. An inquiry conducted in this milieu in 1982 showed that 'half of those questioned (for the most part from older age-groups) had not once been to a theatre, museum or exhibition.'[9] The new generation is more quickly assimilated and the mass of indigenous town-dwellers becomes sufficiently great to make its own norms of living generally recognized and generally accepted. Urban culture triumphs. 'Whereas in 1970, 748 per thousand of the urban and 499 of the rural population had higher and secondary education, the corresponding figures in 1979 were 863 and 693.'[10] The shift is obvious. The more educated youth from the countryside adapts more quickly to life in town.

The third aspect of urbanization in the USSR is the growth of major cities. In 1981 the number of people living in cities with a population of one hundred thousand or over reached 72 per cent in relation to the overall mass of urban-dwellers. The upshot of this was, on the one hand, the comparative decline of a series of small towns, particularly in Central Russia, and, on the other, the concentration of large masses of the proletariat (workers and intelligentsia) in major industrial centres. This is where we find the greatest share of indigenous city-dwellers. We will be able to assess the significance of this fact in the future....

As regards the working class, its composition and structure in the 1970s markedly improved. With each new generation it is becoming, as sociologists admit, 'more and more homogeneous'.[11] The fall in prestige of a series of intellectual (more precisely, engineering) professions, which had assumed a mass character and were comparatively poorly remunerated, helped to stabilize the working class. The mass 'overproduction' of engineers was characteristic of the whole Brezhnev epoch. The official literature acknowledges that disproportions arose in the economy between the number of specialists and the demand for them. The quality of education also declined noticeably. A director, looking at a young specialist, would say angrily, 'What did they teach him in the institute for five years?' Nobody was surprised that, in such conditions, an engineer was paid less for his labour than a worker. The mass withdrawal of qualified specialists into the working class was the logical outcome of such a situation. In 1969, twenty-eight thousand engineers were already 'employed as workers' according to official figures....[13] Thereafter the number of 'deserters' began to grow rapidly.

In the 1960s, 80–90 per cent of school pupils dreamed of going to an institute. According to 1980s figures, 'only 46 per cent of those surveyed expressed such a wish.'[14] Sociologists speak unanimously of the declining orientation to higher education (especially in relation to technical specialisms):

> The reorientation of school leavers away from professions demanding higher education to working professions is a mass phenomenon. It has been recorded in selective investigations in practically all regions of the country and in a series of cases its dynamic can be traced in detail.[15]

Along with the fall in prestige of engineering work, the reduction in vertical mobility in society in the late 1970s has also had an effect. According to Tatyana Zaslavskaya 'only leavers from a limited number of the best Moscow schools' had a chance of entering the most prestigious institutes.[16] In the 1960s, a majority of young people believed that any road was open to them, but by the end of the 1970s they had come to realize the inequality in real opportunities. Official authors concede that children of intellectuals have indisputable advantages in entering institutions of higher education: 'All this leads to the ranks of the intelligentsia being filled more often by children from intelligentsia families, as though the intelligentsia is reproducing itself.'[17]

This situation was the logical outcome of Brezhnev's policy of stability. Social ties became more stable although the development of society was rendered less dynamic. The positive side of all this was that whereas the most intelligent young people from the working class had previously had an absolute desire to join the intelligentsia, they now more frequently remained within their own social milieu. This fact has enormous significance for the overall state of affairs in the country. Back in the 1960s (not to speak of the 1950s) the Soviet working class was replenished primarily from the countryside, but in the 1970s and 1980s it has become to a large extent self-reproducing (or reinforced by those leaving the intelligentsia).

The 'new generations' arriving from the countryside had formerly eroded the working class, for 'organic integration of new recruits into the workers' milieu was a complicated affair, frequently unattainable (or not totally attainable) in the lifetime of a single generation.'[18] The workers' social passivity, lamented both by opposition intellectuals and sometimes by official figures, was quite natural and explicable in the 1960s and the early 1970s. By the end of the Brezhnev epoch, the situation had changed. In the early 1980s the well-known sociologists L. Gordon and A. Nazimova had grounds for concluding, in their research monographs on the Soviet proletariat, that 'fresh reinforcements constitute (and from now on will always constitute) a comparatively minor, "normal" share of the workers' milieu.' This meant it was now possible to overcome the 'infantile disorder' of the primary growth of our industrial proletariat, the more so as by the 1980s the arrivals from the countryside were 'radically different in their social outlook and cultural level from those peasants who moved into the towns in the initial stages of industrializ-ation.'[19] In many cities hereditary proletarians constituted, by the end of the Brezhnev era, up to 70 per cent of the working population. They had a growing consciousness of their own interests and a readiness to defend them. The number of labour disputes increased, although at first 'claims are as a rule presented to middle management.'[20] Nevertheless, amazing events, such as a strike in Kamchatka in 1983 by drivers demanding improved organization of work, have taken place.

By the end of the Brezhnev era we already had a different working class and a different country from the 1960s. Everything had changed. People had changed, the way of life had changed. The consequences of these changes will surely be felt especially acutely by the late 1980s and early 1990s, when the new relations and structures reach full maturity.

As we can see, not everything is changing for the worse. Brezhnev's time had its positive aspects. The ruling circles are very proud of the fact that the well-being of the mass of Soviet people grew appreciably in the late 1960s and early 1970s. But this is only one side of the coin. It is not only about people obtaining television sets, transistor radios, hot water and even cars. A new style of life and a new psychology, more akin to the West's, took shape. And the cause of this must be sought not in the appearance of foreign goods on the shelves of stores, nor in American films, nor in trips abroad. The fact is that modern production, requiring a more intellectual and civilized labour force, rendered unavoidable the Europeanization of thought.

The increase in the value of labour power and the consequent rise in the proletariat's standard of living is an objective tendency in the conditions of the new industrial society determined by the conditions of production. We read in Soviet research devoted to the proletariat in the West that:

> The contemporary scientific-technical revolution has sharply increased the demands on the worker's general and specialist training. The typical figure is becoming the worker who includes in the labour process in the quality of his labour power not just physical skills, the simplest stereotypes of productive-technical behaviour, but his learning. The reproduction of such labour power presupposes expenditure not only on more extended and profound specialist education but also on significantly better conditions of work, housing, nutrition and variety of leisure opportunities.[21]

The same tendency is active in our own society. Research devoted to the Soviet proletariat informs us that:

> A rapid and continual increase in the efficiency of living labour, its productivity, is now a major precondition for the successful progress of the production process. In this lies the economic foundation for increasing the skill and cultural-technical level of the working class in recent decades.

The authors complain, however, that 'the raising of culture and skill and the increasing complexity and stress of work radically extend workers' demands.'[22] In addition there appear demands which from the point of view of official ideology seem 'irrational', 'excessive', 'dangerous' and even 'harmful'.[23]

In several instances the state has attempted to nip this in the bud. Our country is the only one in the world where official censure has been brought to bear on ... fashion. At first they hoped to prevent the wearing of tight trousers: then just the opposite — a struggle was conducted against flared trousers and long hair. Rock music was condemned, not to mention other manifestations of Western mass culture. This all led nowhere. Fashions altered and the authorities, defending yesterday's norms, simply pitted themselves senselessly against the next generation of youth.

Detente also played its role, undermining many of the Russian's traditional prejudices which had earlier been very successfully exploited by the Stalinists (we are surrounded by enemies, the West thinks only of how to destroy us, everything foreign is harmful to us, and so on). The propaganda of the 1970s in fact debunked such notions. Under Khrushchev Coca-Cola was depicted as almost the very embodiment of the horrors of imperialism, but under Brezhnev it was allowed onto the Soviet market.

The American Sovietologist, Seweryn Bialer, insists that detente changed nothing: Soviet society remained 'as it was before the age of detente arrived.'[24] Of course, detente itself was an external factor, but it encouraged the deep-seated internal processes occurring within our society. The *Times* correspondent in Moscow, Richard Owen, observing events at close quarters, noted that the conservative faction of the ruling circles was very disturbed 'by the influence on Russian youngsters of Western life styles, including fashion, pop music and the anti-authoritarian attitudes that tend to go with them.' In striving to counteract this, conservative circles in the period of Chernenko's administration endeavoured to restrict contacts with foreigners and an 'aggressively isolationist mood' prevailed.[25] True, Owen does not say that this campaign succeeded, which is not surprising as the conservatives' successes in this instance were modest to say the least. Despite an energetic press campaign against foreign fashions, films and music, everything remained as before. The newspapers wrote that 'we do not need borrowed passions and borrowed heroes', but Western films continued to be screened — for, as the same author acknowledged, 'they achieved box-office success' and 'Soviet film-makers attempted to imitate them.' Efforts to revive the traditions of Stalin's cinema collapsed because of the indifference of viewers, to whom films on the thirties' model seemed 'patently oversimplified'.[26] Clearly it was a matter here not of the West's influence but of the changing conditions of Soviet life itself, which made the contemporary West seem closer and more comprehensible than Stalin's past. Even the extreme Stalinist, V. Safonov, had the courage to admit this in the pages of *Sovietskaya Kul'tura*. He could not conceal his hatred for youth who dress up in 'foreign rags', in 'jeans with a non-Soviet label highly prized in their circle and blouses soiled with crude designs.' In the end, though, 'is it a matter of rags, my dear comrades? It's a matter of i-de-o-lo-gy!' This is precisely how he writes this word, syllable by syllable, attempting to reproduce his burdensome and hopeless mood. The youth no longer believe in the values of the older generation — unlike in his day, when young people 'were united with the old'.[27] Such a difference is inevitable. Both the youth and older generation had previously been raised in the same kind of social conditions. Now they embody two distinct stages in the development of society.

The changes occurring in the field of culture should also be borne in mind. Much is written in the official press of the population's increasing culture, with references to the growing number of people with higher education, the rising circulation of newspapers, books, and so forth. It is of course difficult to determine the actual cultural level of the people through purely quantitative indicators: it is also important to know what they read, how they read, what they go and see at the cinema, what they watch on television. All the same, it is impossible to dismiss purely quantitative indicators. G.G. Dadamyan, the leading Soviet specialist on the sociology of art, writes:

> Society's widening cultural horizons bring changes in the types of cultural behaviour. The desire of millions of spectators to have 'been', 'seen' and 'heard' leads to a variety of 'booms' in art. The last fifteen to twenty years have been characterized by a rapid growth in attendance at all forms of visual art.[28]

Thus from 1950 to 1978 attendance at theatres rose by 1.8 times, at museums by 5.5 times and at concerts by 2.1 times. The growth of visits to museums is especially heartening, as the cultural values presented in them are more indisputable (in the theatre and at concerts not only good, but hopelessly bad art can be shown, but the content of museums is tested over time). Moreover, whereas in 1950 museums came below the theatre and concerts in the number of visits, by 1978 they already occupied first place. 'At present there is among youth a heightened interest in and attraction to spiritual values' — a fact that became generally recognized in sociological literature.[29] And shifts were happening not only in the town but also in the countryside.

Of no less interest is the 'book boom' of the 1970s. By 1983, according to press figures, Soviet people had accumulated in personal libraries 'a vast fund of books' amounting to 30 million volumes.[30] Typically, a variety of ideological literature lies on the shelves of bookshops at the same time as there is a tangible shortage of most other kinds of publication (including handbooks).[31]

Television plays a special role. The social consequences of its spread have been discussed elsewhere. They are not the most important thing here. Mass production of television sets began in the USSR in 1955. Then there were roughly eight hundred thousand sets for the whole population. The TV was a luxury item. By 1966 there had already been a six-fold increase: five million sets (and 27.8 million radio sets). Over the period 1966–79 the position changed once again. In 1979 alone, 6.44 million TVs were bought, which is more than there had been in the entire country in 1966.[32] Production continued to increase. From 1971 to 1980, 'with overall growth of 2.3 times in the production of goods with a cultural-domestic and economic purpose, the production of colour TVs increased almost fifty-fold.'[33] Even allowing that such high rates of growth were possible only because of the extremely low reference point (in 1955 there were four TV sets per thousand inhabitants in the USSR as compared with 318 per thousand in the USA, and 66 radio sets per thousand compared to 974 in the USA,[34] and we hardly produced any colour TVs at all prior to 1971), these figures are evidence of the growing significance of television in everyday life. Sceptics say that television is just one of the channels for official propaganda, but this is untrue. People do not watch television for the sake of propaganda. But if they do watch it, it is indeed there to see. In other words, it is as a source not of the state's propaganda efforts but of cultural information that viewers mainly watch television, as the statistics relating to viewer interest in different programmes, films or shows bear witness. Official propaganda programmes are not very entertaining, to judge by their popularity; foreign films enjoy increasing demand; and so on.

Let us return, though, to Dadamyan. He writes:

> Judging by the number of published books and pamphlets, gramophone records and cassette tapes (in 1978 the figures were 178 m., 207.9 m., and 2.9 m. respectively) it is possible to come to the conclusion that a fundamentally new cultural situation came into being in our country in the 1960s and '70s.[35]

It is extremely difficult to judge how far the real cultural level of the people has risen on the basis of such data but *the general cultural situation* has clearly changed.

In this respect the resettling of large masses of people in the towns played an enormous role. Urban conditions facilitate access to cultural values – at least in principle. Though we may doubt how *deeply* the new culture has penetrated the masses, the *breadth* of its dissemination is beyond doubt. Perhaps the sociologist was correct who suggested, stressing the rise of a qualitatively new situation unprecedented in Russian history, that the cultural level of the masses became on average somewhat higher during the 1970s than the cultural level of the ruling elite.

The 'policy of stability', implemented by Brezhnev, held back the restructuring of production but did not hinder the profound natural processes occurring in society. In consequence the socio-cultural level of our country began to overtake the economic, which inevitably gave rise to new contradictions.

By the end of the 1970s roughly two-fifths of all workers (more than half among young age groups) had received a full secondary or higher education. The number of workers with higher or incomplete higher education increased. By 1984 no more than 18 per cent of the working class was poorly educated, and as a rule these were people approaching pensionable age. Simultaneously the structure of employment and the character of work had changed. Gordon and Nazimova revealed that whereas in the 1960s the sectoral structure of employment in the USSR corresponded to the 1900–1910 level in Western Europe, by 1980 the structure of employment in our country was approximately that of the developed industrial countries in the West and Czechoslovakia in 1960. This is proof that society had reached a qualitatively new level of development, although the gap between ourselves and the West was still quite significant.

By dividing workers into several categories depending on skill, technology and the complexity of labour, Gordon and Nazimova detected important shifts. In the late 1950s, early industrial technology little different from the level of the 1930s and '40s (and in several cases from the pre-October level) still predominated in our country. In other words, the technical equipment of Soviet industry was basically the same as in Stalin's time; 52 per cent of workers were employed in primitive manual labour. By 1979, the situation was quite different. 52 per cent of workers were involved in developed forms of industrial production, and 13 per cent in the scientific-industrial type of new technology. Workers involved with primitive machinery of the Stalin-era type constituted no more than 35 per cent (among young people, 24 per cent). There were even more noticeable changes in respect of complexity of labour. In the late 1950s, 57 per cent of workers were employed in complex labour demanding professional training, but by the late 1970s this had risen to 70 per cent. In the Soviet Union (as in the West) the differences between the advanced modern strata of the industrial proletariat and its traditional groups were reinforced. Thus on the one hand, there had occurred a qualitative shift in the structure of employment, but on the other, society required still more radical shifts.

Gordon and Nazimova remark that the growth in education appreciably surpassed that in skill. By the 1970s there existed a 'well-educated majority' who were denied the opportunity fully to realize their learning by Brezhnev's policies, which had provoked a fall in the economy's rate of growth and a deceleration in technical progress:

During the 1970s, employment in all of the most simple, unskilled forms of industrial work fell by only two percentage points — from 32 to 30 per cent. Meanwhile the growth of mass education continued at the former rate so that the proportion of people with only primary or lower education fell in 1979 to 19 per cent. This difference gave rise to a situation never before encountered. For the first time in society there were rather more unskilled jobs than workers of that cultural type who, in the past, would easily have filled the vacant positions.

This radically changed the social and psychological situation in the country:

> While a majority of workers possessed pre-industrial skills, they looked upon their position as normal and acceptable. It is precisely when such skills become the lot of a minority that they turn into a source of social tension.[36]

So workers became divided into two basic groups. A *bloc of skilled labour* was gradually formed, uniting the engineering and technical intelligentsia and workers in modern production. A common way of life, similar social situation and common interests led little by little to a drawing together of these groups (when the wages of engineers became too low, the widespread transfer of engineers to workers reinforced existing ties even further). Considerable social stability is characteristic of the bloc of skilled labour. As research has shown, a significant portion of young people from the families of skilled workers who transfer into other socio-professional groups at the commencement of their working lives 'afterwards returns to the social stratum from which it has come.'[37]

At the same time there continued to exist an important *mass of unskilled workers*. The social ties in this milieu are rather weaker and the level of its structural organization remains very low, so it is impossible to speak of a 'social bloc'. A significant section of this mass is made up of those who have left the countryside. In Moscow the prevalence of migrants who do not even have a permanent residence permit, the so-called *limitchiki*, has created an extremely complex situation in many work collectives. Only the marginal people of the Third World can be compared to the *limitchiki* in their social self-consciousness and the precariousness of their existence. In January 1986, Boris Yeltsin, the recently-appointed head of the Moscow Party organization, spoke quite candidly about this problem. Although the word *limitchiki* is not in the dictionary, any Muscovite knows its meaning. Enterprises bring workers into Moscow from other towns 'according to quota' (*po limitu*):

> *Limitchiki* are promised flats, and they come from all over the country, as a

rule with a 'specific' reference. Having got their accommodation, they leave. The enterprises request another 'quota', thus completing the vicious circle. Enterprise collectives remain unstable and they receive less accommodation.[38]

The areas in which *limitchiki* settle are distinguished by a high level of crime, they earn rather lower wages than native Muscovites and their prospects for advancement up the social ladder are restricted. Russian workers who resettle in the highly developed Baltic republics find themselves in a similar position. As Estonian sociologists have noted, poorly and averagely skilled native Russian workers

> are stuck rather more firmly in their social position than Estonian workers in these socio-professional groups. Within five years almost half of Estonian workers in this group have left it, chiefly by joining a higher socio-occupational stratum of workers. The Estonian workers' milieu is also more intensively represented in the non-manual labour group, primarily among the ranks of the intelligentsia.

Meanwhile for both Estonians and Russians in the bloc of skilled labour 'a high degree of similarity in social position' is typical.[39]

The mass of semi-skilled workers appears to be the Soviet proletariat's past; the bloc of skilled labour, its future. But there was already a marked tendency for semi-skilled workers to head for the way of life and, in part, the social values of higher working-class strata. In the 1960s, comparing their own position with that of the poor peasantry in the post-Stalin period, they considered themselves successful, but in the 1980s they are conscious of the fact that they have the right to more interesting and profitable work, and are not satisfied with their position.[40] For its part, the bloc of skilled labour pursues a whole series of changes which would reinforce its position and allow it to participate in decision-making. The chief desire of this bloc is to achieve a structural reform of the economy – which might then have political consequences. The slogan of 'market socialism' finds many supporters in this milieu. Semi-skilled workers, however, are interested in an immediate rise in status, an increase in wages and redistribution of income in favour of less well-off groups. Equality is of rather more interest to them than social restructuring. Both are dissatisfied with the situation that has arisen, but in different ways.

In such circumstances the experience of the West and the Third World holds great value for us. Soviet workers imagine themselves to be a more-or-less homogeneous mass.[41] In the 1980s the position proved rather more complex. *The fate of reform in our country depends, in the final analysis, on whether a strategy of change in accord with the interests of both fundamental groups of workers is successfully elaborated and put into effect.* Although these interests are far from identical they have a whole series of common features.

Over the period of the Brezhnev administration, a large section of the population came to enjoy European norms, living standards and culture. A single, European type of need was formed. This applies, of course, not to the whole country, but to its most important parts. Under Khrushchev youths wore trousers from the 'Bolshevichka' factory, but under Brezhnev they began to wear American jeans. To some this fact might seem of little political significance, but it is no less important than the fact of the appearance of dissidence. What is more, these facts are fundamentally similar.

The essence of the problem is that over the period 1965–75 there was not only a comparative rise in the people's standard of living, about which much has already been said, but a *displacement of the traditional model of demand.* The paradoxical consequence was that, despite an indisputable improvement in life, more and more people began to experience dissatisfaction with their social existence. At first glance this seems inconceivable, and narrow-minded bureaucratic consciousness, on encountering such ingratitude, is plunged into despair: 'They are just greedy for what they haven't got'.... It is actually rather simpler than this.

In 1977 it was calculated that:

> In a rational budget, the amount of income necessary to meet a person's rational needs at present would be, according to the estimates of Soviet economists, in the order of 200 roubles a month on average per head of population in the USSR.[42]

In the same year the average wage reached 155 roubles per month — which incidentally meant a more than threefold increase since 1946.[43] Obviously an average worker was in no position to satisfy completely his 'rational needs' even with a considerable rise in wages. Add to this the inequalities in people's incomes and material payments; imbalances in consumer supply and demand, or in other words the disparity between the quantity of paper money in the country and the rather small amount of attractive goods on the market; the fact that many goods have to be bought from speculators, that the average person is frequently forced to pay various forms of 'extortion' and illegal excess payments to all sorts of grabbers whose services he needs, and that he has to pay twice the market price thanks to the absence of meat and other essentials in the state shops;[44] add to this, finally, that apart from 'rational' needs there are also 'irrational' ones and the conviction grows, first, that the figure of 200 roubles was clearly too low and, second, that even if it is accepted, the average Soviet worker in 1977 could only satisfy, at best, 70 per cent of his needs.

All the same, in 1946 the average wage was 48.1 roubles (converting the sum to new 'Khrushchev' roubles); in 1955 it was 71.8 roubles; in 1965 it was 96.5 roubles. People's incomes were lower, then, in 1946, and yet nobody died of hunger! What is more they felt more contented. How can this be? People can live in different ways.

The results of a sociological investigation in Lithuania in 1975

> showed that 40 per cent of families questioned still had no refrigerator, 63 per cent no vacuum-cleaner, 62 per cent no art objects [for the statistician, art objects and vacuum-cleaners are both the same — B.K.], 74 per cent no tape-recorder. Only 30 per cent, however, explained their absence through the insufficiency of the family budget, and 43 per cent considered it possible to do without them. They did not plan to acquire them in the near future, preferring to save their money.[45]

I must apologize to the reader for the style of this and other such quotations — unfortunately, by no means all authors of official literature treat the Russian language with due respect. But it is not, of course, a question of style. The above-mentioned 43 per cent of those surveyed are pictured as consumers of the old, traditional type who relate to the norms of existence of the 1940s. It is clear that these people must *feel* themselves rather more fortunate than others: one group needs 200 roubles to live while earning 150, whilst this group earns 130 and makes do with 100. The first is discontented with life, the second, on the other hand, is satisfied with it. So increasing personal incomes in no way leads to an automatic rise in 'rational needs'. A little is enough for one in the second group. This is no Buddhist or aesthete concerned with the mortification of the flesh, but simply a person who considers the poverty of the Stalin epoch a normal state of affairs, and a minimum sufficiency an abundance and luxury. The trouble is that the traditional type of consumer, so appropriate to the traditional system of management, is gradually disappearing.[46]

In the early 1960s, traditional consumers were still predominant. According to calculations made at the time, each member of a family needed to spend on average between fifty and fifty-five roubles per month (this criterion lay at the heart of the social programme of the 24th Congress of the CPSU).[47] But for most of our people such an income level was unattainable right up to the period of economic reform. The authors of an official study of the Soviet proletariat acknowledge that:

> It is sufficient to compare this figure with the data on wages quoted above to be convinced that in the 1940s and '50s the ordinary working family and the majority of Soviet people had no possibility of spending such sums. A monthly wage of 50 roubles (at today's prices), typical for the early 1950s, meant that a family of four with two workers received on average only half the necessary sum. By the end of the '50s wages had increased considerably, but still gave a family of four on average only 80–90 per cent of its necessary means.[48]

And this was at the minimal level of needs, reduced chiefly to physical survival. The turning-point was 1965–66, when the average wage of workers and employees rose to between 95 and 100 roubles a month. This meant that the average working family had reached, according to official estimates, the level of 'minimum sufficiency'.[49]

Western sovietologists concede that major changes were occurring in the late 1960s:

> The gains were substantially greater in the 1950s and 1960s than in the 1970s, and they varied considerably among republics, but over the period through 1978 per-capita consumption for the USSR as a whole grew, on the average, 3.2 per cent per year. Soviet families, particularly urban families, acquired more and better housing, enjoyed improved diets, and gained access to a wider supply of goods and services, especially consumer durables.[50]

It was only in the 1970s that consumption began to slow down, and after 1978 Western experts could no longer detect any signs of further growth. At the same time, however, social concepts of well-being began to alter. Old-style consumers were totally satisfied with what had been achieved — indeed, with their insignificant demands, they should have had a feeling of living in material abundance: they had even more money left over, had built up their savings and felt insured against any misfortune. The population's income had grown rapidly. 'In 1965 only 4 per cent of our population had a per capita income in excess of 100 roubles a month, but in 1970 the figure was 18 per cent, and by the end of the Tenth Five-Year Plan it was around 50 per cent.'[51] Of course one hundred roubles is half as much as the two hundred discussed at the end of the 1970s, but then it is twice as much as the fifty roubles required for a 'normal life' by the standards of the Khrushchev era. It seemed that social harmony had been achieved and the happiness of the Soviet people assured. But unfortunately the old-style consumer cannot but come into contact with the new, and bad examples are well known for their infectiousness. New-style demand, which began to form at first in particular social groups closely linked to the development of the scientific-technical revolution and with more intellectual forms of labour, little by little became the general norm.

'The transfer of most families into their own apartments', declared sociologists, 'radically altered the structure of demand.'[52] A large scale programme of house building, expanded under Khrushchev and continued, although less effectively, under Brezhnev, played a major role not only in improving workers' living conditions but also in changing their way of life and psychology, bringing them closer to the European average. The 'demonstration effect' had great significance: you see cars on the street, beautiful things in shop windows, a TV at your friend's, you hear a tape-recorder in a neighbour's room.... This all affects you. Old people still stand their ground and swear at people 'stuffing themselves', at those who want to buy children oranges (when you can make do with potatoes) or imported games (what's wrong with our Matrioshka, our traditional Russian doll), or keep food in the refrigerator (when you can hang it up outside the window), or watch television (when you can listen to a loudspeaker on the street). But young people have adopted European standards from the outset. They do not want simply to exist, but to live like human beings, and make use of the benefits of modern civilization. At first, people who have made the transition to new-style consumption can count upon accumulated resources — the voluntary abstinence of preceding years has not gone to waste. These resources do not last long, but people are initially content. Their life is better than before. The real growth in wages may have been evidently lower in 1970–76 than in the preceding Five-Year Plan, but there was in any case some hope in savings.

After a while, however, queues for oranges form in exactly the same way as the queues for potatoes (and the latter do not disappear either), and the TV repeats all the words that stick in your gullet and which had previously come from a loudspeaker in the street. The old problems do not go away, but are reproduced at a higher level, making them even more acute. In the samizdat almanac *Varianty*, V. Chernetsky and Yu. Khavkin wrote ironically about the consumer society characterized by a chronic shortage of consumer goods.[53] It seems that in many ways the situation had become worse. Previously there had been no money, now there was money and no goods. This was even more annoying! People were furious.

The slogan of the consumer society — 'what was a luxury for our fathers is the norm for us' — acquires an ironic meaning. What was an unnecessary luxury for the old is an unavailable shortage for the young. Norms of consumption have qualitatively changed but the fundamental conditions of life, its contradictions, remain as before. A new conflict arises.

We have spoken about Europe's overall needs, but it must be remembered that these demands are not satisfied. We spoke of the European life-culture, but it should not be forgotten that this culture is in contradiction to the living conditions and material possibilities of many people. In other words, *the contradiction between the ideal and the reality*, which dissidents have attempted to express politically, is, for the broad mass of people, *taking place at the level of material existence*. This is very important. Propaganda tried to interpret this fact. A theory was put forward that the state did not have the time to satisfy the extraordinary desires of the people. The term 'the outpacing development of needs' appeared. The growth of needs, it turns out, 'is happening much faster than the rise in well-being.'[54] If something is not there, the masses are to blame. People should not wish for too much.

This theory is not only primitive, it is quite inconsistent, as it ignores what is most important. We have seen how mistaken it is from the data of the 1975 Lithuanian survey. Even some official authors have recently begun to dispute it, calling for a repudiation of 'this simple scheme'.[55] It is not that needs have grown, but that there has been a qualitative change in the *type* of needs. This is indirectly acknowledged even by some researchers who start out from the theory of 'outpacing growth'. They note that in the 1970s there occurred 'the formation of a new kind of demand'.[56] In other words, a whole complex of needs had taken shape relating to European (more accurately, Europeanized) people. In our view, the existing system is simply in no state to satisfy fully these needs.

The comparative rise in wages did not in itself make people happy. Hot water and even one's own car cannot be life's goal. As a writer in *Literaturnaya Gazeta* remarked, with some justification, it is impossible 'to measure a good life, good and evil, with comforts and wages. As if one cannot live badly with a "Zhiguli"' — the most popular Soviet car.[57]

Soviet sociologists recognize that 'the contradiction of unfulfilled expectations' was a feature of our society in the late 1970s and early 1980s.[58] The population's dissatisfaction with social and living conditions was very well expressed in the official literature. 'Housing, health care, organized leisure and children's pre-school education' are all among 'insufficiently satisfied needs' identified by researchers.[59] And popular discontent is provoked not only by the lack of this or that institution but also by the way these institutions work. We have, for example, a very high overall number of doctors. In 1970 there were more than 950,000 doctors of all specialities in the USSR, as compared with 484,000 in the USA, and 50,000 less than this in West Germany. The numbers of doctors per 10,000 people were 36.2 in the USSR, 22.5 in the USA and 25.1 in West Germany. In France and Japan there were fewer. 'More than one third of all the world's doctors' were in the USSR.[60] Despite this, West Germans and Americans have a significantly higher regard than Russians for the medical system. The fact is that the organization of medical care in the USSR is universally recognized as being absolutely outmoded. Like the whole system for servicing people's cultural, living and social needs, 'it was founded in the 1930s and has undergone only insignificant alterations since then.'[61]

Under Stalin, when the people's standard of living was extremely low and little attention was devoted to individual consumption, collective consumption, directly controlled by the state, developed comparatively swiftly. This was part of the overall policy. Even those Western specialists inclined to the view that the real incomes of ordinary Soviet citizens were no higher or even lower in 1953 than in 1928 acknowledge that 'only education and heath care, treated as investments in human capital, had experienced real advances.'[62] Even in the 1950s and early 1960s the relevant Soviet institutions were regarded as among the most advanced in the world. In the 1960s and early 1970s, Left liberal and social democratic governments in the West (partly influenced by the Soviet experience) began to reinforce and extend the social security system, achieving impressive successes. The Soviet leaders, on the other hand, leaning towards the Western model, began to devote more attention to individual consumption, sometimes neglecting to modernize the social services. At first people were happy, since their position was genuinely improving, but a desire gradually arose for higher-quality work from the social services, the prestige of which (very high in the 1930s) had suffered a precipitous decline. A return to the ideal of collective consumption could be clearly discerned, but at a new level. Moreover, in the USSR a society of 'private consumers' had simply not been successfully established. As social structures stabilized in the 1970s, people became much more aware of their collective needs. At the same time evidence is provided even in official press reports that the quality of education and the health service was generating more and more overt dissatisfaction. In 1983, *Izvestia* (nos. 295–296) published a sensational article, 'Surgeons among the potatoes', in which it was reported that doctors had been sent by provincial authorities to do agricultural labour. As a result, many sick people were not receiving prompt attention and some operations were being botched. The flood of letters which poured into the newspaper after this article speaks for itself. The official press was forced to confirm that 'tearing doctors away from their prime task has, alas, in many places become a habit and standard practice.' Literally everyone is sent to bring in the harvest, sometimes even the head of a surgical unit. The local bureaucracy has no consideration 'either for doctors or for the sick', and openly acts 'to people's detriment'.[63] In order to get help — if it can be got — 'people sit for several hours. On some days, the doctor can see up to 180 people!' When an urgent operation is needed 'the ambulance' goes 'to the surgeon in the field.'[64] What made the letter-writers especially angry was the fact that even in the 1940s, despite the country's extremely severe economic plight such conditions were not usual. As for the doctors themselves, they 'do not believe that the disorder which is setting in can be altered.'[65] And they rightly take the view that publicity in newspapers cannot prevent a repetition of such outrages — as the newspapers themselves admit.

This situation is not accidental. It became possible only through a real change in the priorities in the political system, a devaluation of the social significance of medical institutions and the growing contradiction between society's level of development and the condition of the social services. The question of how to organize one set or another of state institutions is inseparable, in our conditions, from general political questions. Half measures in a particular sphere cannot resolve it. Thus the problem of the health service is connected to the state of the pharmaceuticals industry, scientific and educational institutions, the allocation of state expenditure among different branches, and so on.

But the most important factor, it should be recognized, is not discontent at the quality of health care or the operation of public transport, but people's dissatisfaction with their own work, which is widespread among both skilled and unskilled workers. 'The need for self-expression through labour' has grown steadily among our people in the 1970s and '80s, declares *Sotsiologicheskie Issledovaniya*.[66] Unfortunately, where there is bad management, 'lack of rhythm in production' and bureaucratization of the economy — all especially typical of the last five years of Brezhnev's administration — people simply cannot gain satisfaction from their own work. A letter was published in *Izvestia* from the former leader of a brigade of fitters, V. Demyanishin, under the evocative heading 'I beg you to answer — why?' Why, the author of the letter asked, are we forced to manufacture useless products — 'Vega' refrigerators that nobody buys? 'We convert expensive metal, paint and polystyrene for no purpose. And we get neither moral nor material satisfaction from the labour that we invest in thankless tasks.' The factory fulfils the plan, although this is 'not valour but a crime.' The workers are leaving in droves: in a single year, 22 per cent left — and they were 'the most skilled'.[67] The *Izvestia* correspondent A. Zinoviev (not to be confused with the writer!) uncovered an identical situation at a garment factory in Ufa. The women workers, he reported, were 'depressed in the knowledge' that nobody wanted to buy the overcoats they manufactured. The foreman, M. Galliamova, declared that, although the plan was being fulfilled and overfulfilled, 'hardly anybody derives any satisfaction from it.' And a seamstress, V. Nikul'chenko, said angrily: '"Why do our technologists agree to put such absurd patterns into production? We wouldn't wear such overcoats as the ones we make. So why do we offer them to the customer? I'm ashamed to work like this."'

Brigade leader Demyanishin complains

> What sort of conscious discipline can I summon from workers who have known for a long time that they are manufacturing a product of no use to anybody? ... Why did I, a person used to working, to being useful to people, end up in conditions which are a profound insult to me as a worker?

Izvestia, in its printed comment on the letter from the former brigade leader, declared categorically — and typically — that 'the Editorial Board finds difficulty in replying to the questions you have posed.'[69] Later the paper organized a meeting between Demyanishin and the Minister, but he was equally unable to give an intelligible answer to the former brigade leader's questions.

It is a bad business. What Demyanishin wrote to *Izvestia* about is not his personal problem, it is a social problem — and, as indicated above, all the more so as a 'growing interest in the content of labour' is typical of the modern proletariat.[70] Incidentally, sociologists acknowledge that consumer dissatisfaction is also to a significant degree engendered by the fact that people have little opportunity to assert themselves 'in the work and occupational sphere.'[71] The less a person is content as a producer, the more he demands in the form of compensation from society as a consumer, and the more excessive his demands seem from the point of view of 'realistic', officially recognized norms.... Western sociologists noticed this phenomenon back in the early 1970s and, through an analysis of capitalist society, came to the conclusion that the 'explosive potential of this discontent' with work is a threat to the whole system.[72] One way or another, this problem has proved important, and not just for the West.

Many Westerners suggest that in the Soviet system, 'nearly everyone seems to have found ways to turn its shortcomings to individual advantage.'[73] The traditional conclusion is that serious changes are impossible in the USSR. It is quite true that people adjust to the conditions of life and know how to make use even of its least attractive aspects. But it does not follow that people like the situation. If workers 'take away' 'superfluous' parts or materials from factories, this does not at all mean that stealing is considered a virtue or even the norm. Just the opposite. Soviet writers in the 1980s spoke directly of the growth of 'social discontent' provoked

> by problems that are not invented but really exist, by needs that are socially justified and not excessive, by political maturity and not backward views, by readiness to make a contribution to the development of society and not social dependence.[74]

This fails, however, to take into account the fact that discontent is directed not only or mainly against the system, but against oneself. This is a very important aspect. Neither sovietologists nor official Soviet writers have properly considered the social significance of the fact that an enormous number of people are suffering from remorse. As Marx wrote: 'Shame is already revolution of a kind.... Shame is a kind of anger which is turned inward. And if a whole nation really experienced a sense of shame, it would be like a lion, crouching ready to spring.'[75]

The new generation of the working class is more educated than those that preceded it. It is much more conscious of the contradictions of its own position and the meaning of social problems. Official social scientists believe this 'engenders a series of social problems.' Conflicts arise: 'An "overdeveloped" young person often gives an enterprise a lot of trouble and becomes an undesirable figure.' He stands up for his rights and protests, since 'he runs up against the limits of the opportunities to prove himself as an individual.'[76] Labour discipline deteriorates. As a rule, the official press condemns such people, but other voices can be heard. In the Novosibirsk journal *EKO*, V. Yadov declared that 'some tendencies that are traditionally considered to be negative make me optimistic as a sociologist.' In workers, especially the young, 'a healthy, critical foundation is developing'; they are 'becoming more self-assured, independent and rational' and striving for 'an active part in management.'[77] The last point poses the sharpest questions. Simply raising wages and subjecting the work of the bureaucratic apparatus to some regulation is not enough to change the situation; it is essential *to broaden the rights of workers qualitatively, to humanize and democratize production relations as a whole.*

In 1985 *Literaturnaya Gazeta* conducted a sociological survey among young people. The information gained as a result plainly showed a rise in discontent. It turned out that young people react rather more sharply than the older generation to irrational production targets, refuse overtime working, and above all try to understand the causes of their dissatisfaction. The quality of the labour force rapidly increased during the 1970s but the opportunities for workers' self-realization did not.

> Very many tried and tested ways and methods of management are now proving to be inactive. A young worker intuitively realizes his objective value and demands self-respect, albeit in an elementary sense — that his labour be well organized, intelligently utilized and applied in normal conditions.

This type of individual, created by the natural development of society and production, does not give in to manipulation and demands self-respect precisely as an individual. *Literaturnaya Gazeta* also noted another factor, the decline in vertical mobility in our society at the end of the Brezhnev era, which generated disillusionment and irritation among wide social strata:

> It now takes on average seven years for a skilled worker to rise in status. And for a typical engineer the step up to the next rung of the ladder of responsibility takes ten years. Some reach pensionable age without having gone beyond even the stage of 'ordinary' or junior research officer.[78]

This situation is related to the results of Brezhnev's 'policy of stability of cadres' and the fall in the rate of economic growth. In essence, all such processes are partial instances, expressing the basic contradiction. As Lenin remarked, people remain society's prime productive force, and it is in them that the contradiction between forces and relations of production is, in the first instance, reflected. The rising quality of the labour force has become incompatible with the old organizational structures.

Yadov stresses that:

> It is primarily a question of the objective necessity to increase the masses' participation, albeit indirect, in management. It is difficult not to see links between the radical problems of the economy and the democratization of production.[79]

But it is one thing to desire democracy and another to realize it in practice.

A. Zinoviev (not to be confused with the *Izvestia* correspondent) has said on many occasions that the system reproduces in millions of copies a definite type of individual. This is a sociological axiom, but the satirist has missed the chief point: at a certain stage, the system begins to produce a type of individual that it cannot fully satisfy. It was Marx once again who discovered this sociological paradox. The state needs a certain type of individual — without this, modern production is simply not feasible — but (here is the question): What sort of state do these people need?[80]

Things are suddenly not so simple. For all the comparative stability of economic and political relations in the country, social relations during the Brezhnev period changed and became more complicated. The social organism continued to evolve at all levels according to the laws of self-development. A situation, so to speak, of *static development.*

A major social factor in the 1970s was the formation of *small privileges.* This phenomenon has been little studied. Its essence is more or less as follows: A person receiving between 120 and 180 roubles a month, a wage close to the national average, cannot usually be seen as belonging to a privileged group. But if, to earn this, he either generally does nothing or performs useful work to the value of twenty or thirty roubles, then it becomes clear that in fact his wage represents a form of unearned income. One could exaggerate and say that idlers have been transformed into a special social group! This group is extremely conservative and treats with hostility even the mot moderate attempts to increase the system's efficiency (for such attempts first of all threaten their special position: they cannot work under any circumstances — they have lost the art). This group moreover exists chiefly within the lower echelons of the bureaucracy (an official's work does not lend itself to assessment for quality). This allows them more or less actively to sabotage any reformist initiatives from the centre. Thus in Brezhnev's time not only reformist but anti-reformist tendencies found some mass support, although anti-reformist moods were not, of course, so widespread. It is however a crucial point that the conservative bureaucracy at the lower level could from the very beginning successfully counteract even the most moderate efforts at changes 'from above'. The experience of the first post-Brezhnev years showed that it was extremely difficult to fight this group. Its resistance could be broken only by eliminating 'cushy jobs' at the lower end of the apparatus by sharply cutting back the number of cadres. However the higher tiers of the bureaucracy within each state institution actually strove to do just the opposite. Staff cut-backs proceeded very laboriously and slowly. It was moreover never possible to determine precisely by what principle the dismissals were being carried out. In several cases those who worked the best were forced to leave.

Returning to the question of the lack of correspondence between the needs of individuals and their social opportunities, we should note first of all that not everybody is conscious of this contradiction. For many, it remains at an unconscious level. But its effects are then all the more destructive. This has been partly grasped by official propagandists. Their great fear is that 'negative sentiments have accumulated in the sub-conscious precipitating mistrust, doubt and discontent.'[81] They see the reason for such phenomena, however, in the influence of Western radio — as if Soviet life itself cannot give cause for discontent. In fact, such feelings are most characteristic of people who never listen to Western radio: this kind of thing has not been engendered and cannot be engendered by propaganda. It is occasioned by and reflects the course of life itself; it reveals the objective social conflicts in our society. As C.G. Jung said: 'The unconscious is nature, and nature never lies.'[82] As history has shown, unconscious discontent can at times take strange and terrible forms, which only makes it the more dangerous. Psychologists say that 'in any critical situation the unconscious sets people, and consequently their conscious, in motion.'[83] It pushes millions of people to simultane-ous elemental actions, which often have the awful destructive power and the fateful inevitability of natural disasters. A hurricane is blind, but it never errs, precisely because it is blind; it just goes wherever it must go.

We have put this in general terms, but it is nevertheless obvious that the Brezhnev period was a time in which elements of unconscious discontent were assembled. Instability of cadres and petty sabotage of production, often exposed in the press, were spreading. There were isolated instances of 'wildcat' strikes, even a growth in crime. It was all evidence of the increasing complexity of the social situation. For many, unconscious discontent became conscious. The prime role in this was played not by anger at the economic disorder, not by a revolt of the stomach, but by protest against bureaucratization, against recurrent administrative despotism, against injustice. Here, one great peculiarity of the Russian national consciousness should be remembered. A Westerner believes in freedom, a Russian in justice. For millions of people the widespread corruption of Brezhnevism's later years was an indication that the existing set-up was inconsistent with the most important human values, and therefore had to be changed.

The new social situation is inevitably provoking shifts in mass consciousness. But it is necessary to be very careful here. Up to this point we have talked about processes happening at a very deep level. *Social unconsciousness is rather more flexible than social consciousness.* Human thinking possesses a fair degree of inertia. Sometimes people simply do not perceive changes, or to be exact they take place with a marked delay. 'Time,' psychologists observe, 'is needed to take in and assess a new situation.'[84] Psychological processes usually lag behind social processes. While people are not conscious of change, psychological inertia dominates society, and it is as if they are living in the past. Clearly this cannot continue indefinitely. In the last analysis it is not psychological but social factors that are decisive. But it would be incorrect to reduce one to the other. The way people lag behind events can be seen even in the case of the most elementary and obvious changes. A sociological investigation has noted

the gap between the rates of technical re-equipping and the system of retraining workers. A disturbing fact is that in reconstructed sections only 11.0 per cent completed study courses about the new equipment, and 24.6 per cent productive-technical courses; and 62 per cent of workers underwent no retraining at all.[85]

If there is a delay in even the most essential and pressing results of the technological revolution (an increase in working class skill is linked, among other things, to an increase in its intellectual level), then this applies even more to long-term psychological, cultural and ideological effects. It does not follow, though, that such effects can be ignored. They are present — and, as they say, better late than never.

It is difficult to establish what people actually think. Soviet censored literature has recently provided a range of interesting materials, but their conclusions cannot be called indisputable. Even the authors themselves recognize that 'fear or unwillingness to provide a correct answer on the form' was typical of most of those surveyed during the investigation.[86] In a study of 'rumours' by postal questionnaire, about half of those surveyed simply refused to answer some questions. People prefer to hide their opinion (but this is also significant: it means they have something to hide). They mechanically carry out official rituals without attaching any special meaning to them. The real difficulty is not to guess that people are wearing a mask but to understand what is hidden behind the mask.

Vladimir Vysotsky, the great poet of the Brezhnev epoch wrote:

> What do I do not to miss a kind face?
> How, by chance, do I find out they're honest?
> They have chosen to dress in masks,
> So as not to break their faces on the stone.[87]

What can one learn from official surveys of public opinion? The censored authors acknowledge that in the 1970s there was a marked decline in the effectiveness of the activity of the state propaganda apparatus. This question was in fact at the centre of the June 1983 Plenum of the CPSU Central Committee. The journal *Politicheskoe Samoobrazovanie* complains that 'negative situations for propaganda can arise and are arising.' In the journal's opinion, this is explained by the contradictions between propaganda formulas and the real consequences of 'previous and current economic activity.'[88] We are witnessing a clear 'moral deterioration' of the old slogans in new socio-economic conditions and a plainly visible lack of correspondence between word and deed.

Most of the propagandists' complaints about the various new difficulties which arose in the 1970s and early '80s are not exaggerated. A representative of the state trade unions from the 'Elektrosila' factory, writing in *Trud*, described the 'disgraceful' behaviour of workers who permitted themselves questions such as: 'What does the union do for me? I only pay the dues!' The poor devil complains that the workers — 'and, I dare say, not only in the shops of "Elektrosila"' — 'simply don't know what the unions do for the workers' (!), and that therefore 'we must talk more and write more about it' (!!) so that 'every union member' can realize 'how much the union does for him and his family.'[89] This is really rather funny. If the workers — the members of the union! — do not see its value in their everyday life, then they are simply not going to believe newspaper articles: personal social experience is always more convincing than information gained second-hand. If one is inconsistent with the other, the newspaper version will be doubted (all the more so as the unions' inability to defend workers' rights was openly acknowledged even by Andropov).

Everyday experience works persistently against conservative slogans. Nicholas Lampert, analysing seventy cases of labour conflict recorded in the Soviet press, noted that in only two of these did the union take the side of the aggrieved workers against the management. The concurrence of the union's and management's position was recorded 'in the great majority of cases.'[90] This is no secret to the workers themselves. Nevertheless by the late 1970s the reaction of union officials to this situation was rather less conciliatory. This is shown if not by workers' increasing consciousness of their rights then at least by a certain *demand for rights*. People began to take a more decisive stand in defence of their rights. There was a much greater number of complaints and protests, so many that they clogged up the bureaucratic machine: 'Complaints go in a heap to the central newspapers, to the city soviet, to the regional committee. More. Still more!' And, already, 'high levels that are supposed to resolve questions of quite a different order have begun to be affected.' But the complaints have not a 'malicious' but a 'totally law-abiding' character.[91] People with complaints, 'envoys', arrive in Moscow from the provinces and leave no stone in an institution unturned. Lack of faith in local authorities makes such expeditions unavoidable: in the workers' opinions, even the power of the courts does not ensure an objective investigation: 'the courts do not always examine the arguments and sources of evidence presented to them.'[92] Officials stand their ground and 'seekers after truth' do not retreat. An *Izvestia* correspondent complains: 'Indifference, lack of concern for people's requests, formalism and bureaucratism, when displayed at the outset, can cause an avalanche stretching over many hundreds of kilometres.'[93] As 'seeking after truth' becomes more and more a mass concern, its social meaning changes and disillusionment in the actions of bureaucratic bodies is made all the more volatile. It is curious that the human rights dissidents of the 1970s totally ignored this new and growing sense of justice and gave not a moment's thought to its historical significance, although here we see the appearance of a similar need (with the difference that mass 'seeking after truth' is a more important social symptom than actions 'in defence of rights' by a few hundred intellectuals).

Let us return, however, to the postal questionnaire mentioned earlier. Its data are of undoubted interest. In the course of the investigation the question of people's relationship to the mass media was studied, as well as their relationship to 'spontaneous forms of social information', rumours and so on. Let us start with the first. V. Losenkov, in his analysis of the results of the survey, stresses that 'the audience is inclined to be highly critical' with regard to the mass media.[94] Strange as it might seem, people show a greater interest in foreign than domestic political information. It would be natural for the opposite to be the case and for people to be rather more interested in events which directly concern them. Losenkov writes: 'The strained international situation can provoke more intense interest in an audience than a favourable situation taken as a topic of information about life within the state.'[95] Such an explanation does not seem satisfactory. Things are obviously rather simpler. People believe the domestic political reports of newspapers, radio and television less than they believe the reports from abroad. This recalls the old archetype of Russian national consciousness: even a person with a negative attitude to the domestic policy of the Russian state, identifies with its foreign policy. This was absolutely typical of old Russia (such writers as Pushkin, and even to some extent Herzen, are examples). I think that something similar has happened in our country in the 1970s, at least among the workers.

In Losenkov's view, 'inadequate or insufficient official information' about events in the country, 'irregularities in the operation of the mass media and propaganda', and people's dissatisfaction with the official version of events all give rise to 'rumours'.[96] Alongside these reasons he mentions 'the ideological immaturity of sections of the population', which in official jargon means a disparity between the ideological aims of the authorities and public opinion. This contradiction is revealed with particular clarity by an analysis of workers' attitudes to Party and production meetings. A survey of workers who made 'critical remarks' at such meetings gave amazingly impressive results: 'only 3 per cent of those questioned said that shortages were totally eliminated as a result of their critical interventions.'[97] Seventy per cent of young workers not belonging to the Party do not in general attend meetings, considering it meaningless. We read in the pages of *Sotsiologicheskie Issledovania* that negative assessments are spreading beyond individual 'poor superiors' and are 'being extended to various social institutions.'[98] Workers believe that it is not just a question of 'isolated temporary shortages' but of more profound contradictions. The journal of course reassures us that these 'subjective assessments' do not correspond to reality. We will leave this declaration to the consciences of the authors.

An analysis of rumours also gives very strange results. It turns out from Losenkov's book that the higher the level of education, the more a person is inclined to believe rumours. Men believe rumours more than women, young people more than old men and women. Rumours are of most interest to school-pupils and students and of least interest to pensioners, who represent the 'single and clear exception' to the general mass. The author explains this exception by the fact that 'pensioners' contacts are narrower and less intensive than those of young people.'[99] This is unconvincing, the more so as he provides no evidence for his thesis. Both pensioners and young people have a varied circle of acquaintance, and pensioners have more free time and consequently more opportunities for contacts in their circle. In general, the results of the survey cannot but induce bewilderment. Everything should be the other way round. Vysotsky's lines come to mind:

> Rumours do the round of houses,
> Like flies darting here and there,
> While toothless old women
> Implant them in our minds.

It turns out that toothless old women are not like that. Strange. Something is not quite right. Losenkov himself remarks that 'from the point of view of the modern development of means of communication, rumours are of course an anachronism.'[100] But these 'anachronistic' types of social behaviour ought to be more typical of old people. Losenkov is clearly getting things confused.

We find the explanation in Yu. Sherkovin's article 'Spontaneous processes of transmitting information' which attributes measures of 'active opposition to rumours' to 'the organization of counter-propaganda'.[101] It follows from this that official literature actually places in the category of rumour all unofficial information — the source of which might be Western radio broadcasts, samizdat, personal experience, a leak of information from state institutions, and so forth. Everything then falls into place. There is nothing surprising in the fact that pensioners, educated in the spirit of Stalin, are more inclined to trust government propaganda.

One important question concerned the degree of confidence in unofficial information. In general a majority of people decided not to answer this, but a significant portion of those surveyed, especially people under thirty years of age, declared that 'more often rumours prove to be true.' Among workers of all ages this answer was given by 19 per cent, and among intellectuals by 20 per cent. It is notable that Losenkov himself acknowledges that a significant number of 'rumours' are actually true and that 'in any case' the rumour, true or not, 'originates and is engendered in relation to totally real, frequently quite acute and complex problems.'[102] Nevertheless, official authors insist that rumours must be combated. Conservatives are especially frightened that 'aggressive rumours' are acquiring an even wider circulation. Many authors, it is plain, are profoundly pessimistic: any attempt to refute unofficial information that has gained a wide currency only serves, in Sherkovin's words, 'to spread the opinion being refuted.'[103] Losenkov comes to the still more distressing conclusion that 'reading the newspapers, watching the television and listening to the radio has no impact whatsoever on the assessment of the rumours' authenticity.' The state means of mass propaganda does not have at its disposal effective methods to combat unofficial information transmitted 'by word of mouth'. The situation is deteriorating, and the people

> are ceasing to believe that the channels of information are in a condition where they can always throw sufficient direct light on topical questions. Hence the lack of interest in and even mistrust of part of the mass information reported.

Hence, we should add, the gulf between the comparatively high level of attention to foreign political news (most of our people cannot verify it through personal experience) and the lower confidence in domestic reports: the latter are easier to verify. What interests people is thus a matter not of the level of 'conflict' but an item's truthfulness. The 'information vacuum' and mistrust of newspapers cannot but give rise to 'rumours' which answer questions ignored by official journalism. 'This lowers the prestige of the "silent" local media even further in the eyes of the population' and leads in turn to propagandists, in Losenkov's expression, losing 'faith in the possibility of an audience.'[104] As doubts about the truth of propaganda accounts of events multiply, people look for an independent assessment of what is happening. Journalists, meanwhile, find themselves in an increasingly difficult position. Changes in social life have engendered shifts in social consciousness and in relation to information. The turn to the 'policy of openness' — glasnost — announced in 1985–86 was not only a logical outcome of these shifts, but the only means of winning back favourable disposed mass audience for the official organs.

The picture of society drawn by sociologists in the 1970s and early 1980s differs significantly from what was seen in Stalin's time. The monolithic unity of consciousness has receded into the past. The term 'monolithism' is itself no longer employed. And it is obvious that dissidents and activists in unofficial political groups have not been the only vehicles of social discontent. People a long way from the dissident milieu often felt just the same (otherwise the problem of dissent itself would not have arisen).

The question can be posed more broadly, not necessarily in connection specifically with the Soviet situation. In *any* system, the combination of conscious and unconscious discontent in the course of a social struggle can be a great danger to the ruling groups. Unconscious protest is a destructive force, conscious protest can become a creative force. Social strata with a high degree of internal structural organization are capable of achieving the highest forms of political consciousness, and meanwhile the broad masses in many countries, even if they remain at the level of spontaneous discontent, have been able to provide an important stimulus, through their actions, to the formation of the advanced strata's political alternative. When conscious and unconscious have united, revolutions have happened. So it was in France in 1789, in Russia in 1905 and 1917, in Hungary in 1956 and in Poland in 1980.

Returning to our current situation, it should be remembered that an important part of our population is still unaffected by the European psychology and culture of everyday life. This is already a minority, but it is still quite significant. There is no need to suppose that these people are content: they are becoming more and more conscious of the fact that they are poorer than the rest. There is an enormous gulf between Moscow and the Russian 'hinterland'. The backward regions of the Soviet Union could be called, by analogy with the Third World, the 'Third Country'. The problems here are very acute, although of a different kind. The people of the 'Third Country' are too oppressed by the struggle for existence to speak out in defence of their rights, but they have a very powerful feeling of social injustice.

The combination of these factors creates a dangerous situation. Our history is not especially reassuring. In most cases those who have tried to implement reform from above after a protracted period of conservative administration have come to resemble the fellow sitting by a flask with a genie in it, thinking how he could most carefully remove the stopper....

Andropov's coming to power after Brezhnev's death in 1982 signalled a major defeat for the conservatives. The masses saw in the new leader a man capable of taking decisive charge of the situation and ensuring a break with the past. Andropov acknowledged honestly that the plans for the first years of the Five-Year Plan had not been fulfilled and that the country was in a serious position. Observing that he had 'no ready solutions', he advocated a search for new ones.[105] It was now officially possible to talk not just about the necessity of a deep-going economic reform, but even about more sensitive questions. Andropov emphasized that he was for a 'significant change in the political and ideological superstructure as well.'[106] Andropov's stay in power did not, however, last long. His death in 1984 and the emergence of the hard-headed Brezhnevite, Konstantin Chernenko, in the post of General Secretary began to impede the process of reform. Moreover the far from homo-geneous character of the coalition founded by Andropov was revealed. It united all those representatives of the ruling elite who were discontented with Brezhnevism — reformists, technocrats, and conservative moralists protesting against the corruption engendered by the 'epoch of stability'. While Andropov was alive his enormous personal authority, political experience and iron will enabled unity to be maintained within his bloc. But the contradictions were caused by objective factors. Even under Andropov these had proved an important brake on the transformations then beginning. The fourteen months of Chernenko's 'neo-Brezhnev-ism' were characterized by stagnation in the economy and political life. But it was already impossible to avoid changes. The real problem was not whether reforms would be implemented, but how and by what forces they would be carried out.

The most recent change of leader, in spring 1985, brought advocates of the new course into power. Mikhail Gorbachev came to power after Chernenko's death with the support of Andropov's coalition. Conserva-tives in the Brezhnev mould were removed from the political stage. Brezhnevism could not stave off the changes, it could only delay them. The policy of stability had generated problems that did not exist in the early 1970s. The social situation and economic environment had changed. Brezhnev had created a mass of difficulties for his successors.

He had simultaneously made efforts at radical solutions unavoidable.

The prospect of technocratic measures in the spirit of 1965 and moderate reformism from the top now held little attraction even for the highest leadership of the state. At the 27th Congress Gorbachev declared that 'radical reform' dependent upon 'the democratization of society' was essential.[107] The ideas of the reformist faction, which had argued for a transition to directing the economy through plan and market and to more liberal political procedures, had now become the official creed. Political prisoners began to return from the camps. The mass media regained the interest and often the confidence of its readers by publishing candid and pointed material about problems whose existence would have been flatly denied the day before. At the same time, the practical economic solutions embraced during 1985–87 remained extremely contradictory. They were the product of a compromise between technocrats and reformists which was frequently unsatisfactory to both parties. There is much evidence to indicate a new rapprochement between technocrats and conservatives, now cleansed of the most odious figures from the Brezhnev epoch. The middle tier of the bureaucratic apparatus energetically sabotaged even those measures approved by the overwhelming majority of the leadership. Gorbachev aptly termed this the 'braking mechanism'. The conservative grouping, which was predominant at many levels of the apparatus could not for all that challenge the General Secretary overtly without destabilizing the whole system and thus threatening its own position in the process. Gorbachev, too, had to avoid the risk of destabilization. As the situation developed, the role of the broad popular masses in the process of change assumed ever greater significance. Only the masses' participation in politics could secure a real victory for structural reform.

In the early 1980s, the views of the ideologists of official reformism underwent an important radicalization. In 1986 the Novosibirsk journal *EKO*, which had become the centre of attraction for advocates of change in the last years of Brezhnevism, published an article by Academician Tatyana Zaslavskaya which testified to a significant shift in the positions of reformist experts. Zaslavskaya had initially reduced the role of the masses to support for initiatives from above, but she now realized that social justice can only be achieved 'through a struggle between the interests of different groups and strata' while 'the unwillingness of social groups to give up voluntarily the baseless privileges which for certain reasons they possess' should be remembered.[108] Thus the question of the necessity of class politics, and the formation of a new strategy of radical reforms comparable with the revolutionary–reformist strategies of the more advanced left-wing organizations in the West and Third World, was placed on the agenda. Zaslavskaya spoke of the broad unification of forces in favour of creating 'a society of social justice.'[109]

Unfortunately the programme advanced by Zaslavskaya and those around her was too narrow for the task in hand. Their demands expressed primarily the interests of the highest part of the intermediate strata, the most energetic managers and the scientific elite. In their idealization of the market they were quite prepared to allow a significant fall in the living standards of the lower orders as the 'cost' of perestroika. The market mechanism of redistribution on the Hungarian model was what the top middle strata looked to for the realization of their vision of justice. Some of the proposals of the reformist technocracy were clearly reminiscent of monetarist prescriptions. The criticism of traditional bureaucratic measures made by Zaslavskaya, Bunich, Popov and other representatives of this group sounded very convincing, but the narrowness of their own social positions was evident.

Real changes were occurring in society. The press became significantly more free, although the censors periodically reminded everyone of their existence. A new political environment had come into being in which people began to say what they thought without fear. Historians and theoreticians held fascinating and candid discussions about the country's past, and many Soviet citizens gained the right to travel abroad. However, all these changes only directly affected the intellectual elite and the technocracy. For a majority of the population there was no radical improvement in their lives, and moreover the economic situation continued to deteriorate. At the 19th Conference of the CPSU in summer 1988, Academician Leonid Abalkin confirmed that 'a radical turning point in the economy had not taken place and that it had not emerged from its state of stagnation.'[110] Rates of growth were proving even lower than in Brezhnev's time, inflationary tendencies were being fuelled, consumer goods were still in as short supply as ever — in many cases, even shorter.

The economic difficulties were explained by a whole series of factors, but the major cause was the inconsistency and contradictory nature of the measures being implemented. The technocracy was concerned first and foremost with extending its rights while demonstrating that this was the only road to universal good. The reformers, in order to maintain the 'political equilibrium', had to make continual concessions to the most conservative circles in the bureaucratic apparatus, even though these concessions at times brought the reforms themselves to naught. No general reform took place. Even where new decrees (for example, the law on state enterprises) were enacted, they were extremely difficult to carry out because of contradictions in the formulations. Brezhnev's old economic mechanism, which, for all its absurdity, had lasted two decades, was finally readjusted and partially dismantled. But a new co-ordinated mechanism did not arise in its place.

Attempts seriously to alter the general structure of investments in the economy, or to review the correlation between demand and accumulation, were not even envisaged in the reform process. Such measures would inevitably have fractured the equilibrium between the various apparatus groups, and the leadership (whose own stability depended on this equilibrium) accordingly continued to experiment within the framework of the old structure — not realizing that by doing so it was already condemning its experiments to certain failure.

For their part both the technocrats and the reformist intellectual elite found themselves in a very ambiguous position. The conflict with bureaucratic conservative forces had compelled them to seek support 'from below', but any autonomous mass movement provoked serious misgivings among the reformers. They fought against the bureaucracy without breaking their links with it, and they preferred to use the methods of the apparatus. At the same time, they wanted to see the workers as their active allies, but decided against meeting halfway the demands rising spontaneously from below. The reformist elite aimed for greater differentiation in ownership, the masses demanded greater equality. The elite carried out liberalization while the lower orders wanted mainly democracy.

It is not surprising that the gradually emerging policy of glasnost and the liberals' calls for the masses to become more active were more and more often directed against the liberals themselves. The numerous Left groups, which came into being after the January 1987 Central Committee Plenum had proclaimed a course towards broadening civil liberties, initially saw themselves rather as radical allies of official reformism, but a year later this tendency had changed. The Left began to develop its own ideas. Unlike the liberal experts, who gambled on the fullest possible development of the market while retaining traditional authoritarian structures, the Left insisted that the market would be no more capable than was centralized planning of resolving every problem. And the Left saw its most important tasks as the defence of workers' social guarantees and the struggle to preserve the environment. They counterposed to the ideology of the free market the idea of a democratically regulated economy. Such regulation can and must be based on the market, but not subordinate to it. The goals of society must not be dictated by the state of the market, they must be democratically formulated by taking into account the whole diversity of social interests. It is quite natural that in such conditions the key question is that of political and economic democracy, of the masses' self-organization and of self-management.

The 19th Conference of the CPSU proved the decisive stage for the new reformism. Having raised so many hopes and expectations, it urged people on to energetic autonomous activity. When it became clear that the election of delegates was taking place everywhere under the control of the apparatus, and that lower Party organizations were being granted at best a consultative vote, a wave of protest erupted throughout the entire country. The movement took as its rallying cry the formation of a Popular Front, a new mass organization capable of defending the interests of ordinary people. Mass meetings took place in Yaroslavl, Omsk, Kuibyshev, Krasnoyarsk, Moscow and Leningrad, and in Yuzh-nosakhalinsk strike action was even involved. The Left groups that had earlier been united in loose and unstable organizations — the Federation of Socialist Clubs (FSOK) and the All-Union Socio–Political Club (VSPK) — at last gained the opportunity to form a unified and powerful movement.

The prospects of the struggle for democratic socialism in the Soviet Union were now linked with the Popular Front. For the first time in a whole epoch, the Left in Russia was again showing itself to be an independent political force capable of leading the masses and of formulating its own strategy. Against the reformism of the progressive elite was ranged support for the masses' self-organization and the class interests of the workers; to the policy of apparatus combinations, the movement of ordinary people; to the pursuit of ready-made Western remedies, the idea of self-management; to technocratic irresponsibility, a new ecological consciousness; to a passion for the 'achievements of realistic capitalism', solidarity with socialist forces in the West.

The reformist revolution is only just beginning and has no guarantee of success. Numerous organizational, theoretical and tactical questions of the Popular Front movement remain unanswered. However, the lessons of history have not been to no avail. The Soviet Left is aware of Solidarity's major errors, its lack of theoretical analysis and ideology and its organizational weakness; nor does it wish to repeat the mistakes of Third World revolutionaries who subject the masses to the authoritarian will of a 'revolutionary vanguard'. The key task today is to find the balance between spontaneity and organization, between general democratic demands and socialist ideology. This is already a practical task which must be resolved every day, in our every concrete action.[111]

Notes

1. R. Kaiser, *Rossiya: vlast' i narod*, 'Ardis', 1976, p. 566.
2. *Problemy Vostochnoi Evropy*, no. 11–12, 1985, p. 90.
3. *Regional'nye osobennosti vosproizvodstva i migratsii naseleniya v SSSR*, Moscow 1981, pp. 48, 47.
4. By the term 'average European way of life' I understand not only the Western 'average European standard of living' but precisely what is common to *all* of Europe, East and West — what is characteristic to an equal degree of West and East Germans, French and Czechs, Austrians and Hungarians.
5. *Regional'nye osobennosti*, p. 51.
6. Robert F. Byrnes, ed., *After Brezhnev: Sources of Soviet Conduct in the 1980s*, London 1983, p. 190. Of course, changes have occurred at different rates in different parts of the country. We will analyse chiefly the processes which have taken place in Russia. As regards the other republics, according to the estimates of Western researchers, 'the inequality between regions tends to remain over time' (Jan Ake Dellenbrant, *Soviet Regional Policy*, Stockholm 1980, p. 124).
7. The home of democracy has always been the town. It is sufficient to recall Ancient Greece. Rome's annexation of extensive agrarian territories was the downfall of the urban republic. The instability of democracy in France in the nineteenth century was also caused by the predominance of country over town. It was the same in Russia. Urbanization creates favourable conditions for democratization. Such conditions existed in Russia neither in 1905, in 1917 nor later.
8. *Vechernyaya Moskva*, 25 January 1986.
9. *Sotsiologicheskie Issledovaniya*, no. 4, 1982, p. 116.
10. Zh. Toshchenko, *Sotsial'noe planirovanie v SSSR*, Moscow 1981, p. 139.
11. *Sotsiologicheskie Issledovaniya*, no. 2, 1982, p. 12.
12. *Sovietskaya Rossiya*, 6 April 1984.
13. *Voprosy planirovaniya i prognozirovaniya vysshego obrazovaniya v SSSR: Tezis soobshchenii na vsesoyuznoi nauchnoi konferentsii, aprel' 1973g.*, Moscow 1973, p. 66.
14. *Sotsiologicheskie Issledovaniya*, no. 2, 1982, p. 14.
15. *Sovietskaya intelligentsia i ee rol' v stroitel'stve kommunizma*, Moscow 1983, pp. 201, 202. It is very important that these facts are mentioned in this book in particular — one of the most mendacious in Soviet sociology.
16. *EKO*, no. 3, 1986, p. 19.
17. *Sovietskaya intelligentsia i ee rol' v stroitel'stve kommunizma*, pp. 186–187. See also: *Trudyashchayasya molodezh': obrazovanie, professiya, mobil'nost'*, Moscow 1984; *Molodezh' i vysshee obrazovanie v sotsialisticheskikh stran*, Moscow 1984.

18. *Sotsial'noe razvitie rabochego klassa v SSSR*, Moscow 1977, p. 24. See B. Kagarlitsky, *Dialektika nadezhdi, ch.III*, (excerpt in *Problemy vostochnoi evropy*, no. 7–8, 1983, 'Industrial'naya despotiya'); A. Zorin in *Across Frontiers*, Spring–Summer, 1986.

19. Gordon and Nazimova, p. 41.

20. *Sotsiologicheskie Issledovaniya*, no. 2, 1982, p. 171. With regard to changes in the social life of the Soviet working class, see also V. Dobizhev and V. Lel'chuk, *Nekotorye problemy izucheniya rabochego klassa SSSR perioda razvitogo sotsializma*; *Istoriya SSSR*, no. 5, 1982. These authors also note that in the 1970s 'the prime tendency became reproduction from its own base, an increase in the proportion of hereditary workers, including native town-dwellers' with all the consequences that flow from this (p. 47). Over the period 1977–83 there was a clear turn in Soviet sociology towards more concrete analysis of the social structure of the Soviet working class, which had been almost ignored until then. In the West this question was touched upon by W. Leonhard.

21. *Stachki: istoriya i sovremennost'*, Moscow 1978, p. 15.

22. *Sotsial'noe razvitie rabochego klassa v SSSR*, p. 134.

23. One Soviet sociologist ironically quoted some lines from *King Lear*, (*Znanie - sila*, no. 9, 1984, p. 19).

24. Byrnes, p. 14.

25. *The Times*, 28 June 1984, p. 12.

26. *Sovietskaya Kul'tura*, 28 July 1984.

27. *Sovietskaya Kul'tura*, 23 August 1984. It is typical that this article discusses not Moscow but Ryazan', where it would be difficult to envisage the direct 'influence of the West'.

28. G.G. Dadamyan, *Sotsial'no-ekonomicheskie problemy teatral'nogo iskusstva*, Moscow 1982, p. 81.

29. *Problemy truda v sel'skom khozyaistve*, p. 72.

30. *Knizhnoe obozrenie*, 19 August 1983, p. 11.

31. See ibid. The aforementioned Stalinist, V. Safonov, asserts that the contemporary youth 'reads rather less than people of the same age twenty, thirty, or forty years ago' (*Sovietskaya Kul'tura*, 23 August 1984). This is true. Such changes are still evidence of the *raising* of the cultural level, for people no longer want to read any old thing like Gogol's Petrushka. Normal selective reading, which corresponds to the needs of the citizens of a developed industrial society, is replacing the 'Petrushka effect' which is typical of people who combine literacy with an extremely low general culture.

32. See *Voprosy ekonomiki*, no. 12, 1982, pp. 125–6; *SSSR v tsifrakh v 1979 godu*, p. 19.

33. *Voprosy ekonomiki*, no. 1, 1983, p. 100.

34. See J. Elleinstein, *Storia del fenomeno staliniano*, Rome 1975, p. 203.

35. Dadamyan, p. 81.

36. Gordon and Nazimova, pp. 130, 81.

37. *Trudyashchayasya molodezh'*, p. 167.

38. *Vechernyaya Moskva*, 25 January 1986.

39. *Sotsial'naya struktura. Osobennosti popolneniya osnovnykh otryadov intelligentsii*, Tallin 1981, p. 79.

40. It should be remembered that the chances for unskilled workers to improve their position are not very great. In the estimation of sociologists, they enjoy only

'highly restricted mobility' (*Trudyashchayasya molodezh'*, p. 182).

41. See B. Kagarlitsky, *Dialektika Nadezhdi*, part 1, ch. 3 (*Problemy Vostochnoi Evropy*, no. 7/8, 1983 under the pseudonym of V. Krasnov).

42. Toshchenko, p. 107.

43. See *SSSR v tsifrakh v 1979 godu*, p. 171.

44. By way of comparison: in 1977 a kilogram of butter in a state shop in Moscow cost on average two roubles, but in the market in Volokolamsk four or five roubles – and its proximity to Moscow helped keep the price down! Western authors, referring to unnamed Soviet sources, claim that 'prices on collective farm markets exceeded state prices by 37 per cent in 1965, 55 per cent in 1970, 75 per cent in 1975, and 100 per cent in 1979' (Byrnes, p. 196).

45. Toshchenko, p. 156.

46. The data from a mass survey in 1978 show that people who relate to the traditional sort of consumption constitute no more than 20 per cent and in this group 'most people are over forty years of age' (*Znanie Sila*, no. 9, 1984, p. 20). Thus it is clear that it is a question of a social type that is dying out, while still very much alive.

47. *Materialy XXIV s'ezda KPSS*, pp. 43, 274.

48. *Sotsial'noe razvitie rabochego klassa v SSSR*, p. 146.

49. Ibid. To the extent that the reality of Stalin's epoch diverged from the lofty phrases of advocates of a strong state about the fortunate lives of simple people under the 'great leader'.

50. Byrnes, p. 188.

51. *Osnovy planirovaniya ekonomicheskogo i sotsial'nogo razvitiya SSSR*, Moscow 1983, p. 134.

52. *Znanie - sila*, no. 9, 1984, p. 18.

53. See *Varianty*, no. 3, 1979: N. Abrikosov and E. Vol'nyi, 'Dvizhenie - vse!'.

54. *Sotsial'noe razvitie rabochego klassa v SSSR*, p. 179.

55. *Znanie - sila*, no. 9, 1984, p. 18.

56. *Sotsial'noe razvitie rabochego klassa v SSSR*, p. 177.

57. *Literaturnaya Gazeta*, 14 September, 1983, p. 4.

58. *Politicheskoe samoobrazovanie*, no. 4, 1983, p. 119. The contradictions of the new situation are especially acutely felt by the youth, for whom 'a high initial level of consumption' is typical (*Znanie - sila*, no. 9, 1984, p. 19).

59. *Sotsiologicheskie Issledovaniya*, no. 1, 1982, p. 11.

60. *SSSR v tsifrakh v 1979 godu*, p. 83.

61. *Sotsiologicheskie Issledovaniya*, no. 1, 1982, p. 11.

62. Byrnes, p. 192.

63. *Izvestia*, 28 January 1984.

64. *Sovietskaya Rossiya*, 29 July 1984.

65. *Izvestia*, 28 January 1984.

66. *Sotsiologicheskie Issledovaniya*, no. 1, 1982, p. 20.

67. *Izvestia*, 24 September 1983.

68. *Izvestia*, 13 October 1983.

69. *Izvestia*, 24 September 1983.

70. *Sotsiologicheskie Issledovaniya*, no. 1, 1982, p. 21.

71. *Znanie - sila*, no. 9, 1984, p. 20.

72. Harold L. Sheppard and Neal Q. Herrick, *Where Have All The Robots Gone?*, New York 1972, p. x.

73. Schroeder, in *Soviet Economy in Time of Change*, vol. 1, p. 313.

74. K.I. Mikul'skii, *Ekonomicheskie zakony sotsializma i sotsial'naya aktivnost' trudyashchikhsya*, Moscow 1983, p. 91.

75. Marx and Engels, *Collected Works*, vol. 3, p. 133.

76. *EKO*, no. 8, 1983, pp. 114, 115. The journal authors point to this peculiar form of 'partial' strike as a refusal to fulfil plan targets (see ibid., p. 118). In *EKO*, no. 8, 1985, N. Maksimova recalled instances where entire brigades refused to leave for work, invoking the privileges granted by the law for the giving of blood.

77. *EKO*, no. 6, 1983, pp. 117–8.

78. *Literaturnaya Gazeta*, 20 November 1985, p. 12.

79. *EKO*, no. 8, 1983, p. 125.

80. Compare Marx: the bourgeoisie not only forges itself 'the weapons that bring death to itself; it has called into existence the men who are to wield those weapons' (*Manifesto of the Communist Party*, p. 73).

81. *Komsomolets Donbassa*, 27 September 1983.

82. C.G. Jung, *Analytical Psychology: its Theory and Practice*, London 1968, p. 186.

83. A. Sheroziya, *K probleme soznaniya i bessoznatel'nogo psikhicheskogo*, Tbilisi 1973, p. 18.

84. *Politicheskoe samoobrazovanie*, no. 4, 1983, p. 120.

85. *Sotsiologicheskie Issledovaniya*, no. 1, 1982, p. 89.

86. V.A. Losenkov, *Sotsial'naya informatsiya v zhizni gorodskogo naseleniya*, Leningrad 1983, p. 80.

87. Vysotsky's enormous popularity is an important sociological fact. The poet expressed what the people were thinking.

88. *Politicheskoe samoobrazovanie*, no. 4, 1983, pp. 119, 120.

89. *Trud*, 1 October 1983: Yu. Sidorov, 'Ya — chlen profsoyuza'. This material is very instructive for, whether intentionally or not, the author acknowledges the fact of friction between workers and state union officials. Another question: if, as the author concedes, many workers see no sense in being members of a trade union, why don't they leave it? The authorities declare that union membership is voluntary; from Sidorov's article it is possible to draw another conclusion.... Further, Sidorov recalls that the union pays part of the cost for workers to go away on holiday. But it gets the money for this primarily from membership dues!

90. Lampert, pp. 159–60.

91. *Izvestia*, 24 July 1984.

92. *Sotsialisticheskaya zakonnost'*, no. 6, 1984, p. 19.

93. *Izvestia*, 28 August 1984.

94. See Losenkov, pp. 46, 75.

95. Ibid., p. 48.

96. Ibid., pp. 76–78. A typical example of the unacceptability of the official version of events was the reaction of wide social strata to the Chernobyl atomic accident in May 1986. The newspapers had to engage in repeated polemic with anonymous 'spreaders of rumours' — without any great success.

97. *Sotsiologicheskie Issledovaniya*, no. 2, 1982, p. 167.

98. *Sotsiologicheskie Issledovaniya*, no. 3, 1983, p. 108.

99. Losenkov, p. 80.

100. Ibid., p. 76.

101. *Sotsial'naya psikhologiya*, Moscow 1975, p. 193.

102. Losenkov, pp. 81, 83.

103. *Sotsial'naya psikhologiya*, p. 193.

104. Losenkov, pp. 83, 85. 'The policy of openness' in the mass media which began to be implemented after the 27th Congress of the CPSU reawakened the interest of part of the population in the newspapers and television; but it also gave rise to new contradictions. First, the press now confirmed a whole series of facts that had been categorically denied for several years — and moreover they had only recently imprisoned people for the disclosure of such information in samizdat (for example, on 15 April 1987 *Literaturnaya Gazeta* reported that the USSR was in fiftieth place in the world according to the level of infant mortality — behind Barbados ...). Such candidness in the newspapers certainly did not always engender confidence in the press as a social institution: by reporting such information journalists acknowledged that they had previously been lying — and might thus begin to lie again with the next change in the political conjuncture. Second, the reader, used to seeing the authorities' point of view in the newspapers, was disorientated by the multitude of journalists' opinions, not knowing in whom to see 'the leadership's mouthpiece'. Third, the journalists themselves, having gained great freedom, felt no genuine social responsibility. The censor's control was sharply curtailed but the tasks of journalists in the new conditions remained unclear. It was unfashionable to appeal to the authorities but it proved even more irrelevant to appeal to nobody. As a result the entire press, with rare exceptions, aimed at increased circulation, sensational exposures, etc., and not at any kind of social values.

105. *Materialy Plenuma TsK KPSS*, 22 November 1982, Moscow 1983, p. 11.

106. *Materialy Plenuma TsK KPSS*, 14–15 June 1983, Moscow 1983, p. 15. Interestingly, Andropov twice repeated the same thought during the course of the Plenum.

107. *Materialy XXVII s'ezda KPSS*, Moscow 1986, pp. 33, 54.

108. *EKO*, no. 3, 1986, p. 25.

109. *Izvestia* 18 April 1986 (T.I. Zaslavskaya, 'Taktika Peremen'). In the mid 1980s a debate unfolded in western Marxist literature over the assessment of official reformism in the countries of Eastern Europe. Some were initially mistrustful of the market ideas of reformist experts, although it is difficult to deny the progressive character of these ideas in the given historical situation. A Left-radical economist concedes that: 'No matter how much we are dissatisfied with both market socialism and the status quo, the present historical choice — in the absence of other real alternatives — is still between these imperfect models' (Peter Bihari, 'Hungary: Towards a Socialist Market Economy?', in *Studies in Political Economy — A Socialist Review*, no. 18, Fall 1985, p. 35). It should be added that the perfect model is altogether impossible, or, more precisely, it is not true to life. It is quite clear that no solution can be found that is capable of dealing with all problems. Market socialism is not the final and ideal arrangement of society — such an arrangement can only exist in utopias. The real alternative in Eastern Europe at the end of the twentieth century is not between plan and market but between an economy controlled by bureaucrats and technocrats (including those exploiting

market methods) and an economy of workers' democratic self-management. This economy will itself require a market, but the social role of the market, its relationship to the plan and its structure will be very different depending on the chosen model.

110. *Izvestia*, 30 June 1986.
111. The question of Left forces in perestroika is examined in more detail in Part II, chapter 1, below; also in the article 'Different Perestroikas for Different Folks' (*New York Times*, 7 September 1988).

Conclusion

In the late twentieth century, the word 'reform' has become almost as popular on the Left as the word 'revolution' used to be. Nevertheless, the rehabilitation of reformist principles does not yet signify that the true path has been discovered. What is needed is not a list of desirable changes nor an appeal to moderation and common sense, but a realistic reformist project. Precisely such a project has often been lacking among both radical and moderate reformists. Too often the supporters of change have confined themselves to declarations of their principles, while rejecting attempts to elaborate a consistent strategy. In practice this has meant political ineffectiveness, opportunism, and reformist utopianism, which differed little from revolutionary utopianism.

History has confirmed the supposition that democratic socialism cannot come about as the result of gradual reforms, but it does not follow from this that reformist activity is useless. On the contrary, it is an essential stage in the revolutionary struggle, allowing the alignment of class forces to be altered and a new socio-political situation to be created. The Left must grasp the opportunities opened up by reformism, while not forgetting the limited character of these opportunities.

The starting point of the old reformism was the idea of a gradual movement towards socialism, while that of the new is the realization that a revolutionary crisis is necessary for the triumph of the new social relations. Nevertheless, an immediate transition to democratic socialism has proved implausible in the 1980s – in the West, because the proletarian revolution has been postponed and the masses have directed themselves towards change within the system; in the Third World, because of the insufficient development of the productive forces and economic dependence; in countries such as Poland, because of their geo-political position.... This situation will not last forever, but it is real. On the one hand the need for socialism is growing, on the other the opportunities for revolutionary transformation remain limited. In such conditions reformism must fill the historical gulf between the structures of the old crisis-ridden society and the still 'unattainable' new world. The transition to the revolutionary stage of struggle by the Left in our epoch is only feasible on the basis of successful reformist activity.

It should be acknowledged that this is not an easy task. First of all, a decisive reorganization of the Left itself is required. But self-criticism must not be transformed into self-denial. In the mid-1980s, many Left organizations in the West found themselves in severe crisis, as they were unable to carry through such a reorganization in time and were consequently overtaken by events.

Right-wing forces proclaim a revival of the spirit of primitive capitalism. In fact, we are simply witnessing the exhaustion of post-war neo-capitalist forms, their collapse and return to archaic models. This is evidence not of a rise but of a decline. The Left, however, has been unable to capitalize on the new situation and in many cases has even made concessions. The reason for this must be sought in the contradiction mentioned above: on the one hand, Western society has already fully matured and is even 'overripe' for socialist transformation; on the other hand, the revolution has been postponed and it has not proved possible to win the support of the masses for 'pure' socialist politics. This has led to demoralization and confusion.

Events in Eastern Europe have also had an influence in the West. The stagnation of Brezhnevism proved a more demoralizing influence on the Western Left than the atrocities of Stalinism (typically, debates about Stalin and totalitarianism became especially fashionable in the 1970s: the new interest in Stalinism was the subtext behind efforts to find the initial causes of the collapse of the Brezhnev experience). But Brezhnevism is not the final phase in the history of the Soviet Union, summing up the entire development of our country. Society continues to exist and survive, and to generate social and historical experience. It is becoming obvious that this new Soviet experience is vitally necessary if the ideological crisis of the Left in the capitalist world is to be overcome. But this time it must not be the experience only of the ruling groups' political course, it must also be the experience of the social activity of the masses.

Brezhnevism was not a uniquely Soviet phenomenon. Throughout the whole world, the 1960s and 1970s were an epoch of stable compromise. Persistent economic growth was able to satisfy the lower classes without affecting the interests of the ruling groups. The different factions of the bourgeoisie and bureaucratic groupings were able to coexist peacefully. But this happy reconciliation of different classes and social strata became impossible when the limited nature of resources, and the crisis of traditional methods of management, began to affect economic growth. In some countries it became unstable, in others it was brought completely to an end. The failure of Brezhnevism and Gierek's policies, the defeat of centrism in the West, the Third World's increasing difficulties, all testify to the worthlessness of the old prescriptions. The epoch of compromise was replaced by a time of confrontation in which the whole world was faced with the same choice — either radical reforms, or reaction.

In civilized Britain, reaction took the form of Thatcherism. Britain had been the first to follow a neo-capitalist, Keynesian path of development, and was now the first to encounter the problems of the new crisis. Acute class conflicts replaced the traditional compromise between capital and labour supported by alternating Conservative and Labour governments.

Thatcherism became a reality precisely because of the severe crisis experienced by the British bourgeoisie, which had lost its class unity and historical traditions. It is a bloc of transnational corporations and lumpen-bourgeoisie, or in other words forces located on the periphery of the social structure with an interest in destroying the compromise on which post-war British society had been founded. The technocratic attempts at modernization undertaken by Wilson and Callaghan had not only failed (and led to the downfall of their governments), they had given rise to a significant lumpen-bourgeois stratum, unable to become involved in the evolving structure. Wilson's technocracy generated opposition just as did that of the Shah of Iran, the only difference being that in the former case the collapse of modernization brought the lumpen-bourgeoisie to the surface, and in the latter, the lumpen-proletariat. The bourgeoisie, incapable of modernization and blaming everything on the trade unions and the state, hoped to regain what had been lost by defeating these institutions and appropriating their rights and share of social resources (it was a question, of course, of defeating the social and not the repressive apparatus of the state; the latter required the strongest possible reinforcement).

Transnational corporations in their turn proved able to exploit the rise of the lumpen-bourgeoisie for their own ends. The victims were nationalized industry, the working class, the education system, and so on.

Debates about modernization continued, but Britain fell further and further behind her competitors. Lumpen-bourgeois nationalism combined splendidly with the policies destroying traditional national institutions for the benefit of international capital. It is no coincidence that, in the mid-1980s, Thatcher's government found itself in successive conflicts first with Oxford University, then with the House of Lords, then with the Church of England and then with the Monarchy. It is difficult to suspect lords or bishops of Left radicalism, but their historical conservatism has proved to be incompatible with Mrs. Thatcher's anti-social right-wing radicalism.

Meanwhile the Labour Party was unable to counter Thatcherism with a bloc of national progressive forces, or at least mobilize modern proletarian strata. The triumph of reaction was made possible by the absence of a radical reformist initiative.

It is easy to suspect that in Britain — with its deep democratic traditions, developed political culture and (despite all its difficulties) sufficiently strong economy — the triumph of reaction might be only relative. The choice between radical reform and reaction is a global one. It is quite clear that in countries that do not possess such a rich democratic experience, the consequences of a reactionary solution might prove somewhat more severe.

The danger of a return to the past is as serious for the East as for the West. It is symptomatic that General Jaruzelski's regime has not been able to re-establish the order which existed in Poland prior to Solidarity. The new power has proved rather worse. In present day conditions, the defeat of reformist politics in Soviet-type societies is capable of provoking a return to Stalinism.

The technocratic-reformist measures proposed by Gorbachev's advisers do not eliminate the conservative bureaucracy. They only push it to the socio-political sidelines. The lumpen-bureaucrat excluded from the new structures is as dangerous as the lumpen-bourgeois. The Brezhnev faction has been crushed, but conservative resistance to the changes continues. An economic policy in the spirit of Brezhnev is inconceivable — it was precisely its collapse which led to the change of course. The revenge of the conservative groups can only take the form of an overtly neo-Stalinist reaction, which would be an utter tragedy for the country. Are the technocratic and moderate currents which came to power after Brezhnev's death capable of withstanding this challenge? There is every reason to doubt it. Moderate politics contains too many contradictions, its social base remains too amorphous and its supporters are frightened of too much. Only radical reform, supported by the masses, can present a genuine alternative to neo-Stalinism.

When we compare historical processes in various countries we can detect that, for all their differences, they have much in common. Thanks to this, the Left throughout the whole world can not only make use of common experience, but achieve a definite unity on the most important strategic questions. Specific features of the new reformist project will of course turn out differently in different countries. In the industrial societies of the West, socialists argue about the development of reform into revolution (frequently coming to quite pessimistic conclusions), whereas in the Third World it is a question of the transition from revolution to reform. The Polish experience, also of considerable interest to other countries, is proof that features of revolution and reform can be combined in a single social process.

The entire experience of history teaches us that it is both possible and necessary to formulate the most general principles on which a radical reformist project can be based. What are these principles?

1. The principal distinction between the new radicalism and traditional social democratic politics is that radical reforms affect not only the sphere of distribution but also the sphere of production, management and ownership. They must be directed at securing an *irreversible* shift in the social structure. One should not however be gratified with illusions: achieving the irreversibility of reformist transformations is not always possible.

2. The starting point must be the realities of the class struggle. In everyday politics, conflict does not directly occur between classes, but between social blocs formed on a class basis but not identical to classes. It is essential to work for the creation of a revolutionary-reformist bloc capable of implementing changes and developing while altering along with the historical situation. All programmatic demands and slogans must be subordinate, not to considerations of some sort of abstract rationality or ideological 'purity', but to precisely this task. Only the modern skilled proletariat can be the prop of the movement for structural reforms. The task consists in reconciling its interests with those of other social strata who are in favour of the changes, and of uniting around it broad strata of workers.

3. The necessity of a whole series of transitional stages must be taken
    into consideration, both in the formation of the reformist bloc and
    in carrying out the practical changes. Attempts to realize the entire
    reformist programme at once and incapacity to go beyond the limits
    of the first, preliminary stage are equally ruinous.

4. The starting point must be the Marxist democratic tradition in its
    broadest sense, which is not reducible to an apologia for the
    commune-state. This tradition entails a recognition of all forms of
    the masses' democratic participation in the government of the state
    — from direct workers' control to parliamentarism.

5. Recognition of the market as an important element of the socialist
    economy should not turn into market fetishism. The socialist
    conception of planning does not contemplate the worship of
    elemental market forces (which is typical of bourgeois conscious-
    ness) but the utilization of these forces for the creation of a more just
    society and system of workers' self-management.

Having grasped the unity of the revolutionary-reformist process and
its multi-stage character, we must inevitably acknowledge also the
necessity of temporary retreats. The democratic Left encounters such
questions throughout the world. French socialists, the Sandinistas in
Nicaragua, Solidarity in Poland have all made a serious effort at revolutionary reformism. A common problem which has confronted forces
striving to implement limited but radical changes at the first stage of
their struggle is an inability to retreat. They all thought for some reason
that having gained initial success they would then be able to go from one
victory to another — forgetting that the opposing side will draw lessons
from what has happened, regroup and counterattack. Reform, like revolution, cannot tolerate 'pauses', but success is unthinkable without tactical
manoeuvring. Unreadiness to retreat in such conditions means an inability to fight right up to victory. Thus at a given moment, successes
have necessarily turned into defeat or crisis.

This time, however, defeat has been as limited as victory. French
socialists lost the 1986 elections but maintained sufficiently stable positions to put up serious resistance to the Right. Solidarity was banned but
not smashed. In Nicaragua the pro-Stalinist faction achieved the introduction of martial law but was not able to secure definitively and irre-

versibly the Cubanization of society — the struggle for a democratic outcome to the revolution continues.

The contemporary world is in crisis. The results of the struggles happening everywhere cannot be predicted in advance. This book, and particularly the chapters devoted to the Soviet Union, might therefore seem incomplete to many readers. We are actually stopping in a very interesting place. But the fact is that theory must stop at just this point — or rather, it must be turned into practice. Let us recall — paraphrasing Lenin's words — that it is rather more interesting actually to participate in the process of change than to study it in theory. The level of the preceding theoretical analysis must be corroborated by the results of today's practice. There is no other way.

The outcome of the contemporary world crisis depends on the ability of progressive forces to present humanity with a genuine alternative. The advantage of the present epoch is that, along with its difficulties and misfortunes, it also provides a chance of real change. This is the positive side of the crisis. The Chinese indicate this concept by the unity of two hieroglyphs: 'danger' and 'opportunity'. The question is which one comes out on top.

PART TWO

1

Perestroika: The Dialectic of Change

To Western observers, Soviet society at the end of the 1970s seemed hopelessly conservative and arguments over the 'unreformability of Communism' became commonplace among dissidents and the liberal intellectuals who sympathized with them. Pessimism reigned even among official experts, many of whom, on their own admission, 'had fallen into the depths of despair'.[1] There seemed no prospects for the future of the country other than an expectation of slow decay. However, with the coming to power of Mikhail Gorbachev, the general mood rapidly changed. People who, until recently, had had no faith in even the possibility of reform, began to speak confidently of its irreversibility. The experts were gripped by reformist euphoria and the Western press, of both Left and Right, began to write of the success of the changes in the USSR with unprecedented enthusiasm. Although nobody denied the difficulties being encountered by perestroika — particularly the opposition of the bureaucratic apparatus and the complex economic situation of the country — nothing was capable of shifting the general mood of triumph. Hopeless pessimism was transformed into so much unbridled optimism, although the actual dynamic of social development was much more complicated and contradictory than was generally recognized.

Soviet society has never been as monolithic as it was presented by Stalinist ideology or the oversimplified Western conceptions of totalitarianism. Numerous interest groups, forming both within and outside the apparatus of power, have always exerted influence on decision-making and engendered a variety of conflicts. In Stalin's time these conflicts were one of the reasons for the mass 'purges' within the Party when the executions of prominent party and state figures signalled changes in the relationship of forces between different groups within the apparatus. Under Khrushchev the terror was brought to a halt, but a continuation of the open struggle between factions led first to the downfall of the all-powerful Minister of State Security, Lavrenty Beria, and later to the removal of Stalin's 'veterans' Molotov, Malenkov and Kaganovich. In the last analysis, Khrushchev himself was a victim of this struggle.

It was not simply a matter of clashes between people sharing power or of a conflict of opinions. Each of the participants in these events leant for support upon definite structures in the apparatus and championed their interests. It was precisely the lack of faith of the broad bureaucratic 'mass' in Khrushchev's programme of reforms, and the absence of a social base for it outside the apparatus, which led to the fall of Khrushchev in 1964.

At the moment of Brezhnev's accession the reformist faction in the ruling circles had practically no serious backing. The rehabilitation of victims of the terror in 1954–56, the debunking of Stalin's 'cult of the personality', the loosening of state control over cultural life and the vital extension of individual rights in that period were a very great historical achievement, but it should be remembered that all of these radical measures also played a major role in the struggle between apparatus interests by weakening the position of one faction and structure and promoting the role of others. Khrushchev's early success was connected with the unanimous desire of the ruling circles to put an end to the omnipotence and irresponsibility of the repressive organs at that time, and to place the reorganized state security service under Party control. At the next stage the impulse for continuing the political (but not the economic) reforms was the striving of the younger generation of apparatchiks to strengthen their own position and to edge out and discredit Stalin's 'old guard'. From the moment these goals appeared to have been achieved, the reformist potential of Khrushchev's thaw was exhausted and those people who had risen to their positions thanks to destalinization were interested not in continuing the changes but in preserving stability. Since Khrushchev, carried away with his own reforms, did not wish to take this into consideration, he was removed from his post and replaced with a more suitable leader — Leonid Brezhnev.

The most important peculiarity of the Brezhnev period consisted in the ability of the leadership at that time to maintain a stable compromise between factions in the apparatus while simultaneously raising people's standard of living. It was necessary to guarantee significant and consistent economic growth so that each social group could increase its share of the cake without affecting the interests of others, and to a certain degree this objective was achieved. In the late 1970s and early 1980s workers' incomes grew rapidly and their way of life changed. There was a sharp increase in the number of privately owned cars, nearly every home acquired a television and refrigerator and millions of people continued to be rehoused from the 'communal quarters', where several families shared a kitchen, into normal, modern accommodation. The quality of building and the general provision of living space also improved. It is characteristic of the period of Brezhnevism that there were virtually no major strikes or disturbances comparable to the events at Novocherkassk in 1962 when the Khrushchev leadership was forced to send in troops to crush workers' protests against a rise in prices.

All of these social successes were achieved with a simultaneous growth of the armed forces and a rapid expansion of the government apparatus (which, from the point of view of the bureaucrats, served as the most important indicator of progress). Military-strategic parity was gained with the USA and the influence of the USSR in the world, particularly with developing countries, increased rapidly. Contrary to the popular view which formed towards the end of the Brezhnev era, the 1970s were undoubtedly one of the most prosperous and successful periods in Soviet history. What means were employed, and at what price these successes were achieved, are another question....

If Khrushchev attempted to blend political reforms with the maintenance of the traditional principles of economic management then Brezhnev, at first, chose to do directly the opposite. Political stability had to be combined with economic reform, the intention of which was to broaden the rights of the intermediate link of the economic apparatus and to form a layer of 'Soviet managers'. This reform, begun in 1965, could have accelerated the growth of the country and, at the same time, have satisfied the technocrats whose specific weight within the ruling circles was steadily increasing in proportion to the modernization of society. However, it very soon became clear that, in practice, the reform was only exacerbating contradictions between the economic and Party apparatuses within the economic apparatus itself. It is not surprising, therefore, that the Brezhnev leadership which valued stability so highly rapidly curtailed the changes. By 1970 the reform had in fact ground to a halt.

The reform was accompanied by hopes for improving the efficiency of the economy. Insofar as these proved to be without foundation, however, Brezhnev and his supporters were forced to make maximum use of other, extensive factors of growth. Enterprises had no real incentive to renew equipment (it was quite enough to fulfil the plan with the old machinery, and reconstruction placed the fulfilment of the plan under threat). As a result massive centralized investments in new enterprises became necessary. All of the material, labour and financial resources that existed in the country had to be used to the utmost in the realization of this programme. Not surprisingly, the economy began to 'overheat' fairly quickly. The rapidly rising volume of money in circulation was not guaranteed by the supply of goods and the means devoted to the construction of new enterprises did not bring the planned return: building works dragged on because of the inefficient organization of labour, construction costs were rising all the time and the incipient shortage of money was concealed with the aid of the printing press. In order to receive additional resources, ministries were compelled to undertake new construction before completing the old. In the first half of the 1970s official propagandists loved to say that the whole Soviet Union had been turned into 'a gigantic building site'. By the end of the Brezhnev period they preferred not to recall this image. Many projects remained uncompleted over the course of several five-year plans, the cost of labour had increased fantastically, and there was a shortage of building materials, labourers and energy resources.

The maintenance of fixed prices for food, despite an extremely low productivity of agricultural labour and an uninterrupted expansion in effective demand, led to the state being forced to pay millions in subsidies while the population had to stand in queues complaining about the shortage of produce.

For a time all such problems were offset by increasing links with the West. Detente was a vital necessity for the Brezhnev leadership, and during the 1970s the Soviet economy became significantly more 'open'. However, the position occupied by the Soviet Union in the international division of labour clearly did not correspond to the status of our country as a strong industrial power. 'The basis of our exports,' wrote the economist A. Byko in *Literaturnaya Gazeta*,

> was, and still is, raw material resources, primarily oil and gas, which account for approximately 80 per cent of our hard currency exports. The sharp upward trend in world prices in the 1970s led to an almost twelve-fold increase in the price of oil and it seemed that such a situation would be maintained, at a minimum, until the end of the century. So why change the structure of exports and seek new reserves?

In its turn the imported equipment, acquired with 'petrodollars', could not be utilized with sufficient effectiveness 'because of bad management, chronically unfinished projects and slowness in familiarization'.[2] Despite the income from oil, the external debt of the USSR and the deficit on the balance of trade with capitalist countries grew appreciably. After the Polish events of 1980–81, Brezhnev's supporters came to the conclusion that it was essential to correct the situation in some way. The rates of growth of imports declined and debts were promptly paid off. Nevertheless the position of the USSR on the world market remained extremely precarious, as was revealed by the sharp fall in oil prices in the mid-1980s.

The years 1979–80 proved fateful for the Brezhnev model. Contradictions and errors which had been concealed over many years began to drift to the surface. Rates of economic growth began to fall appreciably, relations with the West steadily worsened and in Eastern Europe, 'pacified' for a full twelve years after the suppression of the 'Prague Spring', the situation suddenly destabilized. In Poland, the crisis quickly assumed a political character and led to a direct confrontation between the government and Solidarity, but other countries of the Eastern bloc were also encountering serious difficulties. When, in December 1979, Brezhnev decided to send Soviet forces into Afghanistan to save the 'fraternal regime' from the brink of collapse, nobody expected this to be the start of a prolonged conflict; it was perfectly clear, however, that the old political methods were no longer appropriate to the new reality.

The crisis of detente, the beginning of the war in Afghanistan and the events in Poland were, of course, not only the result of Brezhnev's policies. The West had entered a phase of structural changes, and a 'neo-conservative wave' had emerged in the majority of capitalist countries. Brezhnev and his supporters bore direct responsibility for the political failures of their allies in Poland and Afghanistan, but events in the rest of the world exposed the complete inconsistency of the political thinking which predominated within that leadership. With its orientation to stability, it expected, in an utterly irrational way, that the outside world would maintain an unaltered appearance and that qualitative changes were improbable. If oil became more expensive this was 'until the end of the century', if liberals dominated American politics this was an 'irreversible shift', and so on. The Brezhnev elite seemed psychologically quite unprepared for the explosions of the 1980s. Attempts to maintain the status quo through force, as happened in Afghanistan, only complicated the situation.

By the beginning of the 1980s the opinion had formed among the most varied strata of Soviet society that Brezhnevism had exhausted itself. The new generation, which had grown up during the years of 'stability', was more educated and demanding. An inconsistent modernization of the way of life had generated new demands and, in the end, a new dissatisfaction. People felt themselves more independent and demanded respect for their civil and human dignity. The years of 'stability' had passed to the benefit of society: social bonds had been strengthened and people had a better conception of their collective interests. In their turn the contradictions between bureaucratic departments were exacerbated to the point where it became clear that 'the epoch of fine pies' was at an end. The shortage of resources provoked interdepartmental clashes and made planning and decision-making at all levels much more complex. The emerging lag in the field of modern technology produced a feeling of horror among the military especially when the United States proclaimed its idea of 'space-based defence'. Thus not only the lower classes were seized with discontent but also a significant section of those at the top.

A paradoxical situation had arisen. On the one hand, society was fully ripe for change, but on the other, there was no serious movement of any kind for reform. Dissidents had never, even in their better years, proposed a programme of social transformation. Throughout the whole period of its existence, the dissident movement had advanced the slogans of human rights and defence of the freedom and dignity of the individual, but its incapacity to formulate a constructive programme meant that the slogans became ever more abstract and divorced from the real problems of the lives of the masses. As a result the dissidents pinned their hopes more and more on diplomatic pressure from without. It was proposed that the 'free world' should force the Brezhnev leadership into concessions in the sphere of human rights. Such a strategy, for all its questionable aspects, was at least understandable in the epoch of detente. But it became perfectly suicidal in the conditions of heightened international tension in 1979–82.

Compared with the 1960s, when the human rights movement was born, a significant evolution had taken place by the end of the Brezhnev period. After the defeat of the 'Prague Spring', a general move to the right could be discerned in this milieu. Academician Andrei Sakharov, who initially favoured 'socialism with a human face', had, little by little, adopted a liberal standpoint and many of his statements (for example on Vietnam and detente) were utilized by American hawks in their efforts to strengthen their position morally. An even more serious shift to the right took place among the 'new emigration', whose numbers had begun to grow rapidly from the mid-1970s. The most surprising thing is that the dissident movement, though in desperate need of detente, practically never recognized this fact.[3] Many in the dissident milieu welcomed the coming to power in the West of such figures as Margaret Thatcher and Ronald Reagan as a sign that 'at long last a decisive stand had triumphed in the free world'. In practice the immediate consequence of the crisis of detente proved to be a new round of repression against 'anti-socialist elements' and a worsening of the situation with regard to human rights.

By the end of the 1970s the dissident movement was in serious crisis. A significant section of activists had left the country, many had been arrested, some had dropped out of public activity. The most important cause of the crisis, however, was not repression but the absence of a political perspective. While the influx of people into the movement had declined, this in no way signified that there were fewer dissatisfied people in the country. Rather, in the new conditions, protest had assumed other forms.

The characteristic features of the 1979-82 period were, on the one hand, a strengthening of reformist tendencies within the establishment and, on the other, the emergence of a new socialist opposition. Unofficial Left groups existed among the youth back in the 1950s, but under 'mature Brezhnevism', their number was insignificant. People who had suffered for such activity during the 1950s and 1960s had either given up the political struggle or joined the dissidents, losing their socialist ideology in the process. The situation swiftly changed in connection with the crisis of the dissident movement. New samizdat journals began to appear whose authors declared their Marxist orientation, discussion circles sprang up and there was a sharp growth of interest in socialist theory. The intensification of cultural links between the USSR and the outside world in the epoch of detente had had an influence on the ideology of these groups. As opposed to their predecessors in the 1950s, the 'young socialists' had a fairly thorough understanding of the ideas of the Western Left, from Gramsci and Rosa Luxemburg to the Frankfurt School, and they could utilize the experience of the reformist and 'revisionist' movements in the 'fraternal countries' of Eastern Europe.

In many respects the ideas of the Left intersected the projects of official reformist experts, both attempting to formulate a realistic programme of changes on the basis of a socialist perspective. Both recognized the need to combine planning and market principles in the economy and the inevitability and necessity of democratization from above. However, in contrast to the reformist academic establishment, the Left placed an emphasis on self-management of production. If the official experts, with rare exceptions such as B.P. Kurashvili, have advocated a unique Soviet 'managerial revolution', the Left has declared workers' democracy as its aim. Moreover, in the opinion of the majority of young socialists, the supporters of official reformism have evidently reevaluated the potential role of 'Soviet managers'. Workers in the government apparatus were genuinely interested in definite changes but, at the same time, were afraid of them. The industrial management apparatus in the localities was dissatisfied with the departmental bureaucracy at the centre but, at the same time, was tied to it by indissoluble bonds. Relations between the 'captains of industry' and the local Party apparatus were shaped in a similar manner. In the opinion of the Left this limited the reformist potential of the technocracy, even in the implementation of a moderate technocratic project. Successful changes could only be begun on initiative from above, but could only be completed by a mass movement from below.[4] Relying on the intermediate strata not only does not guarantee profound changes in society; it does not even allow the consistent implementation of a programme of limited reforms along the lines of Hungary in the 1970s. (It is no secret that it is precisely this 'model' which has inspired the majority of liberal experts.)

By the beginning of the 1980s such ideas were being developed in the pages of three samizdat journals — *Varianty* ('Alternatives'), *Poiski* ('Searches') and *Levyi Povorot* ('Left Turn'). Radical groups had formed primarily in Moscow and Leningrad, but the demand for such publications also grew rapidly in other cities, particularly among the youth. Nevertheless, the Left was still very weak and had no political or organizational experience. In April 1982 most of the more active representatives of the new Left were arrested. *Levyi Povorot* and *Varianty* discontinued publication, as *Poiski* had done even earlier.

Because of the crisis in the dissident movement and the weakness of the Left, official reformism remained the only real alternative to Brezhnevism. This current had also experienced certain difficulties. The reformist experts mainly clustered around research institutes in Moscow, Novosibirsk and Leningrad. Their mouthpiece became the Novosibirsk journal *EKO* which, under the editorship of Abel Aganbegyan and Tatiana Zaslavskaya, attempted to combine scientific profundity with popularity of exposition. What could not be said in the text because of censorship was often 'spoken' by the wicked cartoons illustrating almost every article. The popularity of *EKO* grew rapidly in the late 1970s and early 1980s although the readership remained fairly mixed. The editors conducted a special investigation to determine 'Who are you, our readers?' In fact *EKO*, like the reformist current itself, had numerous supporters in the most varied strata of society 'from the worker to the minister', but could not count on the support of any broad social group. The apparatus of economic management proved to be divided almost equally between supporters and opponents of reform; in the Party apparatus, groups which were oriented toward change were compelled to coexist with conservatives, whereas the intelligentsia supported the reformist project 'for want of something better'.

The social lack of direction of the reformist programme had its positive aspects. Reformist experts appealed more to an understanding of 'objective necessity' than to specific interests, and this created the feeling of an unbiased approach and an interest in the highest objectives of the state. Moreover, the indispensability of change was indeed acknowledged among the most varied social groups. Even conservatively minded figures saw that the USSR's growing lag in the field of 'high technology' could lead to an undermining of military might and that economic weakness could prove debilitating for a world power.[5]

Paradoxically, what the Left saw as the greatest failing of the liberal experts' project — namely, its vagueness and lack of direction — assisted the formation of a broad and diverse coalition of supporters of change. Credit should be given to Yuri Andropov who, during his tenure as head of the KGB, began the very difficult job of uniting various factions and groups in the apparatus into a block of 'healthy forces'. Naturally, different individuals and groups expected different things from the changes. Some merely hoped to force out the Brezhnev 'mafia' from leading positions and to occupy the empty seats, while others wished to reinforce the military and political might of the country; a third group dreamed of a redistribution of power and rights among departments; a fourth group was sincerely concerned to make Soviet society more free, just and dynamic. In any event, all were united by the understanding that it was 'impossible to go on living in the old way'.

Both those at the top and those at the bottom of society felt they were coming to the end of an epoch. Everyone desired renewal. The problem was that its meaning was not uniformly understood.

It was generally felt that Brezhnev's death came about two years too late. From 1980 the country was already living in expectation of this event.[6] When it finally happened even functionaries could not, at times, conceal their satisfaction.

The selection of Andropov as General Secretary was testimony to the political crisis of Brezhnevism but not yet to its final demise. In his very first declarations the new leader gave notice of his intention to carry through transformations not only in the economic but also in the political sphere. Experts began to elaborate draft reforms, overloading the leading bodies with them. The word 'reform', which had almost disappeared from the pages of official documents, began to appear more and more often in the press. A resolute struggle was launched against corruption, which had become virtually a way of life for Brezhnev's elite. Some activists of Left groups who had been arrested in 1982 were released and their places in Lefortovo prison taken by embezzlers and bribetakers. Meanwhile Brezhnev's supporters, recovering from the initial shock of their leader's death, became aware of the impending danger and began to mount energetic resistance. Not a single one of the reformist projects considered at the highest level became an official document. Reform of the schools, proclaimed in the summer of 1983, was reduced to a list of good intentions and then, in practice, killed off.

Andropov's death and Chernenko's coming to power complicated the situation still further. In the person of Chernenko, the country had gained a leader who openly aspired to make his principle 'Brezhnevism without Brezhnev'. However, the lack of perspective in such a policy was apparent from the very first months. The economic situation continued to worsen and the struggle between departments and groups over the drawing-up of any directive document was exacerbated to the highest degree. The country lived in expectation of a succession of solemn funerals.

The death of Chernenko and the selection of Mikhail Gorbachev as General Secretary in spring 1985 brought an end to the protracted interregnum. The reformist current again found itself at the helm, but of the tasks set at the beginning of the eighties not one had been achieved. Almost another year was required to secure a working majority in the Politburo, Central Committee and Council of Ministers for supporters of the new leader. From day to day the newspapers reported on the permutations within the highest echelons of power. The 'veterans' of the Brezhnev mafia, Romanov, Tikhonov and Grishin, gave up their posts, but it proved much more difficult to undermine traditional bureaucratic 'claims' in the national republics. Here Brezhnevites maintained their positions for a long time, even within the highest Party organs. The protracted struggle of the Moscow reformist leadership against the Kazakh Party leader, Kunaev, ended in December 1986 with his removal as First Secretary of the republic's Communist Party, but this provoked serious disorders in Alma-Ata. Many national-Brezhnevites can look on these events with satisfaction. After Alma-Ata, Moscow became much more careful in similar situations — which helped the traditional leaderships in the Ukraine and a series of other republics to retain their positions.

Nevertheless, the Gorbachev faction was undoubtedly triumphant. The Congress consolidated its success by electing a new Central Committee and the idea of economic transformation and democratization was reinforced, at least in general formulations, in the new edition of the Party programme. The word perestroika was heard from the highest platforms. However, in reality, society felt the changes only after the Chernobyl catastrophe in the summer of 1986.

The atomic reactor accident at Chernobyl revealed at once the numerous weaknesses of the traditional management system and its incompatibility with modern technology. Long before the disaster many specialists had pointed to the economic and ecological miscalculations attendant on the seventies strategy of developing atomic energy. The reactors were built too close to densely populated industrial centres and construction was carried out with infringements of the design. Nevertheless, the Brezhnev leadership insisted on the most rapid fulfilment of the 'atoms for peace' programme, which it saw as the magical means of resolving the aggravated energy problem. When the catastrophe happened it became clear that the power station was being run by incompetent people, that the firefighters, sent to the place of the incident, were unprepared for duty in conditions of radioactive fallout (although the existence of such a danger was mentioned more than once in the specialist literature), and that the local bosses concealed information on the real state of affairs from the highest echelons of power, as a result of which the situation deteriorated even further.

No one believed the first newspaper reports, which patently understated the scale of the catastrophe and often contradicted one another. The confidence of readers was only re-established after the press was allowed to examine the events in detail and without the existing censorship restrictions. The policy of openness — glasnost — and 'uncompromising criticism' of outmoded arrangements had been proclaimed back at the 27th Congress, but it was only in the tragic days of the Chernobyl disaster that glasnost began to change from an official slogan into an everyday practice. The truth about Chernobyl which eventually hit the newspapers opened the way to a more truthful examination of other social problems. More and more articles were written about drug abuse, crime, corruption and the mistakes of leaders of various ranks. A wave of 'bad news' swept over readers in 1986–87, shaking the consciousness of society. Many were horrified to find out about the numerous calamities of which they had previously had no idea. It often seemed to people that there were many more outrages in the epoch of perestroika than before although, in fact, they had simply not been informed about them previously. After the information on the crimes and errors of the contemporary period, new material about Stalin's evil deeds began to break through. Writers, journalists and cinematographers, aware of the new opportunities, rushed to make use of them.[7]

If the first period of perestroika, which lasted from spring 1985 to spring 1986, can be called a time of struggle in the apparatus, events clearly entered a new phase in the summer of 1986. The 'golden age' of perestroika had begun.

Glasnost and democratization became the watchwords of the day. Reformist, left-wing and anti-Stalinist ideas were obviously predominant in the mass media. The old mechanism of economic management functioned as before but the political situation had changed. A majority of representatives of the Brezhnev group had already been ousted from their positions in the Politburo and the 'intermediate link' in the apparatus had gone over to passive resistance, defence of their privileges and blocking the implementation of reforms. Draft changes passed many times through innumerable commissions, one version of the text being replaced by another and endless amendments and elaborations being introduced. The bureaucracy had selected the tactic of filibustering, drawing out the decision-making process to the maximum extent. Many resolutions, adopted at the centre, were not implemented in the regions and every possible 'instruction' and 'position' was devised to limit the reforming effect of the new legislation.

The official programme of changes, based on the ideas of Aganbegyan, Zaslavskaya and their 'Novosibirsk group', was initially quite moderate. It proposed an expansion of enterprise autonomy while maintaining the system of centralized planning, the admission of a small private sector, mixed international enterprises in some branches of the economy and the regulation of the administrative and legal systems. The restraint of this programme was its chief political virtue in that representatives of the most varied currents within the Party elite and the country as a whole could put their names to such minimal demands. For the Left the idea of mixed corporations was rather uncomfortable from an ideological point of view, but this was not a central point and the Left anyway still played no significant role in events.

However, even such a moderate programme proved difficult to carry out in the face of resistance from the bureaucracy, and some sort of untraditional means of pressure on the government apparatus was required. Essentially, even the realization of the most lukewarm programme of economic restructuring demanded radical political shifts. Democratization was to become an *instrument of reform.*

The state of affairs in the economy remained extremely unstable. After Gorbachev came to power the slogan of acceleration (*uskorenie*) of socio-economic development was advanced and enterprises were required to increase their output at any price. In reality, enterprise directors called into circulation hidden reserves of raw materials and components put by 'for a rainy day'. Many managers were working sixteen hours a day. All of this not could fail to yield results. The economic indicators for 1985 were appreciably better than for the preceding year. On the one hand, department heads had demonstrated that there was no need to hurry with the reforms because it was possible to achieve reasonable results with the old management mechanism and that it was only necessary to increase the pressure on directors. On the other hand, directors now had to maintain the achieved level at any price so as to avoid serious trouble. In practice, it was impossible to fulfil the plan according to the traditional indicators while simultaneously redesigning the system of management. Something had to be sacrificed. The opinion spread even among official experts and reform-minded planners that the real restructuring would have to be postponed until the 1990s and that the current five-year plan (1986–90) would have to be extended somehow on the basis of the old mechanism. Meanwhile economic growth in 1985, despite the selfless efforts of workers, engineers and many production leaders, remained highly unstable. Chernobyl showed how unreliable was the old system of management. The catastrophe strengthened the arguments of those in favour of quickening the pace of reform. Moreover, the capitalist world, having overcome the most recent phase of its structural crisis, was experiencing a period of rapid growth. The neo-conservative wave was reaching its apogee and the Reagan administration did not conceal its intention of utilizing the increased economic superiority of the USA over the USSR to alter the military-strategic balance in its favour. The war in Afghanistan continued without any serious military or political successes and the situation in the countries of Eastern Europe remained confused and unsettled. As before, the West treated Soviet declarations about restructuring with mistrust.

Political democratization created the only possibility of unblocking the situation and quickening the pace of change. The press, which had gained quite a lot of freedom, had to ensure independent monitoring of the implementation of decisions and to assist the 'pressure from below' on the bureaucracy. The return to Moscow of Academician Andrei Sakharov and the freeing of political prisoners enhanced the authority of the Soviet government in the international arena and provided evidence to the whole world of the effectiveness of perestroika. Many representatives of the sixties intelligentsia, who under Brezhnev had stayed on the political periphery or bided their time, returned to prominence. The Left also became much more active.

The January 1987 Plenum of the Central Committee had to reinforce the shifts which had been taking place throughout the previous year. By Gorbachev's own estimation, the Plenum 'advanced democratization as the major driving force of perestroika.'[8] A whole series of proposals put forward at the 27th Congress were made more concrete. Gorbachev directly declared the necessity of changing the electoral system in such a way that there would be more officially nominated candidates than seats in the Soviets. The Plenum also discussed the election of enterprise directors and section heads and the creation of self-management organs in production. A special Party Conference on problems of perestroika was called for June 1988, although its powers and tasks were not precisely defined.

Although the reforms proposed by Gorbachev were quite moderate, the intermediate link of the bureaucratic apparatus continued to resist. Implementing even a part of what had been discussed at the Plenum proved extremely difficult. 'Experimental' elections of factory directors were conducted in a series of enterprises which, for some reason, were without a boss. No existing directors, however, wished to subject themselves to this experience, and section heads and administrative personnel were appointed, as before, by the director. Although the new law on state enterprises, which envisaged the democratization of industrial life, came into force on 1 January 1988, almost nowhere did the administration permit workers to intervene in the process of decision-making. In addition, many points of the law had been formulated very vaguely. Councils of Labour Collectives were established in the factories, but in most cases the administration itself laid down their powers and tasks and the method by which they were to be set up. Very often the directors headed the new 'organs of self-management' and turned them into an appendage of the administrative apparatus.

Elections to the local Soviets in summer 1987 took place on the basis of the old electoral system. In several districts an 'experimental' list contained one candidate more than there were deputies' credentials, but even here candidates who finished in last place were given the status of 'reserve deputy' if they had managed to gain more than 50 per cent of the vote.

Nevertheless, in almost every 'experimental multi-mandate district' the electors were able to take advantage of their new rights. In a majority of cases it was precisely the local bosses, who had traditionally sat in the Soviets, who were finding themselves 'overboard'. As *Izvestia* acknowledged, the list of 'reserve deputies' included a 'whole string of leaders'. Among those who had failed at the elections were Regional Committee secretaries, chairmen of the Executive Committees of Soviets and their deputies, and so on. 'Several "leading" candidates made it into the Soviet with difficulty, their fate being decided by a majority of one or two votes.'[9] Even in districts where the old system had been maintained the electorate often acted in an unusual manner. Students at Moscow University voted against a functionary of the university administration responsible for the student canteen. According to a report in *Literaturnaya Gazeta* official candidates failed to be elected in 1,076 districts of the country.[10] It should be noted incidentally, that the press covered these events in detail and even spoke of attempts to 'correct' the voting records which had taken place in certain instances.

The elections testified to the change in the psychological climate in the country. The life of society was reviving. Politics was no longer perceived as a pursuit of the privileged, nor criticism of authority as dissidence. In the conditions of liberalization all political and ideological currents existing in society came to the surface. Right-wing liberal dissidents grouped around the samizdat bulletin *Glasnost* and the Moscow seminar 'Democracy and Humanism'. Russian nationalist and fascist groups united under the banner of the *Pamyat'* ('Memory') society. National minorities also voiced their own demands. In the Baltic states there were demonstrations marking the anniversary of the Stalin–Hitler pact in 1939 by which these territories came within the Soviet sphere of influence. In Vilnius several hundred people came onto the streets and in Riga the demonstrations were much bigger. The Crimean Tatars held a meeting in Moscow to demand rehabilitation and a reversal of Stalin's order expelling them from their native land. The Left groups also underwent rapid growth.

The political situation which arose after the January Plenum was extraordinarily propitious for the Left. On the one hand, its demands coincided completely with the slogans of the day and, on the other, the Left was able to attract a growing number of people to its ranks who were disturbed by the slow tempo of real change. The swift growth of 'informal associations' began back at the end of 1986. The Club for Social Initiatives (KSI) and the *Perestroika* club in Moscow quickly became centres of attraction for the socialist and Left-liberal intelligentsia. Ecological and 'cultural-democratic' groups were formed or gained in strength. The movement in Leningrad developed particularly rapidly. On 16 March, following the call of the 'cultural-ecological' group *Spasenie* ('Salvation'), hundreds of young people gathered at the Hotel Angleterre which had been earmarked for demolition. They were joined by representatives of other ecological and Left groups, pupils from technical colleges and schools, workers and students. Stewards from the *Forpost* ('Outpost') group ensured that order was maintained. Journalists who were present acknowledged that everything was superbly organized: 'there were no excesses of any kind'.[11] Participants in the demonstration were unable to prevent the demolition of the building, but they made the larger point that citizens have the right to influence decisions taken by the authorities. The leader of *Spasenie*, Aleksei Kovalev, immediately became a well-known figure both in Leningrad and beyond. Independent Left groups advanced his candidature for the City Soviet, but the electoral commission refused to register him. In its turn the Moscow press came out in criticism of the Leningrad authorities and in support of Kovalev and *Spasenie*.

By the summer of 1987 it was already possible to speak of a mass movement in which thousands of people were taking part in various regions of the country. The platforms of the different groups varied in important ways, as did the forms of their activity. The desire for unity was combined in many clubs with distrust towards other groups, sectarianism and mutual rivalry. Nevertheless, participants in the movement more and more felt the need to elaborate a common platform and to set practical collaboration under way.

In August 1987 the KSI held a conference in Moscow of the fifty-two leading progressive groups at which the founding of the Federation of Socialist Social Clubs (FSOK) was announced. While preserving their various differences, the groups within the Federation jointly declared themselves in favour of socialist pluralism, self-management of production and the democratization of planning. FSOK's Declaration advanced specific political demands: the abolition of censorship and the right of clubs to stand their own candidates in elections. The economic section remained the least worked-out and it was decided to prepare special documents at a later date which would concretize FSOK's positions on the questions of self-management and planning. The clubs unanimously declared that the reform must be carried out without a drop in workers' living standards and must maintain social provision for cheap accommodation, free medical care, full employment, and so on. The extension of the role of market factors in managing the economy was seen as natural and inevitable, but stress was also laid on the dangers of triumphant technocracy and of a substitution of market fetishism for plan fetishism.

FSOK was joined by clubs not only in Moscow and Leningrad but also in Kuibyshev, Krasnoyarsk, Novorossiisk, Ivanovo, Saratov and elsewhere. Throughout the autumn of 1987 the Federation experienced continual growth. Publication commenced of its samizdat bulletin *Svidetel* ('Witness') — later, in recognition of tradition, it was renamed *Levyi Povorot*. FSOK representatives had an opportunity to speak before foreign journalists at the official Novosti Press Agency, and material about FSOK appeared in several newspapers. However, in November the situation suddenly changed.

On 31 October, Central Committee Secretary A. Lukyanov, speaking at a Novosti press conference in front of foreign and Soviet journalists, reported that at the regular Plenum which had just taken place disagreements had arisen over a speech by Boris Yeltsin, and he had been forced to resign as Moscow Party leader. This report had the impact of an exploding bomb, but public opinion was shaken even more by the silence of the official newspapers. Lukyanov's words were reported in Western Europe, China, Hungary and Poland but Muscovites were obliged, as in the first days of the Chernobyl disaster, to find out the news about events in their own country from foreign radio. Yeltsin was well known as one of the most stalwart supporters of perestroika and his resignation seemed an ominous sign. The Left clubs unanimously protested against the silence of the mass media although, within a majority of groups, there were pointed discussions about what could be done in such a situation. FSOK activists began collecting signatures on the streets of Moscow to a letter demanding complete openness — glasnost — in the Yeltsin affair. Vladimir Kurbolikov from the *Obshchina* ('Commune') club, who had come down from Leningrad, Kovalev, and several other members of FSOK were detained by the police while doing this. The crisis intensified even further when the central newspapers and local Moscow press published the record of the Plenum of the Moscow Party Committee at which Yeltsin had been removed from his post and accused of a multitude of political sins. At Moscow University students held a spontaneous meeting and organized an initiative group which made contact with KSI and FSOK. Many Party organizations in Moscow refused to support the decision of the Plenum.

Later, in January 1988, Gorbachev acknowledged that, because of the 'Yeltsin affair', the Party leadership had suffered serious criticism from the Left and that the removal of the Moscow leaders had been interpreted 'by a certain section of the intelligentsia, particularly the youth, as a blow against perestroika'.[12] In their turn, conservative-minded officials saw Yeltsin's dismissal as a signal for counterattack. Serious administrative pressure began to be exerted on the clubs and several activists were forced to abandon their jobs. It became extremely complicated to engage in any activity on an official basis. Clubs were not able to use premises and their reports did not pass through the press, although back in September there had been no problem with this. The Krasnoyarsk section of FSOK, the Committee for Assisting Perestroika, found itself in an extremely difficult position. After activists from the Committee had accused a series of figures in the local leadership of corruption, the Party Regional Committee took a special decision against this group, and one of its members, V.B. Chetvertkov, was expelled from the Party. Similar events occurred in other cities.

A majority of clubs continued to emphasize the legal character of their activity and their preparedness to collaborate with progressive groups in the Party and state apparatus. This did not, however, prevent them from being accused of 'unconstructive positions' and 'attempts to undermine the foundations'. In winter a genuine Stalinist campaign commenced in the press against the Left. *Komsomolskaya Pravda, Pravda, Vechernyaya Moskva* and *Moskovskii Komsomolets* all came out with attacks against FSOK and individual clubs. *Pravda* also attacked the noted playwright Mikhail Shatrov, who was in favour of a more consistent analysis of the Stalinist past and historical justice with regard to Stalin's opponents (including Trotsky). Judging by the tone of some articles, the conservative groups in the apparatus were seriously frightened by the growth of Left activism after the events of August and November 1987. Liberal journalists preferred to keep quiet in the expectation that this 'conservative wave' would soon pass.

In liberal reformist circles reference was made to Gorbachev's winter vacation and the illness of one of the leaders of the progressive faction, Central Committee Secretary Aleksandr Yakovlev. The Stalinists' counterattack was not triggered, however, by a fortuitous set of circum- stances. Perestroika had entered a new phase and the political delineation of society had been sharpened.

If, during the earlier stages of perestroika, the slogan of change had been capable of uniting the most varied currents within society and the apparatus, it was clearly no longer sufficient. Many representatives of the 'new generation' of apparatchiks, who had been able to acquire import- ant responsibilities during the course of events in 1985–86, were inclined to consider the fundamental tasks of perestroika fulfilled and to regard with apprehension any 'experiments' which might threaten their hard- won prosperity. The comparative warmth in international politics and the Soviet–American treaty on intermediate-range missiles – which to a significant extent were a result of the changes in our country – also, in their own way, reinforced the conservative mood in the apparatus. If many bureaucrats viewed internal political liberalization as a kind of 'price' to be paid for the trust of the West and a resumption of detente, their interest in political change clearly diminished when this goal seemed to have been achieved to a significant degree. Indeed, there were further misgivings, after the November outbursts by young people over the 'Yeltsin affair', that the democratic process had already gone 'too far'.

Of course, perestroika was continuing. The rehabilitation was announced of Bukharin, Rykov and other old Bolsheviks falsely accused by Stalin of creating 'the bloc of Rights and Trotskyites' in 1937. The journal *Oktyabr* ('October') published V. Grossman's long-banned novel *Life and Fate*, and the first issue of *Latinskaya Amerika* ('Latin America') for 1988 carried a short note on Trotsky's life in Mexico. The withdrawal of Soviet forces from Afghanistan was being prepared and the press openly wrote of the failure of the 'Afghan campaign': 'the fundamental goals have just not been achieved'; 'the presence of Soviet forces in the country has lost all sense. Withdrawal is inevitable and logical.'[13]

Nevertheless, the dynamic of events was not as it had been in 1986, and among reformists there was a feeling of some dismay. Many radical slogans were repeated in a ritualistic way without any serious resolve to try and carry them out. Experiments with the election of directors were curtailed (although the law which formally made elections obligatory had come into force). The ideologists of economic reform, dissatisfied with the results which had been achieved, advanced all sorts of new proposals and, having lost their former unity, argued all the more furiously among themselves. In the words of the eminent Soviet jurist, B.P. Kurashvili, the measures taken in the period 1985–87 were so superficial and half-hearted that perestroika risked 'not even reaching its hazily presented final goal.'[14] It was essential to formulate more precisely the tasks of economic and political reform and to develop a specific project.

Whereas, at first, the technocratic and democratic concepts of change had more or less peacefully coexisted it was now necessary to draw a clear distinction. The technocrats, more and more obviously defending the interests of the industrial management apparatus, saw the way out of this complicated situation in the partial elimination of social provision and the importing onto Soviet soil of the recipes of the neo-conservative theoreticians of the West. Nikolai Shmelev, one of the most fashionable authors of this trend, quite candidly defined his programme with the words: 'Everything that is effective is moral.'[15] Together with other theoreticians of the technocratic school (G. Lisichkin, G. Popov and others), he has viewed social provision as a brake on development and a 'survival of feudalism'. The technocrats no longer concealed the anti-democratic character of their proposals. In the pages of *Literaturnaya Gazeta* Lisichkin declared that the starting point of reform had to be the interests of the 'advanced' minority, hampered in its development by the slow, backward majority. The task of perestroika was to overthrow the 'tyranny' of the majority and to assert the superiority of the elite.

The expansion of market relations is the main slogan of technocratic ideologues. In fact, however, the 'market' phraseology of this group should be treated with extreme caution. The structure of the Soviet economy, formed under Stalin, guarantees an absolute monopoly position to the leading enterprises and departments. For decades the major part of investment has been devoured by the factory giants producing means of production. Everything has been organized in such a way that the consumer is subordinate to the producer and this is explained not only by the absence of a market but frequently by the absence of any real choice. The economy is oriented not to the satisfaction of human need but to self-reproduction. This 'self devouring economy', to use the expression of the noted scholar V. Seliunin, cannot become more humane through the proposed reorientation from central directives to profit criteria. The means are changed but not the goal.

In these circumstances the proposed 'playing of the market' can only lead to a rise in prices, inflation and increased exploitation of the consumer by monopolist organizations. It is typical that the technocrats, who continually emphasize that the market will solve a majority of problems, are highly disdainful of structural reform in the sphere of production and of a redistribution of investments, although it is perfectly obvious that without such measures 'normal' market competition would simply not happen.

The concrete recommendations of this school are reduced to the removal of food subsidies and the raising of prices in the name of improving financial health. At the same time they propagandize the slogan of 'self-financing', which is understood in practice as the freedom for monopolists to increase prices. Since January 1987, when a series of departments transferred to the principles of self-financing, the newspapers have begun to report fast-rising prices on the most varied goods and services, from trips abroad and window-cleaning to ... funeral services. Analysing the higher cemetery prices for 1987, the Moscow sociologist A. Rubinov remarked, not without irony, that 'the economic prospects for this branch are "indeed marvellous".'[16]

The essence of the matter is that, under the guise of 'reform', workers are being forced to pay for the economic miscalculations of the bureaucracy, bad management, structural imbalances and the pre-crisis situation of the economy. It is perfectly clear that such proposals cannot find mass support. In data obtained from surveys more than 70 per cent of the population are opposed to them.[17]

The concepts of the new technocratic school have not been accepted as an official perestroika strategy and on several occasions have even been criticized by Gorbachev. However, the influence of its supporters in the apparatus has been steadily growing and particular concepts can be detected more and more frequently in official documents. There is nothing surprising in this. Technocratic ideologists have suggested methods which, under a veneer of radicalism, are completely acceptable to the bureaucracy, and have also proposed the retention of traditional structures within both the economic and political systems of society. Despite its anti-Stalinist rhetoric, the technocratic current has converged more and more with the conservative-Stalinists. The brutal apparatus of political control has proved an essential element in a strategy based on frustrating the interests of society and lowering the standard of living of those at the bottom. It is also patently obvious that glasnost and self-management — the watchwords of the previous stage of perestroika — have no part in these concepts.

It is no accident that G.Kh. Popov, one of the major ideologists of the technocracy, appeared in the press with denunciations directed at Yeltsin while bluntly suggesting that, in this complicated situation, the Left might prove more dangerous than the conservatives. After Yeltsin's downfall the technocrats and Stalinists began to act more often as a united front, propagandizing for a rise in prices and for the elimination of those figures who, in their opinion, were too far to the Left and on whom they had pinned the label of 'vanguardism'. Naturally, both sides have viewed this compromise as purely tactical but the objective dynamic of events has pushed them into each other's arms.

In many factories the workers have begun to demand changes in the organization of labour, glasnost at the workplace, dismissal of incompetent and corrupt leaders, a shortening of working time and an end to overtime. The press reported on strikes and spontaneous meetings in many enterprises towards the end of 1987. In December sharp conflicts arose between workers and the local authorities in Krivoi Rog and Volgograd when an absence of money at the bank and the much tighter financial discipline resulted in the non-payment of wages. The workers protested, proving that they, at any rate, had legally earned their money and could not be held responsible for non-fulfilment of the financial plan. Officials mourned the passing of the 'good old days' when it was possible simply to use force. In accordance with the classical laws of the revolutionary process a polarization of forces was taking place in the country.

In January 1988 the well-known Soviet economist, V. Seliunin, wrote that two years of perestroika had revealed the bankruptcy of the fundamental concepts of official economic science. The reformist current had proved to be in no condition to elaborate and propose to society a radical project that could arouse the enthusiasm of the masses. The major achievement of perestroika remained glasnost, but it could not automatically resolve the country's social and economic problems. Now, wrote Seliunin, 'structural shifts are required in the economy — it is necessary to turn from work for its own sake to people and their needs.'[18] Such a perestroika would, in its turn, only be possible if it maintained the living standards of the masses and developed the industrial, political and local democracy which gives workers the opportunity for real participation in decision-making.

The aimless projects of the first years have proved to be unrealistic. The experience of Soviet society has, once again, demonstrated that the most moderate decision is not always the most sensible. In the place of abstract notions of the 'common good' has come a consciousness of the real conflict of interests in society. 'The struggle is not simply between bureaucrats and non-bureaucrats,' wrote a commentator in the popular journal *Novyi Mir* ('New World'),

> but between social groups on which they both depend for support. The major question is: who is capable of leading the mass forces that have a real interest in *perestroika*, in scientific, technical and cultural progress, and are its fundamental vehicle and thus the vehicle for the general interest — the workers with the highest skills, embodying the most advanced productive forces, and the scientific, technical and humanitarian intelligentsia.[19]

Thus the radical wing of official reformism has finally come to the conclusion, as a result of two years of perestroika, that the changes cannot be completed without the support of specific social interests. However, the strategy proposed by this current — to mobilize the modernizing intermediate strata — in no way solves the problem of finding a mass base for the transformations. Only if the real collaboration of the intermediate and lower strata can be secured within the framework of a radical, reformist project will it be possible to forge a powerful social bloc capable of opposing the bureaucracy. What is needed for this is not a boost to the social egoism of the 'advanced' (and essentially the most prosperous) social groups but, on the contrary, a struggle to gain their utmost solidarity with the wider masses. Such a broad platform is entirely possible. Within it are included political democratization, the development of industrial and local self-management, the maintenance of social provision, a redistributive, anti-bureaucratic policy under democratic control from below, defence of the interests of the consumer, and a gradual reorientation of the economy, taking into account ecological and humanitarian factors, towards the satisfaction of human need.

Socialist democracy must also provide the individual with social and legal guarantees. It is important to change economic priorities in such a way that people really become the major goal. Decision-making must be decentralized and democratic procedures must be created which are incompatible with both bureaucratic and technocratic approaches to administration. Finally, the half-measures which are convenient for the bureaucracy must be replaced with new, consistent, democratic legislation. It is not a question of choosing between plan and market (in any modern society there are both). The genuine choice today is between a developing civil society and bureaucracy. Upon which forces gain the upper hand depends the future of socialism in our country and, perhaps, the whole world.

Notes

1. See the very candid interview with Nikolai Shmelev in *Knizhnoe Obozrenie*, no. 1, 1988.
2. *Literaturnaya Gazeta*, 10 February 1988.
3. At this time the only exceptions were the brothers Roy and Zhores Medvedev, who always emphasized the connection between detente and human rights. It should be said that, in general, the majority of dissidents did not consider that 'the Marxist Medvedevs' belonged to the movement. They continually attacked them, accusing them of all manner of things — even including 'collaboration with state security'.
4. This programme was formulated in the samizdat journal *Sotsialism i Budushchee* ('Socialism and the Future') (*Levyi Povorot*), nos. 3–4, 1980.
5. Significantly, the research of Academician Tatyana Zaslayavska, which proved that the manageability of the Soviet economy was steadily deteriorating, aroused a considerable echo.
6. During this time the following anecdote was popular in Moscow: A person is reading a lengthy newspaper obituary and a neighbour on the Metro asks: 'Already?' The reader replies: 'Not yet.'
7. See Boris Kagarlitsky, 'The Intelligentsia and Changes', *New Left Review*, no. 164, July–August 1987, pp. 5–26.
8. M.S. Gorbachev, *Perestroika i Novoe Myshlenie* ('Perestroika and the New Thinking'), Moscow 1987, p. 60.
9. *Izvestia*, 7 July 1987.
10. *Literaturnaya Gazeta*, 1 July 1987.
11. *Izvestia*, 26 March 1987.
12. *Literaturnaya Gazeta*, 13 January 1988.
13. *Literaturnaya Gazeta*, 17 February 1988.
14. *Izvestia*, 15 February 1988.
15. *Knizhnoe Obozrenie*, no. 1, 1988, p. 2.
16. *Literaturnaya Gazeta*, 17 February 1988.
17. Data taken from the research conducted jointly by the Central Economic-Mathematical Institute and *Literaturnaya Gazeta*. Materials from the research were published in part in the FSOK bulletin *Levyi Povorot*, no. 5, 1988.
18. *Sotsialisticheskaya Industriya*, 5 January 1988.
19. *Novyi Mir*, no. 11, 1987, p. 188.

2

The Popular Front and the 1989 Elections: An Interview

Rick Simon: *What role does electoral reform play in Gorbachev's project?*
Boris Kagarlitsky: The problem is whether we can use the term 'Gorbachev's project' at all because one of the most important criticisms of the reforms is that Gorbachev has nothing that can be called a project. It is a kind of set of political and economic improvisations. The electoral reform is an improvisation because it was announced during the Party Conference and it was not even discussed before the Conference, it was not in the documents proposed for discussion at the Conference. A lot of elements of the reform remain contradictory and the electoral law is still contradictory. Official lawyers are confused and interpreting it in different ways. Another problem is to understand why the law is being implemented. Leading up to the Conference there was a growing conflict in the primary Party organizations between the rank-and-file and the functionaries so one of the ways to ease the tension in the Party structure was to switch the attention to the soviets and turn that potential for discontent from the Party to elections. On the other hand, those people who were preparing the ground for the electoral law weren't quite sure it would be possible to control the electoral process.

Now it seems the process is getting beyond control and is becoming dangerous for the liberal wing of the ruling group as well as the conservatives. Paradoxically, that makes it an important element of a really revolutionary change. While it is escaping the control of the apparatus, including the liberal wing, the electoral process is producing a lot of impulses for deeper social and political change and is becoming an element of a revolutionary process.

RS: *The Western press has emphasized the defeats of the conservatives. Was this process repeated throughout the Soviet Union?*

BK: I don't see any defeat for the conservatives as such — a lot of Party functionaries were defeated but they were not defeated because they are conservatives but because they belong to the apparatus. Let me give one specific example: one candidate defeated in Moscow, Bryachikhin, is considered one of the most liberal in the Moscow Party apparatus and that was why he was psychologically and politically prepared to stand in the elections. His defeat by Academician Oleg Bogomolov represents a big problem for left-wing groups which operate in the district. Being a kind of liberal he allowed unofficial left-wing groups, like the Club for Democratic Perestroika, to operate freely in the district. Nevertheless, he has been defeated and that could be used against him and probably later against us. This means that people were not just voting against conservatives but against anyone who was some kind of official.

RS: *What is the likely composition of the Congress of People's Deputies?*

BK: It is still difficult to tell what the composition will be. A lot will depend on the results from the Central Asian republics which we don't know yet. And we don't know the results from Siberia and some other parts of Russia. We can assume that there will be enough conservative-minded deputies even with all the successes of progressive groups.

It is also very clear that the Congress itself will be very uncontrollable at least to begin with because, on the one hand, there were a lot of officials defeated who were designed to fill particular positions in the Supreme Soviet, so it makes the whole project of controlling the decision-making much more difficult. On the other hand, those elected do not represent any organized opposition, they are just individuals and their ability to reach any agreement or understanding among themselves is also very problematical. So we are trying to form a faction of left-wing and progressive deputies but there is the problem of whether we will get enough support from deputies outside Moscow.

RS: *When will the Supreme Soviet be elected?*

BK: Probably at the end of May.

RS: *Will its composition reflect that of the Congress of People's Deputies?*

BK: People have different predictions. It seems that, in the beginning, there was some kind of list of people already prepared for the Supreme Soviet but some were defeated. It is quite probable there will be some kind of vacuum which can be somehow filled by key personalities. That would also be an important event. In Moscow the Popular Front and those deputies supported by the Popular Front are discussing the possibility of extending the powers of the Congress of People's Deputies. Those powers are not well formulated so there are a lot of contradictions. People are saying the powers can be extended — not just passed to the Supreme Soviet but rather some mass political discussion at the Congress should be organized and some proposals about constitutional reform launched, even before electing the Supreme Soviet, thus getting more deputies directly elected by the people into the discussion.

RS: *How often would the Congress meet?*
BK: Initially the Congress was designed to have no real political function other than to legitimate the Supreme Soviet; to give a better political image to the people in power and some legitimacy to the decisions adopted by the Supreme Soviet. But it now seems possible that the Congress can get some real meaning if it extends its powers and functions to more than the one or two days originally intended.

RS: *Do you think this is an embryonic two-chamber Parliament or one chamber of a two-chamber set-up?*
BK: There is some comparison with the French Revolution with the Congress of People's Deputies being likened to the States General. There are different estates: the Third Estate, represented by those people elected by popular vote, and the privileged First Estate, those deputies not elected but rather selected by the official organizations and who took no part in anything like a popular vote or electoral campaign. So that compares quite closely with the French Revolution. So the Congress of People's Deputies must try to transform itself into some kind of Constitutional Assembly but my personal prediction is not so optimistic — try rather than do.

RS: *The Western media placed a lot of emphasis on Boris Yeltsin's success. What is your assessment of what he represents?*
BK: First of all, Yeltsin is constantly breaking the rules of bureaucracy. On the one hand he is from the establishment which means that he is an official connected with the system and, on the other hand, he is constantly breaking the rules of the system and that makes him much more interesting and popular in the country. So he represents both radicalism and continuity and that's one of the reasons for his success.

The second point is that I think Yeltsin is becoming a kind of real popular hero and although he sometimes makes what I think are political mistakes and is not able to take advantage of all the possibilities in the developing political situation, he anyway gets round him a very broad social base. His slogans are very general, very democratic, very progressive, very much reflecting left-wing thinking and also popular concerns — very close to the mentality of broad layers of the people, but at the same time he tries not to be too concrete so that he leaves his hands free. The real problem with Yeltsin is not his programme or slogans but how those slogans will be interpreted and although there is a real Yeltsin movement growing and sometimes becoming organized, Yeltsin's movement lacks a detailed and well-developed political and economic programme and also lacks real political organization — with its structures, rank-and-file, experts — in comparison with a real political movement. In that sense Yeltsin's movement is sometimes really weak and that is why the movement sometimes depends very much on the support of the Moscow Popular Front which has less people but is a permanently functioning political machine.

One point about Yeltsin's ideology. Some people ask whether Yeltsin is in some kind of opposition to the Party. My point of view is that he is probably considered to be in opposition to the apparatus but he is very much in the framework of the communist tradition and in some senses he is much more communist than most of the official reformers who are interested in the West and everything capitalist — everything connected with profit-making, technocratic efficiency and so on. Yeltsin is a moralist and his moralism is deeply rooted in the communist tradition rather than the Marxist tradition. He is egalitarian and stresses social virtues and moral values and that makes him extremely popular and is a very interesting sign that not just socialist but communist traditions are alive in this country.

RS: *Yeltsin has been described in the* Economist *as a working-class conservative. Do you agree with this?*
BK: Yeltsin is not a conservative. He is neither a conservative nor a reformist, he is simply a populist and a moralist. In the sense that the working class and the great majority of the population are not able and are not ready to accept technocratic reform based on capitalist mentality and capitalist social and economic organization. That's quite clear and that's the power represented by Yeltsin's movement. I am also sure there is nothing conservative in it. On the contrary, it is quite progressive —

that rejection of capitalist economic mentality is connected with very concretely formulated interests in getting more democracy and he is for more political democracy for the people. He is very closely tied to the rejection of capitalist methods of modernization — that is not accidental but quite logical because, on the other hand, those who support capitalist methods of modernization are already now very much interested in authoritarian methods of regulating the political crisis. They understand they cannot get those projects implemented democratically because the majority of the people are against them so they see the necessity of an authoritarian solution.

RS: *What role did the Popular Front play in the election campaign?*
BK: In Moscow the Popular Front is growing very rapidly thanks to the Yeltsin factor. While there was a lot of popular excitement the Popular Front was the only organized force able to influence that movement and also we were the only real political organization capable of controlling the crowds and preventing any excesses. This is also very important as people understood that the Popular Front is needed not just to propose slogans and to agitate but also to prevent it from becoming counterproductive. It represented an element of reason in all that and we consider that to be an important success for the Left. We are no longer marginal. When the Popular Front leadership was on the platform of a rally of 35,000 people organized by the Popular Front, that represented an historic moment — although it was understood quite well that those people were brought to the square by the name of Yeltsin not by the name of the Popular Front.

RS: *What is the composition of the Popular Front?*
BK: The Popular Front is organized by left-wing, socialist oriented groups but, at the same time, there is now a group of right-wing Russian nationalists who have organized the so-called Russian Popular Front. They claim that the Moscow Popular Front is dominated by Jews and left-wingers contrary to the Russian national mentality and so has nothing to do with the Russian people. But events have shown that they are unable to get as much support as the Moscow Popular Front. Those people who claim to be the only representatives of the Russian people are not able to get in touch with the real interests of the people.

RS: *Is this an organization like Pamyat'?*
BK: It is like a moderate Pamyat' but it is more interested in restoring

capitalist relations which is not a primary concern for Pamyat'. For the Russian Popular Front it is a primary concern to restore anything which can be restored from Imperial Russia — from the flag to the social and economic relations. It is not a front but a small organization.

RS: *How has the Popular Front developed as a result of the elections?*
BK: The Popular Front is very strong in some cities — in Sverdlovsk, Kuibyshev, Yaroslavl and in some Siberian cities — and it was very active in almost every industrial city all over Russia. At the same time the Moscow Popular Front has had more success this time than any other. During the Party conference the Moscow Popular Front was much weaker than in Kuibyshev or Yaroslavl or even Sverdlovsk, but now we are reaching more or less the same level everywhere. While in Moscow we probably had more success than in other places, the movement is becoming more homogeneous, having the same level of success every-where, which makes it easier to co-ordinate our activities.

RS: *What is the structure of the Popular Front?*
BK: It is different in different cities, but this too is becoming more homogeneous. There are so-called support groups which can be differ-ent clubs or small organizations but now these are not so important as support groups organized at the enterprise level or in institutions or universities. Now we are building district groups in Moscow for electoral activity. The old clubs are mostly either dissolved or transformed into something functioning at an enterprise or district level.

RS: *Does the Federation of Socialist Clubs (FSOK) still exist?*
BK: It is somehow transformed. Most clubs joined the Popular Front and became primary organizations and most of the people active in FSOK, except the anarchists, are now also very important in the Popular Front.

RS: *Do you think this is the embryo of a multi-party system?*
BK: Everybody says that but we must stress that the problem for us is not to build a new party but a mass movement. The great majority of people is interested not in having a multi-party system as such but rather in having more freedom, more consumer goods, better living and work-ing conditions and so on. If they see that a multi-party system is necess-ary to achieve that well, of course, a majority would support a multi-party system. But now people are quite sure that a multi-party

system by itself cannot solve all those problems and that the problem is that of forming some structures for democratizing the different levels of society, including self-management in the economy and defending social guarantees and the living standards of the people during the economic reform — not allowing the technocratic, monetarist modernizers to sacrifice the living standards of the people for their utopian goals.

RS: *Has the Popular Front a clear concept of economic reform?*
BK: Most people say that our economic concepts are very much influenced by Scandinavian social democracy with its concern for social priorities, redistributive taxation, indirect regulation of the market, and so on. But the difference from the social-democratic concept is that we believe in socialist property which means we also believe in direct investment by the state as an instrument of economic planning. We also believe in workers' self-management at the enterprise level and we think that it is very important to keep a lot of planning structures still functioning and even sometimes elements of the administrative planning system can be kept for some period of time — it is probably better to keep them rather than just destroy them. But there is not just a problem of the method of planning but of priorities and democracy: who is planning in whose interests. So we can formulate different methods and instruments of planning but the problem is also to democratize the system in a way that will allow people to have the final say about the priorities of planning.

RS: *What campaign will you run around the local Soviet elections?*
BK: This will have great importance, for us the autumn elections to the local and Republican Soviets are very important. This is the highest priority for the Popular Front. It will probably be more important than the elections to the Congress of People's Deputies because the local Soviets are closer to the people so there can be more chance of democracy.

RS: *What powers have local Soviets been granted?*
BK: The powers are very limited. But if you change the composition of the local Soviets, if you have democratically elected Soviets, they will fight for more power.

4 April 1989

3

The Popular Front and the Economic Crisis: An Interview

Rick Simon: *What is your overall assessment of the Congress of People's Deputies?*

Boris Kagarlitsky: That is a rather complicated question because the general result is very contradictory and confusing. On the one hand it was an important event which helped to politicize wide strata of society and it also gave people some understanding of what the political debate really is. It has shown the real political differences — at least within the system — and from the educational point of view was very important. But, at the same time, there were millions of people who were very frustrated by the results of the Congress.

There were two very important failures of the progressive forces or progressive tendencies. The first was the failure of the liberal deputies, and liberal intellectuals in general, to achieve anything and form any real credible alternative because while the liberal intellectuals dominated the so-called progressive group of deputies they were not interested in forming any real alternative programme to challenge the strategy of the official circles. At the same time, these people, like Sakharov, Popov and partly Afanasyev — the leaders of the so-called progressive group — were always quarrelling with the official leadership on secondary issues. That was a traditional tactic of Russian liberalism which had already failed once before during the first Russian Revolution and now it seems that these people have learned nothing from history. On the one hand, they are continually alienating themselves from the official leadership through their quarrels and protests on secondary issues, thus assuring that their proposals have no chance of getting through and, at the same time, the only interlocutor that they think about is the same official leadership. They do not think about going to the people or mobilizing the people against the authorities. Their only aim was and is to persuade the authorities to do something which they consider to be rational, so in that sense their strategy and tactics were self-defeating. So here the Congress has shown the tremendous capacity of Russian liberalism to defeat itself.

That was one side of the confusion and frustration. The other side was that the mass popular movement which became very strong in Moscow during the days of the Congress has shown its own ineffectiveness. There was a tremendous mass mobilization in Moscow with rallies of around 150,000 people — the last rally had about 200,000. This happened not only in Moscow but in many other places in the Soviet Union where there were very intensive mass mobilizations. The Moscow Popular Front was also dominating the streets in some ways. But at the same time the mass movement was supporting the progressive tendencies in the Congress while those progressive tendencies were not able to propose any serious and credible alternative and thus the mass movement also became ineffective and was going, as we say in Russian, into the sand; just losing steam. The final result was rather demobilizing.

RS: *How did the Congress deal with the dire state of the economy?*
BK: Well it was not *expected* to change anything in the economy, to tell the truth. People were just thinking about the Congress trying to take power and become a democratic organ, the democratic centre for the reforms; taking the initiative for reforms away from the Party structures into some kind of democratic institution. But that had to fail, so to speak, because the forces of the progressive candidates and deputies were, from the very beginning, not strong enough to achieve that result — that was predictable. So those expectations were just too optimistic: there was a lot of wishful thinking, but still it was the wishful thinking of the great mass of people.

RS: *How do you think Yeltsin came across?*
BK: Well, in some senses Yeltsin was among the biggest losers during the Congress because it was not only the case that he failed to be elected to any key position — it was only through some kind of political trick that he managed to get into the Supreme Soviet — but, more important, Yeltsin has shown himself a weak political figure, unable to enter into confrontation especially with Gorbachev personally, who became very unpopular with radically minded Yeltsin supporters. So there was a lot of

frustration with Yeltsin as well and not only among the left-wingers from the Moscow Popular Front but among the Yeltsinists themselves. But he still seems to be getting a lot of support. Despite all his failures and weaknesses he is still commanding mass support in Moscow and in many different parts of the country — although it is two other deputies, the lawyers Gdlian and Ivanov, who are becoming the leaders or symbolic figures for the more radical wing of the populist movement.

RS: *Because they are directly attacking the bureaucracy?*
BK: Yes, they were stronger in their attacks and they showed that they were not changing their positions because of the decisions of the Party organs. Whereas Yeltsin publicly recognized that, because of the decision of the Party Plenum, he was obliged not to put forward his candidacy for the Presidency, Gdlian and Ivanov openly showed their disobedience.

RS: *You do not think Yeltsin has developed his programme in any way?*
BK: The strongest side of the Yeltsinist movement is the absence of any concrete programme because in this way he is able to consolidate or organize around him a very wide social base, very different sectors of the population; promising everything to everybody, producing radical slogans which are not made concrete in any proposals and also organizing people by proposing symbolic measures which are acceptable to very different kinds of people. And the people in these different social groups understand the measures proposed in different ways.

RS: *You mean the slogans he proposes against privilege?*
BK: Yes, especially about social justice. That's something which is understood very differently. But also saying 'cut the bureaucracy' — that's good but what next? How do you do it? Who is to take over the responsibility, and so on? The questions posed by Yeltsin are quite correct but there are no answers.

RS: *Has the Moscow Popular Front gained in support as a result of its campaigns?*
BK: It seems we are now much deeper rooted in the everyday political life of the city. We have groups not only in all districts of Moscow but are also very much present in the daily life of some districts and have some real influence on the people — though it seems that in some parts of Moscow progress is still minimal. If there were good activists in particular districts and also if events were moving us forward we would of course become stronger. But there were also some negative elements

because where the movement had begun to grow too rapidly, internal differences and heterogeneity resulted in political paralysis of the local groups, especially in the Chedomoshki district which, with the election of Stankevich, is considered our stronghold. At the local level Stankevich reproduced the Yeltsin effect, mobilizing a very wide social base around him and creating on this basis a very broad Popular Front — but as soon as they came to do some kind of concrete work there appeared to be too many differences between them. So now in this district where we were progressing faster than anywhere else we have more problems than anywhere else.

You must understand the difference between the Popular Front as it exists in Moscow, for example, and the concept of the Popular Front in the West. In the West or in Latin America the Popular Front movements co-ordinated political parties or organizations which had already existed for some time; which already had their own political following and their own political culture, programmes, traditions and so on. The idea was just to organize and co-ordinate the political structures, the political forces, which already had their own political identity and thus find some kind of general or strategic identity — or not find it: sometimes it failed. In Soviet terms it is the broadest organization of the Left which has been created before any political party or any political regroupment with any clearcut identity of its own so this has resulted in a kind of permanent identity crisis.

RS: *There was recently a meeting in Moscow with the goal of establishing a social-democratic party. How do you assess this?*

BK: The people who organized this conference were unable to agree among themselves on a very elementary point, which is whether to establish a social-democratic or a socialist party. The difference is not only in the word because the Right is trying to have a socially conscious liberalism while the Left is thinking about a radical self-management model. While there is a chance those groups could find some kind of compromise and come together into a real organization, there is still a very strong tendency towards the formation of two separate organizations: one social-democratic, the other socialist. I think that this would be much more positive in some senses because it would be a chance to overcome that identity crisis. So I am now involved in the project of establishing so-called 'Committees of New Socialists' or 'Committees for the Establishment of a Socialist Party' which are being set up in Moscow and Leningrad and will be set up in some other cities. They could be a real tool for achieving the task of political organization on the Left. On the other hand, all the people involved in that project are still co-ordinating their activity with the social-democratic groups. We will participate, for example, in the discussions organized in Tallinn in July 1989 by the Estonian Social-Democratic Party. This already existing party is, by the way, Russian- and not Estonian-dominated, and is trying to establish some kind of working-class base. You must understand that it is more comparable with classical social democracy at the beginning of the century than with social democracy in the West today — and of course not with that of Dr Owen! But I think it is still a real difficulty to achieve some kind of unity of these forces, especially when you are not just trying to unite different political groups but to create some kind of identity.

RS: *How would the establishment of a new party affect Popular Front comrades who are members of the Communist Party?*
BK: This is one of the worst problems because there are many Party members who are also engaged in the creation of the Committees for a Socialist Party, and we are trying to solve this contradiction. We say that the Communist Party which exists now is not a political party and is not recognized by us *as* a political party but is simply a kind of state insti-tution for political participation. Thus being or not being a Party member makes no difference for us. At the same time there is a problem because the Party leadership does not agree with us on this point, and so could punish Party members who participate in such activity. For the time being we are not too pressed by that problem as it is mainly a logical problem. Politically we are not under pressure because the Party members are very engaged in the campaign for an Extraordinary Party Congress which could in fact split the Party if it goes ahead — because the very aim of this Congress is to produce more open differentiation within the official CPSU; to produce real factions and let them have the chance to organize themselves including factions of people who are in fact social democrats, radical socialists, Marxists, Party renewalists, etc. We think that if this goes ahead and there is a chance of such differen-tiation, some sections of the Party would be forced to come closer to the movement for the creation of a socialist party and would finally have to participate in the creation of a new socialist party. On the other hand, we have very similar tendencies in Komsomol. The Lithuanian Komsomol, for example, has broken from the All-Union Komsomol, and there is the so-called Surgut Movement (Surgut is the place where some low- and

middle-ranking Komsomol functionaries met and produced a declaration calling for very radical changes in the structure of Komsomol and in fact for the formation of a new political youth organization). We are now very close to some people in the Surgut Movement, saying to them: if you want to create a new youth union why not establish a socialist youth union.

RS: *Going back to the Congress of People's Deputies – will it meet more than once a year?*
BK: Well, it's going to meet in September and the deputies from the liberal group are hoping to achieve more during the September session. The problem is that in fact they've lost the opportunities opened by the first session, because now the rules of the game have been fixed. Within those rules they have, of course, the chance to achieve something, but the rules are set so as not to let them win the game in general.

Another problem is that the economic situation is deteriorating. In May and June people were able to concentrate on politics alone without thinking about social and economic issues. Although people are frustrated with politics they are not becoming less active, so a big growth is expected in activism on socio-economic issues – the labour process, labour rights, etc. The working-class movement is still very weak, but it is growing while the national problems are becoming worse, and there is no democratic mechanism for compromise or resolution of those problems. So we feel that the situation in September could be very tense; while in May people were looking to the Congress, and what was happening in the Kremlin was reflected in the country in different ways, in September it will be just the opposite – the Congress will be forced to reflect events happening all over the country.

RS: *Is there a growing strike movement against the effects of perestroika?*
BK: Yes, every week you hear of them. There have been some very important strikes like the miners' strike in Norilsk which continued for some days and was combined with an occupation of the mine and a hunger strike. It was eventually partially successful, as some of their demands were recognized by the management. But, at the same time, it was an economic strike not connected with the democratic movement in Moscow for example, and in other parts of the country. In that sense the labour movement is going its own way and the political democratic movements are going theirs – that is, by the way, one of the reasons to

work for the creation of a real socialist organization which could try to combine both types of activity.

RS: *When you say the strikes are around economic demands, is that around higher wages?*
BK: No, higher wages are never demanded because people are not interested in getting money. They are connected with the attempts of management to force people to work harder for the same amount of money, which is typical of perestroika, or the worsening of labour conditions, or just mismanagement which is paid for by the workers. This is all connected with a kind of *khozraschet*, the transformation of managerial processes in accordance not with the laws of the market in reality but with laws of profitability understood in a wildly capitalist sense. The criteria of profitability are not understood in a modern Western capitalist sense — meaning that you must think about the survival of the enterprise, its stability, long-term prospects etc. — but just in terms of Third World capitalism: getting as much money as possible from exploiting the people harder than they were exploited before. It's a situation described in the first volume of *Das Kapital*. We can discuss whether this system was socialist or not — I think it wasn't — but having shown its inability to achieve the results needed for the new stage of development, the ruling stratum is using the worst of capitalist methods to obtain the same results. In the end, I'm sure they will find out that these uncivilized capitalist methods are no better, because they produce only discontent and chaos.

RS: *How are the workers organizing these actions? Are they going through their trade-union structures?*
BK: It depends. Sometimes they are using trade unions; sometimes they are using the official self-management organs called Councils of Labour Collectives, which have no power at all but are sometimes used as a kind of cover for the functioning of the strike committees. Sometimes they are just setting up strike committees or they are just wildcat strikes without any clear leadership. Also there are some groups called, for example, the Inter-city Workers' Club or Workers' Trust which are more politicized but sometimes still stay apart from the political democratic movement including the political Left. This summer there will be a conference of the Workers' Trust group, at which I am probably going to speak. We have a lot of expectations; we still think that the political left of the democratic movement really needs to be united with the

working-class movement, but the problem always mentioned by the workers is: what can the political Left, even when supporting our aims, do *practically* for our movement? How can you help us? And they are quite right.

RS: *Have the Popular Front organizations tried to link up with these strikes?*
BK: Unfortunately, the Popular Front, which is really a left-wing movement, is very heterogeneous and it is mainly an electoral movement with a social base limited to city intellectuals. There are, first, no organizations of the Popular Front in the Russian countryside, which is very revealing. There are workers in the Popular Front and the number of workers is growing but the workers are mostly active not in their enterprises but at the local political level. The electoral movement will survive in this capacity because you have to win elections and you must have some kind of political machinery to do that. That's fine, but you must not expect this kind of structure to be effective in delivering the goods in different fields; to be effective both in winning elections and in mobilizing people for the economic struggle. We are trying our best to achieve that but it seems that some links are missing in this political chain. So, coming back to my favourite point, we need some kind of party organization which can work through the Popular Front for electoral purposes and for some other purposes like local self-management, local self-organization etc.; in the labour movement at the enterprise level for economic purposes — and which can try and pull those types of activity together.

RS: *Apart from the way the enterprises are being run, what are the major problems facing the Soviet economy at the moment?*
BK: First of all, you could better ask what are the problems *not* facing the Soviet economy — then I would probably be better able to answer you. But to put it another way we are now coming to the worst point for many years because we have the problems typical of a centralized economy, the problems typical of an underdeveloped market-type economy and the problems connected with the transition from one kind of economic management to another. So we are accumulating all kinds of problems. People are suffering from the old system, from the inefficiency of the reforms and from the reforms as such. But I can say that people are by and large not afraid of unemployment, though there is growing uncertainty about the threat of unemployment, because people are still sure the authorities would be afraid to go too far with it as it

would immediately produce a tremendous social explosion. People are mainly afraid of inflation, increasing prices and goods disappearing from the shops, and the attempts of economic management at all levels to force the people to work harder without any chance of getting any reward. All that combined is producing the feeling that perestroika is not only economically inefficient but counter-productive.

RS: *What measures are the Popular Front advocating? Do you go along with Yeltsin's proposals?*

BK: Yeltsin's programme is very general, saying you must cut investment in construction. But how should you cut? What should be the priorities? Why in construction? Why, if it is important to cut investment, do it only in construction? Why 40 per cent and not 35 or 43? To give another example: he says to give more power to the Councils of Labour Collectives, but what specific powers? So, first, we are trying to be more concrete and explain what we want.

I think our position can be formulated as follows. First, the people must not pay the price for economic reform. If you want more efficiency and to cut the labour-force you must first put into action a whole system of retraining, compensation, help with finding new jobs, job-creating investment, etc. Only then can you go into the field of rationalization in the traditional sense. You mustn't have this spontaneous process, it must be planned, so another problem is who is controlling the planning. Thus you must have real self-management at the enterprise level, giving all real power to the workers' collectives including the power to elect or employ the management, then dissolving the ministries and putting in their place associations or organizations of the self-managing enterprises in the state sector. Bigger ministries responsible to a democratically elected Supreme Soviet would function as some kind of intermediary between political democracy and economic democracy. That is one point. Second, you must have some kind of rationing for an economy which is going deeper into crisis: the problem is how to organize the rationing. You must set up some kind of democratic and open body which is responsible for rationing, and have some kind of criteria for rationing. It must not just say to individuals why they are buying 1 kg of sugar and not 2 kg; it must do the same thing with enterprises because rationing is not just a problem of private consumption but also a problem for enterprises. So you must establish democratic bodies in the economy and I think the key thing is in transforming the Councils of Labour Collectives into something like workers' councils.

RS: *Do you think they can be transformed?*

BK: Yes, if they get a chance. The workers' councils in the old revolutionary sense take on all the responsibility of management and distribution — not just the functioning of an enterprise but also some of the responsibilities of the distribution of the produced income, produced goods, and so on.

The other side of the programme is thinking a lot about the municipalization of many branches; transforming state property into community property, thus bringing it closer to the people without privatizing it, without losing its social character or even strengthening its social character because, according to our analysis, state property now is not socialist property. So community property is the key point of the programme which we are preparing for the municipal elections in spring 1990 which could probably be a turning-point and a most important political confrontation, the most important political challenge facing us. We are thus going into those elections with a programme of some kind of municipal socialism, using also Western social-democratic experience together with the experience of the Greater London Council and Bologna. The key point for us is in the formation of community property and a strong community sector of the economy, with a system of self-management and economic democracy and with some kind of direct social control. Through the system of elected soviets, consumers would also be able to have their say in decision-making. Coming back to the idea of cutting investment in construction, the problem is not to cut investment in a centralized way but to transform a lot of construction enterprises into municipal property — then the community itself would decide whether to cut or not and how to cut. That is an important difference between us and Yeltsin, because Yeltsin just says 'cut investment', but that is a centralist decision, a centralist approach. Who will decide? We say the problem is not how much to cut although the local soviets would be obliged to cut investment when they get all those enterprises under their control but the key point is to transfer them to community property, thus making them closer to the people and establishing a democratic decision-making process which would enable us to decide democratically what are the really necessary cuts in the interest of the community. With regard to this I am leading the research group in the Popular Front which is preparing the strategy for the local elections next spring.

RS: *Finally, the unrest in the Soviet Republics appears to be increasing.*

BK: Yes. In the West, by the way, they are talking a lot about Central Asia or Armenia but nothing, it seems, about Moldavia where another hot spot is in the making. So it seems there are almost no republics in the Soviet Union without some kind of national conflict.

RS: *Is it Lithuania that is most radically reassessing its relationship to the Soviet Union as a whole?*
BK: It seems that Lithuania is closer to the point of secession, and it is the Communist Party in Lithuania and Estonia which is leading this process. I suspect it is not for good reasons, because the Party bureaucracy now realizes that the best way of surviving both politically and socially is to lead the independence movement which is not a direct threat to their social position.

RS: *You think this is simply a national-bureaucratic phenomenon?*
BK: Well, there are different components to the movement. There are different people like Kazimiras Uoka, a deputy from Lithuania in the Supreme Soviet, who is representing not just Sajudis but the left of Sajudis; the working class base of Sajudis. That's one side of the coin, and the other side is those people like Brzauskas and Party functionaries who are very nationalist but neither left-wing nor democratic.

It's more like the traditional movements known to historians where you have a broad alliance of very different forces which are coming together to get some concrete results. While the alliance is heterogeneous, it still has some kind of concrete aim which is pulling people together, and they could continue together until that aim is achieved. The problem is that the kind of strategy adopted by the Popular Fronts in the Baltic Republics — the support for the national bureaucracies in their demands and struggle against Moscow — is self-defeating because finally it is the local bureaucracy which will become stronger and more consolidated and influential out of all those processes.

RS: *Do you think this represents a real threat to the constitution of the Soviet Union?*
BK: Well I don't know what a threat to the Soviet Constitution *is*, because it's not like in America where the Constitution is everything and when you say the state you mean the Constitution. In the Soviet Union the problem is not the Constitution, you can change the Constitution very easily; the problem is that the state is a centralist state in reality, although it proclaims itself a federal state. And to tell the truth, if you think about

the Soviet Union as a whole it would not survive if it were transformed into the federal state proposed by the Lithuanian or Estonian parliaments. They want to transform the Soviet state into some kind of eastern equivalent of the British Commonwealth, with Gorbachev as a kind of British Queen, and they say that quite openly. I think it could be a good solution, especially for people in Estonia, but still you must understand that Australia and England are not the same country and not the same state. If you think about the Soviet Union as a state it could survive only as a centralist state. Or you must say 'let's leave them alone and concentrate on Russian problems', and although that seems very democratic and radical we come to another problem. In a sense, things could get worse for many people after the destruction of the initial Soviet Union — especially in Central Asia. Not only economically but partly politically, because even in the Baltic Republics there is still a lot of feeling — especially among the minorities; not only the Russians — that secession could endanger their human rights and there could be in an independent state a situation less democratic for the minorities than it is now. So while in the long term the Moscow Popular Front is not against the creation of new independent national states, and is not against the formation of some kind of commonwealth on the basis of the former Soviet Empire, we are very anxious about processes affecting human rights and we say that our first priority is to defend human rights.

RS: *Do you think these movements will lead to an upsurge of great Russian nationalism?*
BK: Yes, it is already happening — although it is not as dangerous as one might imagine, for Russians are less nationalistic than they're supposed to be. You must understand that there is a lot of feeling that we must solve our own problems, and sometimes people say 'let them go away and let us concentrate on resolving our own problems'. You must not think that Pamyat′ will immediately grow after some kind of secession or semi-secession in the Baltic Republics, but of course they are getting more support because of that process. They are using it.

RS: *Do you think sections of the bureaucracy will push this against the supposed break-up of the Soviet Union?*
BK: Yes, of course. Pamyat′ is very effective in using right-wing populist terms, sometimes even using the terms which must necessarily be used by the Left and which we are not using because we are not dynamic enough in the rethinking of our own strategy. For example, they now

understand quite well the feeling of the people who are very afraid of the offensive of Western capital in the Soviet Union. When you go to Pushkin Square and see MacDonald's, a functionary will turn to the foreigners and say that is the result of perestroika; that is one of the successes of perestroika. Whereas ordinary people are afraid that all those joint ventures and Western films coming to the Soviet Union are not coming with some kind of charity but are coming to get more from exploiting us. It's quite evident they're coming into the country in alliance with the bureaucracy and that it's strengthening the bureaucracy. For example, there is a lot of quite visible anger against the appearance of foreign capital, and unfortunately the Left initially missed that aspect of the process. It was groups like Pamyat' that began to speak about that, using all these facts in their own demagogic propaganda. So now we have to work out our own criticism and alternatives which must be concrete, not just saying 'close the doors', but thinking about the doors which must be reasonably open — probably not for capital but mostly for knowledge and culture.

28 June 1989

Index